<.85   £12.95

The Turning Point

The Turning Point

THIRTY-FIVE YEARS IN THIS CENTURY

The Autobiography of
Klaus Mann

With a new introduction by
Shelley L. Frisch
Columbia University

Oswald Wolff
London

The Mann Family
at their home in Bavaria

On the right: Klaus Mann and Erika Mann; at the table: Katia and Thomas Mann with the younger children.

Klaus and Erika Mann in 1930.

Klaus Mann reflecting over a manuscript.

**Published 1984 in Great Britain by
Oswald Wolff (Publishers) Ltd., London**

Cover design by Cheryl Mirkin

ISBN 0 85496 085 6

Contents

Introduction
by
Shelley L. Frisch

K_{LAUS} Heinrich Thomas Mann—his very name evokes the literary constellation into which he was born on November 18, 1906. His father Thomas Mann had published *Buddenbrooks* in 1901, initiating a long line of literary successes that led to his being awarded the Nobel Prize for Literature in 1929. Just prior to Klaus's birth, his uncle Heinrich Mann completed *Professor Unrat* (The Blue Angel), the best-known of his literary masterpieces. Like his illustrious elders, Klaus felt driven to establish his fame as a writer at an early age. "I must, must, *must* become famous," the fourteen year-old entered in his diary. By the time of his death on May 21, 1949, he had composed and published numerous novels, essays, and biographical portraits that sparkle with wit, insight, and passion for his subject matter; an increasingly urgent call for political engagement marks his later works.

From the start of this career, Mann was attacked in the press for unabashedly exploiting his familial advantage. In fact, much of this exploitation stemmed from the press itself, which saw the potential for catchy headlines in the accomplishments of the newest addition to the literary Manns. The éclat of the young Mann's premiere of his first theater piece, in which he co-starred with his sister Erika, Pamela Wedekind (daughter of the playwright Frank Wedekind), and Gustaf Gründgens (an unknown actor later to become the famed portrayer of Mephistopheles), was matched only by the drama of the following week's tabloid proclaiming that "Writers' children put on an act!" Following up on the publicity attached to Klaus Mann's budding popularity, Bertolt Brecht jested in an essay, "The whole world knows Klaus Mann, the son of Thomas Mann. By the way, who is Thomas Mann?" Thomas Mann signed a copy of his *Zauberberg* (Magic Mountain, 1924): "To my respected colleague—his promising father." Klaus was fond of quoting a cartoon from the satirical journal *Simplicissimus*, showing Klaus Mann declaring to his father: "I am told, father, that the son of a genius cannot be a genius himself. Therefore, you are no genius." During Mann's later lecture tour through America with his sister Erika, the press latched onto his spontaneous joke that he and Erika were twins (they were not); thereafter they were known as the "literary Mann twins."

The formative influence of Klaus Mann's illustrious family was crucial to his development as a writer. All three of his autobiographical works attest to this influence: *Kind dieser Zeit* (1932), his early autobiographical portrait composed at age 26, *The Turning Point* (1942), written in English during his exile in the United States, and *Der Wendepunkt* (published posthumously in 1952), a German-language adaptation of *The Turning Point*. Thomas Mann, affectionately called "The Magician" by his family, looms large in these works, often by way of comparison with Thomas's older brother Heinrich. In the prologue of *The Turning Point*, Mann points out the "painful and productive tension between 'the bourgeois' and 'the artist': the ordinary, practical, and buoyant type of man, on the one hand—the uprooted, sensitive, spiritual type, on the other," resulting in a dialectic interchange that challenged and inspired both Thomas and Heinrich. Thomas was irresistibly drawn to the bourgeoisie, but in the capacity of artistic outsider; his best-known literary embodiment of this dilemma is the young artist Tonio Kröger in the novella of the same name (1903), whose desire to enter into the world of the ordinary Hans Hansen can never be fulfilled. By contrast, Heinrich's contempt for the self-satisfied bourgeoisie dominated, motivating him to write overtly political works challenging the establishment. His Immanuel Raat (*Professor Unrat*) and Diederich Hessling (*Der Untertan*—Man of Straw), both of whom identify with the power of the establishment, are objects of his scathing satire. Klaus's literary production was molded by both Thomas and Heinrich. With the former he shared a passion for Romantic irrationalism and its impact on nineteenth-century thought, especially in the sentiment of a longing for death; with the latter he shared a love of French cultural history, cosmopolitanism and, in his later writings, a commitment to a political stance.

Klaus Mann sought alternative literary models as a means of establishing an identity independent of the Mann heritage. In *The Turning Point's* "Olympus" chapter, he sets up a pantheon of literary giants. His "romantic Olympus" is presided over by the tetrarchy of Plato, Nietzsche, Novalis, and Whitman, who share a transcendental humanism, a vision that is at once tragic and optimistic, and a youthful impulse to restructure the world. Contemporary role models include Stefan George, Rilke, and Cocteau. Mann's remarks about André Gide in the *Wendepunkt* typify his search for literary models: "The encounter with him, not with the man, but with the work...helped me more than any other, to find *my path*, the path to *myself*." His admiration for Gide led him to portray the author's life, literature, and milieu in his *André Gide and the Crisis of Modern Thought* (1943), which so fully mirrors and confirms Mann's own thought processes that it reads like an *auto*biography. The quest for self-definition that characterizes Mann's work as a whole leads to an extraordinary interweaving of autobiography and both fictional and essayistic works, which we will examine below.

It is reported that Cervantes, when asked on his deathbed whom he was depicting in the character of Don Quixote, replied: "Myself." Flaubert declared about his most memorable heroine: "Madame Bovary is me." The poet Malcolm Lowry expressed the sentiment that he was "not a writer so much as *being written*." The title of a recent biography by Dieter Kühn, *Ich Wolkenstein* (1977), underscores the author's awareness that he is writing himself simultaneously with the life of the medieval minstrel Oswald von Wolkenstein. For all of these authors, the act of writing inevitably and inextricably intermingles the composing subject and the created object. In Klaus Mann's biographical works on Alexander the Great (1930), Tchaikovsky (1935), King Ludwig of Bavaria (1937), and Gide (1943), as well as in all of his fictional works, he forges a thoroughgoing identification with the lives he unfolds.

In the novel *Treffpunkt im Unendlichen* (1932), Mann creates three fictional counterparts for himself: the characters Sebastian, Peti, and Richard Darmstädter. Sebastian, like the principal character of most of Mann's works, is the same age as the author (twenty-five). Sebastian finds the ideal partnership in Sonja, who is strikingly similar to Erika Mann, even in her problematic relationship with the dancer Gregor Gregori, clearly modelled on Gustaf Gründgens, who was Erika Mann's husband for a short time. The novel's Peti is Sonja's younger brother, again mirroring Klaus's relationship to Erika. Richard Darmstädter exhibits a wide range of intellectual and temperamental similarities to Klaus Mann. The eeriest correspondence lies in Richard Darmstädter's repeated suicide attempts, beginning at the age of fifteen and ending with his self-inflicted death in Nice. This fictional suicide in the Côte d'Azure uncannily prefigures Mann's own suicide in Cannes seventeen years later under similar circumstances.

Soon after his 1933 move into exile, Mann composed a "lyrical novel" on the life of Tchaikovsky. For an author who had involved himself so completely in the dilemmas of exile, his choice of a nineteenth-century Russian composer as his subject matter might appear alien to Mann's immediate concerns. He felt, however, that Tchaikovsky's life embodied the drama of uprooting. Mann's Tchaikovsky is an exile, not in the narrowly political sense, but because there is nowhere on earth he can call home. According to Mann, Tchaikovsky is the prototype of a man without a country: a result of the loneliness imposed by his type of creative activity, his volatile personality, and his homosexuality. In Russia, Tchaikovsky's works were criticized as being too western, the Germans accused him of Asiatic primitivity, and the Parisians found him overly Germanic. Mann wrote Tchaikovsky's story with the conviction of personal identification: "I could describe all of it; none of it was alien to me," he said in the *Wendepunkt*. Mann even invented an additional, ominous identification between the two artists by altering the actual circumstances of Tchaikovsky's death (the result of a cholera epidemic) to a suicide, carried out by his deliberate drink of polluted water and eagerly awaiting a relief from suffering that death would bring.

The most famous case of Mann's interlacing personal situation and fictional construct is his 1936 novel *Mephisto*. This fine novel has entered the limelight in part because of its cinematic rendition by the Hungarian director István Szabó, which won the 1981 Academy Award for Best Foreign Film, and because of the extended controversy surrounding its publication in Germany. Subtitled "Novel of a Career," the book tells of an opportunistic actor who betrays moral and political principles to rise to the top of the theater world during the Nazi dictatorship. The central character Hendrik Höfgen reminds the reader of the Mephistopheles-portrayer Gustaf Gründgens, who formed personal and professional alliances with Hermann Goering and others so that he might remain center stage in the theaters of Germany no matter who occupied the political platform.

As young artists, Mann and Gründgens shared much that brought them together: an all-encompassing desire to attain to fame in the world of the arts, a fascination with the interplay of art and power, a bond of friendship, and even a familial attachment during the period that Gründgens was married to Erika Mann. 1933 brought their differences to a head. Mann observed his former brother-in-law evolving into "the traitor par excellence, the macabre embodiment of corruption and cynicism," as he recalled in *The Turning Point*. Since Gründgens's behavior typified the conduct of so many others who remained in Germany, and because Mann knew him so well, he chose to develop a character with some of that actor's traits to illustrate one of "the pathetic and nauseous crowd of petty climbers and crooks"; as a *type*, not a *portrait*, as Mann repeatedly explained.

Trouble ensued with the novel's first appearance in print in the exile newspaper *Pariser Tageszeitung*: the editors took the liberty of designating Mann's work a *roman à clef*, the kind of novel whose major interest lies in retransforming the fictional work back into the actual world to which it alludes. Mann's vehement rejection of this designation followed immediately; he explained that although many of the fictional characters in the book bear resemblances to known personalities ("Benjamin Pelz" to Gottfried Benn, "Lotte Lindenthal" to Emmy Sonnemann, etc.), the novel transcends facile portraiture and achieves a literary depiction of the decay of a society.

Mephisto was published in Amsterdam in 1936; like all of Mann's writings, it was banned in Germany during the Hitler years. Even after 1945, however, West German publishers were reluctant to be associated with the book. On May 5, 1949, Mann was informed by his publisher that it would be impossible to print *Mephisto* because of Gustaf

Gründgens's popularity in Bavaria. Mann replied with a despondent letter on May 12, in which he expressed the fear that the climate in Germany had not changed for the better since the end of the Nazi dictatorship, and that there was no future for writers like himself. On May 21, 1949, Klaus Mann committed suicide. The death registry listed as his profession: Unknown.

After his death, the *Mephisto* controversy in the Federal Republic escalated. A detailed account of the ensuing debates and trials spanning over two decades would be impossible within the confines of this introduction; the reader is referred to the comprehensive coverage of this issue by Eberhard Spangenberg, *Karriere eines Romans: Mephisto, Klaus Mann und Gustaf Gründgens* (Ellermann Verlag, 1982) for the particulars of how this novel was twice banned by German courts at the same time that it was receiving international acclaim from foreign editions in over twenty languages. Even though a paperback edition of the work was published in 1981, and became an instant and sustained bestseller, these court rulings have yet to be reversed.

To live in exile is a time-honored fate for writers: Dante, Erasmus, Heine, Hugo, Wilde...the list could be expanded indefinitely. Most of these, like German exiles of the 1930's, remained close to the borders of their native homelands, hoping that they would soon return, that their books would continue to be published at home, and that their reading public would neither desert nor forget them.

Why did Klaus Mann go into exile? According to his account in *The Turning Point*, the two most widespread reasons did not apply to his case. The issue of his past political activities and affiliations need not have posed an impediment to his remaining, as far as the ruling Nazis were concerned; one need only consider the case of Gründgens, who had flirted with Communist ideology in the public arena during the 1920's, but who was nonetheless invited to stay. Reasons of religious background would not have played a role, even though Mann's mother was partly Jewish, because, as Mann calculated "according to the fantastic racial arithmetic adhered to by the Nazis," Klaus and his siblings would have been classified as Aryans. It is in fact likely that one or both of these reasons *would* have been used against the Mann family, but Klaus Mann sought to emphasize how his personal convictions led to his move from Germany rather than second-guessing the peculiar logic of the Nazis. Mann's literary and essayistic explanations for his decision to stay away from Germany insistently invoke the image of asphyxiation. In the journal *Das Wort* he wrote in 1937: "I left Germany...because even if I'd remained in 'freedom,' I would have had to suffocate in the air of the Third Reich." In the *Vulkan*, the army deserter Dieter reflects: "Breathing is becoming unbearable. That's it: you can't breathe ...the overwhelming vulgarity that's poisioning the air—like a colossal cadaver. I had to leave, or I would have suffocated!" *The Turning Point* contains a sober statement that "the fear of suffocation is a plain, cogent reason for any preventive action...You might as well suggest that a reasonable man ought to adapt himself to syphilis, or that he should overcome his prejudice against poison." In the *Wendepunkt* Mann declares that "the air in the Third Reich could not be breathed by certain lungs. Death by suffocation threatened at home." The metaphorical implication of this image for writers is clear: freedom of expression had been stifled in Germany. One can also interpret this suffocation literally, since a favorite tactic of Nazi censors was to throw stink bombs at literary readings they considered subversive.

According to Mann, German writers who chose exile formed a distinctive subgroup among the emigrants. "This roving tribe of sophisticated pariahs" even had its own Legion of Honor, selected by the Nazi government. Each time Goebbels issued an expatriation list, the membership of this group swelled. Mann cynically boasted that members of his own family appeared on all of the first four expatriation lists: first Heinrich, then Klaus, then Erika, and finally Thomas.

In the face of the mass deracination of German literature, Mann considered it imperative to mobilize the illustrious group of newly-exiled writers and assert the continued presence of literature even when uprooted by political circumstance. His ambition was threefold: to introduce the literary talents of the emigration scene to the European public, to make known to the emigrants the intellectual currents of their adopted homelands, and to project a political message to those still in Germany. The vehicle he chose for these goals was the journal *Die Sammlung*. After securing the patronage of André Gide, Aldous Huxley, and Heinrich Mann, and assembling a group of writers eager to contribute their talents, he launched publication of the monthly journal in September 1933. The successes and failures of this journal during its two years of existence are symptomatic of the early exile period as a whole. It involved an enthusiastic cooperative effort of an international community, as is reflected in contributions to the *Sammlung* by Romain Rolland, Bertolt Brecht, Jean Cocteau, Benedetto Croce, Albert Einstein, Christopher Isherwood, Ernest Hemingway, Ernst Bloch, Pär Lagerkvist, Else Lasker-Schüler, and Boris Pasternak. However, the conception of the *Sammlung* also brought to the foreground a fundamental dissension about the nature of the exile mission. The dispute hinged on whether German exile writing should remain clear of explicit political statement, so that access to the reading public within Germany would still be possible, or whether the time had come to take a firm political stand as the unified point of view of the writers. Klaus Mann decided in favor of an unequivocal political stand. As a consequence, four of his major contributors — René Schickele, Stefan Zweig, Alfred Döblin, and his father Thomas Mann — withdrew their support from the *Sammlung*, bowing to the indirect pressure that the propaganda ministry of Goebbels exerted on them via their German publishers. All of these eventually realized that no compromise with the Nazis was possible, and cast their lot with the camp of politically engaged writers.

During this period, Mann continued to write novels, such as *Flucht in den Norden* (Journey into Freedom, 1934), the story of a young woman torn between love and political commitment, who finally leaves her lover in order to fight Hitler in the resistance movement. However, as Mann's sense of commitment to the antifascist movement deepened and evolved into a mission that was to sustain and define him throughout Germany's dark years, he turned increasingly to the publication of non-fictional political statements bearing directly on current events. One notable essay of 1935 appeared in a collection smuggled into Germany, camouflaged as a textbook with the title *Deutsch für Deutsche*. Mann's contribution took the form of an open letter to the actress Emmy Sonnemann, Hermann Goering's fiancée, in which he expresses his outrage that in a time when men were being tortured to death on a daily basis, she could choose to marry the torturer. Mann reminds her of the commitment to moral values that an artist ought to maintain by alluding to Schiller's *Kabale und Liebe* (Cabal and Love, 1784): "Lady Milford threw away her jewels when she realized how they had been paid for. But maybe Milford isn't your specialty." It was especially disillusioning for Mann that the remaining artists in Germany appeared to have abandoned all moral scruples.

After spending over three years hovering near the German border in various European countries, Mann moved to the United States, which was destined to become his most permanent of exile homes. An earlier tour through America in the late 1920's had brought him into contact with eminent personalities from coast to coast, from H. L. Mencken in New York to Emil Jannings in Beverly Hills. He had lectured at Columbia and Princeton, chatted with actors and directors in Hollywood, and lived the most carefree of lives. Now he returned as an exile from a fascist dictatorship, fighting a battle that was incomprehensible to many Americans he encountered. Mann met with frequent disapproval over his decision to leave Germany: it was, after all, his country, right or wrong. Mann recalls in *The Turning Point* that Americans viewed the new wave of German immigrants as "those onerous Cassandras," whose prophecies of doom concerning the future of Europe made little sense. Other Americans, who were better informed about the situation in Germany, went to the opposite extreme of a blanket condemnation of all things German. Mann recognized the onset of a new phase of his antifascist mission: he wished to educate Americans about the evils of Nazism, but at the same time to defend the essential respectability of the German character. To these ends, Klaus and Erika Mann wrote two books in English: *Escape to Life* (1939) and *The Other Germany* (1940), which attempt to clarify the situation of German exiles. Klaus Mann published essays in *Esquire* and *The Nation,* and he founded the English-language journal *Decision,* whose fusion of literary and political pieces took up the goals of the *Sammlung.* Contributors included W. H. Auden, Sherwood Anderson, Somerset Maugham, Stephen Spender, and Jean-

Paul Sartre. Thomas Mann called *Decision* "the best, most colorful literary revue America has ever seen." Unlike many of his fellow émigrés in America, Mann acquired complete fluency in English. For a writer, whose medium is to a degree equivalent to his message, bilingualism can be a mixed blessing. Mann expressed the dilemma of exchanging one idiom for another in the *Wendepunkt*: "Am I not already half alienated from German? Maybe it will lead to my unlearning my native tongue without ever becoming completely at home with the new language...But if I no longer had any language, what would I have left?" The linguistic problem was symptomatic of the split identity Mann was to experience throughout his exile years. Klaus Mann, the intellectual pacifist, now found himself pleading with the American Selective Service Board to be admitted to the army. Klaus Mann, the "citizen of the world," as he liked to call himself, was jubilant when granted American citizenship in 1943. Klaus Mann, lover of German literature, wrote in his diary that he had enjoyed a book by Carson McCullers, but could not bring himself to read the latest work of Alfred Döblin, because it was written in the language that Hitler had polluted.

When Klaus Mann began work on his *Turning Point* in 1941, he was preparing to exchange his pen for a sword. The United States had just entered World War II, and Mann was eager to fight fascism in deed as well as in word. *The Turning Point* closes with his upcoming induction into the American army. Poised as he was for action, why would he elect the inherently reflective genre of autobiography?

Like the narrator Dante in the first canto of the *Inferno*, who considers the age of thirty-five as the "middle of the journey of our life," Mann found this age an appropriate midway station to take stock of his life and his community, to review "thirty-five years in this century," as the subtitle of *The Turning Point* indicates. Self-examination combined with societal analysis had fascinated Mann from the time of his earliest writings. In the introduction to *Kind dieser Zeit*, he labelled his autobiography a contribution to the monumental history of the childhood of the bourgeoisie. He expressed the feeling that his particular childhood was not as important as how it reflected a course of events leading up to World War I. Like Dante's *Commedia*, Mann's autobiographies invite a reading on a superpersonal level, as something greater than the description of an individual life. From the prologue of *The Turning Point*, in which Mann states that "our individual destinies are interwoven with the texture of a vast mosaic" to the close of the final chapter's postulate that "every human life is at once unique and representative," Mann asks us to examine his century as well as himself.

After the war ended, Mann wrote mostly journalistic pieces rather than full-length works. He spent much of his time traveling through Germany on lecture tours, as a means of testing out his continued relationship to his native country. To reestablish contact with Germany, he translated his English-language work on Gide into German, and thoroughly reworked *The Turning Point* into a final autobiographical portrait: *Der Wendepunkt*. This work is more than a mere translation of *The Turning Point*. It includes an additional chapter consisting of letters and essays that Mann wrote between 1943 and 1945, which focus on Mann's experiences in the American army. The "Decision" and "Exile" chapters contain some new material. The two most striking omissions in the *Wendepunkt* are the *Turning Point's* "Olympus" chapter and much of the coverage of Gustaf Gründgens and Mephisto.

A few months before his death in 1949, Mann submitted the manuscript of the *Wendepunkt* to his publisher Querido in Amsterdam, which soon after was acquired by S. Fischer, the publisher of Thomas Mann. The publication of the book became a complicated matter, with S. Fischer caught in the crossfire between its most prominent author Thomas Mann, who demanded publication of Klaus Mann's work, and Gustaf Gründgens, the most influential theater director in Germany, who threatened a boycott of the S. Fischer theater series unless passages pertaining to him were removed. It was only after both Thomas and Erika Mann's vigorous protests, and their agreement to delete those passages, that the work finally appeared in print in 1952. This reluctance typifies Klaus Mann's postwar reception in the Federal Republic, and that of many other exile authors, a situation that is only now beginning to change.

In Klaus Mann's adopted homeland, by contrast, *The Turning*

Point received consistently enthusiastic reviews, in The New York Times, The Saturday Review, The New Yorker, The Atlantic Monthly, The New Republic, and others. Milton Rugoff of The Herald Tribune compared *The Turning Point's* sections on memory to Proust and Wolfe, and praised the book's "unusual alloy" of reminiscence, political insight, and lighthearted causerie. The New York Post admired its "bright, staccato prose," and called it "one of the most readable autobiographies of the season." The Atlantic Monthly described Klaus Mann as an attractive product of the civilized Europe he was fighting to restore, and found that his work met all the tests of the successful autobiography. Without a doubt, Klaus Mann would have prized most highly of all the praise accorded by the man whose esteem had meant so much to him throughout his life: his father. Thomas Mann wrote in the prologue to the volume *Klaus Mann zum Gedächtnis* in 1950: "I truly believe that he belonged to the most talented of his generation; possibly he was the best of them all."

On the occasion of Thomas Mann's seventieth birthday, Klaus Mann wrote a detailed letter to his father describing his first post-war return to Germany, as an Intelligence Officer and War Correspondent for the army paper *Stars & Stripes*. This letter represents an important document about Germany and Germans at the moment of liberation frcm the Nazi regime. Klaus Mann's visit to Germany left such an indelible impression on him that he continued to reformulate the contents of this letter for several media throughout Europe. The selection we have appended in this volume, "An American Soldier Revisiting his Former Homeland," was a broadcast version for Swedish radio in 1947.

The conclusion that Mann reached — *you can't go home again* — applies to both his native and adopted homelands. In Germany, the subject of this broadcast, the continued presence of Nazi ideology confronted him at every turn; he was later to discover that the lack of change in post-war Germany would make publishers unwilling to print the works of an outspokenly antifascist exile, which only strengthened his disillusionment and sense of homelessness in Germany. America had also changed. The liberal president Roosevelt, so beloved by

Mann, was no longer in office, and rise of anti-Communist rhetoric unnerved the intellectual community of which he was a part. This sense of rootlessness was undoubtedly an important contributing factor in his 1949 suicide.

"An American Soldier Revisiting his Former Homeland" is a fitting continuation to and conclusion of *The Turning Point*. His autobiography begins in the Munich house in which he was born, at a time when his personal world and the society of the time were still intact. In the appended essay, we return to that same home—now an empty shell—which again symbolizes congruence, this time between his personal homelessness and the falling apart of the world around him.

For their cooperation and assistance, I would like to thank the publisher Berthold Spangenberg, the Klaus-Mann-Archiv in Munich, and the Columbia University Council for Research in the Humanities.

New York City
July 1984

Prologue

Where does the story begin? Where are the sources of our individual life? What remote adventures and forgotten passions have molded our being? What secret influences have shaped our profiles, gestures, and emotions? What whim or wisdom has provided us with that abundance of contradictory features inherent in our character? Where do we come from? Who are we?

Undoubtedly, we are more—something weirder and greater—than our biography indicates and our consciousness grasps. Nobody, nothing is disconnected. A comprehensive rhythm determines our thoughts. Our individual destinies are interwoven with the texture of a vast mosaic portraying and developing throughout the centuries the same age-old patterns. Every movement we make repeats an ancestral rite and at the same time foreshadows the attitudes of future generations. Even the most solitary experiences of our heart anticipate or echo the repertoire of past or coming passions.

It is a long quest and wandering: we may trace it back to the eerie twilight of jungles, caves, and barbaric temples. The bloody ceremonial of the offering continues in our dreams. In our unconscious reverberate the screams from the sacrificial altar; and the flame consuming the victim still sends its flickering light. Atavistic taboos, parricidal frenzy, incestuous desire, heritage of lusts and manias and fears haunt us, corrupt and inspire us. Our souls are perturbed by crimes whose name and gravity we do not know; our hearts are burdened with the weariness of sunken generations.

What is the source of this restlessness in my blood? Is it the pirate tradition of my Nordic forefathers? Which one of my weaknesses and vices is due to a Hanseatic great-great-grandfather—captain, trader, or judge—whose name I have never heard? What I believed to be my most personal sorrow only echoes, perhaps, the frustrations of men and women whose tragedies took place in the stifling coziness of a provincial little town far away, somewhere on the shore of the Baltic Sea.

A picturesque old town with narrow streets and gray, crooked houses —is this the appropriate background for the prologue of my chronicle? The name of the place is Lübeck. I have nothing to do with it, nor do I wish to go there. Yet I would not exist if it were not for Senator Heinrich Mann, an important member of that community—but not quite "dignified": the family line had already become a trifle eccentric. For if the Senator had been entirely comme il faut, according to Lübeck traditions, he would not have fallen in love with a Brazilian beauty. However, that was precisely what happened when he went there on business, seventy-five years ago. His beloved was the daughter of a German merchant and a native Brazilian. The Senator took her back to his home-town. That the joyful couple had to cross the ocean on a sailing ship, was to me, as a child, the most exciting detail of this quaint romance. It was delightful to imagine my grandfather—whom I never saw—carrying his exotic captive to shore from a picturesque schooner. The Senator—very stately and handsome: all whiskers and stiff white collar of tremendous proportions—discreetly groans under the weight of his struggling brunette. She, struggling in his arms, sings and brandishes a lovely pink parasol—bidding farewell to the Brazilian palm trees still visible on the other side of the sea, while, at the same time, the gray towers of Lübeck already loom in the fog.

They had five children—two girls and three boys. The two oldest sons were named Heinrich and Thomas.

Everything seemed perfectly all right with the Manns, so far. A highly respectable family—nothing to be said against them. Their home was one of the finest mansions in town, and the dinner parties they gave were as opulent as they could be. It seemed a pity, of course, that the Senator's brother was a good-for-nothing—slovenly and neurotic. And then, Mrs. Julia Mann—she was nice enough, to be sure. But wasn't she a little out of place, among the other ladies of the aristocracy? Not that anyone told scandalous stories about her. She was just a trifle different—that's all. Too attractive, too musical, and too capricious for the chilly climate of Lübeck. She played the piano—just a little too well—and sang wistful songs that were lovely but also slightly embarrassing. The two boys, Heinrich and Thomas, would probably be more cheerful and vigorous if they had a mother of good Nordic stock, instead of the Spanish belle. Didn't the two lads look rather fragile and dreamy? Their teachers complained about their lack of discipline, and their fellow-students sneered at them because they were not athletic. Rumor had it that they were in the habit of reading modernist books and producing poetry. Too bad for the Senator. Small wonder that he seemed weary and despondent.

Obviously, there was something wrong with his financial affairs too. Senator Mann, alas, was not as efficient and sturdy as his forebears used to be. He was too sensitive and fastidious—in brief, too much of a gentleman to be a successful merchant. When he died—all of a sudden—it turned out that the wealth of the family had melted away, almost entirely. The ancient firm was dissolved; the attractive widow left Lübeck, where she had always been a stranger. She moved to Munich, taking her younger children along. Heinrich and Thomas followed shortly, after having somehow juggled themselves through school. Now they were free at last—two independent young men endowed with a modest allowance and a profusion of melancholy wit and bizarre fantasy. Both had long since decided to become professional writers.

They were closely akin to and yet infinitely different from each other. Their characters and visions seemed to be the utterly divergent variations of one basic theme. The "leitmotiv" both had in common and assiduously paraphrased, was the blend of races—in their case, the Northern element and the Latin streak—as a stimulus and a problem.

From this fundamental antithesis derived the second one—the painful and productive tension between "the bourgeois" and "the artist": the ordinary, practical, and buoyant type of man, on the one hand—the uprooted, sensitive, spiritual type, on the other. Unending and involved is the flux of attraction and repulsion between those two opposite characters—constantly irritating and enchanting, missing and desiring each other. Emotions vibrate to and fro—a dialectic interchange inspiring and intriguing both sides. For "the bourgeois"—which means the normal citizen who feels at ease in this world—at once admires and distrusts his problematic counterpart, the artist; and vice versa. Both need and despise the other. Eros floats between them, disguised as envy or scorn or admiration. The bourgeois honors and respects, though with suspicious reservations, the "power of the spirit," "the august ideals," "the elating beauty of art," all these lofty results of secret struggle and agony. The creative type, on his part, is moved by an odd blend of reactions in view of so much healthy naïveté. How easy, he thinks, must be the life of those who have no vision and no mission. Those happy fools cannot know what it means to be burdened with Hamlet's curse: the curse of consciousness. How smooth and blank are their faces while my brow is disfigured by the cruel distinction of the creative impulse. How drab and meaningless must be the lives of those who have no vision and no mission.

It depends on the individual case which element predominates in the complexity of these feelings. In the case of Heinrich Mann, the element of artistic pride definitely prevailed: his contempt of "the bourgeois" was more intense than his envy. In fact, so deep and violent was his disdain of the "Philistines" that it could grow from an aesthetic animosity to a moral creed and political program. Paradoxically enough, the social urgency in his later books is derived from a pathos that is essentially individualistic, indeed, anti-social: the radical aestheticism of his youth turned into the social radicalism of his mature age.

The younger of the two brothers, however—Thomas—was inclined to stress his wistful tenderness for the fair-haired and laughing ones, rather than his own superiority and solitary splendor. He was a bohemian with a "guilty conscience"—full of nostalgia for the lost paradise of his patrician childhood; hankering, with a sort of ironic fervency, for what he had abandoned and could never regain—the "bliss of vulgarity." And while the nervous brilliancy of Heinrich Mann's early style seems to defy all conventions and compromises, the complex music of Thomas Mann's prose hesitates and woos, full of tender suggestions, complex connotations, and an intricate humor born out of longing and renunciation.

They lived and traveled together—the brothers and brotherly antagonists. They settled in Munich, after an extensive stay in Italy.

Each occupied a modest bachelor flat in the district called Schwabing, where "the aliens" lived, the Prussians, the painters, the Americans: all those whom the native Bavarians considered completely mad. Their widowed mother lived not far from them, with her youngest boy and two daughters. The Brazilian belle was growing old with surprising abruptness, abandoning her looks, smiles and pretensions as if they were jewels or valuable souvenirs to be sacrificed for the sake of her children. The older of the two girls, Lula, was dainty, reserved, and aristocratic; Carla was rather on the fleshy and voluptuous side. She wanted to become an actress, wore saucy hats, and smoked cigarettes. Her brother Heinrich adored her and later portrayed her in many of his novels. But by that time she had already overcome all her caprices and aspirations, and had atoned for her follies—the eccentric hats, the glaring flirtations, and her inadequate talent. She had committed suicide before her theatrical career really started—maybe because she knew, at the bottom of her heart, that it could never be much of a career.

The two older brothers of that lovely and pitiful creature, however, did start their careers—quietly, without hullabaloo. Heinrich's bold and provocative talent was soon recognized by a small group of radical connoisseurs, while the writings of Thomas already had begun to appeal to a broader public. Heinrich, proud and inhibited, restricted his social contacts almost exclusively to the bohemians. Thomas found his way to some of the more exclusive salons. And while Heinrich moved among the lion-maned artists of Schwabing with the helpless solemnity of a prince who has gone astray, Thomas appeared in society circles as an intellectual outsider—hiding his oddity under a conspicuous display of suavity. He may have felt a vagabond among the dignitaries, but he was an urbane vagabond, to be sure—too polite and well-bred to show his embarrassment when the hostess received him with jubilant heartiness: "Delighted to have you, my dear young friend! We were just discussing your novel—the Countess and myself. What's the name of your book? Budden . . . ? My poor memory! Please, help me, Mr. Mann! Is it Buddenbrooks . . . ?"

The most glamorous and gracious of all the hostesses in the Bavarian capital, Frau Hedwig Pringsheim-Dohm, was to play a decisive part in the young novelist's biography. For in the palatial home of the Pringsheims there was, among other treasures, an extraordinary young girl, called Katja—an only daughter—sister of four brothers, the youngest of whom was her twin.

The Pringsheims were an unusual family, rather startling even to so unconventional a society as that of pre-War Munich. Both Professor Pringsheim and his wife came from Berlin: he, from a Jewish background without much social distinction but with a great deal of money; she from the intellectual elite but penniless. Madame Pringsheim's father, Ernest Dohm, was among the founders of a satirical weekly, "Der Kladderadatsch," which exercised considerable influence during the Bismarck period. Her mother, Hedwig Dohm, was a leading suffragette and a fairly popular writer. She produced numerous novels about misunderstood women who suffered from their husbands and imitated the heroines of Henrik Ibsen's dramas. Her drawing-room had been one of the most colorful meeting places in old Berlin. Franz Liszt was a frequent visitor.

Frau Hedwig Dohm had several daughters; one of them, Hedwig, was strikingly beautiful. She became an actress and played Shakespearian ingenues in Meiningen. When the great Joseph Kainz starred there as Romeo, she was his Juliet, and so incredibly handsome that young Dr. Pringsheim, watching her from his box, promptly decided to marry her. So he did, and built her a princely mansion in the finest district of the finest city, Munich.

He collected renaissance tapestry, renaissance pottery, and renaissance silver. His house looked like a palazzo of the sixteenth century. But it was also the first private residence in town that could boast of electric light. He was a professor of mathematics at the University of Munich—an eminent scholar, if I am not mistaken, highly esteemed by all mathematicians. His fourth passion—besides mathematics, his wife, and Italian antiques—was the music of Richard Wagner: the young professor was among the first to finance the costly festivals in Bayreuth. His contact with Wagner ended when the master made ugly anti-Semitic remarks in the presence of his "non-Aryan" sponsor and admirer. The genius was tactless and ungrateful, and the professor had a violent temperament.

The social style of the house was at once grand and informal. The most clebrated artists and scholars of the period mingled in Madame Pringsheim's drawing-room with the princes of the House of Wittelsbach, opera singers from the Royal Theater, Bavarian generals, visiting bankers from Berlin, and some selected samples of the picturesque Schwabing type. The hostess—a dazzling blend of Venetian belle à la Titian and problematic grande dame à la Hedda Gabler—excelled in the long-forgotten art of perfect conversation, accompanying her sparkling eloquence with cascades of pearly laughter. She was sagacious,. charming, and provocative—whether she discussed Nietzsche and Dostoievski, or the great soirée at the home of the Crown Princess; the new canvas by Franz von Stuck or a recent speech of the Kaiser. Professor Pringsheim, short of stature, utterly brisk and jovial, would shock and amuse the party with the improvisations of his caustic wit. His creaky voice was drowned by the melodious lament of his wife: "Oh, Alfred dear! how terrible you are!"

It was in this colorful environment that the young novelist from Lübeck met the dark-eyed girl who so deeply captivated his imagination, his curiosity, and his heart. He had watched her at a distance before he came to know her socially. She bicycled to the University—surrounded by her brothers like a learned little Amazon leading a troupe of her loyal warriors. She studied mathematics, and combined the ready wit of Portia with Jessica's sweet and exotic looks. She was playfully aggressive and yet gentle; pugnacious, witty, innocent, and shy. The young novelist was enthralled. He saw and described her as an oriental princess, a perspicacious child, an at once savage and delicate flower. Hand in hand with her twin brother, Klaus, a young musician, she roved through the streets of Munich. Everybody was struck by their peculiar charm and puzzled by their rapid dialogues bristling with secret formulas, tender allusions, enigmatic jokes. From their aimless escapades they returned to the familiar palace, their home. There they hid from the vulgar world protected by their wealth and wit, watched and spoiled by servants and instructors. Two bewitched infants who knew and loved each other exclusively; they quarrelled and giggled together, while their mother's tinkling laughter came from the terrace like the soft, gay music of a fountain, and the melodies of Rheingold and Parsifal thundered from the big music hall.

At first the fairy-tale princess was rather chilly and flippant to the young novelist. Gradually, however, his sophisticated flatteries and patient tenderness succeeded in breaking the ice—particularly since the twin brother as well as the majestic Maman were rather in favor of the match. As for her father, he would have opposed every conceivable suitor who threatened to take his beloved child from him. It was a thorny task to mollify old Pringsheim's bilious temperament. Happily, there was at least one thing the capricious scholar and his future son-in-law had in common, besides their mutual devotion to Katja—the love for Wagner's work. The professor did not care for literature, nor was the novelist interested in mathematics or majolicas. But both were under the spell of Tristan and Meistersinger. They could always exchange quotations out of Siegfried or The Flying Dutchman when there was nothing else they wanted to tell each other.

The intricate romance between the two young people developed under the auspices of Wagnerian harmonies. Finally it was blessed by the parents and legalized by a Lutheran minister.

The wedding celebration in the Pringsheim palazzo was a great affair, as can easily be imagined. "All Munich" paid homage to the young couple; the Professor delivered a speech full of acrid jocularities; the hostess looked like a dream of Titian, and even old Frau Mann resembled more than ever a fairy-tale princess, with her dark, musing eyes widened under the crown of myrtle. Pale and lovely and exceedingly young, Katja presided at the sumptuous gathering, with her bridegroom at her side. His face, too, was a little pale but composed and dignified, with his handsome bushy mustache and those peculiar eyes of his—very bright eyes under slanting brows, at once piercing and absent-minded, greenish-gray in color. Erect and slender in his well-fitting dress-suit, he tried to conceal his emotion, smiling and conversing, as amiable and correct as ever. But his bride sometimes forgot to answer. She seemed strangely bewildered—deeply absorbed in thoughts.

Did her heart and mind cling to the past—to all those sweet and familiar things she was going to lose? The games with her brothers,

mother's tea parties; the rituals of kissing her father good-night, opening his egg at the breakfast table . . . The quarrels, the giggling, the
studies, the family gibberish incomprehensible to every outsider . . . the
fairy-tale of her youth?

And now? What awaited her when this party was over? A new adventure and fairy-tale, or bitterness and disillusionment? What did he
mean, her young novelist, when he spoke of a "solemn happiness," a
"delicate bliss" they would experience together? He had a queer man
ner of saying such things—at once grave and casual. "A solemn happiness": that was so like him! He loathed everything soft and slouching.
Happiness—just commonplace happiness would be a little bit on the
slouching side: so much the pensive bride understood. But why had
she been chosen—she, of all women from the Baltic Sea to the Alps—
to share with him his extraordinary lot? Of what form and substance
was the invisible link that connected her with that disciplined dreamer
from a distant Hanseatic town? Did they belong together, she and he,
because both were "different"?—somehow remote from reality; ironic,
problematic, vulnerable, and not allowed to indulge in easy satisfactions
or convenient sentimentalities? Was this the affinity between them:
that both were "exceptional," both artists?

For, obviously, she did not belong to that bright-eyed type whom
the leading characters in his books so tenderly despised and wistfully
desired. She was neither blonde nor ignorant and dashing, but dark-
eyed and reflective and only too familiar with all the torments and
solitudes he described. Their marriage, then, was not the meeting between two opposite elements, two contrasting moods and races. It
rather was the union of two beings mysteriously akin to each other: a
protective alliance to save both from certain destructive forces. His
decision to seek happiness, to accept the joys and responsibilities of
normal life—what was it, at the bottom, if not a defense mechanism?—
a strategic move to overcome that "sympathy with Death" which was
so beautifully and perturbingly woven into the tissue of all his tales.
No discipline or wit would be strong enough to meet his sweet and
deadly temptation, Tristan's nihilistic ecstasy, the Nirvana complex,
the saturnine spell of all romanticism. What power, then, could cope
with that weird attraction? Was Love the magic remedy?—mighty

and creative enough to transform the mortal seduction into a stimulus of life? But how hard it must be to learn the idiom of love; how painful to endure the shame and the sacrifices!

Shall I be brave enough? she mused, very frail and childlike between her sparkling father and pale, straight bridegroom. Is everything to be completely different, from now on? Will it take very long for me to get used to it?

Everything takes long: which is, perhaps, the most cruel and the most gracious quality of life. Life moves slowly. The pivotal decisions may be made in one dramatic moment, but they materialize and develop only gradually: it takes months or years until they assume the weight and the familiar features of reality.

A small apartment in Schwabing, not far from the Pringsheim mansion: was that the enormous change? But the intimate contact with the whimsical father, the loving and brilliant Maman, the chivalrous brothers, continued. Life seemed almost what it used to be.

It was only four or five months later that the bewildering transformation began. There it was—the wondrous experience; the most natural and yet miraculous promise. How heavy and disfigured the delicate fairy-tale princess now appeared. How puzzled and helpless she seemed. Another few months, little mother, and you will know if it is to be a boy or a girl!

It was a girl. They called her Erika. She had the dark eyes of her mother. The young father thought her wonderful.

And before Erika learned to stammer her first "daddy," a brother and playmate arrived—on November 18, 1906. Two of his uncles, Klaus Pringsheim and Heinrich Mann, agreed to be his godfathers. His full name was Klaus Heinrich Thomas Mann.

The Turning Point

CHAPTER ONE

The Myths of Childhood

(1906–1914)

> . . . *a stone, a leaf, an unfound door; of a stone, a leaf,*
> *a door. And of all the forgotten faces.*
>
> THOMAS WOLFE
>
> *La réalité ne se forme que dans la mémoire.*
>
> MARCEL PROUST

MEMORIES are made of peculiar stuff, elusive and yet compelling, powerful and fleet. You cannot trust your reminiscences, and yet there is no reality except the one we remember. Every moment we pass through derives its meaning from the preceding one. There would be no present nor future if the past were blotted out in the minds of men. It is our capacity for recollection which stands between us and chaos—a rather fragile bulwark, we must admit.

What do we remember? How much? According to what principles does our consciousness keep the traces of certain sensations, whereas others are dropped into the abyss of the unconscious? Is there any sort of identity or authentic kinship between my present ego and the youngster whose curly head I have seen in faded portraits? Would I know much about that golden-haired lad without the reports and souvenirs handed down to me by other witnesses? When I try to recall what it may have felt like to bear the silky weight of those curls, I always find myself, curiously, in a room of our house, near a table where my mother kept a collection of photographs neatly displayed in a flat silver bowl. It may have been among these family relics that I discovered the portrait of my former self. Probably I was only six or

3

seven when I lingered, a chubby little Narcissus, before my own image. The boy who rummaged mother's photo album had already lost his handsome mane of gold: he wore a modest page coiffure, with bangs hanging deep over his forehead. His look at the smiling physiognomy of his past was already that of nostalgia.

What, then, do I remember? Who is the lad I recognize in the twilight of that drawing room? Is he the one who wore the silky curls? Or is it already his "aging" brother who wistfully gazes at the splendor that used to be his own? Do I remember the curls or only the reflection they left in the mind of a curl-less child?

Our unconscious responds to certain tokens, secret cues and signs that come to us from nobody-knows-where. There is an aroma, faint and yet intense; a fusion of rubber and a particular sort of linen and lacquered wood, with a touch of flannels and calico, the material of which curtains are made: the curtains of a baby carriage. But is it *my* baby carriage whose soft, swinging rhythm I now feel rocking me, once again? Or is this another delusion? What I now take for my experience may have actually belonged to my younger brother, Golo. I always had a certain proclivity to rob him of his candies and toys; for I was older and bigger. Do I now try to steal the blissful slumber of his babyhood? I already had to walk, toilsomely, step by step, when it was his turn to be wheeled about. No doubt, the baby carriage I recall is the one which I envied Golo. No matter how hard we try to capture the bliss of paradise, it is only our own longing for the paradise lost we succeed in finding.

The baby carriage is the paradise lost. The only happy period in our life is that part of it we spent asleep. There is no happiness where there is memory. To remember things means to yearn for the past. Our nostalgia begins with our consciousness.

How could I ever forget the beloved image which so often helped me to find sleep and oblivion? Night by night I invoked the token of a cradle furnished with sails—a magic bark to carry me far away; through dark woods, over silent waters, straight into the purple depth of a bottomless sky. I must have seen the winged cradle in some painting or heard about it in a fairy-tale. It followed me through years, a symbol of night and escape. Gradually, however, the cradle altered its shape; it became longer and tighter. The vessel on which I now embark for the harbor of forgetfulness has a more sinister form and color. Cradle and coffin, womb and grave are emotional synonyms.

The sleep we keep longing for, the perfect sleep, is dreamless. We are haunted by dreams as soon as we have learned to remember and to repent. At the age of five, or even before that time, I was already familiar with the evil whisper of nightmares. The room which I first shared with Erika, then with Golo, was invaded by apparitions. How I loathed the pallid gentleman who came almost every night to disturb my rest! Sometimes he carried his head under his arm, as if it were a flower-pot or a cylinder. It was most unpleasant, indeed, to have his disconnected face grin and nod at me. So intense were my fear and hatred of this particular visitation that I decided at last to do something about it and discussed the matter with our nurse, Anna with the blue cheeks. The Blue Anna, on her part, talked it over with our father, who felt that effective measures were appropriate to stop the headless nuisance.

He came to see us at bedtime—a rare event in itself!—and developed his proposed strategy. The decapitated guest, he suggested, wasn't really so frightful. He tried to get the better of us by sheer bluff. "Just don't look at him when he comes again!" he advised us. "Then he'll probably vanish. If he still annoys you ask him politely to beat it. Tell him that a children's bedroom is no place for a decent phantom to hang out and that he should be ashamed of himself. This may be enough to get rid of him, but if he still hesitates, you may warn him that your father is very irritable and just doesn't like to have ugly spooks in his house. At this point he'll disappear without making any more fuss. For it is a well-known fact in ghostly circles that I can make myself very unpleasant, indeed."

We followed his advice and the spook presently dissolved. It was an imposing proof of Father's almost superhuman insight and influence. From that time on we began to call him "Zauberer"—magician.

The life of a five-year-old is painful and complicated compared with the beatific coma of babyhood. It seems paradisiac, however, if contrasted with the whirlwind of problems and sufferings we have now to cope with. In a case like my own this contrast is particularly striking; for the relative peace and serenity characteristic of the child in general seems redoubled by the idyllic condition of the period and the social sector to which our family belonged. If the youngster is comparatively carefree even in the midst of trouble and disaster, the child that lives in a protected, prosperous world must deem this universe an almost perfect institution.

The nostalgia of childhood is reserved to the rare hours of reverie and to those five minutes each night when the room has been darkened and the fatigued mind lingers between dream and consciousness. But the early morning finds you awake and buoyant. The cold water in your face is a delightful thrill; the breakfast—a festival. A new day! Your day! Your sun! Your coffee! Your appetite!

The child is strangely akin to the primitive man: innocent and greedy; without guile or mercy; ignorant and creative. As man in the vernal era of antiquity, so the child evaluates and orders all phenomena anew as it were, for the very first time. Naïve and realistic, unable to grasp abstractions, it builds its own hierarchy and myth according to what it sees, smells, and touches. Nothing exists outside the scope of its own interests and perceptions. How could it doubt the unique significance of its experiences? There is nothing with which to compare them.

A rainy day, a journey, the physical sensations of cold, hunger, fever, toothache, or love; the flavor of wines, melodies, or caresses— the whole repertoire of our emotional and bodily life is burdened with memories. The day inevitably arrives—sooner, perhaps, than you anticipated!—when there are no longer "new experiences," only the variations of familiar patterns. After a long time of intense and conscious life you may even reach the point of recognizing the general human characteristics in the unmistakable features of the most beloved individual. Then you perceive behind the singular face of your mother the drama and beauty of motherhood. To the mature and experienced mind the "type" is more essential than its individual representative. The child confounds, on the contrary, the accidental representative with the species. All mothers have to adapt their voices, motions and smiles to the one mother who counts; namely, yours. As the genius of antiquity personified the basic impulses and elements—love, storm, water, war, fertility—the child conceives the mother, the dog, the garden, the milk, the disease.

Even the nicknames made up and employed by the child possess absolute validity. Since we called our mother "Mielein," we never thought it possible one could call her anything else. Is there anyone who does not know who Ofey and Offi are? You might as well not know the name of Jupiter and his relationship with the goddess Minerva. Obviously, Ofey is Mielein's father and, therefore, Offi's husband; for Offi, quite naturally, is Mielein's mother, our spectacular grandmamma with lustrous, near-sighted eyes, a fountain-like, silvery laugh, and a very handsome lorgnette fixed on a silver chain she wears around her neck. Offi has a merciless manner of examining you through her glasses. Many people turn fidgety under her piercing regard, but we don't. Of course not: she is "our" Offi, and the lorgnette is a part of her, her token, just as the owl is the goddess Athena's or the lightning belongs to Zeus.

To fear the great dignitaries of the hierarchy would be as preposterous as to criticize them. They are the way they are and have to be treated with reverence and indulgence. There is nothing frightful about Father: he is gentle and good. Of course, he has his little weaknesses and animosities which you must heed and respect if you want to remain on pleasant terms with him. For instance, he has something against dirty finger-nails and doesn't like you to use your thumb to transfer a bit of food from your plate to the spoon or fork. Curious as it may seem, this harmless procedure is likely to irritate him completely. "For heaven's sake—not the thumb!" he may beg you, looking sick with disgust. "Use the tip of your nose, if anything! Or your big toe! Everything is all right with me—as long as it isn't your thumb."

There are other taboos, all of them irrational but not difficult to observe. You must keep quiet from nine o'clock in the morning until noon, Father's working hours, and again from four to five in the afternoon when he rests. To enter his studio while he is mysteriously occupied there would be as blasphemous as to invade the temple when a secret ceremonial is taking place. To annoy or to hurt your father is an exceedingly serious matter, although he never hits you. His offended silence is embarrassing, indeed, painful enough. Your mother scolds you when you have done naughty things, stained your clothes or eaten sweets before dinner time. Such palpable transgressions are likely to be overlooked by your father. You never can tell what he is going to notice and how he will react. The paternal authority is incalculable—at once touchy and lenient.

It seems so odd and even somehow deceitful to employ these accepted terms: "father," "mother," "paternal authority." For how could I possibly succeed in describing the peculiar blend of moods inherent in the traditional labels? "Father" . . .: that is the ticklish touch of a mustache; the aroma of cigars and eau de Cologne; a smile thoughtful and absent-minded. "Father" means a placid, sonorous voice; the long rows of books in his working room—a solemn, suggestive sight. And music . . . yes, his image and name invoke harmonies; floating, saturnine sounds; the wistful fragment of a melody he used to play at the piano. Shortly before supper, after his evening walk, he would withdraw into the darkening drawing room, and then the fatherly tune would waft, soft and low, through the house, up to the second floor where we sat with our governess.

"He plays so beautifully," said one of us four children. "Does he practice at his desk, between nine and twelve?"

But the governess laughed. "He doesn't practice at all," she said. "He doesn't know how to play, really. He just improvises a little."

What he played in the solitude of the dusky salon could hardly be called an improvisation. It always was the same rhythm, at once drawling and violent; always the same desperate tenderness; always that swelling, weeping, jubilating song: It was always Tristan.

If it is an intricate and delicate task to define the essence and aura of the paternal myth—the mother image is even more evasive and untouchable. For she is closer to us than Father, who always remains somewhat remote. She is the most familiar being—the indispensable one. She teaches you how to pray and to swim and to wash your face. She makes the menu, buys your birthday gifts, goes coasting and skating with you. The motherly hair is soft, rich and dark; the motherly eyes are gold-brown; the motherly hands are fragile and dexterous, helpful, intelligent hands: they can repair the hole in your shirt and, if necessary, can even cut your hair. They also know how to caress and to play and to comfort.

Mother and father are inseparable and yet essentially different from each other—a heterogeneous double-being. Father speaks rather slowly, in an equal, resonant voice; Mother's speech is rapid, jumping from the deepest bass up to surprising heights. She is fond of bitter chocolate and takes her tea without cream and sugar: he prefers things sweet, soft, and milky. Mother is efficient but untidy: Father, dreamy but neat. Mielein does not care if you disturb her at three o'clock in the morning; but she minds your losing your new gloves or being late at the dentist's. The Magician does not even know that you possess gloves or that your teeth require medical treatment; but he disapproves of immoderate speed in eating your soup or pudding and expects you to enjoy the long walks he is in the habit of taking, if possible with the dog and the children.

They are the way they are: there is nothing to change or to wonder about. Father has an unmistakable manner of clearing his throat, especially when he sits alone in his studio, during the working hours; Mother has a rather painful technique of pulling at the lobe of your ear when she thinks you deserve a serious punishment (in fact it hurts more intensely than any one would anticipate). Doctor Cecconi is furnished with his fearful drill, whereas Jennie, of course, has her voluminous bosom.

Fantastic as it may seem, there are, perhaps, readers who don't know who Doctor Cecconi is and even are somewhat puzzled as to Jennie's identity. So I may as well present Doctor Cecconi, the dentist, and our Jennie, "the pearl" who has always been with us; the lusty, versatile chambermaid who actually runs the household. It seems absurd that I should be obliged to mention such fundamental facts. To point out that Jennie is our faithful guardian angel and butler and mascot, is almost as trivial as it would be to mention that Motz is a collie, black, with beautiful white spots on his flanks. All this—the dog, the dentist, the maid; Father's music and Mother's laugh—is self-evident and indispensable. The attributes of life need no explanation.

The odd thing about children is that they don't question the necessity and rightness of the phenomena surrounding them, but think them exceedingly funny. Uncle Cecconi is funny because he speaks with a foreign accent and makes faces to amuse us while he repairs our teeth. Jennie, of course, is big fun with her glittering, greenish eyes, her dynamic efficiency, and the imposing curves of her figure. ("Jennie has such soft, big breasts," I observed, as a child of five. Whereupon the grown-up person who subsequently repeated the story asked me if I considered this phenomenon ugly or beautiful. "Not really beautiful," I replied, musingly, "but I enjoy looking at it.")

Motz was too amusing for words when he transformed himself into a jangling devil as soon as he left the house. Gentle and obedient at home, he promptly began to rave when excited by the smell of freedom. The frantic noise he produced was howling rather than barking. Gyrating, foaming, capering in a veritable paroxysm of nervous delight and fury, he irked adults and scared or beguiled children. Motz was a sensation; or rather, our little party including Motz inevitably attracted a lot of malignant or startled comments. Sometimes, in Munich or in the country, a friendly lady or gentleman would offer us a candy or an apple and talk to us, with that unctuous condescension typical of the grown-ups.

"You look so cute," the friendly stranger would say. "All four of you. Very cute and different. Who is your dad, little fellow?"

The ludicrous question was addressed to Erika, whom the silly grown-up took for a boy. Of course, we didn't answer but only giggled and shrugged. As soon as the idiotic adult had withdrawn, however, we assailed our escort—governess or mother—with excited questions.

Why was that stupid old lady so interested in our father? Why did she call him "dad," without even knowing his name? And what on earth made her say that we were "different" and "cute"? Different from whom? If it was Mielein who accompanied us, we were just told not to bother. "Never mind," she said. "People talk a great deal of nonsense." But the governess or Jennie seemed flattered and animated after incidents of this sort.

"Why, of course," they would chuckle, "you do look kind of different from the other kids. It's mostly your artistic outfit, I suppose . . ."

Our "artistic outfit" consisted of embroidered coats and knickerbockers which Mielein had chosen for us. They were made of heavy linen—very solid and handsome, indeed. But the little boys in the street thought them ridiculous and sneered at us when we passed by—two couples (Erika and I; Golo and Monika), followed by the governess; protected by the hysterical collie.

What fatuity!—to find anything comical or conspicuous about us. Didn't they realize, those preposterous grown-ups and truculent youngsters, that everything we did, wore, or said, was not only normal but, indeed, the very essence of normality? True, Monica was still rather small and silly; but little sisters are "meant" to be tiny and ignorant. As for Golo—one year older than Monica—he was not much taller but infinitely more serious and composed: an utterly dignified little man. No doubt, Golo was the pattern and paragon of a younger brother—nothing to laugh about. Was it conceivable that people, in their colossal dumbness, found anything to object to in Erika and myself? Those gawky strangers should be ashamed of their own glaring folly, rather than to marvel or to jeer at us. For, after all, we were "real," whereas their reality seemed pretty dubious to us. They were only "people": we were—"we."

Our life could not but be exemplary, as it simply was *life*—the only one we knew. Life, of course, needs no justification. There is nothing to criticize or to explain about its autonomous reality: there would be no world but a vacuum if "our" world ceased to be.

We did not need the outside world of the ribald strangers. What could it offer us? It was specious and dreary. In our own realm we found everything we could wish for. We had our own laws and taboos, games and superstitions; our songs and slogans, our arbitrary animosities and predilections. We were self-sufficient.

Anna cooked the soup and Jennie set the table. Anna was less significant than Jennie; but both were indispensable. So was, in a less conspicuous way, the third servant, the housemaid, whose identity often changed but whose character and appearance seemed stable. She was a clumsy thing from the country with huge, bluish hands and a stubborn forehead. Her true importance sprang not so much from the fact that she fixed our beds and cleaned our shoes and coats, but from her ability to teach us popular songs. It was thanks to the housemaid that we became familiar with all those fine, heartbreaking ballads about dashing sailors and abandoned girls. We adored the gloomy tune and the incomprehensible text. Bilious authorities like the governess or grandmamma Offi sometimes disapproved of this sort of musical training.

"I really don't understand why Katja allows the children to pick up such hideous nonsense," Offi would complain, emphatically supported by the governess.

"How perfectly right you are, Frau Geheimrat!" she agreed, all servile hypocrisy. "I've frequently begged Madame to stop this obnoxious mischief."

In cases of this kind Mielein was inclined to take our side, not too openly, to be sure. "You must not contradict Fräulein Betty!" she admonished us, somewhat vaguely. "It may be, of course, that she happened to be a little bit nervous—probably because you anger her so much. In any case, you may sing the ballad for us after dinner, just to find out if it's really that bad."

It was a colossal hit. Mielein and "the magician" almost suffocated with laughter. Finally Father managed to tell us that this was, in his opinion, an unusually moving song, not objectionable at all. However, we ought not to recite it too frequently, partly because Fräulein Betty disliked it; partly because the ballad would remain more effective if we saved it for extraordinary occasions. Christmas might be a nice opportunity, one of us suggested; and our parents laughingly agreed.

Fräulein Betty's smile was rather tart, not to say downright bitter, when we informed her that our musical presentation had been approved of by our supreme authorities.

The governess could hardly be very much of a nuisance as long as Mielein was there to protect our constitutional rights. But the situation became alarming when Mother had to spend a winter somewhere in Switzerland, because of a slight affection of her lungs. She wrote us witty and nostalgic letters, but they were no substitute for her presence. Now there was nobody to pray with us at night (for we wouldn't say our prayers in front of the governess); nobody who belonged to the peak of the hierarchy and at the same time to us. Jennie, Anna, the housemaid, Motz, and we ourselves were all right but lacking in power and dignity. Both Father and Offi certainly possessed plenty of might and glamor; but the latter displayed it too obviously, while the former did not show enough of it. The influence of the governess grew in a disquieting way: in fact, she was on the point of establishing a veritable tyranny.

The governess is one of the central myths of my childhood. She is touchy, proud, and capricious; by turns lovable and forbidding. Her face appears sometimes taut and ashen with bitterness—sometimes beaming with gracious serenity. Everybody seems a little afraid of her, even our parents. Her reproachful air reminds us of the fact that she has had a better time and more obedient pupils in the household of Baron Steiner, who unfortunately moved to Canada.

"I often wish I'd gone along with the Baron!" sighs the governess —whereupon we almost weep with gratitude for her generous patience. She makes us believe that any other governess we might possibly have got would have either left "this sloppy house" at once or imposed truly Draconian rules upon us. We implore her not to abandon us. She is mild and wise: her successor might be a vicious termagant.

In reality, however, they were all alike. They followed each other, an impressive parade, from the legendary Blue Anna up to that vain and whimsical "Fräulein" whom we called Betty-the-Lily because of her delicate character and complexion. The chronicle of our childhood could be divided into five or six great periods according to the changing régimes of those wayward queens. We might speak of the "Blue Anna period" or "the Lily era," just as we refer to the Elizabethan period or the epoch of Catherine the Great. Of course, they differed from each other in minor characteristics, but what they had in common was more profound and essential. All of them cherished the memory of an ideal household with which they had formerly been connected—some brilliant Baron who, alas, had meanwhile transplanted his fine family to the shores of a distant country. They all observed, with the same patronizing smile, that our father and mother were "very interesting people," which tactfully meant that, of course, one could not compare our bohemian milieu with the smart and idyllic set-up in a baron's castle. "Other children" were at once delicate and tough, in contrast to us violent and hypocritical sissies. Other children had fun and knew how to take a beating; they washed their teeth twice a day, went to church, were good sports and worshipped their governess.

We didn't like other children. It was only much later, when I was twelve years old, that we began to have friends. Up to that time we had only ourselves.

Erika and I were sent to a private school, a rather dusty and pretentious little institution where the scions of Munich's "Upper Ten" were introduced into the mysteries of the alphabet and the multiplication table. School, in this preliminary and harmless form, meant neither big fun nor big trouble. The fundamentals of reading and writing were easy enough to grasp. The teacher, an elderly spinster with sour features, was considered a humorous freak. As for our classmates, we had but little contact with them. They didn't know our games and idiom.

Our games were more intricate than the primer, more exciting than the rough amusements popular among kids. There were no "games," really: there was just one vast and complicated phantasmagoria—a mythic system within the myth of childhood, an elaborate cosmology rather than a play. It started with two different patterns which overlapped and gradually merged. The first scheme embraced the realm of the dolls and dogs, whereas the second dealt with our own world and involved the house, the garden, the parents, Jennie, and the governess. The house was transformed into a huge boat that kept cruising over the seven seas.

Fräulein Betty had read to us a melodramatic story called "Captain Spieker and his Cabin-Boy," which seized our fancy so profoundly and lastingly that we often amuse ourselves, even today, by reciting extensive quotations out of that trashy story. In those days, however, we took every detail of the adventurous plot as seriously as the Holy Bible. Our vision of the Big Boat was shaped precisely according to the model of Captain Spieker's vessel. Jennie and the other maids were the sailors; Mielein, a sort of fashionable super-stewardess. Father, of course, was the captain, hiding, most of the time, in the sanctum of his private cabin. There were only four passengers: two capricious ladies called Princess Erika and Mademoiselle Monica, and two gentlemen of high degree, both furnished with fancy titles and staggering bank accounts. Golo and I were exceedingly fond of personifying these stately globe-trotters: it was fun to adapt our conduct to their grand and whimsical style. They were no frivolous playboys, our traveling millionaires—quite the contrary. Two men in their early sixties, they had to carry a heavy burden of responsibilities and paternal sorrows. Ominous radiograms informed them about catastrophic developments of the stockmarket, while secret messengers delivered alarming news as to the behavior of their distant sons. Those young men, utterly naughty and unrestrained, wasted millions for immoderate supplies of candies and chocolate tarts, while the troubled fathers spent their days musing upon the wickedness of the world.

My son Bob was a pretty doll of celluloid, very cute and silly, with wide-open, laughing eyes and roguish little dimples in his cheeks. I adored him and obstinately refused to spend the night without having him in my bed. His function and importance in my life were multiform and complex. First of all, he was my beloved toy and most treasured possession. Secondly, he played the decisive role—together with Motz, the collie—in that extensive and wondrous saga we hatched and developed throughout the years. In this context the versatile darling appeared as the son and savior of King Motz, whose life and realm were periled by two enemies: the ferocious phalanx of the Amazons, led by the governess, and the cohort of nasty street Arabs, the same vicious lot that kept harassing us when we walked and played.

Unfortunately, however, Prince Bob was not as virtuous as he was plucky. When the battle was over, or rather, when a battle was over, for the strife never ceased, he indulged in all sorts of frivolous diversions among which the excessive partaking of cream tarts and rich layer-cakes was the most costly and immoral one. In short, the radiant hero and heir was at the same time quite a problem child and reckless good-for-nothing who caused a lot of scandalous expenses. And it was precisely in this capacity—in his role as gluttonous Prince Charming—that my celluloid Bob was admitted to the elegant sphere of the liner. It was his sparkling personality which linked the two incongruous domains—the streamlined packet-boat and the bellicose dreamland.

The epic struggle between the noble dolls and the ribald Amazons seemed as unending as the aimless voyage of our home floating across the seas. The intrigues and adventures of the two fanciful schemes more and more intermingled. Golo and I, the two troubled magnates, shook our heads over disconcerting news that reached us with regard to the strategic situation at the Motz front.

"Did you read this, your Lordship?" I asked Golo, who replied: "No, your Holiness. Anything new from the battlefield?"

"Ten thousand babies slaughtered," I announced sombrely. "That's about all. And two million lovely little dogs taken prisoners. Everything may be lost, King Motz endangered himself, unless Prince Bob renounces his cherry pies and performs one of his stunning feats."

"Too late! too late!" wailed my honorable colleague. "Woe is us! The good King is doomed. The Amazons come out victorious."

And he pointed at Fräulein Betty, who hurriedly approached from the house.

Games and life are one tissue, magically interwoven. The games assume the vigorous color of reality: reality—the iridescent charm of plays, dreams and songs. The time of childhood, as I now recall it, seems a brilliant sequence of serene rituals and ceremonious pleasures.

There is always something to look forward to. During the morning hours, there is the promise of luncheon: while you are eating your soup, you already dream of the pudding. From September until December you anticipate, joyfully and impatiently, the radiant ritual of Christmas Eve with its bountiful display of beaming candles, spicy cakes, and two hundred gaudy surprises; the beloved ceremonial of the solemn hymns sung in a darkened room before the folding-door opens to reveal the glittering sight of the magic tree. Christmas when everybody overeats of stuffed goose and marzipan; the happy birthday of the Infant Jesus—festival of glee and harmony, the glowing climax of the children's year. The following weeks are still brightened by Christmas souvenirs, which gradually fuse with the expectation of Easter. Of course, the festival of the colored eggs cannot compete with the great joy of the beaming conifer. But it is a great affair in its own way, the serene inaugural of spring. Then there is summer to look forward to, the blessed months of June, July, and August spent in Tölz, a picturesque little town situated near the Alps, by the Isar river.

We have a house in Tölz and a spacious garden where many games can be played that couldn't be played elsewhere. The days of immutable brightness are long but eventually come to an end: the summer lingers in depletion and weariness over the meadows and fields. The summer games become stale when the chrysanthemums display their mellow splendor in the flower-beds. You are glad that winter is near, with snowball battles and coasting and the regular Sunday dinners at your grandparents' home.

Ofey's sumptuous renaissance palazzo always maintained a thrilling flavor of mystery—it was so vast and so rich!—and yet it was, in a sense, the most familiar place, the castle of childhood, the exquisite mansion of souvenirs. It always existed—has never ceased to be. The apartment in which I was born, the modest flat in Schwabing, has long faded away: we left it when I still was a baby. Our second home was situated in a residential district of suburban character, by the Isar river. It must have been a spacious and pleasant dwelling, but somehow it failed to become mythic: in my memory it seems a comfortable waiting-room where we spent several years while "the new house" was in the making. As for the latter, a stately villa on the bank of the river, its picture dominates the major part of my youth. However, it remains "the new house" to me, as I was already eight years old when we moved into it, in 1914.

Four years later, in 1918, we gave up the country house in Tölz, the beloved idyll of so many summers. Tölz is the heart and kernel of the childhood myth, but its reality has become rather flimsy. I have not entered the house since the day we left it. Of course, I still remember the arrangements of the rooms, the shape and color of the furniture, the magnificent view from the terrace. But all details are blurred and transfigured, too intensely imbued with nostalgia and dream.

The only place whose legendary patina was equal to that of Tölz was Grandfather Ofey's splendid residence in the center of Munich. A focus of souvenirs, it is profoundly connected with the inmost essence of my early years, and yet it remained actual and palpable when the house in Tölz had long undergone that wondrous meta-morphosis which transforms wallpapers, windows, stones and stoves into the weightless and indestructible substance of the myth. When I try to retrace the first dining-room where I was taught how to eat, sitting erect at a table side by side with the adults, it is the gorgeous hall in the Pringsheim home that looms up, lavishly adorned with Ofey's potteries. Throughout our childhood his collection meant to us the symbol of fragility and preciousness. For we had been told that each of those gaudy plates, bowls and tankards represented "a fortune" in itself: to break one of them would be "the" unforgivable crime—worse than murder or pulling your brother's hair when you fought with him. To pull any one's hair was, of course, a pretty gruesome thing to do; for, according to the Blue Anna, the immediate consequence was a cancerous disease of the skull. However, to touch Ofey's treasures was even more nefarious—an inconceivable outrage that could not but provoke the most grisly reactions. We were often haunted by the idea that we might be compelled by an evil spell to destroy and to pollute the whole splendor of Ofey's house—the pottery in the dining-room and the lobby, the sensitive velvet in Offi's little salon, the lovely bronze statues in the library, the satin cushions covering the chairs and benches in the music hall. What an infernal joke it would be!—to trample on the tapestry, to spit at the can-vases by Lehnbach and Hans von Thoma, to ransack the boudoirs and bedrooms upstairs. Offi would hurl silvery screams and pluck out her beautiful auburn hair. And Ofey? But at this point our bloodthirsty imagination refused to go any further. The choleric little man might commit the most stunning atrocities in his rabid wrath. We preferred not to test, indeed, not even to gauge the formidable potentialities of his furor. It seemed preferable to overcome our vandal impulses and to remain civilized.

They were charming people, our grandparents, as long as we left alone that priceless junk on the walls and kept nicely quiet at the dinner table. Offi was gracious and glamorous, Ofey—bizarre and impish, a remarkable expert in mathematics and naughty cracks which were "nothing for children." We didn't understand them anyhow but loved to listen to his creaky voice. His voice was indescribably squeaking; his head unbelievably bald. He was the bald little man with the creaky voice. He was Grandfather.

A second grandfather was unthinkable: Ofey concentrated all characteristics and dignities of the grandfather-species in his crisp and picturesque personality. But Offi had a competitor—Omama, the "other" pattern of the grandmother type. For, while Mielein's mother was radiant and self-assured, the woman whom our father called "Mama" was meek and lustreless.

A wan, ashen tinge was typical of her voice, her complexion, her modest dwelling, and everything she did or represented. She seemed constantly haunted by superstitious fears and irrational misgivings. When we had tea at her place, three or four times in the course of a year, she treated us with heaps of dusty sweets, big doses of sodium bicarbonate, and weird anecdotes about seemingly harmless diseases which suddenly reveal their fatal gravity; "cold lightnings" which manifest themselves in the form of transparent balls and look exceedingly pretty when they hurtle through the roof, from story to story, until they reach the cellar where they explode and devastate everything; or about children who were in the habit of making ugly faces and were amusing themselves with the invention of new hideous grimaces just when the clock struck—whereupon their features remained distorted for good.

We appreciated both tales and cookies. In her own humble way, we felt, Omama was as excellent an ancestress as Offi.

Both grandmothers—so infinitely different from each other—were cruelly struck by blows which strangely resembled each other and which befell the two women almost simultaneously, although without any causal connection. Nevertheless, in my memory the two tragedies are tightly linked: I have always conceived them as weird parallels in the chronicle of our family.

The personalities of the two victims are completely blotted out in my mind, I cannot retrace the appearance of Uncle Erik, Mielein's oldest brother, who went to distant Argentina and there found his death "by falling from a horse." Nor do I remember what Aunt Carla looked like—Omama's youngest daughter who was so suddenly killed by apoplexy. All I can recall are their portraits—Uncle Erik's picture on my mother's desk, Aunt Carla's on that of my father. Uncle Erik—very erect on horseback—looked peevish and energetic, while attractive Aunt Carla—smilingly bent over a bunch of flowers—seemed on the point of melting away with wistful tenderness.

The drama in Argentina preceded the ghastly disaster that Omama had to witness from such merciless proximity. It may even be that Erik's death took place several months or a year before Carla gave up her life. But the chronological details are irrelevant. In my recollection the two catastrophes merge. I hear Offi's scream: "My son Erik! My horseman! Murdered by his horse! Bled to death in faraway Argentine!" (An outburst which, of course, I never witnessed in reality but so often imagined that it became real to me.) And even while Offi's theatrical wails resound through the mansion in the Arcis-Strasse, Omama's inconsolable whimper wafts from a dreary boarding house, just around the corner. "Carla! Oh, Carla!" sighs Omama; "Erik! Oh, Erik!" yells Offi.

Finally both mourning mothers leave their respective dwellings—driven away by their unbearable grief and the ardent desire to inform the sisterly neighbor of the horrid event. Brandishing the tragic telegrams and a multitude of black veils, gloves and umbrellas, they rush down the street—each hurriedly approaching the other's residence. They meet just midway between their houses: in fact, they almost run into each other, both being blind with sorrow and natural nearsightedness.

"Oh, Julia! Dearest!" cries Offi. "What a comfort to see you! Do you realize what has happened to me?"

"To *you?*" Omama flashes back. "What are you talking about, Hedwig dearest? Carla was *my* child, after all."

The miscomprehension continues and produces effects of macabre drollery. Finally they understand each other and launch out into renewed, redoubled lamentations. The two tragic grandmothers—the august Offi and the humble Omama—embrace each other, united by sorrow and loss.

"My unfortunate sister!" the one whispers into the ear of the other. Their tears and mourning veils intermingle as they cling to each other in desperate tenderness. Unwittingly, all absorbed in their suffering, they have ascended one of the pedestals with which the city of Munich is so richly endowed. In friendly proximity to a medieval knight of the Wittelsbach clan, they stand in the midst of the Brienner-Strasse—a double monument of despair.

Did I ever believe the stories we had been told concerning the sudden decease of our relatives? This is a ticklish question: it involves a whole complex of psychological problems. We can hardly venture here on an analysis of infantile credulity and infantile skepticism. To say that I never questioned the "adaptation for children" of the family drama as it was presented to us does not mean, necessarily, that I actually believed it. To believe is an action, something you do consciously and deliberately; whereas not to question indicates a passive attitude, a renunciation rather than an active effort. You may refuse to scrutinize the truth, out of sheer politeness, or because you realize the intricacy of the task; or simply because you feel that *it would not be good to know everything.*

Children, up to a certain age, are polite and cautious. Their curiosity is restrained by the instinctive feeling that the truth is, in some situations, dangerous—indeed, pernicious. Besides, they don't like to give the lie to their adult friends. It would be utterly tactless to doubt those well-intended inventions as to the stork who delivers the babies, the Christ-Child who busies himself with the distribution of innumerable gifts, and poor Uncle Erik who broke his neck in the jungle.

Yet, we discriminated, if only unconsciously, between truthful, exciting stories which we loved to discuss and to magnify, and those other reports which one better leaves unquestioned and untouched. Omama's account with regard to the "cold lightnings" was thrilling and convincing, something we loved to dwell upon. But what she told us about Aunt Carla's apoplexy somehow sounded hollow and inadequate.

"How did it happen?" we asked without really expecting any satisfactory answer.

"Did she catch a cold and then walk about without her overcoat? Or what?"

Omama's face grew strangely rigid and vacuous. "It had nothing to do with a cold," she insisted, in an at once tormented and perfunctory way. "It was her heart. Just her heart that broke . . . That's all. Well, children, how about another piece of this strawberry tart?"

Offi's reaction was even more disquieting when we casually referred to those truculent horses in South America. She just turned her face away and for a while sat motionless, as if petrified. After a long, stone-like silence, she murmured something to the effect that it was not only the horses who were dangerous in those distant regions; nobody should force his son to settle down in the wilderness.

No doubt, there was something ominous and uncanny about the apoplexy and the horse. Both were untouchable subjects. We recognized the taboo and respected it.

You discover no truth unless you have decided to seek it. The quest is almost tantamount in itself to the discovery. You will find whatever you look for.

The assiduous Christ-Child will be drowned by a flood of Christmas advertisements. The stork's bill that carries the babies is to be replaced by a more realistic image. And then—be patient! it will not take long!—you may hear all the gruesome details of Aunt Carla's suicide: how she swallowed the poison in her mother's house and then gargled with lukewarm water to mitigate the infernal pains. Her wretched mother, our Omama, meanwhile jogged the door from outside and implored her to open. But the actress-daughter, frenzied with pride, frustration and cruelty, continued to gargle and to die, pacing her narrow room as if it were a stage on which she performed the pantomime of her agony watched and applauded by thousands. But there was only her mother, writhing and whimpering in the dingy corridor.

And we should be informed about Uncle Erik's melancholy adventures. He was so grand and stubborn, our Uncle Erik, and so boastfully extravagant: his gambling debts reached the staggering height of 200,000 marks. So Ofey lost his temper and bought him a farm in the Argentine. He had to go there, or else . . . Nobody could foresee that he would commit the folly of getting married, over there, to a dubious lady whose main interest was in the spacious estate he owned and in a handsome steward she persuaded him to engage. Who knows what actually happened among those three human beings—the uncle, his wife and the South American steward— isolated in a vast and savage country? The only palpable fact is that the native couple got the better of the foreigner. He somehow disappeared, passed away. Nobody ever traced the gruesome details of his tragedy.

Don't attempt to unveil the secrets hidden from you by the grownups. It is out of mercy and shame that they conceal those stories: they are sordid and sad. Enjoy the cloudless skies of ignorance as long as they are granted to you! The apple of knowledge has a bitter taste: sometimes its flavor is that of death and decay. Beware of the serpent who allures you with devilish information as to the making of babies and the Uncle's jungle-romance! Wisdom is sterile: it yields no happiness. But what you forfeit is irreparable and valuable beyond words—your paradise.

Paradise is imbued with the bitter-sweet fragrance of conifer, tonic herbs, and raspberries, fused with the scent of moss that has become warm in the sun—the vast, powerful sun of a summer day in Tölz. The clearing where we spend the morning picking berries lies in the midst of a stately forest, the beautiful wood of fir trees which commences right behind our house. This is by no means a forest among others of a similar kind, but *the* forest—matchless, mythic, representa-

tive, with its solemn twilight, its smells and noises, the perfect formations of its mushrooms and shrubs, its squirrels, rocks, rivulets, and
unassuming flowers.

And here are the children with the dog, and Mother wearing a
summer dress, a pretty garment made of heavy linen, with wide,
puffed sleeves and lavish embroideries. We call it "the Bulgarian
one," as somebody brought it back as a gift from an oriental journey.
Mother is bare-headed, offering the dark richness of her hair to the
caress of the sun. She sits on a felled tree, and Motz rests next to
her, still panting after the hectic fatigues of the ramble. His scarlet
tongue, thin and pointed, elegantly shaped, hangs out of his slavering
mouth. His golden eyes, half-closed, leer gratefully at Mother, who
pats his silky neck, smiling down at him with absent-minded tenderness.

"Children! Pfui!" I hear mother's admonishing voice. "You must
not eat all the raspberries now! Don't you realize I wanted you to
pick them for a particular purpose? Jennie toys with the idea of
producing a raspberry cake for dinner. She'll yell with anger when
there are no berries to cook with. You are indescribably naughty!"

She talks so rapidly and uses such fancy words that we laugh instead
of being scared. Especially the idea that Jennie could yell with anger
strikes us as irresistibly ridiculous.

Even Mielein's threat that she is going to complain to Dad when he
comes to fetch us completely fails to impress us. "He'll probably
kill you," she announces.

We are positive that he won't. Mielein is not going to tell him
anything to the effect that we sneaked the raspberries, to begin with.
And even if she told him, he wouldn't really mind.

"So they swallowed all the little berries, did they?" he would say
with a musing, untroubled smile—and then add, while raising his
brows a little: "I certainly hope they didn't eat anything poisoned."
He often terrified and amused us with gruesome stories concerning
dangerous mushrooms and fruits, nasty fish-bones, and the evil consequences of immoderate greed in general. It was odd and exciting
to watch how he resembled Omama when he dwelt on such didactic
atrocities. The delicate oval of his face seemed to lengthen as if

reflected by a distorting mirror, while his eyes anxiously narrowed. We were never quite sure in such moments whether he deliberately imitated his mother, just to let us have a good laugh, or whether, on the contrary, he couldn't help looking like her and even failed to realize the resemblance.

He appeared at twelve o'clock on the dot to walk with Mielein and the rest of us, across the meadows to the marshy pond where we had our swim before luncheon. The path, soft and serpentine, went through the fields, leaving the village to our right. It was rather tedious to walk in the sultry air of noon. The sky was now covered with rows of white fluffy clouds gathering like swollen pillows between the peaks of the mountains. There was a strong, somewhat intoxicating smell from the grass, which was particularly lush in this boggy region and lavishly speckled with fat, yellow flowers.

This was summer: the seven of us—two parents, four children, one Motz marching through a fertile and drowsy land, a little toilsomely, as the ground was sticky underfoot. This is the summer horizon—fretted by the Alps; the summer steeple looms to our right; the summer shrubs and blooms exhale their sultry fragrance. And this is the summer pond—small, round and black, with plenty of reeds on its edges and sporadic white flowers floating in the middle of the tranquil surface.

It was an ideal bathing place—the pond of ponds, so to speak. Its water had a strong and tonic smell and was so heavy that you hardly felt your own weight once you had dived into its gold-brown depth. Yet, that clumsy baker apprentice from a neighboring village managed to be drowned in our beloved pond. We would never have heard about the depressing incident, if chance and Jennie had not guided us to the place where the baker's corpse was displayed.

There was nothing unusual about taking an evening walk through the cemetery. We went there frequently after our former cook had become the wife of the gardener. It was entertaining to decipher the turgid inscriptions adorning the primitive tombstones. The trite formulas of mourning seemed at once moving and funny to us. We giggled about the baroque names of the dead and the clumsiness with which the surviving relatives expressed their faithful devotion. The uncanny nearness of putrefaction did not frighten us. Death was no reality, just a lurid rumor among grown-ups.

Why did Jennie ever lead us—as though it were by chance—into that dusky chapel where the drowned young baker lay—arranged on the bier between two burning candles? First we did not realize that it was a dead man we saw. We took him for a wax figure, another bizarre adornment for a grave or the church. But Jennie told us the truth. Quivering with excitement, she whispered to us who he was, what had happened to him, and where he was to be buried. She also explained why his mouth was covered by a black band: "It's because his lips are all blue and swollen," she said. But she could not explain the forbidding strangeness of that sallow mask which had once been his face. Nor did she know why his hands, the hands of a working man, appeared so brittle and transparent and so unspeakably noble.

He looked as haughty and self-assured as if he had accomplished something utterly fine and unusual by being drowned in the pond. Or was it the mere fact of his being dead that made him so princelike and precious? Hadn't we been told that all of us have to die? How, then, could death be a privilege? Why was its sight so frightful and beautiful?

We stood motionless, spellbound with awe and apprehension, when Jennie whispered: "Let's go now! You've seen him . . ."

We had seen the dead man, solemnly exhibited between flowers and lights—a new puzzle, a new beauty, a new myth.

CHAPTER TWO

War

(1914–1919)

THERE was no bloody sword. But that our father predicted its imminent coming was weird and exciting enough.

Our summer in Tölz was particularly pleasant that year. Three jolly cousins of ours, Eva-Mary, Rose-Mary, and Ilse-Mary, occupied the neighboring house and garden, together with their delicate mother, Aunt Lula, and their brisk little father, our Uncle Jof, a Bavarian banker. The three girls were good sports and a lot of fun. The seven of us, four Mann children plus three Löhr girls, formed a dynamic and merry team, unflaggingly occupied with the invention of ever-new games and pranks.

A masquerade scheduled for the middle of August was supposed to be the climax of the season. We intended to startle the grown-ups with a theatrical production in the grand style—a veritable festival full of suspense and glamor. Eva-Mary, the oldest, supervised the rehearsals that took place in our garden, under the chestnut tree. Everything developed smoothly, in the most promising fashion. But then a minor incident interfered.

First we thought it just a meaningless caprice of our governess. It was so much like her to interrupt our artistic work, even while Eva-Mary recited her beautiful monologue. The governess looked pale with malice when she suggested with one of her wry, hideous smiles that nobody would be interested in our spectacle, just now. "You'd better forget about it," she said.

Of course, we were thoroughly hurt and surprised. "What's wrong?" we asked, shaking with indignation.

"Do you want us to drop our great enterprise, just because you are in a bad humor today?"

She shrugged her shoulders, all derisive superiority. "This has nothing to do with my humor," she said. "War has been declared on Germany and our Austrian ally." She had a queer way of pronouncing these words, with a sort of cold, perfunctory enthusiasm, as if they were something she had memorized. "Our magnificent Kaiser has taken over the supreme command both of army and navy," she added with flippant triumph, as though this strategic detail would prove the triviality of our project. "But you are much too young, I suppose, to grasp the magnitude of such historic events," she concluded, already on her way back to the house.

Indeed, we were much too young. The report of the governess left us flabbergasted. We sat in the grass and wondered. None of us had the faintest idea of what was actually meant. Could the Kaiser, in his capacity as supreme commander, simply forbid our show? Obviously, this was a problem of pivotal importance. We discussed it at length but finally drew the conclusion that this was too definitely beyond us. Only our parents could help.

We found both on the terrace but not really together—strangely separate from each other. Mielein sat at the table, far away, in the shady background, with a huge newspaper spread out in front of her as if it were a map she had to peruse. As for Father, he stood at the other end of the terrace, leaning against the balustrade, solemnly absorbed in the sight of mountains and sky. It was, indeed, a sunset of rampant beauty, almost alarmingly spectacular, with the horizon ablaze, lavishly bathed in purple, bluish, and silver tints. The jagged curves of the mountain peaks were silhouetted against this feverish background.

Father did not turn his head towards Mielein, nor did he notice our presence when he said in a lowered and yet sonorous voice: "Before long a bloody sword is going to appear in the sky."

After this, we did not have the nerve to ask any questions concerning our show.

War seemed more exciting than any other game we had ever played. The big fun about it was that the grown-ups participated with hectic enthusiasm in this new vagary. Everybody seemed tickled by the strength of the coalition gathering against our country. Evidently, it was the main objective of this game to collect as many foes as possible. "Many enemies, much honor!" The slogan sounded cheerful and arrogant. The shop owners and peasants in Tölz were highly amused as the war declarations poured in. No doubt, our dynamic Kaiser had enough pluck and genius to cope with the whole dastardly bunch of them.

Frau Holzmeyer of the grocery store got a kick out of the thought of how our dashing lads would lick the Russian Bear, perfidious Albion, and decadent, vicious France, the traditional archenemy of the Teutonic people. As for the pharmacist around the corner, he had startling news from his boy, who was a sergeant with the Royal Bavarian Army. According to this initiated young man, Paris was completely undermined and might be blown up overnight: it was up to our Emperor to choose the appropriate moment.

The whole little town was agog with rumors and prophecies. The population seemed at once elated and panicky. Lurid stories concerning the wiles of secret enemy agents were eagerly discussed at the marketplace. The man at the telegraph office flurried the community with suggestive hints at certain messages that had gone over his wire that clearly indicated the drinking water in Tölz and the neighboring places was poisoned. A lady who stopped at the White Horse Inn was almost lynched by the mob because her speech had a foreign accent and she looked uncannily spy-like. The trains were jammed; the hotels, deserted. The tourists rushed to the station as if the enemy troops were already invading the town.

Everybody bustled and flustered and had relatives who wanted to be kissed good-bye before joining the ranks. Our parents—both the Löhrs and the Manns—hurriedly went to Munich to bid farewell to various cousins and brothers. Mielein had to comfort Offi, who was in a state because of Uncle Peter. He happened to be in Australia as the guest of a scientific congress, which evidently meant quite a calamity as Australia had wantonly declared war upon us. He was a physicist and Mielein's oldest brother. The idea that the Australians might keep and torture him as a hostage was rather upsetting.

But nobody except Offi really cared. The thought of one distant uncle could not spoil the sweeping fun of so glorious and general an upheaval.

The governess said that in such great, wonderful days nobody must be selfish: "The whole nation has to make sacrifices," she told us. As for herself, she was proud to have a cousin in the Army Service Corps. If her fiancé were still alive, she would happily give him to the infantry. Unfortunately, however, he had been killed in a motor accident, several years ago. Jennie, who agreed with the governess concerning the necessity of sacrifices, reveled in blood-thirsty enthusiasm. She had a marvelous time when she distributed sandwiches and beer among the uniformed country boys whose train stopped in Tölz on the way to Munich. How coquettishly she flushed and giggled as the lads paid homage to her appetizing appearance!

"It's good that the kids don't understand what it's all about," she whispered to the governess, who looked lean and sallow with envy. "Did you hear that one? Kind of fresh, isn't it? Well, one has to take it, I guess. After all, war is war . . ."

When I try to recapture the savor and rhythm of 1914, I visualize fluttering banners, gray helmets adorned with ludicrous little bouquets, knitting women, cocky fellows in uniform, glaring posters, and more flags—a swelling parade of black, white, and red. Everything struts and blusters and shines. The very air is imbued with the general swagger and the blatant refrains of military songs. Every other day a new victory must be celebrated. Wicked little Belgium is smashed, almost in no time. Staggering news pours in from the Eastern front. France, of course, is on the point of collapsing. Our ultimate triumph seems guaranteed: the boys will be home for Christmas.

People keenly discussed the choice of countries and colonies the Kaiser ought to annex for the Fatherland. The governess promised us China and Africa as if they were toys or cookies. Jennie beamed, constantly surrounded by a minor army of uniformed step-brothers, cousins, and surprisingly well-preserved uncles. The joyful noise of their farewell parties reverberated throughout the house. Mielein often wondered if she should not interfere but then decided against it. It seemed more advisable to forbear, considering the unusual circumstances. In a few months from now—at any rate, before spring—the whole thing would be over.

However, our dazzling Emperor, as unpredictable as valiant, changed his mind and postponed victory, just for the fun of warfare. It was a trifle disturbing because of the dessert which had been removed from the daily menu. We had bravely accepted this measure as a patriotic sacrifice of temporary nature, but in the long run the absence of puddings and strudels was depressing.

Our life underwent other changes, some of them gratifying. Mielein told us, frankly and succinctly, that these were not only great times but pretty tough ones to boot. The new house into which we had moved just before the outbreak of the war was somehow strained and burdened by a mysterious blot called "mortgage." A certain scarcity of funds seemed to result from this weird condition. Two mighty gentlemen, Ofey and a publisher in Berlin, also were involved in the lurid intrigue. Both Grandfather in his castle and father's friend, Herr S. Fischer, turned restive and whimsical, evidently affected by the strain of those trying days. Obfuscated by patriotism and their cranky dispositions, they abruptly stopped sending checks. The Magician, dignified and distrait, seemed to regard this as a mere nuisance, but Mielein was worried. She fired one of the maids and our governess. We hardly missed the former and were overjoyed to get rid of the latter.

There was something breezy and dangerous about our newly acquired liberty—the tough, unbound life without governess and dessert. Our transfer from the exclusive institute in Schwabing to an ordinary school in our own district was another move in Mielein's money-saving policy. Erika and I were separated. She presently became the chieftain among the girls, while my own position in the male class remained somewhat precarious. I could not speak the local dialect, to begin with. Much in contrast to Erika, I never quite succeeded in adapting my tongue to the guttural gibberish which is the idiom of native Bavarians. Although I was born in Munich, the boys in my class took me for one of those "dirty Prussians," which was almost as bad as to be an enemy alien. Besides, they resented my "artistic" outfit and my aversion to scrapping. In short, they thought me a sissy. Yet I don't believe that they really disliked me. The opinion prevailed that I was "crazy as hell" but neither a rat nor a fool. They treated me with a certain ironic courtesy and even were amiable enough never to beat me up.

There was a lot of sadistic violence among the pupils, as well as on the part of the teacher. Flogging was still accepted as a sound pedagogical principle, indispensable in the taming of truculent kids. Our instructor, a squat, muscular fellow with an enormous mustache, was a master in the art of corporal punishment. The last warning he would grant the penitent was to hold the flexible cane just under the nostrils of the trembling youth: the smell was supposed to have a purifying influence on the conduct and character of the sinner. If this ultimate maneuver failed, the gruesome ritual had to take place. With murderous politeness the torturer asked his victim to lie down on the special bench reserved for such occasions. Before following this ominous invitation the criminal was expected to perform a pathetic scene, one of the essential elements of the spectacle: with a considerable display of tears and dramatic gestures, the defendant tried to move the heart of his judge, although he realized, at bottom, the utter hopelessness of his efforts. There was no mercy: the pedagogue silently pointed at the loathsome rack which awaited the whimpering evil-doer.

The flogging was conducted with cruel zest and solemnity. The whole class breathless with delight and horror watched the ignoble procedure. The whining of the penitent began even before the first blow fell: he writhed and groaned while the teacher brandished his supple weapon as if to make sure that it was in good shape. The wails, louder as the first strokes whistled down, gradually increased and grew hysterical and spasmodic. When the nauseous ceremony was over, the victim produced a sort of tragi-comic epilogue, according to the tradition. Rubbing his behind, he kept capering to and fro, in front of the teacher's desk, still sobbing and hurling impressive bits of description as to the unbearable pains he experienced. The teacher smirkingly watched the show, finally cutting it short by an authoritative motion. "That will do," he decided, satisfied, like a lion after his bloody meal. "You may go back to your seat."

I often wondered if the flogging might actually have hurt as much as the victim's behavior suggested. It may be that elements of dramatic conventionalism were involved in the ghastly performance. Yet the punishment must have been painful. My heart contracted with each stroke that went down, and I felt a pang in my stomach at every yell and whimper. It would have been better for me, perhaps, if I had had to endure the castigation myself, at least once in my life, instead of suffering from the torments inflicted upon others. However I have been spared, up to now, the experience of physical maltreatment. The teacher never extended to me his frightening invitation to lie down on the bench. I was doomed to pass through the delicate agonies of pity, mysteriously protected, on my part, by an honorable or disgraceful taboo.

When the evening prayers were said and the bedroom darkened, it was sweet and painful to think of all the bloody goings-on out there, in the trenches. How terrible it must have been when hundreds of thousands of Russians perished in those murderous swamps where the inspired strategy of Marshal von Hindenburg had placed them! For many a night I was haunted and thrilled by the roaring of their helpless protest. And what sort of complicated torture had the Australians in store for the miserable Uncle Peter? They probably treated him as the Negroes were treated in the tale of Uncle Tom's Cabin. Would I ever have to undergo such martyrdom? Poor Uncle Peter! Poor Russians! Poor General Hindenburg! It could be not easy, I figured, to perform such heroic but grisly deeds—compelled to act like a monster on account of professional duty and martial genius. Poor generals who had to become inhuman! Poor soldiers who were sacrificed by inhuman generals! I melted away with pity. Already half-asleep, I confounded myself with those good-natured, ungainly Russians chased through the Australian jungle by the merciless Marshal von Hindenburg who, on his part, intensely suffered from his own nasty efficiency. Finally I visualized myself saving many a gallant soldier—no matter if foe or ally —by virtue of my startling heroism.

My eagerness to take part in the bloody events was not derived from pure patriotism or military ambition. There were other motives involved—curiosity, masochism, pity, vanity and fear. Indeed, fear may have been the main ingredient in this emotional complexity. Not that I thought it frightful to be sacrificed for the sake of a common cause:

on the contrary, I imagined such martyrdom as a sort of enormous, bitter-sweet pleasure. Infinitely more grisly than actual pain is the danger of being excluded from the collective adventure. To be an outsider is the one unbearable humiliation. So strong is the gregarious instinct of man that he prefers every woe to the torments of solitude. It was this innermost fear of moral and physical isolation which caused my martial aspirations and reveries. I kept dreaming of heroic fraternizations, since I knew, at the bottom of my heart, that I was destined for other trials of a different kind. In puerile fantasies I tried to deny and to overcome the intrinsic law of my nature which forever prevents me from belonging to the enviable, if pain-stricken, majority.

Can a bodily disease originate from a certain psychological disposition? Is there a causal link between the almost fatal illness I passed through in 1915, and the general state of emergency? The wing of death which then touched so many of my older and unknown brothers also cast its shadow over my childish face.

Appendicitis assumed in our family the character of an epidemic in surprising contrast to all medical doctrines. First the two "little ones" had to be operated on within forty-eight hours; then it was Mielein's turn, and finally Erika and I fell sick with the same acute inflammation. In the four other cases the operations were carried out just in time: the clinical process was normal and satisfactory. With me, however, things took an alarming turn. When I was delivered at the hospital, the abscessed appendix had ruptured. I recall with terrifying liveliness the endless and painful transport from our house to the clinic, which was situated at the opposite end of the city. My abdomen seemed to burn, to explode, to rave, to burst asunder. The ambulance—an inferno on wheels—carried me much too slowly along the estranged avenues and deserted squares to a destination whose lurid name I knew not but could guess when looking at Mother's tearful face.

Almost needless to say, my grave illness—the fact that "Klaus almost died"—was to become a legend in the grand style. I have often been told—and I never grew tired of listening to such moving reports—how I screamed in my anguish and how appallingly emaciated I was, a veritable skeleton. But I am unable to recall any of these mythic sufferings except the sensation of an almost unbearable thirst. The frantic longing for water supersedes in my memory all other images of agony. The whole episode, as I recollect it, is a fleet but overpowering nightmare of suffocating darkness and torrid heat. It begins in a rocking ambulance and—the next morning, as it were—ends in our garden at Tölz. The tribulation is over; death has dismissed me; the feverish thirst has been quenched. I hold a huge glass of orange juice in my hand. Sprawling on an armchair in the shade of a chestnut tree, I breathe the sultry air of summer boredom and recovery.

I was a hero, for I had survived. My environment—family, servants, and neighbors—evidently appreciated the fortitude and noble courtesy I had proved by resisting the urgent appeal of death. Small wonder that I began to look down at my ordinary brother and sisters who just "lived," a matter of no particular merit, whereas I—a much more interesting case!—was alive, contrary to all likelihood and the most competent forecasts. Small wonder that I was spoiled and fed with all sorts of dainty and nourishing things: it was only fair and nobody must complain; for I had been terribly sick. Indeed, the doctor had said that I was supposed to gain weight. While the daily rations of the ordinary folks gradually but sensibly shrunk, it seemed a gracious gesture on my part when I condescended to accept another sandwich or a third slice of cake.

However, this gorgeous state of being coddled and nursed could not last forever. My privileges dwindled in exact proportion to the progress of my recuperation. When the summer was over I had almost completely regained my vitality, weight, and strength. I was healthy enough to endure every-day life, the stringent life of the third war winter in Germany.

The war had long ceased to be adventurous or elating. It was just daily life and a rather dreary one, too. Admitted that the strategy of General Ludendorff was ever so glorious and cunning, that Albion was perfidious, that the Yankees were not much better and that unrestricted U-boat warfare was one of the inalienable rights of the German people: none of these well-known facts was an adequate substitute for a pound of butter.

To us children, as well as to the average citizen, war primarily meant not enough to eat. With the food situation constantly and rapidly deteriorating, it became a general obsession to discuss all aspects and implications of this one paramount problem: how, where, at what price and risk one could obtain the indispensable victuals. The hoarding of illegal food was not only a necessity but a sport; more than that, a mania. Some people developed the most uncanny skill in tracing devious sources of milk, lard or honey. With unflagging ingenuity they explored the countryside in search of chickens, rabbits, and potatoes. The funny papers and the criminal records were full of stories concerning the reckless wiles employed by the egg-ham-and-butter hunters.

The expeditions to distant farms or to the hiding places of professional food procurers were risky but not without a certain savage charm. As for the "legal" methods of obtaining the necessities of life, they were infinitely more tedious. It certainly was no fun to stand in line for hours and hours to get a quarter-pound of rancid margarine or to be dismissed at last with the cruel announcement that the shop had to close for want of any supplies. I shall never forget the winter morning when Erika and I decided, in a sudden paroxysm of generosity, to present Mielein with the unexpected gift of six eggs. We had discovered a tiny store somewhere in the suburbs where such rarities were available, provided that you had the tenacious fortitude to stand in line from six o'clock in the morning until noon or so. That is what we did, and the reward was worthwhile. We received the eggs—how smooth and appetizing they looked!—as if they were six fragile talismans. Happy and agitated we made for home—beaming in anticipation of Mielein's grateful surprise. I carried the eggs in my cap, as the shopowner had refused us a paper bag. But my bare hands became numb in the freezing cold. The inevitable occurred: the six eggs rolled out of the cap that I clumsily held and broke to pieces before our unbelieving eyes. It was bitter beyond description to watch the beautiful yolks, a mucilaginous rivulet, oozing away between the paving stones. Both of us burst into tears. It now seems to me that our tears froze even while running along our cheeks and adorned our bewildered faces like biting little jewels. Everything was glacial and forbidding and infinitely sad.

It would be an exaggeration to assert that we actually starved, but the plain truth is that we were always hungry. No doubt, this state of constant privation cannot but leave certain marks on one's physical and moral constitution. You don't take wealth and plenitude for granted, once you have known what it means to dream of a sandwich as an almost inconceivable delicacy. Our food and clothes, the shoes, the coal, the soap, the writing paper—everything we touched, smelled or swallowed—was "ersatz," miserable shoddy stuff. It must have been a tough time for our mother—much harder on her than on us. To feed four greedy youngsters and a fastidious husband under such trying conditions certainly was no picnic. She did a magnificent job, unflaggingly ingenious and energetic. What she accomplished is all the more admirable considering her background and past. The fairy-tale princess to whom my father paid homage in "Royal Highness" had to cope with the problems of real want and misery. The "artistic outfit" and handsome marine uniforms she had bought us in 1914 were threadbare and outgrown in 1917. And as for shoes, leather was almost as rare as butter. For a while, we wore heavy sandals with wooden soles. But soon we grew tired of them and preferred to walk about barefoot.

The traditional Sunday dinners at our grandparents' house remained a regular feature of our life in Munich. But now the festive menu consisted of an emaciated bird—a dubious sort of heron with a disturbingly fishy flavor. It was only the solid splendor of the dining hall and Offi's indestructible dignity that kept the whole affair from degenerating into downright poverty. Indeed, the attitude of the hostess was so sovereign and detached that her guests were tempted to take the reduced style of the household for an elegant vagary. The dreary fact that we had to bring our own bread along seemed an amusing comedy, the way Offi handled the situation. Her laugh heartily tinkled as we unpacked our modest provisions.

"If only I had asked my guests all along to come here well supplied with bread and cakes!" she joked. "I might have saved a nice amount of money." And she proudly added, while pouring the tea out of a fine silver samovar into the delicate china cups: "At least as far as tea is concerned, I'm pretty confident that I'll hold on for the duration."

"For the duration." . . . But would the war ever end? Was it possible to imagine a world without war? A world with enough to eat and no victory celebrations? We didn't quite believe any more that things like whipped cream and peace actually existed. Sometimes we would interview Mielein as to those legendary days that ostensibly used to be and were supposed to return.

"What is peace like, really?" we kept asking her. "Is everybody very fat and merry when there is no war? Did people actually eat a whole fish between the soup and the meat, and a huge chocolate cake afterwards? How could they digest so much food? Will we eat layer tart every day when Germany wins the war? Why hadn't she already won? After all, we have Ludendorff and the Kaiser while the others have only cowards."

"Our professor says we'll win before the end of this year. He always spits a little when he gets excited. Today he was spitting like hell when he told us about the German victory and all that. Do you think we'll win before Christmas? Are we going to have long victory vacations when the war is over?"

But Mielein seemed strangely sorrowful. "Nobody knows," she said vaguely. "Of course, your professor may be right. Maybe he isn't though. The war might last thirty years—now, with America in it . . ."

"But the professor says it makes no difference," we insisted. "America or not, he says, we'll lick them."

"Maybe your professor is right," repeated Mielein, still with that musing expression on her face. "But I don't think so, really."

Her opinions with regard to the war and its probable outcome dissented from what our father obstinately believed. They never argued: there was no loud word at table. But we were keen and observant enough to notice the divergency of their views. Mielein had lost faith in the cause and the winning chance of the Reich, whereas the Magician remained grimly confident. He concealed his misgivings and qualms, if there were any, somewhere at the bottom of his heart.

This wartime father seems estranged and distant, essentially different from the father I have known before and after those years of struggle and bitterness. The paternal physiognomy that looms up when I recall that period, seems devoid of the kindness and irony which both inseparably belong to his character. The face I visualize looks severe and somber—a proud and nervous brow with sensitive temples and sunken cheeks. Curiously enough, it is a "bearded" face, a long, haggard oval framed by a hard, prickly beard. He never wore a beard, though, except once in Tölz for a few weeks or months. However, this martial caprice must have considerably impressed me. The wartime father is bearded. His features, at once proud and worried, resemble those of a Spanish knight and nobleman—the errant hero and dreamer called Don Quixote.

I see him leaving his working room—very erect in a tight, uniform-like jacket of gray material. His lips are sealed, as it were, over an ominous secret, and his pensive regard goes inwards. He looks weary and preoccupied. The morning at his desk must have been unusually fatiguing. What uncanny spell is it that forces him to cloister himself in his library, every day of the year, from nine o'clock until noon? Just as Cinderella has to vanish at midnight—leaving one tiny slipper behind—my father is compelled to withdraw as soon as breakfast is over, leaving the fragrance of his morning cigar as a familiar token. A conscientious sorcerer, he ponders over his inventions and calculations. This time, however, he has evidently engaged in a dangerous piece of witchcraft. It is not one of his beautiful stories he is now making up but something more abstract and mysterious. He becomes impatient when visitors ask him questions concerning the nature of his forthcoming work. "It's just a book," he says, with a strangely unfocused look in his eyes. "No, not a novel. Just a book. It has to do with the war."

It sounded weird, as though he were occupied with the invention of new murderous weapons or strategic devices. Had he sacrificed the serene realm of his tales for the sake of black magic?

It was much later, long after the end of the war, when I for the first time perused the queer product of those dismal years, the "Reflections of an Unpolitical Mind." It is easier to understand this book, both its rampant fallacies and saturnine beauty, if one has witnessed and can recollect the circumstances to which it owes its existence. The cruel strain of those days, the bleak seriousness of the author's life, his lack of political training, even the inadequate food and the chilly temperature in his studio during the winter months—all these elements worked together to create the peculiar climate, the perplexing mixture of violence and melancholy, that prevails in the "Reflections."

The book is a spiritual adventure of a highly personal, indeed, singular nature, a literary tour de force and a political blunder of impressive proportions. The ironic analyst of complex emotions hazarded to transcend, for the first time in his career, the original domain of his experiences. His keen and sensitive mind, beset by the war as by a malady, could not content itself any more with the exploration of artistic and psychological problems. The colossal drama aroused and deepened his social conscience. The new political interest first manifested itself, paradoxically, as an ardent and elaborate protest against the political sphere as such. The unpolitical mind, when turning political, deemed it his foremost task to defend the somber grandeur of Germanic culture against the militant optimism of Western civilization. He confounded the reckless arrogance of the Prussian imperialists with the splendors of Dürer, Bach, and Schopenhauer. The deadly ecstasies of Tristan and Isolde became an argument in favor of the Teutonic expansion and unrestricted submarine warfare. However, these erroneous deductions are conspicuously lacking in persuasive power. They seem put forward in an uncertain, reluctant manner, as if the author realized, at bottom, the dubious eccentricity of his own position.

The whole extensive treatise is but one running fight—executed with nervous élan and desperate sagacity. The cause which it extolled and defended was essentially doomed, and the author knew it. One does not believe in a cause which one conceives and describes as insolubly connected with decay and death. One may be attracted by such a cause, indeed, one might even love it, but one can hardly believe in its future. In the "Reflections" a spirited fighter wastes his energies for the sake of a misconception. He meant to protect and to glorify a noble lady by the name of culture while actually risking his soul on behalf of an ugly chimera. The highminded awkwardness of his action is akin to Don Quixote's misguided heroism. There are only windmills where the martial visionary suspected wicked and relentless enemies.

The windmill-foe against whom the polemic artillery of the "Reflections" was mobilized is a mysterious character presented as "der Zivilisationsliterat" (which means "the literary champion of civilization"). His name is never mentioned, but his anonymity is only a seeming one. For the extensive passages quoted from the writings of the unmentionable antagonist are literally derived from an essay by Heinrich Mann.

His biographical study of Emile Zola was published in the first year of the war, just when the tide of jingoism was at its highest. While the whole nation raved about the deeds of our invincible army, Heinrich Mann dared to praise the invincible spirit of the French fighter and novelist. It was in the course of this controversial panegyric that the German champion of European civilization launched a peppery attack on those dastards and climbers who betrayed the cause of humanity by endorsing or tolerating the notorious misjudgment in the Dreyfus affair. The phrasing of the diatribe suggested that its real targets were by no means the late antagonists of Emile Zola but rather certain contemporaries: at any rate, this was the interpretation which the irritable defender of German culture gave to the historic escapade of his civilization-conscious brother and opponent.

The relation between the two deteriorated with the outbreak of the war, which Heinrich considered a heinous adventure destined to plunge the German people into utter disaster. He tried to remain "au dessus de la mêlée," as did some of his French colleagues under the leadership of Romain Rolland. According to the "Reflections," however, he was not yet beyond the turmoil at all but a downright partisan of the Allied cause—indulging in the rhetoric of an average French agitator. Be this as it may, their political feud had long assumed the degree of emotional bitterness which inevitably destroys any personal contact. During the whole war the two brothers did not see each other.

Heinrich Mann, for many years an isolated, though highly respected figure of the literary vanguard, now became something like the representative of a political movement. In 1914, when the liberal German intelligentsia chimed almost unanimously in the martial chorus, he was among the very few who remained clear-headed. Two years afterwards, his grave and flamboyant voice found wider echo, not yet with the masses, to be sure, but with a keen, articulate minority. The pacifistic ethos, at first timid or nebulous, began to take on a more definite shape. A daring group of writers, mostly living in Switzerland, ventured to arraign the devastating slaughter in general and, in particular, the guilt of German militarism. The young poet Klabund, glowing with world-embracing enthusiasm and a virulent tuberculosis, addressed an angry manifesto to Emperor Wilhelm, whom he advised to make peace without any further delay. The satirist Carl Sternheim employed his incisive wit to debunk the slogans of jingoism. It was Stefan Zweig who dared, in 1917, to extol publicly "Le Feu," the anti-war novel by Henri Barbusse. The Alsatian René Schickele—a writer of remarkable courage and delicacy—founded and edited a literary and political monthly, "Die Weissen Blätter" (The White Book), which focused the seditious currents from France, Austria, and the Reich. It was in this meritorious review that Heinrich Mann published most of his literary output during that particular period.

Of course, the average Germans were scarcely aware of such "subversive" goings-on. The vast majority still believed with unabated stubbornness in the cause of the Fatherland and the inevitability of its final triumph. However, the spirit of rebellious criticism can never quite be suppressed: it filters out through devious channels and gradually imbues the atmosphere.

I was not yet eight years old when the war began and just twelve when it ended. And yet even my inexperienced mind was affected by the humanitarian gospel that challenged the thud of official phrases. First there was just a faint perturbation, a latent apprehension which slowly grew and deepened and became articulate. The reluctant process of this inner awakening was accelerated by the message of a certain book Offi gave me as a Christmas gift in 1917. Berta von Suttner's classic anti-war novel "Die Waffen Nieder!" certainly is not a literary masterpiece, but no matter how obvious and trite its plot and style may be, its sturdy emotionalism seized my imagination and actually changed my mind. It was partly, or mostly, thanks to Berta von Suttner's naïve but skillful appeal that I began to grasp certain essential facts and to ask certain basic questions. Could it be that our teachers and the newspapers and even the General Staff had tried to delude and to cheat us for three years and a half? We had been taught, over and over again, day by day, from August, 1914, that war was something great and necessary. Now the Austrian Baroness convinced me that organized mass slaughter was evil as well as preventable. Was it conceivable that the appalling calamity might have been avoided, if only our Kaiser had been less ambitious? Was the responsibility not exclusively with our enemies? And as for those enemies, they were, perhaps, not really so monstrous as we had been told. Perhaps they were just human beings. Such thoughts were dangerous and exciting. They questioned everything we were supposed to believe. In fact, they invalidated the whole system of official slogans and statistics. For if it is true that men are human and akin to each other, no matter in which country they live— who, then, is to be blamed for the disastrous mess? Who are the culprits? Where do we have to seek them, the maniacs, the demagogues, the exploiters?

We heard confused and sinister tales as to a revolution going on in Russia. They had killed their Czar and done away with their generals. If such enormities were feasible, why were they restricted to that distant and savage country? Why would not the other peoples follow the Russian example?

"Revolution! Revolution! Trucks full of soldiers speed through the streets; window panes are smashed; Kurt Eisner is President . . . It all sounds so fantastic, so incredible. And yet it is somehow flattering to imagine that people might later discuss our Bavarian Revolution with the same sort of seriousness we have when talking about Danton and Robespierre. Unfortunately, we could not attend the performance of the magician Uferino. That was quite a disappointment but besides that the birthday was a lot of fun. I now possess the complete works of Kleist and Grillparzer and Körner and Chamisso."

This is the opening entry in a diary I kept from 1918 until 1921. The handsome booklet was given to me as a birthday gift, on November 9, 1918. (The ninth of November is actually Erika's birthday; but throughout our childhood we celebrated our birthdays simultaneously, like twins. In reality I was born one year and nine days after Erika.)

The next note, under the date of November 11, reads as follows: "The armistice has been accepted. Peace, at last! But what now? We are approaching a catastrophe. School has opened again. Our professor got terribly mad because there was so much noise and because Germany has to make peace with her wicked enemies. Yesterday Mielein read aloud to us a very funny story by Gogol. I read the drama 'Atonement,' by Theodor Körner. Very poor stuff."

Staggering things occurred. Our magnificent Kaiser sneaked out of the country, a pitiful fugitive. So did Ludendorff, our great, infallible leader!—and many another hero and commander. It was all very muddled and thrilling and completely different from what we had expected. Germany had lost the war, but our professor said she didn't, really: someone had stabbed us in the back and, furthermore, President Wilson had fooled us with his fourteen promises. As for our professor, he rejected not only the defeat but also the Republic, which resulted from it. The scholarly patriot insisted that the whole Republic was a dirty trick set up by Poincaré, Lloyd George, and the Jews with the design of humiliating and expropriating the Germans. When listening to that pedagogue, one inevitably got the impression that the Emperor and his General Staff were the victims of a treacherous hoax; according to him, there were Jews and anarchists who persuaded our glorious leaders to surrender just when we were on the point of winning and Germany was stronger than ever.

Something was wrong with the peace. Nobody seemed to like it. In fact, people now looked more apprehensive even than during the war. Besides, there was no whipped cream, which had been promised to us as a token of victory. As far as food was concerned, the winter of 1918–19 was at least as bad as the preceding one had been.

In other respects things had become even worse. Didn't peace mean that the shooting was over? But it was only now, after the signing of the armistice, that it began in our very midst.

On February 21, 1919, the Bavarian Premier, Kurt Eisner, was shot dead, just around the corner from our school building. My diary's comments with regard to this incident are rather melodramatic. It asserts that I shed "bitter tears" on account of Eisner's assassination—a statement which may have been somewhat exaggerated but hardly was as completely phony as the family considered it to be. I forget how it happened that my confessional note became known to the others; but I remember that they kept teasing me about my ostensible mournfulness. The truth is that I was disgusted with the callous zest displayed by my classmates when they discussed the event. Eisner, an eloquent idealist with a slouch hat and a Christ-like appearance, had not been popular with the Bavarian natives. They thought him outlandish and suspicious and were rather pleased when a dashing cavalier, Count Arco, "liquidated" the cumbersome highbrow. The murderer was openly praised as a hero, whereas the memory of the victim was revered only by the working men and some radical intellectuals. Heinrich Mann, who had been a friend of Eisner, concluded his funeral speech with the meaningful remark that the late statesman and thinker deserved the honor of being called a Champion of Civilization.

The turbulent interlude of the Communist dictatorship in Bavaria was a direct consequence of Eisner's assassination. In my memory this illstarred experiment seems an obstreperous nightmare, mainly consisting of open cars carrying sinister-looking commissars, and of enormous posters covering the walls with their glaring cartoons and slogans. The whole affair had a savor of artificiality—something carnival-like. It was a fierce carnival, though: all well-to-do people grew jittery and upset. There were many rumors about looted houses, maltreated women, and all sorts of outrages allegedly committed by the Reds. In our neighborhood many homes were searched for illegal weapons: the frightened inhabitants subsequently described the atrocious scenes. According to their reports, the revolutionary bandits behaved like rapacious monsters. It seemed amazing, indeed, that any human being could survive such horrors as were imposed on our unfortunate neighbors. Our own house, incidentally, was spared by the government agents. We took it for a lucky chance at the time, but learned afterwards that the patrols had been instructed to pass over the villa of Thomas Mann. True, it was a capitalistic-looking mansion, and the books of its owner did not correspond with the principles of Marxism. The proletarian officials, however, whom their opponents denounced as a gang of illiterate brutes, were in reality men who respected the talent and integrity of a writer, whatever his political views. The author of the "Reflections" was left in peace by the Reds on account of "Buddenbrooks" and "Death in Venice."

My diary reports, under the date of April 13:

"In the morning there were rumors to the effect that the Communist government has been overthrown. Levin and Toller escaped. They say that Levin has carried half a million marks to Switzerland. Erich Mühsam has been arrested. I went to see the collection of medieval weapons at the National Museum. Fairly interesting."

The rumors were premature: the Reds remained in power for another couple of days or so. Munich was in a regular state of siege and surrendered to the Free Corps of General von Epp only after a fierce and tenacious struggle. To us the civil war meant but a distant grumbling that accompanied our games. My diary entry of May 2 reads, characteristically:

"Before lunch we played baseball and at the same time listened to the noise of the guns. The Red and the White are fighting near Dachau. Later we had a look at the big machine gun posted near our house. There is no bread. Fanny has made a sort of flat cake instead. Seems all right; rather tasty. Read a fine story by Walter Scott."

On May 5, when the troops of General von Epp had already entered the city, I went out to buy myself a copy of Gogol's story, "The Overcoat," and found the streets "swarming with soldiers." On May 8, the civil war was officially declared to be over and daily life resumed its familiar boredom. But the memories of what took place still lingered everywhere, even in that bleak building where I had to learn how to conjugate Latin verbs and how to hate the French. Diary entry of May 8, 1919: "At school again, alas. The professor tells us that a very famous regiment has been quartered at the building. The same soldiers, he says, who killed Rosa Luxemburg and Karl Liebknecht. I didn't like the way he said it—as if it were something to boast of. Day before yesterday five Spartakists were executed in the courtyard of our school. One of them was only seventeen. He refused to have his eyes covered. The professor says such stubbornness proves how fanatic he was. But I think admirable."

Revolution and civil war, peace treaty and class struggle—all these boisterous issues and upheavals upon which I so naïvely commented, affected my real life very little, and only indirectly. I was keen and ambitious enough to take an interest in those things whose paramount importance I began to grasp. However, one essential part of my being secretly and obstinately refused to believe in the actuality and relevance of a world which I still considered, at the bottom of my heart, a ponderous phantasm of the grown-ups. My intellectual status was comparable to that of certain people who lived at the junction between two cultural eras, say, the Dark Ages and the Renaissance. Those puzzled generations harbored a double concept of God and life: on the one hand, their minds were already molded by the rousing message of enlightenment and scientific adventure, while on the other, they still adhered to the patterns and rituals of the ancient concepts. Thus they actually lived in two worlds—the flat orb vaulted by the celestial roof, as old wisdom described it, and the revolutionary cosmos of Copernicus. To the former vision they were bound by piety and tradition: the latter mightily appealed to their curiosity, their lust for progress and knowledge.

The same complexity was characteristic of my own psychological situation at the age of twelve. My callow mind was torn between two incongruous spheres and idioms—the grandiose abstractions of the adults and the palpable mythology of our own experiences. Already attracted by the problems and promises of a ribald and intricate world, I remained faithful to the images and evaluations of infancy. The great games and fairy-tales had not yet faded away. The myths of childhood were still alive.

The validity of Jennie's rank as a myth is, of course, beyond any doubt. She had always been with us—a venerable state in itself. All attributes of her character and appearance were embellished by the patina of primeval intimacy. Indeed, her connection with the family was even older than that of Motz, incredible as it may sound. Rumor had it that Jennie, in the days of yore, had acted as Offi's chambermaid and knew Ofey when he still had plenty of hair and his collection of pottery was only in its beginning. However, it may seem idle to trace her career back into prehistorical epochs. Suffice it to say that the amazing woman had been in Mother's confidence and service long before Father paid his first visit to the palazzo in the Arcis-Strasse. Mielein brought her along into married life as a sort of dynamic mascot and essential ingredient of her dowry. She rocked all of us in her lap, decorated the Christmas tree, set the table when we had dinner guests, advised Mielein in the choice of cooks, flowers, and evening gowns, and was altogether a pearl.

When food began to be scarce, during the war, she excelled in discovering devious "sources" and startling recipes. At the same time, however, she grew strangely irritable and fidgety. Her voice and laugh became shrill; she lost her temper over trifles and quarrelled with the cook and the washerwoman. The cook had to be fired as Jennie insisted that she gypped and swindled. But the next one turned out to be even worse: this time it was Jennie's own ring, an irreplaceable souvenir, that mysteriously disappeared. Mielein began to believe that all wartime cooks were dishonest; for she was missing valuable objects herself. The third one proved more rapacious than all her predecessors combined. Jennie triumphed and raved. "Cooks are crooks!" she proclaimed. She wanted to run the household suite herself, without any thievish assistance. Mielein agreed that this might be the best solution.

"Isn't it awful," she said to us, "what the war does to those good-natured cooks. How corruptible they are! How easily they lose their balance! Even our Jennie, Gibraltar of integrity, seems a bit nervous and agitated."

The story of Jennie's fall assumed epic proportions in our family saga. Her depravity was unmasked by the parting cook. "It's none of my business, Ma'am," that upright female observed, according to all chroniclers who ever described the event. "But I may as well tell you," she said, "*who* is the thief in this house. It isn't *me*, Ma'am: it's *that* one!"

The scene must have been terrific—comparable only to the legendary fights between such superhuman termagants as Sieglinde and Brunhilde or Mary of Scotland and Elizabeth. However, the whole affair, for all its violence, might have ended as a domestic scandal without consequences or significance, if the Magician had not interfered himself. Irritated and allured by the uncivilized noise, he descended to the subterranean premises where the uproarious scene took place. This had never happened before. The effect of his mere appearance was so utterly stunning that even Jennie seemed overwhelmed. When Father asked her to open the door to her room, she obeyed, silently and quickly. It is reported that she looked pale and majestic while striding toward the door, and audibly gnashed her teeth. With her hand already clasping the latch, she announced solemnly: "You'll feel sorry, Herr Doktor. I am innocent. You'll feel very sorry for having suspected me,"—a statement that seems almost insane in its glaring absurdity, considering the sight in store for my parents behind the mysterious door.

There it was, the motley collection of things stolen from us in the course of the years, piled up in a crazy hodgepodge; rubbers and salad bowls, fans and sausages, toys we had separately sought and at last forgotten. She had grabbed, for years apparently, whatever she could get hold of. Neither junk nor jewels were safe from her kleptomania. She stole overcoats, paintings, and hats. Her appalling storeroom contained six umbrellas, twenty silver knives, dozens of shirts and neckties, fine editions of classic literature, two bottles of imported champagne, and Father's treasured walking stick.

"All this belongs to *me!*" Jennie announced. "Don't you touch it, Herr Doktor!" She embraced the room, and everything that was in it, with a wide, truculent gesture.

The walking stick, she insisted, was that of her late fiancé: very much like my father's, perhaps; yet a different stick. She disputed about every item. A ravenous monster, she snatched a bunch of handkerchiefs from my mother: "They are mine!" she shouted. But her fury reached its frightening climax when my father discovered a bottle of his favorite Burgundy.

"My Burgundy!" he exclaimed—heartily moved as by an unexpected meeting with a dear old friend.

"My Burgundy!" she snapped back.

It was at this point, over the Burgundy, that Jennie tried to hit the Magician. She might have seriously hurt him if he had not jauntily parried her outrageous attack. He jumped aside, surprisingly alert, while Mielein stood petrified in view of such a nightmarish spectacle.

This went too far: there are limits. My parents felt that something ought to be done; but it was the cook who did it. She sneaked to the telephone. Before Jennie realized what was going on, the police had their information: a dangerous criminal was to be arrested in the home of Mr. and Mrs. Mann.

Jennie, lifting her hand against the master of the house!—this truly was revolution. Jennie—parading in Mielein's most beautiful hat, glittering with Offi's jewelry, drunk on Ofey's wine, brandishing father's cane: this is the way the world ends, an ancient order cracks, the apocalypse begins. The most revolting things became conceivable when Jennie could transform herself into a vicious freak.

We were bombarded with phone calls and anonymous letters revealing more staggering details. The whole neighborhood had long been wondering how we could allow such scandalous goings-on. Every night another soldier or officer! It was utterly shocking. An elderly widow, tragic and picturesque in her mourning clothes, filled our drawing room with her theatrical wails. Jennie, the widow said, was responsible for the suicide of her husband. "She is a regular demon," stated the veiled matron, with a sort of bleak appreciation; and added, as though out of the impulse to define the matter as precisely as possible: "A murderess, that's what she actually is."

I began to admire Jennie. Her stature grew in proportion to the extravagant record of her wickedness. Evidently she was eaten by vices as by virulent maladies. Her mental balance had been gravely disturbed by the general disorder and catastrophic commotion brought about by the war. Her primitive but receptive mind could not resist the wave of corruption and brutalization that swept and undermined the continent. Why should she not change her lover every other night as he might be killed even before the next rendezvous? Why should she not steal and indulge in fornication as the divine commandments obviously were annulled? If she had lived in a peaceful, orderly period—who knows? She would have got married, perhaps, and led a respectable life. But these were monstrous times. So, naturally Jennie turned monstrous.

It seemed logical, though at the same time surprising, that the judges acquitted her. For that is what happened: the rampant sinner was found free of guilt. It was like a parody of all revolutionary justice. Jennie triumphed because she represented,—with what skillful élan!—the underprivileged class. She lied with gusto and flamboyant eloquence. Everybody was smitten with her popular wit. She stole the show. My parents gave a pitiful performance. The audience booed and hissed when Jennie described how my mother tried to deprive her of that Burgundy, the souvenir from her gallant cousin. "Only one bottle!" Jennie cried, almost weeping. "And they have a huge cellar crammed with champagne and brandy—damned exploiters they are!"

She wore a tight blouse of green satin and looked more stately than ever. Paradoxically, the vulgar magnificence of this outfit was accepted by both the court and the audience as an additional proof of her revolutionary dignity. Even the cook who had been instrumental in unmasking her thievish colleague now did not have the nerve to abide by her accusations. It was the acme of Jennie's worldly career. She enjoyed every minute of it. An aura of victory and at the same time of martyrdom beamed around her festively heated brow as she withdrew from the witness stand—all triumphantly swollen bosom and glaring green satin. While striding toward the door, she darted a withering glance over her shoulder, back at that despondent-looking couple—my unfortunate father and mother.

Was this the last act of Jennie's drama? By no means. A bleak epilogue still was in store for her. Her specious glory tarnished almost as quickly as it had been gained. She became a spook haunting the family to which she had once belonged. At the hour of dusk when the skies and things turn pale, we would see Jennie roving through the streets of our neighborhood. As the evening grew darker, she approached our house and began to revolve round the garden where she used to play with us. We would watch her from a hiding place while she stumbled and mumbled—confiding her grisly secrets to the deserted alley.

How squalid and wretched she looked! We could not see her face: it was hidden by a mangy, discolored shawl. But we recognized, not without shuddering, her famous blouse of green satin, once the token of triumph: now so deplorably threadbare and lusterless. Her figure that had been buxom and alert had become sodden and flabby, softened and soaked, as it were, by many rains, many tears, many drinking bouts.

She would linger in front of our house door as if she were still living with us and had just returned from a merry evening off. No doubt, she looked for her key, rummaging in her little bag with impatient nervousness. There was no key. She would grow angry. We would see her perform a grand and swaying motion with the upper part of her body, rather crazy and beautiful. At the same time she would spit, just at the threshold of our house. We could hear the splashing little noise.

What then occurred was still more alarming. Infuriated by the elusive key and the transitoriness of her mundane successes, she would raise her fists and murmur a malediction. We could not catch the words, but they must have been dreadful: the hissing sound of her voice was enough to give us the shivers. Even more frightening was her face, now revealed as the shawl glided down to her shoulders. Slightly bent backwards, it lay obscenely exposed to the eerie light of a street lamp, a wolfish grimace, bloated under the dirty crown of dishevelled hair; destroyed by misery and wrath; the eyes glassy with drunkenness.

There she would stand for minutes that seemed ages to us, petrified in her savage pose of fury and despair. We watched her, breathless with fear and pity, as she let her arms sink at last, as though suddenly tired or sobered. Her features and body, even her clothes, seemed to sag while she slowly turned away from us, shrouding herself in the worn-out shawl. It was this freezing, pathetic gesture—that helpless attempt to protect herself against the chill of the night—which struck me most deeply and painfully. It made me grasp the merciless, irreparable character of Jennie's decline.

Something dwindled and paled in view of this sodden wreck that had once been our dexterous playmate. Something irreplaceable crumbled and faded away, hollowed out, corroded by unknown, relentless forces. What was this war which corrupted and dislocated our jolly pal Jennie? What were they aiming at, those débâcles and revolutions? What sort of reality was it that got the better of our myth, our childhood?

CHAPTER THREE

Civilized Education

(1920–1922)

THERE are six of us. The two youngest were born in the midst of turmoil and calamity: Elizabeth, in the spring of 1918; Michael, one year later. Thanks to the arrival of the baby couple, Golo and Monika advanced to the position of the "middle ones," while Erika and I were promoted to the rank of almost-adults. We felt like uncle and aunt, embarrassed before the tiny creatures. They were so cute and pathetic, a trifle wearisome when they cried, but most lovable when they smiled or slumbered. Elizabeth, called Medi, had a sweet little porcelain face, whereas Michael, alias Bibi, was rather on the stocky side, sanguine but irritable, frequently beset by violent fits of anger. Father took a fancy to Elizabeth; Mielein, out of a sense of justice and equilibrium, pampered the little boy. The new team absorbed a good deal of paternal tenderness, an inevitable development accepted by us with grim stoicism.

For Golo and Monika the situation was particularly delicate. Evidently, they fell short of Medi and Bibi as far as dainty cuteness was concerned; nor could they compete with the vigor and experience commanded by Erika and me. However, Monika—at once unassuming and self-assured—seemed satisfied with her own little assets. As for Golo, far more complex and ambitious than his female counterpart, he had sufficient energy and imagination to build up an idiom and style of his own. Deeply entangled in the dilemmas and aspirations of his unmistakable Golo-sphere, he also participated, from a respectful and jealous distance, in our games and adventures. It was he to whom I confided all my fantasies, projects, and worries. For he was endowed with the ability to listen, an exceptional gift, even among mature men and women. His silent attention was, perhaps, more intense and productive than my wayward expansiveness. I invented, swaggered, jested, and lamented; he kept quiet and listened. I never learned what transmutations my vagaries underwent in his impenetrable mind. He was my confidant but I was not his: which may have been partly on account of my naïve egotism, partly, because of Golo's pride and sensibility.

It must have hurt him that our intimacy, so ebullient in the realm of dreams and speculations, was much less unrestricted in reality. There, Erika and I belonged together: our solidarity was absolute and indisputable. We acted twin-like in an almost provocative way: the grown-ups as well as the kids had to accept us as an entity. The only aspect of life we did not have in common, the one sphere where we were separated, was that dreary accessory called "school." Erika was not admitted, alas, to the gloomy building where I had to endure so much boredom; nor could I partake in the jolly pranks to which she incited her obedient classmates in the girls' high school. It is, perhaps, on account of this separation that all details and incidents connected with those bleak morning hours have completely faded in my consciousness. School was too dull and insignificant even to provoke seditious feelings or the bitter-sweet pathos of martyrdom. Neither a horror nor a stimulus, it was just a nuisance.

The most obnoxious crime committed by the gawky Philistines who acted as our teachers was their way of treating the Greek, Latin, and German classics. Even the most exciting drama, the sweetest poem, tarnished and turned hopelessly vapid when touched by their clumsy fingers. Happily, the very selection of reading matter was such that it did not really make much difference how the schoolmasters handled it: most of the stuff was a deadly bore, anyhow. Almost none of the material we had to study at school was apt to seize or enrich my fancy. Whatever literary background I possess is certainly not due to the sleepy old Wilhelms-gymnasium.

The voices of the great poets fuse in my memory with the voices of those who first transmitted them to me. There are certain masterpieces of the German romantic school which I cannot reread without hearing, once again, the intonations of Mielein's swift and sonorous voice. She was wont to read aloud to us, as long as we were youngsters and it still meant an effort to us to read by ourselves. There was nothing ceremonious about these occasional reading hours. The whole set-up was cozy and informal, with Mielein lying on her sofa and the cook from time to time dropping in to ask questions concerning the dinner menu. However, such domestic interruptions could not break the spell emanating from Grimm's fairy-tales or the wondrous caprices by Tieck, Brentano, and Hoffmann.

Mielein was very good at evoking certain eerie moods; but, of course, Offi was more masterly and dynamic. Our literary contact with her began comparatively late: I must have been about twelve when our enterprising grandmamma suggested, one wintry Sunday afternoon, that she might as well read a story by Dickens to us, in order to shorten the long hours between luncheon and tea. She chose the "Christmas Carol" and it was a hit. Subsequently the "Dickens hour" with Offi became a regular institution. For several years to come, Dickens and Sunday afternoon meant the same thing to us.

Offi, the former star of the Ducal Theater in Meiningen, displayed considerable skill in characterizing the colorful variety of human types created by the genius of Dickens. Her voice sounded tinny and quarrelsome when she impersonated a cranky spinster: it became unctuous or harsh, creaky or melodious, according to the respective character and situation. She was matchless in aping quaint originals and gave us the shivers with her realistic performance of grisly villains. In short, it was a first-rate show and we enjoyed it intensely. We shrieked with laughter over certain episodes in "The Pickwick Papers," were thrilled by "David Copperfield," and, for one reason or another, thought "A Tale of Two Cities" more startling than even "Oliver Twist."

Nobody could compete with Offi's theatrical training and impetus. Yet in a sense it was even more elating to listen to Father's steady and vigorous voice. Sometimes—not very frequently, though—he would ask us, with a sort of solemn casualness, whether we cared to hear a fine tale, after supper. "Unless you have any other engagements," he added, half banteringly, half out of absent-minded politeness.

We had no other engagements. We considered it a great treat and privilege to be admitted to his workroom, where the scent of his cigar pleasantly fused with the faint odor of glue wafted from thousands of books. The book-cases were overcrowded. More recent publications covered the chairs and sofas. The Magician shook his head humorously at the disquieting plenty. "The productivity of my dear colleagues assumes the character of a calamity," he would observe, at once sorrowful and amused. "I really need a new book-case, upstairs, perhaps, in your little breakfast corridor."

We could not help giggling. It was so very much like him to refer to the first floor lobby, where we had our morning tea, as "your little breakfast corridor." And how typically Magician-like!—this earnest interest in the placement of the new book-case. In general he seemed completely aloof from what went on in the house. Neither the new ice box nor our repaired bicycles could arouse his curiosity. But as soon as his private, particular sphere of life was concerned—his wardrobe or library—he seemed meticulously concerned in every detail involved. It irritated, indeed, offended him to see a tiny item on his spacious desk removed from its traditional place; the same Magician who would overlook a new set of arm-chairs in another part of the house was likely to complain when the blind eyes of his Homer bust were not properly dusted.

This gentle pedantry in respect to his own belongings became even more obstinate when the item in question happened to be a family relic from Lübeck. Baroque monstrosities like stuffed bears or golden tankards were treasured throughout the years, in memory of past birthday parties or long-forgotten business jubilees. At bottom, of course, he was fully aware of his weakness; it was not without self-irony that he indulged in it. Characteristically, he would not allow the hideous bears or bowls to disturb the harmony of his sanctum. Those bizarre adornments were reserved to the dining room or the lobby. The only souvenirs of Hanseatic derivation exhibited in his studio were a couple of tall candelabra, each with seven ornamental branches.

They were placed in front of a glass door, just behind the desk. In the evening, when the door was covered by a green velvet curtain, the big candlesticks produced a gorgeous effect, the faded gold of their branches profiled against the flowing darkness of the draperies.

"Well, you'll find a place to sit down, somewhere," Father said, confident and distrait. Whereupon he seated himself in the huge arm-chair, next to the floor-lamp. And then the great entertainment began.

His favorites were the Russians. He read to us "The Cossacks" by Tolstoi and the strangely primitive, childlike parables of his latest period; we heard stories by Gogol and even one piece by Dostoievski, that uncanny farce called "A Ridiculous Tale," describing the experience of a high official in St. Petersburg who gets deadly drunk at the party of an inferior colleague. The Magician was exuberantly amused by the macabre antics developing out of this situation. Sometimes he had to interrupt his lecture for a minute or so, all shaken and overwhelmed by his nervous delight.

On other occasions he chose more innocent or more romantic material. It was thanks to him that we first became familiar with the lusty wit of Tom Sawyer. Or he would enthrall us with one of the jewels of the great German tradition, that serene and lucid novelette by Mörike on Mozart's journey to Prague, or Goethe's "Fairy-Tale," unfathomably suggestive, full of magic allusions and playful fantasies.

No doubt, these eventful evening hours in Father's workroom meant a stimulus, not only to our imagination but also to our curiosity. Once you have tasted the charm and solace of great literature, you become avid for more stuff of that kind, other ridiculous tales and suggestive parables. So you begin to read by yourself.

We had never had a chance to travel, except between Munich and Tölz. At the age of thirteen, I knew neither the sight of the sea nor any big city, save the one where we lived. Now books became the magic vehicle that carried me to distant spaces, never-dreamed-of scenery. The cities of Bagdad and Isphahan revealed their thousand-and-one secrets imbued with the scent of musk, blood, and roses: the spell of the Arabian Nights was more compelling than even the vast appeal of the American prairies. Sure enough, it was wonderful to lie in ambush behind exotic plants in the company of plucky Redskins. For a while I was crazy about the Leatherstocking Tales. But the landscape of fantasy is endless and multiform. I traveled with Gulliver to the giants and midgets; with Jules Verne up to the moon. Mowgli, the exquisite human youth among the wolves, snakes, and monkeys, introduced me to the hiding places and hunting grounds of the Indian jungle; I dwelt with Robinson Crusoe on the desert isle. The air was tonic and crisp in the Nordic realm of Selma Lagerlöf: the wings of her wild geese became the magic carpet on which I cruised over the fjords and rocks of fabulous solitudes. Walter Scott was my chivalrous guide through the castle and forests of old England: thanks to him I became acquainted with many a valiant lord constantly engaged in romance and feud.

It often seems to me that it was only then, when I was thirteen or fourteen, that I really knew how to read. How fastidious and desultory have I turned since that time! Nowadays I have to overcome dastardly inhibitions before I venture to read a ponderous novel from cover to cover. In those distant days the most extensive dramas and epics seemed too short rather than too voluminous. I did not content myself with reading one book by a particular author: as soon as my interest was aroused in a certain poet or story teller, I greedily consumed his complete works—ten volumes by Henrik Ibsen, twelve volumes by Gotthold Efraim Lessing or Friedrich Schiller. Neither the stringent gravity of Friedrich Hebbel nor the mighty dimensions of Goethe's versatile amplitude could frighten me away. Undaunted and insatiable, I plunged into the diffuse grandeur of romantic epics and didactic poetry.

My own callow writings naturally echoed the moods and intonations of what I had been reading. As a producer of literature I was no less diligent and unflagging than I used to be as a consumer. I don't know how many notebooks I may have filled with dramatic sketches, lyrical outbursts, and narrative fantasies: it seems to me that my poetic output must have comprised more than a hundred "volumes," before I had reached my fifteenth or sixteenth year. I wrote love stories and mystery stories and historical tragedies. I wrote about subjects utterly remote from my own experience. I wrote without any objective—just for the sake of writing. Nobody read the stuff, except Golo, who knew it mostly by heart. Sometimes I compelled him, by means of mental or physical pressure, to carry a bunch of my childish-looking notebooks to the offices of a local newspaper or publishing house. He desperately tried to convince the doormen that these manuscripts were the immortal work of his inspired stepmother, Miss Natasha Huber. But the guardians at the gates of glory dismissed him with a paternal grin or some juicy invectives. Golo and I complained together about the meanness and ignorance of our compatriots.

Gradually I ventured on autobiographical themes. As the scope and intensity of my inner adventures increased, I grew tired of the idle and irrelevant patterns I had hitherto copied. After having indulged in so many meaningless masquerades, I began to hanker for self-identification. I finally tried to articulate, honestly, if with a turgid and inadequate vocabulary, the worries and aspirations that really beset my mind. Why are we in this muddled, fantastic world? What is the intrinsic meaning of all the tragedies and antics we witness? What is behind and beneath the boisterous lies and slogans? What is genius? Am I a genius? Why not? Where is God? What is God like? Is God a reality or just another illusion? Can God be good since His world is so conspicuously evil?

I was about fourteen years old when I composed a lengthy treatise demonstrating the nonexistence of God. The mere fact, I asserted, that there are many Gods, Allah, Jehovah, the Catholic deity and the God of Martin Luther, whom I had been taught to worship, irrefutably proves that there is actually none. Whereupon I sardonically referred to God's embarrassing situation in wartime. How could it be explained that both antagonistic parties implored the same divine authority? The Lord received the contradictory requests without intervening in favor of either group. There seemed to be something utterly confusing, indeed deceitful and unfair, about such lofty detachment. *Whose* God was he, after all? The God of the Kaiser and General Ludendorff, or the God of Monsieur Poincaré and President Wilson? Evidently he was either a partisan God or altogether callous and aloof. How could he otherwise acquiesce in such dreadful goings-on as wars, revolutions, railway accidents, grammar schools, and the like? I am not quite sure if I actually quoted Stendhal's ambiguous remark, which Nietzsche called "the only atheistic crack I would like to have made myself." Said the author of "Le Rouge et le Noir": "The only excuse for God is that he does not exist."

I drew the succinct conclusion that God is just a contrivance to exploit and tame the underdog, including inspired schoolboys like myself, and ended with the traditional challenge: "If you exist, God, why don't you avenge my blasphemy? I don't believe in you, God!— can't you hear me? Why don't you shatter me with your lightning? I know the reason, my Lord: you can neither hear nor shatter *because you don't exist.*"

I failed to grasp, at the time, that such puerile swagger paradoxically implies the actual existence of God, as does, for that matter, Stendhal's uncanny flippancy. To denounce Him, already means to recognize His being. In fact, I am inclined to believe that the sacrilegious protest against God is more akin to a truly religious attitude than is the perfunctory piety of many a church-goer.

But, again, how trite and inconsequential are even the most passionate doubts compared with the enormous fact of God's evident and inexplicable presence! How pitiful, the audacity of us puny sinners!— considering the colossal scope of His plans. He is patient. He waits and listens—motionless, inaccessible. Silently he endures the hollow prayers and blasphemies rising from our planet. All this has no more relevancy than the rattle of tinny bells. In glacial stillness he awaits the valid evocation, the authentic lament. He awaits the truth, the blood, the essence of our being. Nothing less will do. Nothing less is accepted. He will extort the bloody truth from us: he will squeeze us until we yield it. Lightnings are toys: mythic junk to frighten the women and children. The Lord is not spectacular and dashing. He is slow and tenacious and great. He is appallingly great.

Go ahead and tease the Lord, little brawler! There will be no punishment, no reaction: not now, silly dwarf! Not yet! The tribulation is long. Don't you realize what may be in store for you? The God whom you now provoke will make you writhe and whimper. He will answer you. You shall hear his voice. Wait and see! The wounds, the tears, the wasted efforts, the frustrated hopes . . . But what do you know about suffering? You are only fourteen.

Only fourteen! . . . Your boyish face, blank and fair, tries very hard to assume a tragic expression. Brooding over your diary, just before dinner time, you seek to vocalize what burdens and inspires your heart. Finally you write down these words:

"Night falls, once again. Another night!—how dull! . . . I must, must, *must* become famous!"

Youth is appallingly selfish. A lad of fourteen, like an animal or a genius, has a remarkable ability to overlook all problems and phenomena save those which directly appeal to his appetites. Never before nor afterwards in my life have I been so intensely narrow-minded as during the period from my thirteenth until my seventeenth year. So absorbing was my concern in art and literature that I became impervious to all social or political issues. Even as a child I had been more observant and realistic. The upheaval of 1918 and the turmoil of the following months were the last political events I witnessed with the naïve keenness commanded by children alone.

After the collapse of the Bavarian Soviets and the subsequent establishment of a half-military, half-bureaucratic dictatorship, my interest in politics dwindled. I read hardly any newspapers and, if at all, exclusively the theatrical column. Even such stirring events as the assassination of our Foreign Minister, Walter Rathenau, in 1922, left me more or less cool. The death of Kurt Eisner, three years before, had impressed and shocked me much more. Yet, Rathenau was more important than the late Bavarian Premier, not only as a statesman but also as a literary figure. Moreover, he happened to be an old acquaintance of my family and a great friend of many writers I liked. The dastardly crime committed against him by a gang of nationalistic brutes, marks one of the most disquieting developments in the pre-Hitler history of the Reich. Needless to say I was disgusted; but I was not disgusted enough. Even the obnoxious way in which my schoolfellows discussed the incident, failed to excite me really. I certainly loathed the murderers and wholeheartedly despised those who stupidly extolled their crime. But at the same time I prided myself on being utterly detached and disillusioned. What could one expect, after all, of those homespun cretins? They were mean and ignorant beyond words.

I deemed Munich a bore and altogether barbarous—maybe because it happened to be the only city I knew. Besides the Bavarian capital, in that time, had a poor reputation among liberals. It was considered the most reactionary place in Germany—a center of the counter-revolutionary tendencies smouldering all over Europe. Flippant editors in Berlin used to run the dispatches from Munich under the caustic heading: "Atrocity stories from a savage land!" The people of Munich, in their turn, stubbornly believed that Berlin was ruled by a conspiracy of Jewish bankers and Bolshevist agitators.

Politics were void and depressing: I refused to bother with them. How much did I know about crucial issues like the occupation of the Rhine and Ruhr zones by the Allied armies? Only what I learned from the glaring posters displayed all over the city. I studied them carefully; for some of them carried grisly cartoons and captions arraigning the outrages ostensibly committed by colored troops. I recollect in particular one rampant account to the effect that a single Moor had raped not only scores of virgins and children but, as a climax of depravity, a handsome mare, sole and treasured belonging of an upright Rhenish peasant tribe. This sordid fabrication haunted me for years, replacing in my mind certain images out of "Uncle Tom's Cabin." The exorbitant potency of the dark-skinned satyr beguiled my imagination, whereas the so-called "national disgrace" utterly failed to impress me. A beautiful poem or painting seemed more significant to me than the "black pollution" of Düsseldorf or the devaluation of the German mark. It made but negligible difference whether our pocket money consisted of twenty pfennigs or twenty marks: it always sufficed to pay for a pencil or a bit of candy.

At home, things had picked up somewhat since the gloomy days of 1917. Of course, decent food was still scarce; but the period of foul potatoes and cabbage was over. Our domestic style began to resume a certain degree of bourgeois elegance, mainly thanks to Mielein's untiring skill. We children never asked ourselves how she managed to keep the extensive household going, not on a lavish scale but pleasantly and smoothly enough. All of us took it for granted that she was able to do miracles, assisted by the Magician, who, of course, was notably wonder-working in his own way.

The useful collaboration of the thaumaturgic couple was particularly evident in the case of those profitable letters they jointly produced for the United States of America. Or rather, it was Father who actually wrote the text—sketchy surveys of conditions in Germany—whereupon Mielein, in no time, rushed to the post office to have the valuable item registered. It was addressed to an exotic institution by the name of "The Dial," a bountiful demi-god on the other side of the ocean, benign and wealthy enough to acknowledge the receipt of registered mail from Munich by sending, in its turn, the most delightful tokens. It always was a little Christmas-like when those handsome American checks arrived and Mielein got her bicycle out of the cellar and rode apace to Herr Feuchtwanger's little bank. There she received a stunning lot of good, solid German inflation-cash for that flimsy stuff the Americans use as money. Mielein beamed and the Magician smirked. Next Sunday we had a goose; and all of us got new raincoats.

We had sold the country house in Tölz and invested the returns in war bonds, a fine patriotic deed, undoubtedly, but also a bitter loss. The sums from German publishers became depressingly meager. However, the Magician said, optimistically, "There is nothing to worry about, as long as we have 'The Dial.'"

He had almost completely regained his suavity and steady equilibrium: the morose wizard, delving into the depth of the Germanic soul, gradually became a wartime memory, like the banners, the songs, and the cripples. The time had come when he little by little found his way back to those more serene tasks and projects he had abandoned in August, 1914. Now, with the war over, he could concentrate, once again, on what inevitably remained the crux and heart of his life, the story-teller's age-old, meaningful craft.

He had engaged in two narrative enterprises when the war broke out and estranged him from both. Now he wavered between the two fragments, both of which seemed attractive. What should he finish first?—the memoirs of the impostor Felix Krull—another ironic paraphrase of his traditional theme, the ambiguous implications of the artistic mission; or a short story dealing with tuberculosis, love, and the thin air in a Swiss mountain resort. Krull was screamingly funny, but the sanatorium romance looked rather promising too. A sort of macabre pendant to "Death in Venice"—that was what it might turn out to become. One could call it "The Magic Mountain"—not a bad title, indeed, for a weird and humorous improvisation. There was quite a bit of material—Mielein's letters from her sojourns in Davos and Arosa, and his own diary notes written during his visits up there . . . What a delicate choice!—between the spirited swindler and the inspiring tubercles . . . Finally the decision was made in favor of our good dog Bauschan!

For it is always wrong to precipitate matters. Life is long and gives you plenty of time to carry out many projects. If you cannot make up your mind which one of two topics you ought to tackle first, it might indicate that the moment is not propitious for either. However, there are innumerable things worthwhile to write about; there is, for instance, the dog, a droll and amiable mongrel with golden, expressive eyes. The extensive walks in Bauschan's company were the most tonic relief during these trying years. It may be a good idea to give the good-natured animal a token of gratitude. Bauschan deserves to be immortalized.

There is no need of a plot. All that has to be done is to describe, with serene thoroughness, Bauschan's familiar looks, the antics he is wont to perform, his little escapades and adventures. The scenery by the Isar river yields a pleasant background, unassuming and yet picturesque. It will be good to dwell on many details characteristic of those friendly paths so often walked in cheerful or pensive moods, while Bauschan amused himself by chasing a bird or a mouse. The story, "The Master and His Dog," may prove entertaining enough, for all its lack of suspense. A story is not likely to be a bore if it mirrors, precisely and without false pretensions, an authentic aspect of reality.

This is an idyllic moment in the author's life, and it seems appropriate, therefore, to produce an idyllic tale. Let the others, the younger and bolder ones, revel in ecstatic visions and glaring experiments!

Bauschan is more interesting, indeed, more real than is their expressionism,—this nebulous blend of optimistic-revolutionary and mystic-apocalyptic tendencies. A long literary career is rich in vicissitudes: there are ups and downs. So this is one of the quiet periods—a breathing spell and recreative interval. It is neither possible nor desirable to remain always in keeping with the requirements of the vanguard. If the fashionable devices happen to be incompatible with one's own innermost tastes and trends, the best thing to do is to withdraw, for a while, from the center of literary events. Never mind their calling you obsolete and pedantic! The hectic glory of the post-war generation may prove less solid than your cautious growth. Time marches on.

Time marches on: wait and see! To rove with Bauschan through the hunting-grounds of the Isar valley is, perhaps, more creative an exercise than to partake in the shrill performance of political life. The author of the "Reflections" might easily have become the official champion of the reactionary German elite. But he rejected, calmly and politely, such flattering propositions. The affinity between him and German nationalism, if it had ever existed, was of transitory and partly erroneous nature. Even in his most Teutonic moods he had nothing in common with the gangster methods and hollow slogans of those despicable patriots. Yet his conscientious mind needed time to prepare the crucial conversion in favor of the Republic. Lingering between two political adventures, he turned unpolitical, once again.

As far as I can remember, political issues were scarcely discussed at our dinner table, during that particular period. This may be a mistake on my part: perhaps I just failed to listen when the grown-ups talked politics. However, it seems to me that cultural subjects prevailed when the Magician had guests.

We children classified and judged the friends of our parents as if they had been comedians hired for our fun. Some of them we thought brilliant—veritable stars in the field of sparkling conversation, while others were ever so dull. None of them realized how mercilessly they were watched. They took us for well-bred, rather bashful youngsters who scarcely participated in the colloquy but kept a respectful silence. In reality we were the most cruel critics flaying every gesture and anecdote. We exchanged pitiful glances when a joke didn't click, or nodded like appreciative connoisseurs when we deemed the humorous effort successful.

Sometimes the most celebrated jester turned out to be a flop, or a notorious bore was surprisingly witty. Then we would say, after dinner: "What a pity! Björn was not at his best tonight." Or: "Professor Litzmann was almost gay, for a change." It sounded as if we had discovered flaws in Caruso's voice or gold in the organ of an anonymous chorus girl. But in general the accepted hierarchy remained valid: the favorites lived up to their reputations; the bores were as boring as ever.

As for Björn Björnson, son of the Norwegian classic, he was fabulously entertaining. We worshipped him on account of his foreign accent, his magnificent, snow-white mane, and his countless stories about Henrik Ibsen, Edward Grieg, and the whole Scandinavian Olympus. A talker in the grand old style, he completely bewitched us with his gales of laughter and eloquence. Björn was indeed almost matchless.

There were various categories of guests: the grand passers-by who spent just a few days in Munich; the temporary intimates who showed up very frequently during a certain period but subsequently made themselves scarce until they disappeared altogether; and finally, of course, the real friends—those who always were around and always will remain.

Björn, who spent his life between Norway and Italy, was a glamorous representative of the first category. Others "dropped by" on their way from Vienna to Berlin: Jacob Wassermann, for instance, at once somber and roguish, all dignity and pensive weightiness; or Hugo von Hofmannsthal, whose poems enchanted me when I was still a child, but whose personal charm, an iridescent, nervous attraction, I failed to grasp at the time. Besides, there were the travelers from the north, "en route" from Berlin to the Bavarian lakes, Vienna, or Milan. S. Fischer, the distinguished publisher, amused us because of his patriarchal jocosity and exaggerated lower lip. Gerhart Hauptmann looked like Goethe in a state of intoxication—majestic and absent-minded; the impressive arch of his forehead marked by a movable network of furrows: his eyes, under lifted brows, at once pallid and domineering. It was fascinating to watch his face, a vacuous but arresting mask, while he punctuated his indistinct eloquence with fumbling gestures. His utterances, when soberly analyzed, turned out to be trite and confused. However, they seemed full of inspiration and mystery, thanks to the suggestive pantomime accompanying his stammer.

Hans Pfizner was a wartime friend who appeared but rarely in the period I am talking about, and definitely withdrew as soon as my father joined the liberal camp. The romantic composer, a noble but anemic imitator of the German masters, was doggedly conservative, not to say a downright reactionary. The intellectual contact between him and my father lasted about as long as the latter was occupied with the "Reflections." In fact, the chapter devoted to Pfizner's music—in particular to his opera "Palestrina"—is one of the finest things that curious essay contains. As for Pfizner himself, he can hardly be counted among our favorite guests. A dwarfish little fellow, fidgety and tormented, he was not the type to conquer a bunch of critical youngsters. Our heroes were of a different stamp—the two Brunos, for instance: Bruno Walter and Bruno Frank.

As for Bruno Frank, I ought to have included him among the myths of childhood: we made friends with him when we were tiny kids and he was gloriously young. We loved him because he was at once glamorous and warmhearted, and read poetry to us in a thundering voice, and wore colorful dressing gowns and enjoyed fooling around with us. Later we loved him also on account of his books, from which emanates the same vigorous urbanity to which his personal charm is due. Both the Magician and Mielein seemed particularly animated when we had Frank for dinner. His visits—frequent but irregular, for he traveled a lot—were familiar as well as exciting. He was the uncle-like jester we had known from our earliest years: but at the same time there was something adventurous about him—a tinge of mundane eccentricity and buoyant elegance. We had been told wondrous tales about his successes and the staggering chances he took at the gambling tables of Monte Carlo, Cannes, and Baden-Baden—fabulous reports that could not but increase his appeal.

The glory of Bruno Walter was different but no less enchanting. The great conductor was our neighbor in that friendly suburb where all people knew each other after a while. But no one would have dared to approach him when he rode by street car to the central district where the opera is situated. I visualize him as he was wont to stand on the platform of the trolley car absorbed in thoughts; his face rather pale and tired under the slouch hat; his eyes, musing and unfocused, wandering into space. There was a strange aura around him—not forbidding but inaccessible: the magic echo of music.

In the circle of his family or as our guest he was cordial and unassuming. He worshipped and pampered his handsome daughters, Lotte and Gretel, our two dearest friends.

We saw them every day: they were like sisters to us. Gretel, the younger one, was exactly my age. Dark-haired and racy, she strikingly resembled her father: her gold-brown, eloquent eyes, her smile and speech were like his. She was musical and graceful; at once flippant and gentle. I was crazy about her. Without her consent or knowledge, she became "the young poet's first love" and had to behave accordingly. I expected her to be much more cruel and capricious than she actually was. In fact, it may have embarrassed her not a little to see herself styled, in the poems I wrote for her, as a wayward belle, untamable and effulgent, very Carmen-like.

Lotte, too grown-up and experienced to be bothered with poetry, graciously accepted the role of the unselfish confidant. At the same time I could not help being attracted by her milder splendor as well. If Gretel was a piquant brunette, her sister could be counted among the dreamy blondes, wistful, tender, and unusually appetizing. Both seemed all too thrilling and admirable to me; for they possessed not only their own personal glamor but also the fascination of a strange and marvelous world—the opera, the symphonic concerts, intimacy with illustrious singers, the whole enthralling realm of music and the stage.

Music was something beautiful and elating, especially when conducted by Walter. The theater bewitched us—whether the play produced happened to be by Shakespeare or by Sudermann: whether the actors did a fine or a mediocre job. But the opera, magic combination of drama and symphony, was the unsurpassable pleasure, the dream of dreams, the ideal. The opera as a form of art may be a monstrous bastard. Evidently, the "musical drama" is by no means the supreme development of aesthetics it was conceived to be by Richard Wagner and his followers. But the dazzling display of colors and harmonies, ballet, tragedy, and vocal beauty, spectacular staging and sublime emotions, cannot but mightily appeal to all naïve, impressionable minds: children, artists, and women will always be spellbound by the blend of theatrical and musical effects.

The Munich opera flourished under the leadership of Bruno Walter. He gathered around himself a plethora of magnificent voices: Delia Reinhardt's sweet and soulful mezzo, the amazing soprano of Maria Ivogün, Bender's velvety bass, Carl Erb's tenor, strangely melancholy and moving, the vigorous baritone of Gustav Schützendorf, and scores of others. The famous institute, widely praised from the days of Bülow, Mottl, and Levy, lived up to its high tradition, once again—for the last time, perhaps.

The two seats at the extreme left of the first row were permanently reserved for the "Herr Kapellmeister Generalmusikdirektor Professor" Bruno Walter. It was from this privileged spot that we were allowed to witness a profusion of great performances. The glorious cycle of operatic impressions opened with "Hänsel und Gretel," that engaging fairy-tale, only a trifle corrupted by Humperdink's redundant orchestration in the Wagnerian style. For years it remained a moot question between Erika and myself which opera had the precedence of the other: "Hänsel und Gretel" or "Undine," Lortzing's musical stage version of the beautiful story by De la Motte-Fouqué. Erika was extremely ambitious on behalf of "Undine": she insisted that her first opera surpassed the entire repertoire in splendor and importance. "Undine" was her personal property: I have never had a chance to hear this opus myself. Yet its score as well as its plot seems thoroughly familiar to me, thanks to Erika's meticulous and lively reports.

"The Flying Dutchman" belonged to both of us; for we went together to see him, invited and accompanied by the Magician himself. It is, perhaps, on account of this early impression that I have maintained a certain predilection for this, so to speak, "pre-Wagnerian" product of Wagner's genius. The substance both of drama and music, molded by the pure romanticism of Lortzing, Marschner, and Weber, strikes me as more truthful and persuasive than the forced grandeur of "The Ring" or the artificial popularity of "Die Meistersinger." The

drama of the errant captain and his high-minded Senta is, to my feeling, more authentic and moving than the ponderous ecstasies of the
subsequent works. The opening scene is as colorful and enchanting as
it could be. I am exceedingly fond of ghost-ships and of their singing
sailors. In the production we saw, the uncanny character of the vessel
was effectively underlined by means of flitting lightnings and bluish
flames. It was most enjoyable and exciting. I still feel sorry for Erika,
who was placed so much to the left that she could hardly catch a
glimpse of the lurid splendor. Of course, she burst into tears: what
else could she do, considering the magnitude of her loss? But when the
Dutchman appeared and beautifully deplored his misfortune, Erika,
forgot hers.

How many unforgettable hours! What a multitude of visions and
melodies! "Rigoletto" and "Lohengrin," "Butterfly" and "Aida," "Frei-
schütz" and "Don Pasquale," "La Bohème," "Figaro," and "Der Rosenkavalier"—what gorgeous wealth of beauty and emotion! I fell in love
with Carmen and thought it was the singer, a certain Luise Willer,
who had seized my heart. She was a sturdy brunette—remarkably
buxom and saucy. I sent her a pretty heart made of marzipan and re-
quested her autograph. She accepted the heart and was gracious enough
to give me an autographed portrait. It was the first and the last time
in my life that I presented a lady with a marzipan token of my devotion and asked a "vedette" for her signature.

We were captivated, bewitched by the opera. When Walter's seats
were not available, we would stand for hours—first, in front of the box
office; then, at the entrance of the theatre, to be among the first when
the doors would fly open at last; finally, of course, throughout the
show itself. I recollect that we once spent ten hours standing during a
single day, for the sake of "The Magic Flute." There is, alas, no artistic treat that could now induce me to accept such hardships, not even
"The Magic Flute," which I still consider one of the finest and most
curious things ever written.

It was almost as wonderful a performance as when Bruno Walter
managed to spare an hour or two to explain to us, at the pianoforte, the
charm and structure of an opera. He played and talked and sang; he
improvised, sparkled, elucidated; he made us laugh and weep and al-

most understand. We would sit around the piano—Gretel, Lotte, Erika, and I. Everything was good and cozy, within the room and without: the piano with the portrait of Gustav Mahler; the three girls absorbed in listening; and, outside, the familiar trees, the familiar paving-stones, the pavement of the Mauerkircher-Strasse: just an ordinary street in the city of Munich, not very picturesque, rather ordinary, but trustworthy and likable as seems everything one has known and used very long.

The faded picture revives. The melodies, voices and smiles—everything breathes and moves, animated as if by magic. Indeed, my nostalgia evokes, once again, what seemed sunken and lost—the laughs, the whirring sounds, the motions of hands and lips. Walter impersonates a humorous character, Papageno, the clown of "The Magic Flute." He is very funny. Our hilarity resounds throughout the house. Frau Walter rushes downstairs—all fluster and disapproval in her spectacular dressing gown. She laments and scolds: Bruno ought to change his clothes, it is high time for the opera; Gretel hadn't yet learned her lessons; Lotte ought at last to write that letter; and as for us, the Mann children, why, we had nothing in mind but mischief, as was generally known. But she could not help laughing as Walter answered her with the comic pantomime of Papageno, whose mouth has been locked by the three cruel ladies.

We were fond of Frau Walter. Her scolding had the character of a half-jocular rite, something prickling and tonic, like a cold shower or sturdy blast. In fact, we rather enjoyed it.

"Let him just finish the act!" we begged her. "Just the first act!" Please please please! It's so much fun! Please please!"

Naturally, she surrendered. "Ten minutes," she decided, and added with a surprisingly tender smile: "Of course, I'd like to hear Tamino's aria myself . . ."

And she sat down, next to Gretel.

"The Mann children"—who, according to Mother Walter, had nothing in mind but mischief—became gradually quite notorious. We established a veritable gang, with Erika, the Walter girls, Ricki and myself as its nucleus. . . . But I suddenly realize, not without dismay, that

I have not even introduced Ricki as yet. What a glaring omission! It annoys me all the more as I feel this sort of neglect to be symptomatic of a serious danger inherent in the autobiographical style. There is a certain tendency, common to most authors of memoirs, to dwell almost exclusively on those contacts the writer may have had with so-called celebrities, while more or less overlooking his friendships with less distinguished individuals. This falsification, or falsifying stress of certain elements at the expense of others, can spring from facetious vanity and snobbishness, but more often than not results from less contemptible considerations. An autobiography is necessarily incomplete. Among those innumerable experiences which enrich and shape a human life, the author has to select the most relevant samples. Modesty may induce him to prefer such material that is apt to yield some new information regarding men or matters of general significance. For, being modest, he realizes that his report, say, of a meeting with Bismarck or Edison is likely to arouse a certain interest, for the sake of those illustrious personalities: whereas nobody cares whether the author's anonymous friend happened to be a good sport or a bore.

To introduce a personal friend who is unknown to the reader, virtually means to present a fictive character. The literary technique of allusions and abbreviations which is applicable in reference to well-known figures, necessarily fails when it comes to persons whose names and destinies are meaningless to the reader. In such a case the author of an autobiography will bungle: unless he changes his approach and adapts the tactics of the novelist.

When mentioning Bruno Walter, I may take it for granted that the majority of my readers are more or less acquainted with his talents and activities. In fact, I can even go further and presuppose that people know approximately what type of a man he is, what he looks like, and so on. But the face of Ricki is blank. Nobody has an inkling as to his appearance, character, or background. I have to go out of my way and build up his personality, as does the writer of fiction whenever a new actor enters the scene of his story:

Descended from a highly cultured, well-to-do family of Jewish extraction, Ricki was a handsome and sensitive lad. We knew him from early childhood, as his parents were on friendly-neighbor terms with ours. He looked savage and delicate, somewhat like a neurotic gipsy, with a tangled mass of dark hair falling onto a low forehead; black, bushy eyebrows over a pair of violent eyes set very close to each other. He was witty and naïve and quivering with that attractive nervousness typical of certain hyper-aristocratic dogs and horses. His face was all softness and sensual innocence, but his hands seemed appallingly old—wrinkled and lean; restless, jerky, tormented. Ricki was a constant problem and unending fun. He loathed school and simulated the most complicated maladies, in order to be sent to the country. He wanted to become an artist and shocked his family by his macabre vagaries jotted down on paper. All his paintings and sketches showed an uncanny lot of crippled beggars and emaciated little girls guiding their blind grandfathers through barren landscapes. He loved children and cats and the mountains, and we loved him. We went to school together, and skiing, swimming and skating; we romped about and pulled silly tricks and read poetry and heard music together; we discovered sex— "so that's the way they make babies!"—and giggled about the grownups, and thought ourselves quite big and important—together.

We founded a theatrical club, Erika, Gretel Walter, Ricki, and I. First it was a fairly humble enterprise, just one-act plays, performed in the lobby of either our home or Ricki's, with the respective parents as audience. Little by little, however, we grew more ambitious and ventured on the jewels of dramatic literature—Lessing, Molière, and Shakespeare. We played "Twelfth Night": Ricki was weird and comic as Malvolio, and Erika's Viola was solemnly page-like, musingly tender and very beautiful in her timid grace. It was upon this occasion that she discovered her love for the theatre and decided to become an actress. The big show took place in Ricki's family mansion. It was a sumptuous affair, followed by a masked ball. Lotte and Gretel were not allowed to participate. Frau Walter was against our theatrical exercises. "Another mischief!" she complained. "Those Mann children! Nothing but monkey business!"

She was not completely mistaken, alas. Indeed our tricks became more and more risky. We got a tremendous kick out of doing forbidden things and mystifying the grown-ups. Our specialty was faked telephone calls. We thought it funny to call up Mrs. Meyer and make her believe that Gretel was the maid of Mrs. Ruderer, who wanted Mrs. Meyer for dinner, next Wednesday, at seven o'clock. Mrs. Meyer, only too pleased, promised to show up on the dot. She would wear her best and bring Mr. Meyer along. It was too amusing for words.

Erika excelled in imitating voices: she was like one of those imps who bamboozle men, adopting ever new intonations and appearances. It was amazing how tinny her voice could sound: how peremptory, ringing, or bland. She could talk like a Saxonian cook or a Prussian secretary or the opera singer Delia Reinhardt. Her speech was precisely that of a foolish little waitress when she called the local matinee idol, Bert F., a good-looking juvenile. The young "beau" was half-flattered, half-bored when she confessed her passion. Gracious and distrait, he granted the rendezvous she was begging for. It was quite a coup when we invaded his flat, the whole gang of us. He took it nicely. We made friends with him. It was wonderful to be on familiar terms with a real actor. What a sensation!—to watch the magic ceremonial in his dressing room: the breath-taking transformation of our pal Bert into Don Carlos, Prince of Spain, or Mortimer, the lover of Mary Stuart. I admired Bert. He was at once brisk and weary: a veritable hero with a tinge of interesting "morbidezza." I decided to become an actor and altogether like Bert.

The friendship with him was all the more delightful as we concealed it from our parents. The same went for night clubs, detective films, and salacious books. Actually I liked Tolstoi or Hölderlin infinitely better than some sordid pulp magazine. However, the mere fact that I was not supposed to read the trash considerably increased its attraction. The streets were more interesting after midnight—not because any unusual things were likely to take place but because we ought to have been home in bed. It was the notion of "sin," the illegal action as such, that beguiled us. The more wicked, the better! Chocolate candies are dainty. But stolen sweets must even be daintier!

Bert incited our ambition by telling us how skillfully he could steal when he was a youngster. "Wait and see what we are able to do!" we swaggered, and a few days later asked him for a party while our parents were out of town. The entertainment consisted exclusively of stolen things: from the sausages to the Vermouth everything was cribbed.

How could we have let Fräulein Thea into our confidence? She was the new governess for Medi and Bibi, a sturdy and ethical female: we ought to have known the type. Naturally enough, she lost no time in revealing our viciousness as soon as our parents came back. She told them everything—about Bert and the robberies, and that we often walked through the streets at night. We thought her perfidious, but she just did her duty. Every upright "Fräulein" would behave the same way when confronted with the dilemma whether to let down some irresponsible youngsters or to partake in their transgressions by concealing them from the unsuspecting authorities.

As for the now enlightened authorities—our parents—they may have been somewhat less unsuspecting than Fräulein Thea believed. Their forbearance did not prevent them from keeping their eyes and ears open. They were patient but vigilant. Of course, they realized that our habits and hobbies were not altogether ideal. However, they depended on our sound moral instinct and their own civilizing example, rather than on punishments and tirades.

Fräulein Thea's report came not so much as a surprise but as sad confirmation of their own misgivings. It looked as if we were on the point of actually running wild. No doubt, we needed a drastic lesson.

The drastic lesson turned out to be fairly mild. We were sent to a country school. It was no reformatory with iron discipline our parents had chosen for us, nothing like that. On the contrary, the place where Mielein delivered Erika and me, on a chilly morning in March, 1922, seemed pleasant and cozy enough, an experimental youth community of the most advanced type.

The institute was situated in a hilly region of Middle Germany, called the Röhn, not far from Frankfort-on-the-Main. The scenery was barren but not without an austere sort of charm. In the tonic air of a mountain valley—a particularly crisp, breezy air, as I well remember— a group of boys and girls lived and worked together, under the guidance of a tolerant and rather helpless professor. The teachers were men and women of high intellectual ambitions—some of them frustrated artists. The pupils came from various milieus and cities, mostly from Frankfort or Berlin. Among them prevailed, as the uniting element, the spirit of what we called the Youth Movement.

This typically German phenomenon—the bombastic self-glorification of youth as an autonomous form of life—is difficult to explain to anyone who has not experienced both its absurdity and its charm. Conceived as a sort of romantic revolution against our mechanized era, it contained inspiring, truly progressive elements along with the germs of evil. Undeniably, there was something wholesome and promising in that tendency away from the city, back to nature with rucksack, a guitar, and no liquor. But these harmless penchants were tainted by a lot of nebulous pretensions. The Youth Movement did not content itself with challenging our drab materialism by means of spectacular costumes and medieval songs: it indulged in all sorts of muddled and boisterous slogans, until it finally degenerated into a dreary conglomerate of reactionary currents and devices.

When I came in contact with this curious movement, it had already passed the climax of its career. What began, years before the War, as a sweeping upheaval, soon became a rather sterile pellmell of quarrelsome youth factions—nationalistic organizations, religious groups, or vegetarian societies. Yet these diffuse trends and energies still exercised a certain influence upon the style and principles of experimental pedagogy. The atmosphere in a Free School Community like the one to which we now belonged was palpably imbued with the mannerisms and postulates of the Movement. I suppose that never before in history —not even when the wise men of Athens worshipped and inspired the adolescents—were young people as consciously and arrogantly young as were the German generations preceding and following the World War. To proclaim "I am young!" meant a war-cry and a program. Youth was a conspiracy and a challenge. When we met in our ascetic rooms, or outside, in the woods, or at the candy store in the village, we would exchange mystic signs, meaningful smiles and glances: "I am young!"

"So am I."

"Good for you. The old ones are swine and idiots."

"Right you are. To hell with those over forty. As for myself, I feel unusually young today."

It was upsetting and hard and wonderful to be young, a constant problem and immeasurable joy. We felt indescribably sorry for those who had wantonly forfeited this chosen and trying state. How old-fashioned to hate one's teachers! They deserved pity, what else? Our professor for instance, what a deplorable chap! At least fifty, and still tries to be our comrade! He couldn't be more pathetic.

In reality, he was a decent man full of the best intentions. But he was lacking in the intuition and authority indispensable to cope with a lot of half-baked boys and girls. He tried very hard to reconcile the grandiose aspirations of the Youth Movement with a modest degree of academic routine. His efforts were foiled by our restiveness. The school, his lifework and pride, disintegrated little by little. In the end our parents thought it best to let us come back to Munich.

Erika stayed at home. As for, myself, I insisted, surprisingly, on being sent to another country institute. There was something about life in a community of young people that seemed utterly attractive to me. I wanted more of this at once unbound and gregarious existence; more friendships, more discussions, more wandering through the woods and summer nights spent in front of romantic bonfires.

The Odenwaldschule, near Heidelberg, was a pedagogic institute of high standing and great reputation. Its leader, Paulus Geheeb—one of the Founding Fathers of the Free School Movement—combined profound experience in all matters educational with strange, childlike naïveté. With his wide, pensive eyes and spectacular beard he looked like a hermit who lives on herbs and wisdom. In fact, Paulus' body was nourished exclusively by fruits and vegetables: his spirit, by the philosophies of India, Hellas and the great German period, from Herder to Schiller and Kant. The bungalows where we had our working and living rooms bore the names of Geheeb's lofty patron saints. My own quarters were in the Plato House, while Paulus had chosen the Goethe House as his residence. However, his favorite place was the hedged part of the garden where he kept animals—the beautiful deer and birds to which he was so tenderly devoted. "In the company of my children," he was wont to say, "I recreate myself from the adults: with my animals, I recreate myself from the children."

Yet he was fond of both children and adults, in his bland and oblivious fashion. Faith in the fundamental goodness of child and man was, indeed, the essential tenet of his pedagogy. His educational method was based on the premise that human beings are, or can become, decent and reasonable. He believed in democracy as the most effective way to secure discipline. The pupils of his school formed a veritable parliament which decided all important issues affecting the life of the community. This autonomous body determined the legislation and hierarchy of the institute; if need be, it could expel objectionable members or even annul a measure taken by the chief himself.

It was a colorful crowd that gathered in this animated and idyllic "Pedagogic Province," to use Goethe's term in reference to an institution conceived and conducted in Goethe's spirit and taste. Paulus had no prejudices or preferences. With equable benevolence he welcomed the sons and daughters of industrialists and penniless bohemians; neurotic wrecks and infant prodigies. There were the children of celebrated Italian singers, Dutch coffee magnates, and Indian rebels; the scions of the French Communist leader, Marcel Cachin, and of an exiled Russian nobleman; the sons of Austrian poets, Chinese scholars, and American bankers. The first thing a child learns in such motley environments is tolerance and politeness. A high degree of urbanity is required where many different types have to adapt themselves to one rhythm and style. National or social arrogance becomes a fatuity under such circumstances.

I made friends with young people from various countries and milieus. We admired each other, criticized and pampered each other. We were conspicuously congenial and altogether too sophisticated for words. Our ideas and poses, everything we did was a trifle hectic and sometimes glaringly theatrical. In other moments, however, our pathos was undoubtedly genuine.

I was sincere when I burst out into rhapsodic cries of gratitude—praising Life for being so gaudy and enigmatic. My longing for guidance was as spontaneous as was my aversion to discipline. I was truthful when I cursed even the modest amount of social responsibilities the Odenwaldschule imposed upon us. Nor did I lie when I started up in the middle of the night and stumbled to my desk, still half-asleep, to jot down these words:

An unknown voice, sweet and stringent, wakens and blesses me.
Whence does it come, this irresistible call?
Welcome, my guide!
Here I am!—ready to follow, no matter whom.
Whoever you are, you may help me to find myself.

CHAPTER FOUR

Disorder and Early Sorrow

(1922–1924)

THERE is always the same disorder: from time immemorial—the old sorrow and primeval joy.

The depths of organic life are disorderly, a maze and mire of lust and suffering and rampant energy. The roots of our being are tangled in boggy grounds, soaked with sperm, blood, and tears, unending orgy of lechery and decay, sorrowful, lustful. The spaces of the microcosm resound with the groan of orgasms and agonies as battlefields do with the cries of the wounded and victors.

Behold! from the smoldering darkness rises the River God—the Satyr and Bull, ebullient with potency; covered with mud and foam; panting with desire; guffawing, weeping, quivering in raptures; blind and ravenous—all aimless fervor; torrential, wayward, irresistible.

He is not the child-god, coquettishly toying with the miniature bow and arrows. He is cunning and fierce, a merciless hunter, a shark. But he is also a jester, fond of masquerades and all kind of banter. I have watched him in many disguises, dazzling or disfigured. He may appear bland and tender, until his whisper becomes a yell and his features turn wolfish. Angelic and fiendish by turns, he is the motive power behind masterpieces and murders, antics and tragedies. He fertilizes and devastates, spreading delight and panic. He kindles the heart: rhapsodic words gush from the lips he touches. He addles the mind: his path is covered with the traces of crimes and the ashes of suicides. Irrational and irresponsible, he transcends the categories of ethics, logic, or aesthetics. Moral evaluations are not applicable to his autonomous being. He is neither good nor evil. He is infinite energy for both evil and good, disorder and harmony.

Was my generation—the post-War generation in Europe—more disorganized and frivolous than youth is in general? Have we been unduly sex-conscious and unrestrained?

We grew up in a time of sweeping changes and uncertainties. How could we be infallible when everything failed and fumbled around us? Civilization boggled along, aimlessly, as it were. Nobody had the faintest idea what would happen next. Sometimes it looked as if utopia were around the corner: in other moments we anticipated the collapse of all values and institutions.

Yes, we were familiar with apocalyptic moods, versed in many temptations. But I am unaware of any such things as "vice" among the realities we experienced. Loneliness or lust are realities; so are hunger, boredom, or jealousy. But what is vice? What does the notion of sin actually mean? I am unable to grasp the sense of a pompous abstraction.

We could hardly deviate from any ethical norm, for the cogent reason that there was none. The moral clichés of a smug and prosperous society—a nauseous blend of obsolete taboos and morbid inhibitions—crumbled under the blows of War and Revolution. The hypocritical etiquette of the bourgeois era seemed done away with, for good. Indeed, we deemed the old morality so definitely passé that we did not even bother attacking it any more.

We were not debunkers. Preceding generations had done a terrific job in sapping the mendacious ideology of the ancien régime, the regime of virtue and exploitation. It was from iconoclastic geniuses of the late nineteenth century that we learned the disparagement of the intellect and the cult of Eros. In the midst of emptiness and disintegration there seemed nothing stable and worthwhile, except the lustful mystery of our own physical existence. With so many fine words and dreams having palled upon us, we sought a new theme for our carols —and found the Body Electric.

What we called our "somatic consciousness" gradually assumed the character of a philosophic system, an inevitable development, considering the German tendency to systematize even chaos. A young writer

by the name of Wolfgang Gräser launched the formula of a new
"sense," the "body-sense," which he asserted to be the integral experience of his generation. The intensified awareness of one's own
physiology, this philosopher pointed out, could not but bring about a
whole set of unprecedented sensations. He coined terms like "somatic
melancholy," "physical pride," "organic intuitions," and explained why,
in his opinion, these particular sensibilities essentially differed from the
usual psychological patterns. According to this thinker, men had repressed or neglected, since the days of Hellas, their physical appetites
and reactions: hence the unbalanced state of our civilization. The one-
sided spiritualism of occidental culture was arraigned as the root and
center of all evil. War and revolution, while revealing the hollowness
of ideas and the wretchedness of the human race, might also be instrumental in reaffirming the intrinsic truth and dignity of our being. Confronted with the crude necessity to struggle for his existence, man may
be brought to remember his primeval nature. The abandonment of
intellectual complacency was the prerequisite without which there was
no hope for a sound equilibrium. No abstractions would do. It was only
under the auspices of a new physical comradeship and universal solidarity that the spirit of reconstruction, the ultimate renaissance, could
be born.

Wolfgang Gräser—who, incidentally, was destined to die young,
without having produced a second book—was not a creative thinker,
but he aptly defined certain tendencies floating in the air of his period.
The newly stressed "somatic consciousness," the emphasis on the instinct at the expense of the intellect, was, indeed, the one element uniting the most divergent types and attitudes of youth in the nineteen-
twenties. Philosophically it manifested itself as a sharp reaction against
the past century's scientific optimism and shallow faith in human reason as the universal regulator of life and the guarantor of progress.

The "somatic credo" was nebulous and dynamic. It embraced dangerous trends, along with beautiful and wholesome impulses. Every
movement whose essential function it is to challenge the absolute rule
of the intellect contains the potentialities of irrational violence: it may
degenerate into a menace to civilization itself. The anti-intellectual attitude of the post-War generation was not free of such ominous impli-

cations. Our disparagement of logic and discipline foreshadowed the
coming glorification of naked brutality. The idolatry of the body anticipated the oppression of the intellect. The erotic freedom obstrep-
erously claimed and enjoyed by my contemporaries prepared the triumph of the most cynical materialism. We sneered at the restrictions
of an obsolete morality; but the coming barbarians would betray morals
altogether, for the sake of their obscene "racial" doctrines.

Needless to say, I had not the faintest inkling, at the time, as to the
ghastly distortions our sex-mysticism might eventually undergo. I could
not help noticing, though, that our new philosophy—or rather, the
particular mood in which many of us indulged—sometimes expressed
itself in rather unpleasant forms. The praise of physical virtues irritated and bored me as soon as I found militant connotations involved.
Also, I disapproved of the frantic interest in sport, which was another
symptom—the most powerful one!—of the anti-cerebral current. Sport
seemed dull and puzzling to me: I never could understand why people should lose their minds and money over prize fights or football
games. Happily, these coarse aspects of the new direction played but a
negligible role in the educational scheme of the Odenwaldschule.

Yet some of the younger boys had athletic ambitions and amused
themselves with ball games, throwing the discus, and other exercises. I
liked to watch them when they ran and jumped. There was one lad
among them whom I liked to watch in particular. His name was Uto.
He was sturdy and deft but by far not the strongest or most dexterous
one of the lot. Nor was he especially handsome. But I loved his face.
He had the face I love. You may be smitten with many faces when
you live long enough and possess a responsive heart. But there is only
one face you love. It is always the same. You recognize it among thousands. And Uto had that face.

He might have been of Slavic extraction, with his high-set cheekbones and narrow eyes. Or rather, he looked like a little Swede with a
drop of Mongolian blood. His bright hair appeared sometimes strawy,
as if dried out and paled by the sun. In other moments it seemed
honey-colored, with rich golden tones. His lips, too, were dry, and his
knees and hands were always covered with scratches. His eyes had the
color of ice—drifting ice in a river, shimmering in the air of a crisp

winter morning. They were not blue, his eyes, but of a radiant gray; an extraordinary gray, indeed, with a tinge of silvery green: lustrous with innocence; at once limpid and unfathomable.

I addressed verse to him, which he did not read. I called him by the names of Hellenic champions and demi-gods, which sounded funny to him. Still he appreciated my devotion and was impressed by what he thought my erudition. He was bland and humble; vain enough to accept my homages: too naïve to recognize my hero-worship.

He said to me: "You're the first friend I've ever had. It's swell to have a friend."

His face was blank and cool. He was lonely and ignorant as are the animals and the angels.

I wrote on a scrap of paper: "I love you."

He read it and grinned. "That's a good one!" Then, suddenly turning serious: "But of course you do. Friends must love each other."

I told him that I might have to quit school. My parents had written me that they wanted me to come home.

He refused to believe it. "You wouldn't do that to me," he said. "You wouldn't leave me alone. You're my friend. Your parents will understand when you tell them. They couldn't make you come home and leave your friend here, alone."

I had lied to him. My parents didn't want me to come home; quite the contrary. I was supposed to stay at the Odenwaldschule for another couple of years, long enough to prepare myself for the "Abitur," the pivotal examination and prerequisite for any academic career in Germany. But I didn't want to make the Abitur. I didn't want to stay. Surely, I liked the place and was gratefully devoted to old Geheeb. And yet, I couldn't bear it any more. Uto was so much stronger and lighter than I was, and I envied him so. He was all vigor and serenity: no problems existed for him. But to me, the cosmos was but one problem, impenetrable and disconcerting. I could not decipher the hints and signs of my destiny.

. . . "My parents insist," I told Uto. "I'm afraid this will be our last Sunday morning walk."

. . . What sorrow drove me away? What disorder awaited me?

My parents were mildly alarmed about my sudden return. However, they agreed that I might as well take private lessons at home until I would be in shape to face the examination. An erudite spinster and a jovial professor in retirement were appointed to brush up my rather incomplete knowledge of irregular verbs and arithmetical formulas. The old girl was gaunt and withered; I felt infinitely sorry for her. As for the professor, he was simply a rat. His face, all puffed up and of pink complexion, seemed that of a jolly fellow; but his tiny eyes, snapping insidious sparkles from behind his pince-nez, revealed his true, unpleasant character. His name was Geist, which means Spirit. I loathed Professor Spirit. He didn't think much of me, either. Of course, he acted like the embodiment of cordiality whenever we saw each other. Slapped my shoulders; grinned at me; gave me that understanding-good-old-uncle twinkle: "Hello, pal! Not prepared your lesson, once again—huh? Ha ha ha! I used to be young myself. Let's have a good laugh together." That kind of stuff. But behind my back he said filthy things about me. I had no discipline, no moral equilibrium: that's what he told my parents.

Maybe the era was a little shaky as far as moral equilibrium is concerned. Was it my fault? Was I to blame when the period, at once hectic and weary, seemed predisposed to all sorts of intoxications? The collective organism which is society was avid for lust and oblivion, depleted after the orgy of hatred and destruction; still bleeding from many wounds.

The bloody uproar of the War is over: let's enjoy the carnival of the inflation. It's loads of fun and paper: printed paper, flimsy stuff—do they still call it money? For five billions of it you can get one dollar. What a joke! The Yankees are coming—as peaceful tourists, this time. They purchase a Rembrandt for a sandwich and our souls for a glass of whisky. Messrs. Krupp and Stinnes get rid of their debts: we, of our savings. The profiteers dance in the palace hotels. Let's join them! Didn't we have something called Revolution? Another trickery and illusion . . . But why shouldn't we pretend to be brothers?—united, not by democracy, but by the galvanizing rhythm of jazz. Let's make our descent into hell accompanied by the syncopated yelling of a Negro band! Until that day—it may be tomorrow!—

we want narcotics and kisses to forget our wretchedness. Let's go to bed with each other! Or fool around in the parks if there are no beds. Boys with girls, boys with boys, girls with girls, men with boys and girls, women with men or boys or girls or tamed little panthers— what's the difference? Let's embrace each other! Let's dance!

Millions of helpless, impoverished, bewildered people capered and swung in a delirium of hunger and hysteria. Dance was a mania, a religion, a racket. The stock market danced. The members of the Reichstag hopped about as if mad. The poets were convulsed with rhythmic spasms. The cripples, the prostitutes, the beggars, the re- formers, the retired monarchs and astute industrialists—all of them swayed and skipped. They danced the shimmy, tango, fox trot, and St. Vitus' dance. They danced despair and schizophrenia and cosmic divinations. Mary Wigman—all angular loftiness from top to bottom —danced Bach, Beethoven, and Brahms. They danced with Negro masks, Gothic helmets, and no clothes on. They danced ecstasies, hangovers, orgasms, intoxications, and nervous tics. They imitated Isidora Duncan, Nijinsky, Charlie Chaplin, the motions of pugilists, and the tormented pantomime of imprisoned animals in the Zoo. Jazz was the great balm and narcotic of a disconcerted, frustrated nation. The fever was indomitably expansive—a mass frenzy akin to certain contagious excesses in the Dark Ages. Small wonder that the pulsating heart of the country, the capital, was affected most perturbingly.

Corruptible and always hankering for sensations, Berlin absorbed political and intellectual currents from everywhere. It was its function and force to organize whatever moods were floating throughout the land; to focus and dramatize the desires of a diffuse and inarticulate people. When the general vein was dashingly patriotic, the capital surpassed all other places in vociferous demonstrations. When the vogue was cynical-apocalyptic, Berlin did a great job in displaying misery and vices on a colossal scale.

"Look at me!" blared the capital of the Reich. "I am Babel, the monster among cities! We had a formidable army: now we com- mand the most riotously wicked night life. Don't miss our matchless show, ladies and gentlemen! It's Sodom and Gomorrah in a Prussian tempo. Don't miss the circus of perversities! Our department store of assorted vices! It's phe-nom-e-nal! An all-out sale of brand new kinds of debauchery!"

When I first came to Berlin, for a short visit, in 1923, the inflation already was approaching its staggering climax. The aspect of the city was dismal and yet gaudy, bluffing with the hectic flush of its nervousness.

I had the time of my life. To be in Berlin meant a constant thrill in itself. My enthusiasm transformed the bleak squares and avenues into a labyrinth swarming with mysteries and adventures. What fun! —to stroll along those fabulous streets whose very names were charged with risky allurements, Friedrich-Strasse, Unter den Linden, Tauentzien-Strasse, Kurfürstendamm. It was exciting to swallow the greasy borscht in one of those Russian restaurants which then sprang up at every other corner. Was this portly waitress an exiled Grand Duchess, a niece or cousin of the late Czarina, perhaps?

I was keenly interested in the backgrounds and tragedies of the innumerable refugees teeming throughout the city. Were they innocent victims, or were they laden with crime? Had they been reckless and narrow-minded when still powerful and at home? Had they provoked their somber destiny? And how somber was exile, really? I figured it rather harsh but not without epic features. To escape from the GPU, at night, over snowy roofs; to arrive in Warsaw or Bucharest, with no possessions but two priceless diamonds; to open antique stores and night clubs everywhere between Cannes and Los Angeles; to weave political intrigues and kiss the beloved icons in squalid hotel rooms; to rush from country to country haunted by nostalgia and Soviet agents: it could be no easy life, to be sure. And still, it attracted me, in a weird, irrational way. True, I felt sorry for those errant noblemen and professors. But, at the same time, I could not help envying them a little.

My feelings towards the prostitutes were of a similar nature. I never watched them without thinking, "poor women! how wretched and wicked you are!" But I did so out of a sense of duty: it wasn't my true reaction. No doubt, I used to be more honest as a little boy, when the grown-ups asked me if I thought Jennie's bosom beautiful, and I answered: "No, but I enjoy looking at it." That was really the way I felt about the wandering whores. Pitiful creatures, all right; however, it was enjoyable to watch their garish procession.

Some of them looked like fierce amazons, strutting in high boots made of green, glossy leather. One of them brandished a supple cane and leered at me as I passed by. "Good evening, Madam," I said. So she whispered into my ear: "Want to be my slave? Costs only six billions and a cigarette. A bargain. Come along, honey!"

There were girls among them who couldn't have been older than sixteen or seventeen. Others had wrinkled faces under their make-up. I was told that some of those who looked most handsome and elegant were actually boys in disguise. It seemed incredible, considering the sovereign grace with which they displayed their saucy coats and hats. I wondered if they might be wearing little silks, under their exquisite gowns. Must look kind of funny, I thought—a boy's body with a pink, lace-trimmed shirt. Not very pleasant, though. Were there Russian princes among those picturesque, if somewhat revolting hermaphrodites? Or the sons of Prussian generals who, in such a bizarre mode, protested against the rigid principles of their fathers?

The romanticism of the underworld bewitched me. I was magnetized by the scum. Berlin—the Berlin I perceived or imagined— was gorgeously corrupt. I wanted to stay much longer. But how? I had no money. Something had to be done.

Not that I intended to wash dishes: I was more ambitious. The ideal solution, I thought, would be a job that yielded not only cash but fun and glory to boot. Why shouldn't I have a chance in one of those cabarets with mixed, informal programs, as they flourished, at the time, in the fashionable districts of Berlin?

Among my new friends was an aging mime whom I knew to be on the most cordial terms with the lady who ran a popular establishment called "Tü-Tü." So I called on him and informed him of my intention. "You must help me," I begged. "You with all your contacts."

"Of course," chuckled my friend, strangely animated. "Nothing could be easier." He went to the telephone and called the "Tü-Tü." "Hello, grandma!" he said to the patronne—old jester he was! And then explained to her all about me—how remarkably brisk and handsome I was, and how gifted, and that I wanted to recite some poetry: "His own stuff, if you please! All made by himself! Imagine!" Could she use me in her new gala-program, tonight? She could. I was beside myself with excitement.

There was no time to think of my repertoire: the few hours were completely filled by hunting for a tuxedo. I arrived just in time at the "Tü-Tü"—shivering and sweating in my borrowed clothes that were too large for me; my feet aching in dress-shoes which, in their turn, were not large enough.

I found the patronne, a gaunt, elderly woman, in her dressing-room, all absorbed in her make-up.

"Here I am!" I announced, as cheerfully as I could.

"The privilege is mine," she said, unsmilingly; then, peering at me with a withering expression of disdain: "Who are you, anyhow?"

I stammered something to the effect that I was the young poet whom that friend of hers so warmly recommended: whereupon a tart smile altered her face, then died. She examined me from top to bottom. "So *that's* what a young genius looks like," she observed at last. "Never mind. After all, what really counts is the talent." And she concentrated on her eyelashes again.

Several minutes passed while she worked on her face with lipstick, rouge, and several tiny brushes. Evidently, she had forgotten my presence. I cleared my throat, coughed discreetly; but she didn't react. I waited another minute; then pulled myself together and said, "I beg your pardon, Ma'am . . ."

She remained motionless; just glanced at me askance, "Oh, our genius is still around," she said, while picking up her powder puff. "You'd better beat it, young man. It's high time for your number."

My hands became moist and shaky. "Already . . . ?" I asked, suddenly out of breath.

"It's almost nine o'clock," she said gruffy. "Would you please let me finish my make-up? Somebody will show you to the stage."

I don't know what happened next and how things could develop with such nightmarish swiftness. Before I realized what was going on, I found myself on a stage. There was a curtain—a fine, heavy tissue of green velvet, as I recollect distinctly—and presently the curtain went up, and there was that gasping emptiness in front of me and within my reeling mind. I didn't even remember the poem I wanted to start with. My voice must have trembled in the most comic and deplorable fashion as I produced a whispered, "Good evening, ladies and gents!"

Somebody laughed, down there in the shady depth of the orchestra. My eyes, which got gradually accustomed to the dim light, discerned the silhouettes of some people scattered throughout the house. "The audience . . ." I felt, terrified and enchanted. And I began my recital.

The opening number was a saucy ballad dealing with a countess and a gang of sailors she received in her boudoir. Nobody laughed, moved, or talked when the poem was over; only that stone-like, disconcerting stillness.

Hastily I began another poem; then a third and a fourth. My voice grew more and more monotonous; my verse, increasingly daring. The silence in the house remained, a thundering billow of stillness, as it were, drowning my pathetic flippancies.

It was a flop with a vengeance; it was the essence of nonsuccess, the complete lack of response, the washout in its nightmarish extreme.

The next day I went back to Munich.

Years afterwards the friend who had introduced me to the "Tü-Tü" told me about the pedagogical trick he pulled. "You were such a little fool, at the time!" chuckled the old jester. "Such a highbrow ass! So, of course, as soon as you'd left my humble home that afternoon, I scurried to the phone and called the patronne, once again. 'Now, listen, honey pie,' I said to her, 'now, without kidding: that so-called sensation I just recommended to you, really is an ambitious young chicken who hasn't the faintest idea what's what. Thinks our racket is nothing but cash and fun—little fool he is. Well, we know better—you and I. So why not teach him a lesson?' . . ."

They taught me a lesson, all right.

There was no Tauentzien-Strasse in Munich; nor any streamlined parade of perversities. On the Spree River, everything had that uncanny dash and punch—even prostitution: whereas on the Isar a leisurely tempo prevailed. Munich, serene, beautiful, and obtuse, entirely lacked the feverish verve of which the Berliners could boast. If Berlin somehow maintained the snappy rhythm of the Empire, in the midst of disaster, Munich never quite lost its savor of enjoyable sloppiness—apocalypse or not.

Berlin had no Bohemia. The artists were too commercial to be veritable bohemians; the bourgeoisie, too smart to be outright Philistines. But in Munich the traditional antagonism between the "decent citizens," and the "crazy good-for-nothings" remained a stimulating feature of the community. The brewers and shopkeepers never ceased to be shocked by the eccentricities of those long-maned clowns who wore slouch hats and used fancy words. The bohemians, in their turn, unflaggingly taunted the well-fed, beer-bellied hypocrites.

We formed our own little bohemian set: a pretty callow sort of café society, to be sure; yet we thought ourselves mighty sophisticated. A young chap named Theo introduced us into the swanky night clubs we had hitherto only gazed at, longingly, from outside. Now there was that slick young man, Theo, to pay for the drinks and dinners, throwing a few billion marks on the table with a grand and absent-minded gesture. He looked like Sir Galahad and gambled successfully on the Stock Market. Theo was naïve and clever, sentimental, boastful, and generous, a typical son of his time, class, and country. His father was a humble clerk at the very bank that financed Theo's risky ventures. Theo treated us with champagne, lyrical outbursts, and patronizing smiles. He arranged masquerades in his bachelor's flat and romantic picnics on the shores of Alpine lakes. Sometimes he almost spoiled our fun by stressing rhapsodically how much fun it was. "This evening will become a glorious piece of memory!" he would exclaim, in the midst of a merry feast—whereupon the smiles froze on our faces. We exchanged embarrassed glances when Theo tactlessly praised our "jolly little circle." We were ever so gay, he insisted, making us feel dreary. "A typical post-War circle," Theo said. "Cynical, disillusioned: but full of pep." He was amazingly clumsy.

The pillars of the circle were our friend W. E. Süskind and an attractive girl from Norway. She studied art, twittered like a canary, and was excitingly disorganized. Theo thought she loved him and called her "my little singing-bird." She flirted with me to annoy Süskind and Theo. She was shrewd and primitive and altogether delightful. Süskind wrote a story about her. He was in the habit of writing stories about the girls he fell for. He had a good deal of talent. The story in which he immortalized Erika, was indeed a remarkable piece of writing. Unfortunately, it could have no happy end; for Erika was impervious to his wooing. So Süskind revenged himself by having her assassinated. The conclusion of his plot was rather lurid, with Erika sitting in an armchair and looking peevish because her lover had killed her. Of course, Süskind could never have done such a nasty thing, really. He was much too fussy and delicate. He didn't kill Erika but, instead, dedicated a fine essay to her. In this treatise, called "The Dancing Generation," he tried to define the basic tenets of all little post-War circles, including our own.

The Walters had moved to Vienna. A venomous press campaign, not without anti-Semitic savor, disgusted the great conductor with his position at the Munich Opera. Lotte and Gretel occasionally came to visit us, though. Theo took them to the Green Boat or the Regina Bar and was smitten with their personalities. "A definite asset to our group!" he announced, beaming with satisfaction because the world was so colorful and his speculation with Austrian schillings promised to be a hit.

Ricki, too, joined our party but exceptionally. He was in one of his hermit streaks and gnashed his teeth when he heard a jazz band. He usually gnashed his teeth when he disliked something—a disquieting habit to which one had to get accustomed, for the sake of Ricki's company.

There were other occasional participants in our meetings. Most of them were older than Erika and I, veritable grown-ups, like Bert F., the accomplished matinee idol; or that muscular young lady who was running a school of gymnastics; or certain young literati who already had a book or two to their credit. I was tickled to death when I could read to one of those experts a few samples of my own production. I recollect one evening in W. E. Süskind's apartment when I recited my verse in presence of a real critic, an Austrian journalist who "covered" literary events for the Viennese press. So I cried out my poor rhymes and muddled ecstasies, and when I had finished the expert said: "Your poems are lousy, young man. But you must go on." I remember distinctly the unctuous sound of his voice. I didn't know whether I should be offended. But in the end I decided to take his oracle as flattering.

It was an animated clique, all right, as whose patron saint and stooge Theo spent his money. However, it took on its definite shape and flavor only when it was joined by Pamela Wedekind, the daughter of the late poet, dramatist and crusader, Frank Wedekind.

Frank Wedekind was the classic of the "roaring Twenties" in Germany, although he died in 1917. The rugged intensity of his dialogues anticipated the shrill accents of the expressionistic school. The baroque atrocity of his plots foreshadowed the actual excesses of the War and post-War era. His insights and dislocations were strikingly akin to what we believed in ourselves. Sex—the liberation, the "sanctification" of the sexual impulse—was the gist of his credo. He propagated the "reunion of beauty and morality," paraphrasing his message in manifestoes and songs, stories, dramas, and farces. He scandalized the zealots, was vilified by the critics, sneered at by the ivory-tower snobs. An inspired quack and clownish reformer, he traveled from city to city impersonating the tragi-comic heroes of his didactic harlequinades, those stunning horror plays with "Weltanschauung." A generation was spellbound by the paradoxical grandeur of his work and personality. He meant to us what D. H. Lawrence meant to our contemporaries in the English-speaking world.

It chanced in the house of my uncle, Heinrich Mann, that I was presented to Wedekind's widow, Tilly Wedekind, and her daughter Pamela. Tilly was gentle and beautiful, a drowsy angel with remarkable legs. The demoniac playwright married her when she was just eighteen. A role in one of his dramas was given to her, just a minor part, for that matter: the character of a young page who saves the persecuted heroine by exchanging clothes with her. Subsequently it was this very heroine, Lulu, the embodiment of elementary passion, whom Madame Wedekind impersonated, with her husband acting as her partner. In the play, he tried to tame her indomitable force and was crushed. In reality, of course, he was infinitely stronger than she was. He taught her how to walk, talk, sing, smile and weep. He animated her supine loveliness as the legendary sculptor, Pygmalion, animates his marble. She opened veiled, wistful eyes; she danced on a rolling ball, kissed her hand to the audience, she radiated and seduced: she was Lulu.

Poor Tilly! She was so childishly coquettish. But her voice, at once melodious and hollow, sounded as if it came out of a hypnotic trance. Her alabaster brow, under auburn hair, seemed lost in forgetfulness. Sometimes a transient shadow altered and darkened her smile. The merry widow, the inconsolable widow, shuddered as if touched by other-worldly vibrations. What apparition frightened and caressed her?

"Don't you feel well, mama?"

This was Pamela's voice—well trained and metallic. She bent slightly forward to touch the hand of her mother.

Mama had a faint, apologetic smile as if conscious of guilt. Her eyes wandered, trying to avoid the radiant regard of her daughter, which reminded her so strikingly of her late husband's gaze. How painfully familiar she was with ambiguous smiles, the suggestive play of the Mephisthophelean brows, the tyrannic tenderness of this casual clasp!

"I am all right, dear," Tilly said, aghast, once again, in view of the weird resemblance.

"I hope so, mama," said Pamela, stressing every syllable with uncanny exactness.

Pamela idolized her father. It was his authority which had molded not only her thoughts and tastes, but also her poses and intonations, the style and substance of her character. She wanted to become an actress, to continue the Wedekind tradition. While preparing herself for this task, it was her favorite exercise to recite songs, accompanying herself at the very guitar that used to be his own.

Curious, unforgettable picture!—Pamela sitting under her father's deathmask, on a couch in his former studio. His stony face dominates the room with its aquiline nose and the white, sightless eyes staring

into space under the slanting brows. Pamela's face is but a softened
and rejuvenated version of the paternal features.

She remains motionless, her bold, adolescent head turned sideways,
away from us, as if listening to mysterious instructions wafted to her
from—where? She sits erect in her black, tight-fitting dress, an inspired school girl; her face blank and taut with attentiveness, while
her fingers glide automatically over the chords of the instrument.
Finally she announces as ceremonially as if addressing a vast audience:
"I first sing for you 'The Blind Boy,' one of my father's favorite
songs."

Her voice sounds glassy and bland when she begins:

> O ihr Tage meiner Kindheit,
> Nun dahin auf immerdar,
> Da die Seele noch voll Blindheit,
> Noch voll Licht das Auge war . . .

Pamela, Erika and I became inseparable. Her friendship was as
excessive as was her filial devotion. There seemed something hectic
and forced about all her emotions or, rather, her mode of exhibiting
them. However, the theatrical presentation of feelings does not necessarily affect their authenticity. Certain characters, such as Pamela's,
are "unnatural by nature": the passionate presentation is tantamount
to the passion itself.

She could be ravishing, and sometimes she was involuntarily funny.
In other moments she seemed dismayed and saddened without any
conceivable reason. She would fling her face into her hands and
abruptly burst into tears. When besought to explain her conduct, she
would weep even more convulsively. In the end she managed to
stammer a few syllables to the effect that someone had referred to
her father in the course of a conversation, several hours ago. "I can't
bear it." And she covered her face again with her ten spread-out
fingers as behind a red, trembling fan.

It was on the occasion of such an outburst that I first noticed the
curious shape of her hands. Up to that moment I had never dared

question any detail of her appearance, hypnotized by her self-assurance and histrionic skill. Now I saw that her fingers were short and broad, with blunt, spatular tips. And I remembered that these were Wedekind's hands—the helpless and brutal hands of all those characters he used to embody on the stage himself.

So Pamela had inherited these cursed, terrible hands that seemed sore and aching and always sticky with blood. Hers were these admirable, lovable hands which now protected her tearful face.

I asked her if she didn't think it a good idea to marry me.

We were of the same age, Pamela and I, just eighteen, at the time of our engagement.

"If you only were a little older!" my father complained. "You're just too callow, that's all." And my mother sighed: "What are we going to do with you?"

My poor, puzzled parents! I had just disclosed to them, under dramatic circumstances, that I was through with Greek grammar and arithmetic. My method of passive resistance was simple and effective. I stayed in bed and informed the family that I was undergoing a major psychological crisis. When Professor Geist showed up, I told him to go to hell.

My parents were rather upset. How about the "Abitur"? My academic career? My future? I pointed out to them—not rudely but obstinately—that I didn't give a damn for my academic career but had made up my mind to become a dancer. Yes, indeed,—a ballet dancer: what's so funny about it? Something like Harald Kreuzberg, whom I admired so much. He would give me lessons, perhaps. In two or three years from now I might be wealthy and celebrated: dancers make loads of money, some of them.

Mielein and the Magician—though accustomed to all sorts of vagaries on my part—seemed rather worried this time. My mother sadly observed that she had always hoped her oldest boy might become an architect. She could content herself with a physician, an artist, or even an opera singer. But a dancer, of all things?

As for my father, he had no prejudices against the profession as such but only wondered if I was fit for it. Wasn't I rather on the gawky side? He suggested that I think it over, once more. It was April now. The family council decided to adjourn any further discussion until September or so. Then the problem should be faced squarely and a solution be found. But where and how was I to spend the interlude? I did not want to resume my studies. Nor did my parents think it a good idea to have me hang about in the house, without any purpose or schedule. They seemed relieved when I made a suggestion, on my own.

How about Heidelberg? I submitted. Once, on a trip from the Odenwaldschule, I had stayed there for a while and found the place attractive. Above all I was smitten with a spooky-looking old house situated on the Neckar River, a former monastery of the Dominican friars; now in the possession of Baron Alexander von Bernus, the poet, alchemist and student of occultism. Wasn't Bernus an old acquaintance of ours? Why not ask him if he wanted me as a paying guest? It would be cozy and stimulating, I thought, to spend a few months in such quaint surroundings. The scenery was delightful. The Baron's reputation was apt to arouse my curiosity. Besides I might attend some courses at the University, perhaps . . .

The Baron, who was by no means in the habit of receiving strangers in his private residence, may have been astonished by my father's request, especially as the relations between the two men were far from being intimate at the time. Yet the master of Stift Neuburg agreed. He just wanted to find out, perhaps, what kind of a lad it was who wished to partake in the conventual life of the castle.

It surely was an odd community of which I became a member when moving into the ancient chapter house on the bank of the Neckar River. As for Bernus himself, he looked and acted precisely the way in which the popular fancy wants a poet to behave and look. His face —pale, soft, and flabby, but not without a certain dreamy energy—was framed by a mane of rich, silky hair. He had begun his career as a bohemian but soon abandoned the idle games of aestheticism for more profound experiences. After a period of apprenticeship with various esoteric organizations, he joined Dr. Rudolf Steiner, the founder and high priest of the Anthroposophic movement. Henceforth the Baron devoted his time to the exegesis of Steiner's poorly written gospel and the promotion of Anthroposophic wisdom. Besides he was occupied with deciphering the secret idiom of the stars and producing Paracelsian concoctions.

The Baroness certainly matched her husband as far as metaphysical training is concerned. She too was initiated into the arcana of magic roots, supernatural hygienics, and the meticulous hierarchy of the cherubim, demons, and minor goblins. She was an arresting personality—the Baroness Imogen von Bernus, mistress of Stift Neuburg. At once roguish and august, she resembled an intellectual grande dame of the French rococo, an analogy she underlined by the capricious mode in which she wore her fine, silvery hair. Besides, she liked to drop occasional remarks hinting at her relation to certain distinguished individuals of the eighteenth century period. In fact, she once confided to me, laughingly but by no means as a joke, that she was the reincarnation of a famous courtesan at the court of King Louis XIV—a noble, if light-minded lady of unusual talents who enjoyed the favors of many a royal personage.

A little chat about metempsychosis was nothing extraordinary in the daily routine of Stift Neuburg. Of course, everybody knew that the Baron, during his last sojourn on this planet, used to be the buxom chambermaid of Goethe's mother in Frankfort. A red-haired anarchist who stayed with the Bernus family as their permanent guest, prided himself on having been Robespierre. In his present incarnation, however, he played a certain role in the upheaval of November, 1918, but subsequently withdrew from the political scene. For he had it from "usually well-informed sources" that there would be no World Revolution until the tenth day of August, 1929. A reliable ghost had told him so—employing a helpful peasant boy as his mouthpiece.

The peasant boy, Max Pricklhuber, worked with the Baron in the laboratory. An efficient lad, notably gifted both as chemist and medium, small wonder that the spirits had a penchant for him: he was conspicuously handsome. Nobody would have suspected the huge, sinewy youth of having mediumistic talents. Yet such was his sensibility to the appeal from other-world regions that he was sometimes struck by mystic energies under the most awkward conditions. It chanced that the voices and apparitions would haunt him when he was lying in the

bath tub pleasantly relaxed. I would often see young Pricklhuber raving through the corridors of the castle, naked, dripping with water, his
hair disheveled, his eyes widened in panic. He looked frightful and
admirable in his trembling bareness, bellowing, gesticulating, snorting:
an antique hero hit by a holy insanity.

The only sensible person in the midst of this bedlam seemed the
young daughter of the Baroness, a peevish little thing called Ursula
Pia. Sober and precocious, she looked after the household, the stable,
the orchard and her own schoolwork, while the adults were absorbed in
their weird and whimsical studies: What archangel will take over the
cosmic government in 1950? What repercussions is this change to have
regarding the developments of alchemy? Will it be possible, under the
new constellation, to discover what even the great Paracelsus had
sought in vain—the Stone of ultimate Wisdom?—the supreme formula
which transmutes the ordinary metals into the desired substance,
gold . . .

"They're batty as hell—all of them," muttered Ursula Pia when she
dropped by to deliver the mail or a cup of tea in my room. "Why do
you stay here, anyhow?" she asked suspiciously. "Are you nuts too?"

Was I nuts? What an embarrassing question! And why did I really
stay? It seemed difficult to explain. I could hardly make it clear to the
little girl that I had chosen the castle as my temporary residence, simply because there seemed no other place for me. So I just observed,
with a sort of suggestive vagueness: "It's so quiet here . . . and I'm
kind of fond of this view."

The scenery at which I pointed was indeed superb. In serene brightness the Neckar River flowed through the most idyllic panorama of
gentle hills, lush meadows, and stately linden. At a distance you could
discern the famous Castle of Heidelberg on the other side of the river
—a fragile silhouette in the silvery haze.

"Gorgeous, isn't it?" I sighed, overwhelmed anew.

"It's all right, I suppose," she said dryly.

A queer kid she was, Ursula Pia. Her eyes were strangely pale and
yet intense in a wan little face with inflamed nostrils and a turned-up,
tiny nose. She was at once grave and nimble, a cat-like creature with
the attitude of a matron.

"I just wonder what you're doing here, all day long," she said, flippant and still with a certain motherly concern.

I became elusive, once more. "Lots of things," I said, while still looking out of the window.

There was a greenish flash in her eyes, rather uncanny; full of distrust and curiosity. "Magic stuff?" she asked in a pressed little voice as if there were some sordid mystery she wanted to be let into. "Sorcery?" she insisted, with a disgusted grimace. "The same kind of monkey business, I guess, dad and ma fool around with, as soon as I leave them alone in that so-called laboratory?"

I tried to explain the difference to her. "Your dad," I said, "wants to transform one thing into another—mushrooms into sleeping tablets, for instance. Now, that's not exactly what I am after—I want to make something new—do you get that? something pure and beautiful and alive. A dance, perhaps; or a poem; or a melody."

The little girl shrugged her shoulders, pursed her lips and produced a brief, whistling sound—soft but penetrating and somehow very frightful.

"Poets . . . dancers . . . sorcerers . . ." she said, shaking the upper part of her body as if under an icy shower. "It's all the same to me. The same waste of time; the same mess; the same bore." After a pause she added: "Of course, I could practice magic too—if I cared to. But I don't. Not a bit. I just don't think it's worthwhile. Horseback riding is worthwhile. Or watering the garden. The rain is worthwhile; so are some of the things our teacher tells us about: what a flower looks like inside, or what kind of clothes people wore, hundreds of years ago. There are plenty of things worthwhile. But magic? Puh! It stinks." And she made a disgusted grimace.

There she stood, a neat and stolid thing. No doubt she could do her bit of magic as efficiently as the next fellow, a little better, perhaps. But she didn't bother. The sorcerer's child was fed up with sorcery.

And how about the Magician's son? What was wrong with me? Did I actually hope to contribute a new device to the repertoire of poetry and witchcraft?

"Well, it's getting late," observed Ursula. "Dinner time, I suppose." But she didn't move.

The day was over, all right. This was the hour when the river was wan, the foliage shivered, and a mystic chill descended from colorless skies. The stillest hour when the curfew has ended its wail; the hour of forebodings and caresses, "l'heure exquise, l'heure bleue—" there it was, wafting its message from the sleeping well and the juniper tree into this room and straight into my heart.

Don't look now, Ursula Pia! This is sorcery. We are motionless, you and I—pallid and petrified in the eerie dusk: but the things begin to talk. The crimson blooms in the vase, the lilac bush in the garden, the candle, the crucifix, the pictures on the wall—they whisper and sing and tell stories. Those whom I love the most, smiling in ebony frames, exchange meaningful glances: Mother, Sister, my betrothed, and a child with high-set cheekbones and limpid eyes. Whom do I love the most? Don't listen now, Ursula! Close your ears and your eyes! For this is the River God's voice.

Behold! he rises from darkness, heaving the weight of his purple flesh; his prodigious brow wreathed with vine, the antique flute in his hand, the token of Pan and the Satyrs. Beware of his savage allurement, little Ursula! Avoid the spectacle of his pranks and grimaces! He is the archwizard: his breath and touch bewitch the animals. Don't watch him when he stumbles through the park, magnificent and obscene in his drunkenness. He addles the mind: his path is covered with the traces of crimes and the ashes of suicides.

Look at him, Ursula! There is no chance to escape—neither for you nor for me. His grip and spell are inescapable. He blinds and deafens and inspires us; he entangles us in his great disorder; he sweeps us away, billow-like, irresistible. Where does he carry us, the holy monster? When will he release us from his clasp, the wanton deity? Never mind, little sister! Accept it! Bear it! Enjoy it!

"We don't know the way," I said aloud, to my own surprise. "Take it, little sister! But take it easy."

"I'll try my best," she said, with gentle determination. "So should you, young man. You must try very hard, or you may go astray. For you are easily fooled and easily wounded."

What was that? Was I hearing things? How could this little girl babble such Pythic stuff? How much did she know? How far had she followed me into my reveries?

But this was neither the place nor the hour to ask questions. Hadn't I been told that Ursula Pia could practice magic, if she wanted to do so? Didn't I know this was an enchanted house? And the river outside, the Neckar, was enchanted too—the cradle of poetry and romantic madness.

Don't ask questions! This is the hour of stillness and divination. The message from the well, the inaudible call from the juniper tree delights and calms the vulnerable, seducible heart. A breath of lilac and evening soothes the sorrow, transforms the disorder into harmony. For one transient moment everything fuses and integrates: the crucifix, the flowers, the beloved faces and desired lips, the mask of the River God, the aimless lust, the wordless suffering, the dances yet to be danced, the tears to be shed, the unspoken, unspeakable prayers.

CHAPTER FIVE

The Devout Dance

(1924-1927)

THE Walpurgis Night of the inflation was over. We had to adapt ourselves, once again, to reasonable figures and modest standards. A spirit of sobriety and disillusionment prevailed; in other words, we had quite a hangover.

At the same time, however, there was a new confidence—a mood of reconstruction and "Let's start all over again!" which gradually spread out and became stronger and finally replaced the hectic bustle of the past few years. The German people began to awake and to recuperate from a nightmare that had been inflicted on them, violently upsetting their moral standards and their bank accounts. They had no Kaiser any more, no German Alsace, no fleet, no army, no generals, no decorations, no titles, no colonies, no illusions. But they had a future.

A youngster of eighteen years wanted to start a literary career. How did he tackle this problem?

Since he happened to be a son of a noted writer, the most obvious thing to do seemed, of course, to exploit his father's prestige and contacts. But his vanity, or his sense of honor, prevented him from doing so—at least, for a while. He concealed his name when he submitted three literary essays to one of the most exacting periodicals in Germany, "Die Weltbühne." The editor, Siegfried Jacobsohn, was a legendary character in the literary milieu of Berlin; a tiny man, almost dwarfish, he displayed terrific energies: both his acute wit and inexorable seriousness were widely feared and admired. Surprisingly enough, he felt there was something worthwhile in those aphoristic sketches by a nameless lad: he accepted all three of them.

Unfortunately, however, he soon found out my identity and insisted on featuring my name, which provided "Die Weltbühne" with a tiny sensation and probably was the pivotal mistake of my literary career. For from now on I was labeled, the precocious son of a distinguished father, the easy-going heir of a great spiritual tradition.

I was smart enough to gauge the opportunity, but too callow to sense the inherent danger. Everything seemed so easy. How curious! People were interested in what I had to offer. The most respectable papers—Berlin's august "Vossische Zeitung" and the eminent journal of Frankfort—printed my short stories, my reflections on country schools, French poetry, and the miracle of being young. I began to make a little money: it was lots of fun. I rushed from Heidelberg to Frankfort, from Frankfurt to Berlin, back to Heidelberg, and to Berlin again.

There I moved into a fairly expensive hotel at the Kurfürstendamm. My decision was made: I was going to write a book. Or rather, I intended to make a collection of the stories I considered particularly successful, and to submit the whole bunch to a publisher. Just one more item was needed to round off the whole thing. So I cloistered myself in my luxurious apartment (with bath and an unpaid bill) and ventured on the composition of some arty "legends."

A hundred years ago, there lived an attractive mystery boy by the name of Caspar Hauser. He was dumb and timid and without guile; for he had spent the first sixteen years of his life in a pitch-dark cave and only learned to speak when he was seventeen. Rumor had it that he was a royal prince buried alive by his jealous relatives. Other observers insisted that he was an astute impostor or just a half-wit. At any rate, he was assassinated, only a few years after his liberation, which seems to bolster the prince-theory. Thanks to this cruel death, his figure later assumed a sort of mysterious halo. The speechless youth was extolled by many a poet as the incarnation of melancholy and innocence.

A few whimsical sketches around this enigmatic problem child were, in my opinion, precisely the right kind of arabesque to wind up the pell-mell of my narrative extravaganzas. Opus One was ready. I called it "Before Life," as I felt that my life had not really started as yet.

What my stories mirrored was only its reflection, the dream-like delight and awe in view of its vast approach.

I walked about in a constant haze of bewilderment: So that's what it is like to be grown-up, to have a job and money trouble and quarrels with colleagues and a love affair. . . . How curious! How real!

Yes, I had a job, or something like a job, with one of the leading morning papers in Berlin, the "Zwölf Uhr Mittagsblatt." I was the "second-string theatrical critic," which means that I had to cover the minor theaters in the suburbs, the music halls, and some of the vanguard experiments. It was grand to attend, say, a performance of the "Prince of Homburg," by Heinrich von Kleist, at the former Royal Theater in Steglitz, near Berlin—to sit down in the midst of all these respectable gentlemen of the press, swollen with the feeling of my own importance. I enjoyed it tremendously. To rush to the editorial offices as soon as the show was over; to jot down some gracious or flippant lines which would be read, just a few hours later, by all those busy people in the subways, the busses, the cafés, the hotel lobbies—I certainly got a kick out of it. I could not help feeling, at the bottom of my heart, that this new position of mine really was but another hoax I tried to pull, another trick to bamboozle the grown folks.

It tickled me to find out how far I could actually go. One of the young actors in Berlin—an unusually gifted chap with the features of a transfigured pugilist and a striking, metallic voice—was the subject of my particular admiration. I indulged in paying homage to his genius, secretly convinced that the boss would omit the rhapsodic passages. But my lyrical outbursts were published in their entirety and no one seemed to find them objectionable or ridiculous. Nor did any one question my right to attack a popular vedette or celebrated mime. I remember, for instance, that I once was exceedingly nasty about one of the most distinguished representatives of the classic theatrical style, the famous character player Ferdinand von Bonn. There was nothing Mr. von Bonn, or anybody else, could do about it: the critic of the "Zwölf Uhr Mittagsblatt" just didn't like his performance. Had they known how I inwardly chuckled! The big hoax! It worked!

It was a busy winter, full of work and hope and excitement. I got loads of fun out of my job, and Erika was even more enthusiastic about hers; she spent innumerable evenings playing a speechless lady in the Max Reinhardt production of G. B. Shaw's "Saint Joan," although she had already played leading roles in matinees. So strong was our determination to find everything wonderful and exciting that we even loved the two dreary rooms which we had chosen because of the modest rent. The building was situated in the district called the Old West: it was one of those architectural nightmares typical of a period and an attitude that has become popular as "the gay Nineties." They may have been quiveringly gay; but what remains of them couldn't be more depressing. It is to the gloomy façades of these bourgeois fortresses that Berlin owes her appearance of pretentious ugliness. There is nothing quite as hideous in the history of modern architecture as what is known as the style of the "Gründerjahre" in Berlin—which means the epoch following the victorious war against France, in 1870. It was the most prosperous and the most vulgar period Germany ever passed through. Our home in the Uhland-Strasse was one of the monuments testifying to the devastating influence which the excess of wealth and the absence of spirit can have on the developments of a culture.

I can still see it and smell it: it all comes back, I can touch it, as soon as I close my eyes. The little candy store at the corner, the old woman who sold newspapers just in front of the house; the entrance, bleak, wide, and pompous; the ghastly mosaics adorning the walls of the lobby; the staircase of phony marble, the worn-out carpet, and then— third floor, to your right—the door with the humble little brass plate, "Frau Hedwig Schmidt; widow."

She was our landlady—the "little patronne," as we used to call her; a jewel of a woman—good-natured and somewhat down-at-heel; slovenly, generous, and indulgent; her chubby face with its childish features and innumerable wrinkles framed by an abundance of restive curls. She was an intimate friend of ours, the coziest creature I have ever known. How she beamed with pride when I sold a story! She was sorrowful but never grew impatient when our bill assumed disquieting proportions. When we awakened her, at three o'clock in the morning, to borrow one mark fifty pfennigs for the taxi driver, she would welcome us with a drowsy grin: "Those kids! They're crazy as hell..."

In December I took a leave of four weeks or so. Munich seemed beautifully provincial after the buzz and blare of Berlin. I enjoyed the placid regularity of home life. Every day I spent eight or ten hours at the narrow desk where I had once struggled with mathematics and irregular Greek verbs. The task I had now to tackle was no less intricate but definitely more gratifying.

I ventured to write a play. A play about my dreams and memories and longings. About the things I was familiar with and loved and understood. A play about young people, of course. A play for Erika and Pamela. There also would be a role for that young actor with the metallic voice. And a part for myself as well; but I didn't intend to play it. The idea that I could ever appear on a stage to impersonate my own double, seemed almost as absurd as it would have been to ask my old teacher, Paulus, to play the picturesque character who obviously wore his features.

"The Old One," all beard and mystery, supervised the lurid institute which I had chosen as the background for my dramatic fantasy. I called it, somewhat enigmatically, an "asylum for fallen children." Half ballet-school, half sanatorium (with a touch of jail, brothel, and monastery), it gave shelter to a bunch of forlorn youngsters, gentle creatures, just a little bit depraved and derelict. They sang pious songs with chirping little voices, rehearsed their group dances, and were casually looked after by a neurotic quartet of four older boys and girls—Anja and Esther, Jacob and Caspar—who had probably also begun their careers as "fallen children," under the guard of the Old One. Needless to say that all four of them were madly in love with each other, in the most tragic and mixed-up fashion. Anja loved Esther, and Jacob loved Anja, and Caspar (who was something like Anja's step-brother) loved everybody, and Esther loved no one, really. But then, of course, she fell in love with Erik—she just couldn't help it: it was one of those things. For Erik was wildly attractive, the veritable incarnation of sex appeal. A sailor, an adventurer, an enthralling brute, he invades the conventual dance academy. With his sweeping appetite for love, food, and fun, he bewitches and upsets the bitter-sweet idyll of Anja and Esther and the anemic kids. The emotional relations among the members of the little group become perturbingly complicated. Esther shouts at Anja, out of sheer hysteria. Anja suffers silently. Caspar is rather depressed but talkative and composed. Jacob goes so far as to fidget about with a gun. Erik is all reckless zest and fine amativeness. The Old Man smirks, and feeds his animals (as Paulus used to), and understands everything. The children sing. Esther and Erik finally run away together. Anja and Caspar (both are somehow related to the Old One) exchange plaintive remarks with regard to the destiny of man in general and of our post-War generation in particular.

I called the play "Anja and Esther" and dedicated the book edition to the metallic juvenile whom I wanted to play the sailor. The very evening I had finished the script, I insisted on reading it aloud to an intimate family party gathering in my father's studio. When I had read the first act, which dies away with an eerie note, very much à la Maeterlinck or Strindberg, there was a dismal stillness, until my father, from his arm-chair in the corner, mercifully murmured: "Strange. Very strange, indeed."

"Rather on the morbid side, I suppose," my mother added, with a cheerfulness that sounded a trifle forced.

Aunt Lula, however, inquired in a brittle little voice, her dainty face rigid with disapproval: "I must confess that I am somewhat puzzled as to the relation between those two young ladies, Anja and Esther. Why are they so conspicuously fond of each other?"

Whereupon my father suggested, apologetically: "Well, you see . . . a sentimental friendship, between schoolmates . . ."

Everybody agreed that my romantic play had a great deal of atmosphere.

I went back to Berlin but didn't stay there long. As soon as I received the first check from my publisher, nobody and nothing could have held me in Germany. To travel! to see the world! . . . I was hankering for the sight of other skies, for the melody of foreign languages.

The trip to England with W. E. Süskind had been decided upon for months. I thought he would be an ideal guide, as he spoke English fluently enough, and had read D. H. Lawrence and Aldous Huxley (neither of whom I was familiar with at that time), and because he was my friend and sensitive and clever.

What a sensation when we crossed the frontier and I found myself, for the first time, on foreign soil, surrounded by people who spoke in a foreign tongue! It was only Dutch—closely akin to German. Yet the ungainly chap who offered us hot coffee and cigarettes seemed the embodiment of exotic fascination. I remember that Süskind, at least as excited as I, observed, with one of his fumbling and expressive little gestures: "Out of Germany! It's a prison—there, behind us . . . A prison—that's what it is . . ."

I was to think and to remind him of this remark, eight years afterwards.

London was a disappointment. I didn't see it, really. I was blind. I saw a gloomy boarding house, and a few things in the British Museum, and armies of taxicabs—quaintly shaped and yet so surprisingly nimble —and endless streets, parks, squares, and bridges. But I did not see London. I was waiting for Paris. London was something overwhelmingly big: it confused me, got me down. Paris—the unknown city on the other side of the Channel—was more real to me than London in all its huge reality. Walking along the Thames, I was hankering for the Seine. I persuaded Süskind to shorten our stay. We decided to return by plane to the continent.

The first impression of Paris. . . . But this I cannot describe. It would be as if you tried to analyze your first meeting with the person you were predestined to love, long and passionately.

Undeniably, I came to Paris with a lot of preconceived enthusiasm— determined to find it gorgeous. But this favorable prejudice might have turned into bitter disappointment if the city had not lived up to my high expectations. However, I found the reality of Paris even more enthralling than I had dared imagine.

It's not that I had any sensational experiences during this first stay. I just fell in love with the city—with its smells and noises and colors, the sight of its squares and streets, with its melodies and the civilized nonchalance of its people, and, of course, with its light.

I suppose it was the light, more than anything else, that captivated me right in the beginning, that pearly haze everything in Paris is bathed in. It is as if the atmosphere had adapted itself to the fastidious standards of a mellow civilization. There they are—lavishly dispersed all over the royal spaciousness: the solemn shadows of Poussin's classic landscapes, the infinite variety of grays as Monet has known and caught them, the serene tints of Renoir—smiling rose, vigorous blue, and voluptuous white; the nervous violence of Toulouse-Lautrec's glaring posters, Géricault's fervent black, Bracque's beautiful browns and yellows, and the morbid blue of Picasso. What an abundance of shades!

Why does one fall in love with that city? Because of the nacreous pallor that sometimes transfigures the trees and statues in the Luxembourg gardens; because of the sacred massiveness of Notre Dame, and the fragrance of anise and red wine and female perfumes in the little bistros, and the obsolete glamor of certain restaurants and theaters and hotels, and the shabby coziness of Montmartre, and the ludicrous pretensions of Montparnasse, and because of the Madeleine, and those noisy terraces on the Boulevards, and because of the charmingly hoarse voices of the prostitutes and the duchesses, and the treacherous innocence of the pimps and the poets; and because of the brioches and the mousse au chocolat, and the Champs-Elysées, and the Camembert cheese, and the preposterous grandeur of the Eiffel Tower, and the view from Sacré Coeur; and because of the babas au rhum at Rumpelmeyer's and the spicy scent in the Halles, where the vegetables are even more magnificent than the piles of roses and carnations. One loves it because of Balzac and Jeanne d'Arc, and the Boulevard St. Germain, and the brothels, and the many monks, and the yellow covers of the books, and the exquisite window displays, and because of what Proust has written, and because of Offenbach and Heine and Molière and the Ballet Russe and Louis XIV and the cheap hotels and the Panthéon and the arcades of the Rue de Rivoli with those dreary English bookshops, and because of the many pissoirs—they are so convenient—and the many fountains and trees and gardens—they are so beautiful. One loves Paris because of the supple cats and the garrulous concierges and the accordion music of the dancehalls; because the traffic is such a mess but nothing happens, and because you get wine with your food, and everybody speaks French, and the Place de la Concorde constantly turns about, never ceases to move: a gigantic carrousel with all its statues and flowers and bicyclists and the Egyptian obelisk as its brittle but powerful center.

That's why one loves Paris—not for the sake of adventures. Berlin and New York and Shanghai may be adventurous cities, but not Paris. It is mature and beautifully balanced and not eccentric at all. How, then, could it be adventurous? The night life in Rio or Cairo or Buda-pest is "adventurous," which means that it is dangerous and sordid. But the night life in Paris is charming because it is a natural and in-tegral part of life in general. All things concerning sex are handled with that perfect casualness which is the proof of real civilization.

He who seeks adventures in Paris, will be disappointed. But I didn't seek adventures. I wanted to live in Paris. So I was not disappointed. No one who wants to live there will ever be disappointed.

Süskind returned to Munich, precisely on the day for which the end of our journey had been originally scheduled. He was an orderly boy. I was not. I stayed behind, all by myself, or rather, I found new com-pany to stay with.

The light of Paris enchanted me: I wanted to see the light of Mar-seilles. Somehow I managed to go South. The Train Bleu carried me towards the blueness of the Mediterranean.

Marseilles has more violent lights and deeper shadows than any other European city (outside of Spain). The golden Madonna, mag-nanimous protectress of the seamen and prostitutes, scintillates at her rocky lookout post. The main street of Marseilles, called "La Canne-bière," a charming travesty of the Parisian Boulevards, glows and glis-tens as if in a furious effort to prove its importance as a metropolitan avenue. You pass the picturesque square of the Old Port, ablaze with brightness; turn to your right, and presently go astray in the maze of narrow streets—receiving you with the blare and stink of massed, primitive vices.

The marvels of Marseilles, already imbued with the savor of Africa, made me avid for the real thing, the miracles of the Arabian landscape.

I went to Tunisia and from there to the interior. I stayed at Biscra and Cairouan. I saw the Sahara and thought it more beautiful and more terrifying than even the ocean or glaciers. I was intoxicated by the colors and smells of the Arabian towns and villages. The palm trees enthralled me, and the heat, and the rampant gibberish of the native lads. It was thrilling to ride on a camel's back. What curious creatures the camels are! so grave and lofty and yet so ludicrous, with their long necks and sad, stupid eyes.

Whenever I think of anything bewitched and fairy-tale-like, of exotic scenery and hypnotizing sounds, it is Tunisia, my first visit to that country, that presently comes to my mind. I recall the massive, elegant domes of the mosques; the bustle and scurry in the shadowy bazaars where the gaudy junk literally flows from the cave-like stores over the pavement. I was fascinated by the sweetish perfumes, dubious candies, colorful garments, and fanciful products of Moroccan leather. The bearded salesmen amused me with their transparent wiles and thunderous eloquence. They tried to be so cunning and astute. But in reality it was I who cheated them in the end. For I relished their glib persistence like a vaudeville act and had an excellent time sipping that aromatic concoction which they called café Turque—until I abruptly discovered that I had forgotten to take any money along.

I stayed as long as I possibly could, or even a little longer. When it had to be, I embarked grudgingly for Palermo.

Italy was definitely an anticlimax. In Palermo one hankers for Tunisia. At Naples, one remembers all the exciting stories one has ever heard about that much-vaunted city. I thought it depressingly dull, although I was persecuted by a gang of veritable apaches and almost assassinated in a sinister sort of maison de rendezvous.

Disappointed by Naples, I renounced the usual excursion to Capri.

Rome failed to impress me. How heavy and theatrical is the Eternal City! Its classic splendor has withered—tainted and numbed by the blight of Fascism.

Yes, it is Fascism that spoils even the most perfect monuments of the Renaissance and Baroque. The magnificent palazzos are cheapened by the cocky blackshirts who guard them. The dreary grimace of the Duce disfigures the most graceful façades.

I loathed Fascism in 1925 as I loath it now; but at that time my aversion was purely emotional, lacking in intellectual foundation. Fascism irritated me beyond words. I was repulsed by its insipid rant, long before I grasped its devastating impact.

I have never liked Italy, as I knew it only in the state of Fascist degradation. No doubt, I would deem Germany a hideous, despicable country, if I had not been there before the outbreak of the Third Reich. But the only Germany I knew, was as yet uncorrupted by the Nazi plague.

Quite a few things had happened while I traveled abroad. Field Marshal von Hindenburg, the dreary Victor of Tannenberg, was elected President of the Republic, as Friedrich Ebert's successor, which was shocking news. In general, I was but faintly concerned with political matters. But this development somehow struck me as ominous and offensive. The senile brute and reactionary squire—our President! I didn't like the idea. Suddenly I felt that I ought to have been in Germany during the election. Now my voice was wasted—one vote less for the decent liberal candidate.

But, happily, there were other events that helped me overcome the transient anxiety. Infinitely more exciting than that old bore Hindenburg, for instance, was, the publication of my two first books—the slim volume of short stories, "Before Life," and the romantic play, "Anja and Esther," in a neat binding of delicate lavender blue. What a thrill! My desk was burdened with fan mail and newspaper clippings. The first letters from young people and women and colleagues who had read my stuff! I relished every word as a sign of beginning success—a token of future triumphs.

The most encouraging message came from Stefan Zweig. The tireless promoter of striving talents gave me one of his most hearty and heartening pep talks: "Go ahead, young friend! There may be prejudices against you because of your famous parentage. Never mind. Do your work! Say what you have to say!—it's quite a lot, if I am not mistaken. I expect a great deal from you. I want you to think of my expectations when you write your next book."

I did certainly think of him. And it helped.

My bags were crammed, not only with French literature and Arabian souvenirs, but also with bundles of notes I had jotted down, in London, Paris, Marseilles, and Tunisia. Even more profuse were my heart and mind—pregnant with experiences I wanted to communicate: overflowing with tunes and images and the beautiful echoes of human voices, all of which I hankered to articulate.

I was avid for self-expression. No fragmentary account would do. This time, it had to be the real thing—the complete confession: nothing short of a novel.

So I sat down and wrote a novel, "The Devout Dance."

What was the novel about? About a young man, of course, and his adventures; his restlessness, his sorrows, his elations; a young man, and this time—the anarchy and promise of the twentieth century. He was a child during the great war, and in adolescence finds himself confronted with a messed up, but colorful world. So he plunges right into the mess and the splendor.

My hero and double, the devout dancer, is a well-bred boy, descendant of a patrician family, but isolated from all bourgeois traditions. At once weary and enterprising, he toys with the idea of committing suicide but promptly changes his mind and runs away, to Berlin. There he makes friends with all sorts of bohemians, good-natured prostitutes, sympathetic flotsam. For a while he earns his living by reciting poetry, dressed up as a sailor, in a cabaret called The Puddle. Then he meets Niels (who might as well be called Erik), whereupon things turn even more disorderly. Niels is truculent and divinely naïve. The devout dancer worships him. He quits his job and follows Niels from city to city, in a crazy zigzag, through half of the continent. Somehow the devout dancer always manages to have a certain minimum of money. In his own dreamy way he is rather smart and resilient, no fool or saint, to be sure.

So he strolls about—floating, forlorn, hazardously uprooted; an intellectual vagabond and ecstatic tramp. He is childish and sophisticated, genuine but coquettish, saturnine but reckless, lascivious but without guile. Always in a haze of melancholy, in a delirium of loneliness, he keeps exploring, insatiably, the sordid little secrets of the underworld, the great treasures of world literature, and the landscapes of human faces. He is disorganized and wasteful: rich in imagination, poor in discipline. He knows how to love and to renounce. He is lonely because he seeks freedom, nothing but freedom, extreme independence. He jeopardizes all his privileges, betrays his responsibilities: for what? For a dazzling chimera called Life, life as such; as unending movement, sensual spell, meaningless miracle. He thinks he is strong enough to get away with his risky ecstasies without any guide or goal; without security, home, or lasting human relations; advised by nobody and nothing except his own impulses and visions, completely isolated and completely free.

By no means is he lighthearted or frivolous. The thought of death is powerful in his mind, although he summarizes his credo: I believe in this life. But the life he means is a sacred adventure, a devout dance.

He is very young.

I was very young when I thus portrayed and exaggerated my own shortcomings and potentialities.

Erika was young, and so were Pamela and Gustaf Gründgens, when we all met in Hamburg to produce my play "Anja and Esther." Gründgens was the versatile star of the Hamburger Kammerspiele, a literary theater of high standing. The leader of the institute, Erich Ziegel, had a proclivity for controversial experiments. But Gründgens was the one who sparkled with ideas and was inexhaustible in producing stunts and sensations. The idol of Hamburg's theater fans, he captivated the audiences with his inspired stunts and ever-new disguises. He was morbid and mysterious as Hamlet, irresistible as Schnitzler's Anatole, sinister in Strindberg's dramatic nightmares, flamboyant in Schiller's "Don Carlos," utterly sophisticated in the farce by Oscar Wilde, taut with hysteria in expressionistic fantasies, quivering with wit and rhythm in the musical comedies by Offenbach. He managed to appear slender on the stage, although in reality, he was rather on the flabby side. He looked strikingly attractive if his role required good looks; and, if necessary, transformed himself into a stooping old man. He was by turns bland and violent, ribald, tragic, timid, or feline. He was all talent, no substance: the most ingenious performer I have ever seen.

In a typical sudden caprice he fell in love with my play, particularly with the idea of having it produced with Erika, Pamela, the author, and himself in the leading parts. I received urgent telegrams from the management of the Kammerspiele to the effect that my personal ap-

pearance was indispensable to guarantee a success. I was bewildered,
tickled—and easily persuaded.

Gustaf invaded our hotel rooms as a neurotic Hermes, light-footed
in his worn but elegantly shaped sandals, wearing his monocle with
striking nonchalance and his shabby leather overcoat with as much
sovereign grace as if it were a beautiful antique garment. He was
haunted by his vanity and persecution mania, and a frantic desire to
please. There was something very grand and very pathetic about him.
He was mangled by inferiority complexes. His face, without the mask
of make-up, was strangely wan, as if covered with ashes. He glittered
and suffered and seduced. He wanted to be loved, but no one loved
him. His eyes were icy and soft like the eyes of a rare and royal fish
who had jewels in place of eyes.

His attitude, voice and gestures changed as soon as he entered a
stage. I felt helpless when I compared my own gawky efforts with
Gustaf's experienced bravura. His part was that of Jacob, the gloomy
one in love with Anja. But he paid little attention to his own lines.
Indefatigable and omnipresent, he supervised all of us, encouraging
Erika with looks that seemed plaintive with admiration; teasing Pamela
because of her pretentious mannerisms; stimulating me with clever
little pieces of advice: "More bitchy, Klaus!—if you know what I mean
. . . not so stiff! More life! Take two steps to your left, just before you
have to say this line . . . two bitchy little steps—look—like this . . ."
How easy it seemed when he did it!

The premiere took place in Munich and Hamburg simultaneously.
In my home town the play was received with a sort of chilly curiosity.
Our circus in Hamburg, however, stirred up quite some hullabaloo
from the Baltic Sea down to the Danube. All newspapers were running
stories about the "children of famous poets staging a big show in
Hamburg." Some of the articles were insidious, others were patronizing. But all of them meant publicity for our venture in the Kammerspiele. "Children of famous poets" drew crowded houses, and the
public interest still increased when the "Berliner Illustrierte," by far the
most popular German magazine, carried our portraits on its front page,
which was the most spectacular publicity available. The picture showed
the two girls and my own solemn face; Gustaf's portrait was removed:

he was no poet's child and altogether not interesting enough. What a moment of deadly embarrassment when he discovered the outrage! He sat motionless and erect, his lips tightly closed, his features numb with anger. No word, no gesture: only the mute complaint of his jewel-like eyes. I was afraid he could never forgive us, really, for this insult of which we were the innocent cause. Later, when portraits of Gustaf Gründgens adorned more than one magazine front page, I often thought of his tart smile, the beautiful performance of dignity and grief he displayed when his colleagues, in the little restaurant of the Hamburger Kammerspiele, gloated over his conspicuous absence from our group picture.

I enjoyed leading an actor's life with all its ludicrous intrigues, excitements, and ambitions. It was grand, as long as it lasted. I was exceedingly fond of the atmosphere in the canteen, sticky with smoke and gossip, and of the sweetish aroma of make-up, dust, and feverish expectations that made the air in the narrow dressing rooms so sickening and delightful. How wonderful was the tension of the last minute before the curtain rises! It's a thrill like that before a dive into icy water. And then, there it is—remote and yet frightfully close, that gaping darkness—the enemy you must conquer; the wild animal you must tame; the lover you must embrace: the audience.

I can still see myself standing with Gustaf behind the scenes, shivering in anticipation of our cue. Gustaf looked rather striking, with his eyes glimmering under the baroque crown of his purple wig. He seemed absorbed in listening to the dialogue on the stage, the passionate whisper between Anja and Esther. "Isn't she wonderful?" he breathed. "Her voice . . ." And I knew whom he meant—

I loved the theater. But, of course, to love it is not enough. You must become addicted to it as to a drug, or you must give it up. It has to be your cross and agony, your heaven, your love, and your life, or it will be nothing to you whatsoever.

Even while I was in Hamburg, and had to play every night, and enjoyed it, I was interested in all sorts of things that had nothing to do with the theater. I had friends outside of the theater, too. In fact, I found most likable company in the circles of a certain degraded jeunesse dorée, sons of patrician families that had become penniless during the inflation. They still lived in the stately villas where their parents had once represented the dignity and wealth of the Hanseatic tradition. As exiled princes, melancholy and proud, they roved through the bleak spaciousness of dusty drawing rooms and abandoned gardens. There was one young fellow among them I used to be particularly fond of. He had a long, bony, sensitive face and the nervous slenderness of an aristocratic greyhound. His name was Ramon. He had a lot of grace and a strange sort of humor—wistful and bizarre.

Ramon and his friends were somehow different from the young men of similar milieus in other German cities. They possessed more nonchalance and self-irony than one usually finds among Germans. It was good to talk books and music or just silly stuff with them, after all that hectic blare in the Kammerspiele. We had a grand time when the whole gang of us strolled through St. Pauli, the "wild district" of Hamburg, not quite as wicked as the quartier du Vieux Port in Marseilles, but amusing enough, a sweeping display of turning lights, female flesh, sailors' uniforms, and exaggerated vulgarity. The contrast to the dignified stillness of the residential quarters was striking. What a curious and paradoxical pleasure!—to see the sons of a decaying aristocracy, well-bred, melancholy, and playful, mingle with the plebeian crowd in a sinister joint called "Three Stars" or in that monster department store for cheap pleasure, the "Alcazar."

Hamburg was delightful. The theater, St. Pauli, "Anja and Esther," Gustaf's assiduous tricks, everything was charming, for six weeks or eight. But it was my mania—or a kind of fear of anticlimactic developments—to break up situations before they might become stale. I ruined (and sometimes saved) human relations, professional opportunities, studies and pleasures, by rushing away, just in order to move, to change, to remain alive.

I wanted to write a new story. Something on children, two boys and two girls. Yes. And about their mother, a widow. Life in the country. Children play games and talk fancy stuff. Yes. And then, mother has an affair. Naturally. The vagabond—savagely attractive. Invades idyll. Fools around with kids; seduces widow. Of course.

But the lover was missing. I called him, clamored for him, employed all sorts of devices to catch his face, his voice, his appearance. But he refused to show up. The only lover who presented himself was the too-familiar ruffian—disheveled hair, radiant grin, the irresistible vitality . . . No more of this! This time, I needed a more subtle character. Something more nervous, more cerebral and refined. But, of course, he ought to have sex appeal. Intellectuals have no sex appeal, that's the trouble with them. Not for me, anyway—and, therefore, not for the widow. She waited, and I didn't know for whom. Poor widow! We were quite in a fix, she and I.

I tried very hard to help her. I traveled about, seeking a lover for the wistful matron. She led her dreary life with the kids—patient and meek, but secretly disappointed. I had created her, and now I let her down. It was not very gallant.

I went from Hamburg to Berlin; from Berlin to Munich, Vienna, and Nice. Finally I went to Paris.

It was a long sojourn and a magnificent one. The unique city seemed more hospitable and graceful than ever, in that glorious spring of 1926. Life was smooth and colorful and comparatively inexpensive. The depreciation of the franc was just considerable enough to make things easier for noncapitalistic visitors of my own type and to add a faint touch of helplessness to the splendor of the metropolis.

Paris was swarming with foreigners of all races, colors, and social backgrounds. They brought the foreign exchanges of five continents and were treated by the French with a sort of ironic tenderness. The luxurious cafés on the Grands Boulevards and the Champs-Elysées, the night clubs of Montmartre and the terraces of Montparnasse—all hotels, theaters, vehicles, restaurants, beauty shops, book stores, art galleries, and Turkish Baths were jammed with the motley crowd from Tokyo and Birmingham, Detroit and Tunisia, Rio de Janeiro and Hamburg, Shanghai, Stockholm, and Kansas City. It was a veritable invasion—peaceful but overwhelming—of pleasure-seeking Babbitts, frustrated painters, stingy professors, flippant journalists, ladies of the monde or demimonde, drunkards, scholars, art collectors, dressmakers, loafers, philosophers, criminals, millionaires, celebrities, and nobodies. Never again in my life have I met (and lost) so many people as in that spring of 1926, in Paris. I met people of all nationalities, even French-men. What a host of casual acquaintances, brief and passionate friend-ships! But some of these new relations were to last and to grow and to assume great importance for my further life.

It was in that fine and eventful spring that I met the young novelist, René Crevel.

His personality and work strikingly contradicts the accepted pattern of what a young Frenchman of letters is supposed to be. René was neither slick nor scholarly. His compelling charm was not devoid of tragic and violent features. There was something indescribable about his eyes—huge, shiny stars widely opened as if in constant bewilder-ment or delight. They had no color—just light. Terrific things occurred in their limpid depth: blasts of other-worldly electricity were succeeded by sudden darkness as if clouds of sorrow fell from a grievous fore-head over these radiant orbs. Then there would be new flashes of golden and bluish-green sparks.

He was gentle and generous, but could turn truculent, indeed, cruel, when irritated by pettiness and meanness. His fervent integrity re-acted against everything low and ugly. The qualities he loathed most implacably were those he considered typical of the class from which he was descended himself, the bourgeoisie of the Third Republic. No fiendish vice seemed so unpardonably hideous to him as the avarice and smug obtuseness with which he thought his own family tainted.

His attitude, even his appearance, was molded by this furious resent-ment against his relatives, especially his mother. As his mother wore black exclusively, René preferred loud colors and rough material for his clothes, which made him look half like an apache, half like an eccentric from Oxford, with his bushy hair, thick lips, and those stun-ning eyes. He spent his days with Americans, Germans, Russians, and Chinese, because his mother suspected all foreigners to be crooks or perverts. He drank gin and whiskey as the smell made her sick. He attacked Christianity because she went to church. She was fervently patriotic: he reveled in disrespectful jokes about France and her sacred traditions. She was a puritan: he shocked her with dirty jokes. His whole being was a challenge to her tastes and convictions. He enjoyed discussing his father's suicide, for he knew that Madame Crevel tried to conceal this disgrace. Not only had Crevel Sr. taken his own life—hanging himself in Madame's tidy salon, just when she expected guests: he had been mad, a hopeless paranoiac, according to the story his son liked to tell, shaken by desperate merriment. What a delightful idea of Monsieur and Madame Crevel to have a son under such circumstances!

Sometimes I was perplexed, even shocked, by the vehemence of his judgments, the abruptness of his intellectual somersaults. He was infantile and rather frightening when he plunged into one of his diatribes against Christianity, and it was terrible to hear him discuss his mother. He described her as a veritable paragon of meanness and hypocrisy. I can still hear the rapid flow of his words, gushing with a sort of angry enthusiasm from his innocent mouth. In his impetuous eloquence the coarse and witty argot of the Parisian suburbs was surpringly intermingled with the vocabulary of Siegmund Freud, Arthur Rimbaud and the Surrealists. He chided and cursed like a young god annoyed by human viciousness and intoxicated by earthly wines. Besides, he lisped a little.

There he was, sitting on my bed, in a very blue shirt and gray flannels, his face bent down to the sheets of his manuscript—the opening chapter of his new novel, "La Mort Difficile." It was easy to recognize the features of his own mother in the venomous portrait of Madame Dumont-Dufour, the mother of his problem hero, young Pierre. The merciless intensity of this literary attack seemed all the more perturbing as I knew that Madame was dangerously ill. When he had finished reading, I asked him whether his mother's state had improved. He said, No, she is in a pretty bad way, indeed: "She may die very soon."

I also asked him what was going to happen to Pierre, the leading character of his story. He smiled, and had a peculiar way of looking at me without seeing anything, staring right through me as if I were a cloud or a ghost or nothing. "I'll kill him," he said, still with that proud and absent-minded smile. "What else is he good for? Pauvre petit . . . I'll do away with him, somehow . . ." Later he told me that he would let him swallow sleeping tablets and make him die somewhere in the streets of Paris, on a bench. "For the son of Madame Dumont-Dufour has no place in which to live or to die."

Thus his difficult death kept growing in the very kernel of his organism, a murderous fruit that would burst open when it is ripe and soft, and drown with the effusion of its purple juice the delicate heart that nourished it.

But when I met him, he still was eager to live, to accomplish something, to play, to love, to fight, and to create. Indeed, he was dynamic enough to conquer my drowsy belle, the motherly ingenue surrounded by four healthy kids, awaiting the seducer. The character I had been seeking so long for my story—there he was: incalculable, dashing, lovable and complex. His gift and challenge is not only the physical adventure, that monotonous ecstasy Erik and Niels had to offer. The inquietude he bears and transmits, is more spiritual and profound. He seems winged by extramundane powers—puerile, iridescent, chivalrous—as he invades the bedroom of the nostalgic widow: "Me voilà! I am the most experienced and yet most naïve creature on earth—a young European intellectual."

To be a young European intellectual—it was an attitude, an ambition: it almost became a program. The concept of European was meant, and accepted, as a protest against German nationalism, while the term intellectual defied the fashionable idolatry of "blood and soil" (Blubo). The patriots attacked us as "uprooted internationalists"; the Marxists, as irresponsible bohemians. We were denounced as "cultural bolshevists," "pornographic scribblers," "naughty kids," "traitors to the Fatherland," and "enemies of the proletarian cause." We stuck together, called ourselves "the youngest Germany," and endured the general affronts with a sort of coquettish stoicism.

The pretentious plural, "we," suggests a collective effort that hardly existed in reality. There were just a few of "us"—a handful of striving talents, derelict and muddled. What we had in common were certain tastes and animosities rather than stern convictions. All of us were addicted to the same sort of sensual curiosity and haunted by the same doubts and uncertainties. The restlessness, the great inquietude, was the program.

There was no group in the traditional German sense, nor was there a movement according to the French pattern. The informal comradeship connecting a group of young writers in Berlin, Munich, Zurich, Vienna, and some other places, was rather like the natural solidarity among such young English poets as W. H. Auden, Christopher Isherwood, Stephen Spender, Louis MacNeice.

Playful and open-minded, we floated between the classes and nations, even between the literary camps and tendencies. The obstreperous interlude of Expressionism had obviously reached its end: the new formula of revived Naturalism ("neue Sachlichkeit") was only in preparation. The prevailing mood was that of the "creative pause," to employ a popular slogan coined by a second-rate German philosopher. Everything fluctuated and faltered. Nothing seemed definite or impossible. We looked around, we played, we wondered, we waited. . . . "You are like bewitched princes," a witty critic once said to me. "Expressionism was your palace and home, which you have abandoned. Now you stand lingering at the crossroads uncertain where to go."

There were so many directions, so many promises, so many dangers. We could not make up our minds. We toyed with the most divergent formulas: we tried to reconcile and to fuse the most contradictory experiences. Our attitude was molded by an abundance of incongruous devices. We tried to be urbane and seditious, sacerdotal and flippant, progressive and romantic. We were mystic and cynical. We wanted everybody to be happy but were appallingly lacking in social consciousness. We pretended to be "good Europeans" but neglected or ignored the fundamental problems of our own country. Our light-minded chorus accompanied the gradual disintegration of the continent. We enjoyed the colorful scenery about us and failed to notice that, in reality, our devout dance was taking place in the midst of a social and moral vacuum.

We were exceedingly busy and ingenious, but all our activities were somehow inconsequential. We launched magazines, edited anthologies, dedicated books to each other, had our plays produced all over Germany, attacked hostile groups, praised our friends, and shocked the Philistines.

All of us were extremely fond of lecturing. We delivered lectures in literary salons, book stores, theaters, and concert halls. I traveled about, lecturing in Prague and Vienna, Zurich, Dresden, Hamburg, Breslau, Berlin, Frankfort, and Magdeburg. I lectured alone or with Pamela (who sang Frank Wedekind's songs), or with Erika (who recited the verses of our friends), or with my fellow-representatives of the Youngest Germany, who recited their own stuff. I read an extensive paper, expressly composed for such purposes: it was called "Today and Tomorrow" and neatly summarized my views with regard to life and literature, Europe, God, the nuisance of bourgeois morality, the limitations of Marxism, the mystery of sex, and the intricate adventure of being a young European intellectual.

Problems of a similar kind were the dramatic gist of my second play, "Four in Revue." The premiere took place at Leipzig, co-starring Gründgens and Erika, Pamela and myself: two happy young couples, so to speak. For Pamela and I were still engaged to marry, whereas Erika had meanwhile become Frau Gründgens. Followed by the curses of Saxonian critics, we embarked on a nation-wide tour which a dauntless agent had arranged for us. We were booed at by the Berliners, abused in Munich, applauded in Hamburg, and discussed as interesting freaks in Copenhagen, where we appeared under the sponsorship of the leading newspaper, "Politiken." Sometimes our performances were a struggle with the audience, rather than a civilized entertainment. We sneered at the critics, quarreled with our agent, roared over our fan mail, and ruined our reputations.

The newspapers went to town over our obstreperous publicity and completely forgot that the whole ballyhoo owed its existence to them. True, I was too vain and immature to reject the offering of a shoddy halo which I confounded with fame. But I would have been sensible and modest enough not to run after this frothy kind of popularity, if it had not been imposed on me by the same scribblers who later taunted me on account of my complaisance.

The main reason for both the flattering and insulting noise was, of course, my father's steadily growing success. In the time I am speaking of, he was more in the public eye than ever. If "Buddenbrooks," that epic swan song of German romanticism needed a long time to be recognized by the masses, "The Magic Mountain" was promptly hailed as the first German novel of great European dimensions.

It is against this background of solid glory that one should conceive the tawdry glamor surrounding my own start. The truth is that, at the age of twenty, I was unduly well known and unduly disparaged. Incessantly flattered and teased, I amused and revenged myself by behaving the way I was apparently expected to.

What I failed to realize was the amount of embarrassment my eccentricities caused my father. For, almost needless to say, his name was somehow drawn into most of the satiric write-ups with which the German press used to honor me so lavishly. I remember a cartoon in the "Simplicissimus" showing me postured behind my father's chair. He looks at me askance, full of grief and suspicion, while I observe, according to the caption: "I am told, father, that the son of a genius cannot be a genius himself. Therefore, you are no genius."

The poet Berthold Brecht began a sparkling article with these words: "The whole world knows Klaus Mann, the son of Thomas Mann. By the way, who is Thomas Mann?" Anecdotes about our family life were made up by some witty half-wit and circulated by dozens of papers. In exceptional cases they happened to be true. For instance, the dedication my father wrote in a copy of "The Magic Mountain" that I found among my Christmas gifts: "To my respected colleague—his promising father." I was careless enough to show this pleasantry to a friend who, on his part, repeated it to a journalist. Subsequently it was quoted in all gazettes between Bremen and Budapest.

It wasn't really as funny as all that, but somehow characteristic of my father's attitude towards me at the time. It was an attitude of observant irony, half-amused, half-skeptical; indulgent, understanding, and moderately curious as to what was going to happen next. I am sure his confidence in the fundamental soundness of my character has always been firm enough to prevent him from being seriously perturbed with regard to my future. But he probably was more irritated, at times, than he wanted to show or I liked to notice. No matter how provocative our follies became, he stuck to his tested principle of letting us do as we pleased, watching our risky games with sympathetic detachment and admonishing us, from time to time, with a frown, a sorrowful smile, an apprehensive silence. He never seemed to remember exactly with whom I lived, which book I was working on, or where I had been spending the time since he had seen me last.

"Where do you come from, just now?" he would ask me, at the dinner table, with a sort of cordial vagueness. Then my mother would interfere, very much accustomed to act as mediator between him and a world whose extraneous details constantly evaded his mind.

"Why, Tommy, you know very well that Klaus has just come from Darmstadt, where his play has been received very nicely, indeed."—Or, "But, darling, didn't I tell you only yesterday that Klaus has had a very interesting time in Paris with his friend Crevel? But you know Crevel —the nice one, with the bushy hair and beautiful eyes. Of course, you know him quite well: we met him at this ghastly party at your publisher's house, when we were in Paris, last spring. He talked so rapidly; you couldn't understand him at all. . . ." And then my father would say something about René which proved that he knew much more about him than I had expected.

We sometimes suspected him of having more insight into our affairs than he usually showed. On other occasions his aloofness bewildered us. But just when we began to wonder if he cared at all, he surprised and touched us with a casual gesture. It may have happened that he completely ignored a nasty criticism about me published in a magazine which I knew he was in the habit of reading. He discussed the weather, while inside I was raving with tempests. But after dinner—just when my mother said, "Well, I suppose that's all, children!"—he would shake his head with a sort of half-bantering grief, and sigh: "Yes, yes, the world is full of malignant stupidity—we ought to get used to it. Every morning we have to swallow one venomous toad at least. I think it was Flaubert in whose diary I found this revealing remark . . ."

The constant coming and going in our house seemed to amuse rather than to disturb him. Besides, he performed quite a bit of coming and going himself. Good-natured and conscientious, not without a certain ironic solemnity he accepted the social implication of fame: the lectures, literary meetings, banquets, and conferences. Nobody was astonished when he withdrew after luncheon, with a nonchalant wave of his hand: "Good-bye, then, children. See you early next week. Didn't Mielein tell you? That Goethe festival in Frankfort . . . Quite a nuisance, indeed; but it has to be. I better hurry; the afternoon train leaves at three . . ."

Nor did he lose his poise when my mother exclaimed: "Oh dear me! I've completely forgotten to tell the chauffeur that Erika arrives at nine-forty. Or was it at ten o'clock? I must find the wire she sent me! She said something about a friend she may bring along, too—if I am not mistaken." Then he would raise his eyebrows, politely surprised and pleased: "Is that so? Erika comes tonight . . ." And he added reflectively: "It's pretty long since I last saw her."

Everybody brought his friends along: sometimes our house looked very much like an informal country hotel or the headquarters of some playful conspiracy, bustling with intrigues and arguments, long-distance calls, flirtations and quarrels, people reciting poetry or perusing the timetable of the trans-European express trains or just talking to each other in that rapid gibberish that most of our friends picked up from the Mann family. In the midst of this general turmoil, my mother was the only person thoroughly initiated into the various worries, tastes, and schedules of her children and her children's friends. She seemed to forget or to mix up the simplest matters but actually remembered and organized the most involved affairs. With a fervent concern for my father's well-being always dominating her mind, she managed helpfully to take part in all our troubles and in the troubles of those we cared for. She knew when Gustaf had passed through another crisis, and was familiar with the inward struggles of my brother Golo, who attended a country school, and with the progress of Michael's violin study, and with Ricki's distress because of that lovable but agonizing girl he happened to be so frantically fond of, and with the trying problems involved in W. E. Süskind's new novel.

Of course, there were periods of high tides and low tides in the gregarious life of the house. It may have happened—not very frequently, though!—that all of us were away, entangled in work and adventure in some distant part of the country or the continent. Then the house must have been comparatively still, with my father observing his schedule, as unchangeable as the meticulous rites of a strategic movement or a religious service. It always seemed strange to me and quite touching, the idea of the Munich house in its state of placid tranquillity. I liked to imagine my father coming home from his walk, entering the drawing room (but not before he had exchanged his dirty shoes for a pair of slippers!) and kissing my mother's hand with half-humorous gallantry: "How have you been, my heart? Have you driven the very old ones to the theater?" The "very old ones" were my grandparents. It was one of my mother's innumerable duties and privileges to drive them about in the car and to provide them with entertainment. So both the Magician and Mielein chuckle a little, and then they have their supper. I wondered what they may have been talking about—whether they discussed things that had occurred long ago, or rather the things to come: our things. I wondered whether it was we they discussed, with a sort of serene apprehension, in that touching tête-a-tête of theirs.

In such moments of faint and pleasant nostalgia I liked to remember a scene insignificant in itself but strangely moving, and which I could never forget.

I visualize myself coming down the stairs from the entrance of our house and crossing the garden while Hans, the chauffeur, and the open car stand waiting for me outside, in the Föhringer Allee. It is one of my many departures: I don't know where I am leaving for: I am just leaving for some unknown destination, and I carry a bag and an overcoat and some books. Just when Hans, with a polite little bow, opens the door of our Buick, my father appears at the window of his room, in the second floor of the house. It must be four o'clock in the afternoon, the hour of siesta. He wears his dark dressing gown and starts to let down the blinds of the window. But he interrupts himself and falters as he notices the car, my luggage and myself, down in the alley. How distinctly I recall the picture! My father, standing up there, framed by the square of the window, beckoning at me with a tired and serious smile.

"Good luck, my son!" he says, and adds with a sort of solemn jocularity: "And come home when you are wretched and forlorn!"

CHAPTER SIX

"Rien que la Terre"

(1927–1928)

I<small>T</small> WAS all the fault of Horace Liveright, really.

He had ventured on the American edition of my story, "Kinder-novelle" (The Fifth Child, 1927), and, for one reason or another, thought it a good idea to ask the young author to the United States for a few lectures. The letter I received from Boni & Liveright, Publishers, New York, was couched in a cordial but noncommittal fashion, just an inquiry as to whether or not I would be inclined to consider a journey to the U. S., some time next year, perhaps.

I had never thought of crossing the Atlantic, nor did the note from the publishing house sound definite and urgent enough to change my mind in this matter. It reached me when I was traveling about with our theatrical group: which explains my failure to acknowledge its receipt. It was only several months later that I remembered the invitation.

It was a sultry night, in the middle of August. Erika and I walked together along the picturesque shores of the Lake Starnberg. We were then living with some friends in a modest hotel in the country. Every night, Erika drove out there, as soon as she was through with her performance at the State Theater in Munich.

For years it had been her dream to play Queen Elizabeth in Schiller's drama "Don Carlos"—the childlike princess from France who becomes Philip's wife, the stepmother of Prince Carlos and the object of his unfortunate passion. At last the beloved part had been given to her under the most promising circumstances. The show was presented as part of a dramatic festival by which the City of Munich hoped to attract the tourists. Erika was co-starred with none other than Albert Bassermann—widely recognized as Germany's most eminent actor. She did a beautiful job—not only in "Don Carlos" but also in other plays.

Wasn't she very happy? She should have been proud and pleased and at the same time eager for more work, new roles, new opportunities. Surprisingly enough, she seemed restless and worried.

"I don't know what's wrong with me," she complained. "Everything works out nicely, and still I feel low." There was a short stillness before she added: "The Lake Starnberg is fine. Munich is fine, and the State Theater. But I'd rather be somewhere else. Ten thousand miles from here."

"Not a bad idea," I said. "There are plenty of things to run away from."

I thought of my nasty critics and my capricious fiancee, Pamela. Just some days ago she had informed me, bluntly and emphatically, that she was in love with Carl Sternheim, the aging playwright and satirist. It seemed that she even toyed with the idea of marrying him. What a baroque thing to do! Sternheim was famed, not only for his sparkling comedies and highly original style, but also for his flippant aggressiveness and quarrelsome arrogance.

"Maybe Ricki wasn't so wrong, after all," I observed, musingly. Ricki had abandoned Europe, his family and his accustomed life—all of a sudden and without any apparent reason. With dogged obstinacy he spurned all financial support from his wealthy people—out of sheer defiance and, perhaps, in order to punish and impress his cruel lady friend. In Mexico he worked as a truck driver; now he was washing dishes in New York. The letters he wrote from there had an odd undertone of bewilderment, indeed, of fear, echoing, as it were, the fierce grandeur of that distant city.

Apropos New York—wasn't there a certain gentleman who had recently expressed his desire to welcome me on the Hudson River? Why shouldn't I go, after all? Or rather, why shouldn't we? For there could be no doubt that we would go together, if at all.

So we composed a cable to the unsuspecting Mr. Liveright: "Enchanted by your friendly invitation which reached me only today stop ready to leave in four weeks with well-known actress Erika Mann who happens to be my sister stop intend to spend winter in U. S. . . ."

Horace flashed promptly back: "Infinitely sorry you didn't make up your mind sooner stop season now overcrowded postpone journey to next year . . ."

But we had already startled all our friends with the news of our imminent trip. It would have been much too awkward now to withdraw the story. The only thing to do was to send a second cable, even more cheerful than the preceding one: "So happy . . . intend to arrive New York about the first of October . . ."

The Boni & Liveright staff must have been flabbergasted. However, they got in touch with a lecture agent on our behalf. Surprisingly enough, the foolhardy impresario seemed interested: a third message informed us that a lecture agent committed himself to arranging our tour and guaranteed a minimum of $1500. It sounded fabulous. Erika bought herself a fur cape, a bumptious gesture of which I entirely disapproved. "Besides," I said, "you won't keep it long. It will be stolen from you, naturally it will. Probably even before we arrive in New York. Fur coats are precisely the kind of stuff international gangsters are crazy about."

We hunted advance payments from newspaper editors and letters of introduction from our friends. It turned out that practically everybody had a few cousins somewhere in the United States. Transatlantic cronies sprang up like mushrooms: some of them had seemingly made a point of coming to meet us right at home. Our friend Christa Hatvany (who later became known under her maiden name, Christa von Winslë, as the author of "Girls in Uniform") presented us to her American friend Dorothy Thompson, a brilliant young newspaper woman. Dorothy said it was a swell idea for two youngsters like ourselves to find out what things look like on the other side. "You'll have a marvelous time," she predicted.

"You'll have a hell of a time," was the prophecy of another American —a red-haired chap by the name of Sinclair Lewis. We met him through his publisher, Ernest Rowolth, famed for his fine record in eating whiskey glasses, while his American author, Mr. Lewis, was rather in the habit of emptying them. He admonished us not to go to the United States, because of prohibition. "Why should you exile your self, voluntarily, into that dry inferno?" he grumbled. But we insisted on going, in spite of his spoken and written warnings.

The books by Sinclair Lewis were about all we knew of contemporary American literature: "Main Street" and "Babbitt," along with some of Upton Sinclair's novels, had influenced our vision of life and people in the United States. But neither the sturdy criticism of Sinclair Lewis nor the elaborate indictments of Upton Sinclair were powerful enough to blot out completely the first decisive impressions we owed to the American genius: the puerile vigor of the Leatherstocking, the feverish acuteness of Edgar Allan Poe's delirium, Mark Twain's tonic wit, and the rhapsodic tenderness of the "Leaves of Grass."

We were eager to see the land of the open spaces and towering cities, Walt Whitman's "athletic democracy," the land of Lincoln and Sacco and Vanzetti, the land of stunning mixtures and contradictions: the vast country from which publishers sent friendly cables and Chaplin bewitched the world, and handsome pilots embarked, with nonchalant heroism, to their lonesome flights across the ocean. We wanted to see the Main Streets and the prairies and the skyscrapers, and how prohibition worked, and if Negroes were really lynched. The Mississippi River attracted us, and the tawdry glory of the movie stars, and the staggering tales about organized crime in Chicago. Broadway and the Golden Gate attracted us, and the Henry Ford plant and the Capitol. We wanted to see America.

Was this journey just another hoax, a risky attempt to bamboozle the grown-ups, on a large scale this time? No doubt elements of this kind were involved in our reckless adventure. From the very beginning of our trip we could not help feeling that we duped the respectable folks, once again, by presenting ourselves as a couple of serious lecturers—without even speaking English . . . Yet this tinge of jest and masquerade does not completely explain our erratic obsession. To my retrospective view, the merry escapade of 1927 appears as a light-minded prelude to graver experiences we were destined to pass through. A dress rehearsal of exile—that's what it actually was.

The rehearsals are sometimes more thrilling than the performance proper. That is to say, in rehearsing the show the actors may anticipate all the fun and excitement, yet without suffering from the painful suspense of the opening night or the bleak monotony of the repetitions. It can be fairly amusing to play the uprooted vagabond, as long as you do have a home to return to. Tourists are welcome everywhere—particularly if they happen to be twenty years old and not quite devoid of wit.

How hospitable we found the world when we were a couple of vagrant youngsters! Everybody treated us with the most gratifying kindness. Our own naïveté and that benevolent fairy called Prosperity protected us from all evil. Somewhat later, in 1929, our American friends might have received us with sour faces and sealed pocketbooks. But in September, 1927, Wall Street and culture still flourished: the Statue of Liberty beamed with joviality as her imposing figure loomed in the silvery mist, and there it was—the sky-line of Manhattan: much-vaunted, oft-described, and yet stunning—a hazy mirage, titanic and elegant.

This was the city I was going to like best among all cities, except Paris. I knew it right away, when we rode from the harbor to the Astor Hotel. There was the electrifying contact which announces, or already is, love—the startling delight at the first glimpse. "Aren't they wonderful!" I exclaimed, in view of the skyscrapers. "I didn't imagine them that beautiful!" I must have sounded quite awe-struck, as if I were speaking of Gothic cathedrals or Egyptian pyramids. Everybody laughed—Ricki who had come to meet us at the pier, and a highly polished emissary of Princeton University, and Mr. Donald Friede, who presented himself as the partner of Horace Liveright and was just as urbane and dapper as he could be, his pleasant face adorned by the most attractive little moustache I have ever seen in my life.

And then, at the Astor, the journalists roared with laughter when we told them that Sinclair Lewis had warned us against the trip because of prohibition, but that we liked it here nevertheless, and were eager to meet American poets and to see Brooklyn Bridge and the Metropolitan Opera, and that we were twins, Erika and I. The twin gag was a rash improvisation: we had made it up in front of the Statue of Liberty, without considering the consequences. "The Literary Mann Twins!"—it was under this heading that our portraits appeared in the afternoon papers. Everybody seemed touched and tickled by this cute and surprising detail: that we were twin-born, notwithstanding the great difference in appearance. In the long run, it became cumbersome. We were labeled as a couple of facetious freaks, an adventurous double-being.

We must have been utterly funny. The journalists guffawed, the headwaiter smirked, the elevator boy grinned, the room maid giggled, Donald Friede smiled, and Ricki laughed and cried: "It's good you're here, you foolish globe-trotters. I've been kind of lonely . . ."

And then we plunged into the exploration of that vast labyrinth and vociferous mystery—New York City.

We roved from Harlem to Wall Street; from Chinatown to the German district; from Central Park to Brooklyn; from the Bronx to the Village. We were spellbound by the rhythm and blast of this new splendor, by the unprecedented pattern of beauty which is the streamlined Gothic of New York City. We enjoyed taking our meals in the midst of the breath-taking noise that fills a Broadway cafeteria, or in the luxurious peacefulness of a palace hotel. We were crazy about the large, tasty oysters, so popular in this country but a symbol of extravagant feasting in Germany. We liked grapefruit hardly known back home, at the time; and we heartily approved of the American way of serving oysters and grapefruit and everything nicely chilled, lavishly garnished with ice. The abundance of ice cubes, iced water, iced fruits, iced fruit salads, and so forth, struck us as one of the most obvious advantages of the American culinary style compared with the European.

We got a kick out of riding in the subway—aimlessly: just for the fun of it. It was so much more rapid, we thought, and better organized, too, than the U-Bahn of Berlin. The great views from the tall buildings were thrilling, and so were Coney Island and the Battery and the Burlesque shows and the many exotic restaurants, Russian and American and Syrian and Italian. We had a grand time watching the Negroes dancing, and sauntering through the Metropolitan Museum or the modern art galleries on Fifty-Seventh Street. It was fun to be present at a glamorous evening in the Metropolitan Opera, although we thought Madame Jeritza pretty poor as Carmen. And it wasn't bad to sit about, for an evening, in those smoky Greenwich Village dives that reminded us so cozily of Schwabing and Montparnasse. We were incredibly fond of meeting people—as many of them as possible. (I may add, in parenthesis, that it has long become hard for me to understand that insatiable appetite for new faces, new contacts, new flirtations, discussions, quarrels, and reconciliations. Among all follies of youth this gregarious mania now strikes me as the most incomprehensible one. The day inevitably comes when you realize that a lot of acquaintances are unlikely to offer you anything but still more bitterness and disappointment. As long as you are eighteen or twenty-two, however, you jump at every contact as if it were the big affair of your life.)

Gradually we became familiar with some aspects of New York life. The respectable people asked us to dinner parties, while the Villagers introduced us into the curious underworld of the speakeasies. Then there was a third group—the most attractive one—who gathered for improvised meals in our Astor rooms—colorful chaps, shabby but full of punch: Ricki's pals and colleagues.

He worked then as an errand boy in a flower store. The salary was poor, so terribly poor, in fact, that he often saved the nickel he was supposed to spend for his car-fare, because he was hungry and wanted a sandwich more than anything else. It had happened, before we came to New York, that he begged in the streets for a few cents or a cigarette or had to spend a night on a bench, in Central Park or on Times Square. True, in his particular case such hardships were the result of desperate romanticism, rather than of inescapable circumstances. However, they were actual and painful enough; besides there were many among his friends who had to bear the same sort of life, by no means out of any masochistic whim. We met quite a few of them—all types of eager, derelict youth, native or foreign born; Italian, Jewish, Russian, Irish, or German: but all subjected to the same callous system that allowed any one to become President of the United States or to starve to death.

We sought and relished, though not without apprehension, the gross contrasts of life. There was something exciting and frightful about spending the afternoon with a bunch of penniless tramps—and then to rush home, to the Astor, and change clothes for an opulent dinner party, say, at the palace of Otto H. Kahn.

It was Kommer—Rudolf K. Kommer, the amiable mystery man

from Czernovitz (Rumania)—who had introduced us to the modern
Lorenzo de Medici (with silvery mustache and downtown office). We
were considerably impressed, not so much by his patronizing chat as
by the stunning display of Rembrandts and Mantegnas in his princely
mansion. The millionaire, pleased by our awe, was all polite serenity
and condescending blandness. However, we never felt really at ease in
his company. He had just too much money: the thought of it was
faintly irritating. There are people who cannot help making insipid
cracks about physical deformities in the presence of hunchbacks or
midgets. Thus we were constantly tempted to discuss, at the table of
Otto H., the disquieting, indeed, untenable phenomenon of enormous
wealth.

It was in Greenwich Village we felt most at home. Horace Liveright
was an initiated and zealous guide—at times somewhat stagy perhaps
but good company, even when indulging in his innocuous mannerisms.
He loved parties and took us to many of them, but, it seemed, always
the same. There always was a plenitude of attractive girls, and all of
them seemed rather fond of gin, and there were Swedish hors d'oeuvres,
nicely arranged on a desk or the top of a gramophone. The whole
set-up was informal and gay and ever so bohemian. After supper a few
couples would dance—there wasn't much room but that made it still
more amusing—while others had a look at slightly lascivious pictures:
no coarse stuff, to be sure, just artistic extravaganzas, with a certain
flavor . . .

We chat with Joseph Brewer, chief of the Brewer & Warren publishing firm. While treating each other to anecdotes about funny people in
Paris, Louis Galantière, American-French man of letters, entertains
the party with Gallic songs—sprawling on a couch, with one arm resting on the shoulder of a tipsy belle and his other hand pulling the
strings of a guitar. Ernest Boyd, meanwhile—exceedingly red-bearded
and intelligent—has a heated argument in several languages at once.
What we are able to catch is just rugged fragments of the violent
conversation: ". . . lousy amateurs . . . no style . . . don't know how to
write . . . to hell with Joyce . . . tries to copy Picasso. . . . Hemingway
should be ashamed of himself . . . who is Gertrude Stein, after all? . . .
lot of bunk. . . . Joyce, after all, is a genius . . . to hell with Picasso.

. . . Gertrude Stein—merde alors. . . .. Mencken ought to know better.
. . . Henry James? "Polizei!" . . . Nathan's "Katzenjammer" . . . Ezra
Pound? Quelle blague! . . . To hell with Yeats . . . a genius . . . I may
talk it over with Knopf . . ."

Who is the other fellow? Waldo Frank, perhaps? People tell us he
has a lot of talent. Ought to read his stuff. But this one isn't Frank.
Not at all. A new face. Ought to read his stuff. A terrific talent, most
probably. Or is he a publisher? Or a painter? Looks like a musician,
though. Or is he just the husband of that handsome dame who now
joins the group? But who, then, is the dame? Is it Anita Loos? Nonsense. She is in Vienna. Everybody seems exceedingly sorry that she
is in Vienna. We are sorry, too. For we did read her stuff. It must be
Eva Herrmann since it isn't Anita Loos. Of course it is Eva Herrmann, the girl who looks so bland and innocent—all fragility and
sweetness—and yet makes cartoons which are amazingly malicious.
We ought to look at those things she does. But not now. Please, not
at this moment! To tell the truth, we are a little dizzy. There must
have been something wrong with that gin—with the sweetish one we
drank out of tea cups, in that damned speakeasy. Maybe there was
nothing wrong with it: we had just too much . . .

"I still refuse to believe that Vanity Fair is controlled by Babbitts . . .
Dadaism . . . lot of hot air . . . poor old Virginia Woolf . . . if only
Mencken could make up his mind!" . . .

H. L. Mencken's name went as a leitmotiv through all literary conversations among Villagers. He already was a legend: his fame reverberated in Europe and from there back to his homeland.

We found him buoyant, nervously brisk, and a great talker. The
hours we spent with him, in his apartment at the Algonquin Hotel,
were most pleasant and stimulating. He was keenly interested in all
aspects and developments of German culture, his old hobby and spiritual predilection which, at that time, did not have as yet the somewhat
ominous connotation it assumes in 1942. He was brilliant in an informal way, vigorous, gay, and witty. We loved it when he burst into a
terrific thunderstorm of abusive words at the mention of prohibition.
What hair-raising nonsense! he bullied, while we feasted together on

mutton chops and exquisite red wine. What an outrageous thing—this so-called prohibition! The thought of it made him lose his temper. We admitted that it probably was pretty awkward—a tiresome kind of law, we agreed, full of sympathy. But he insisted that it was a crime and the absolute peak of idiocy. "Schweinerei!" he grumbled. "Quatsch! A filthy racket—that's what it boils down to. A racket—backed by hypocrites and half-wits." Then he added, a little more cheerfully, that, as far as he was informed, there was no American citizen—mind! not a single one!—who would never touch any liquor because of the prohibitive laws. "I know hundreds of Americans more or less intimately," he said. "Perhaps thousands; but six or seven hundred at least—conservatively counted. All of them drink liquor—including the President, and my mother, and those virtuous spinsters . . . to hell with all of them. I beg your pardon, Miss Mann. Well, let's open another bottle. Prost."

We had a penchant for curiosities with a macabre tinge. Dracula was tops. No theater in Europe, not even the Grand Guignol, offered such a profusion of first rate horror devices. We were spellbound by the weird physician who was supposed to cure poor, sweet Lucy from her anemia, but who in reality . . . He cut an uncanny figure as he bent down to the invalid, piercing her with his look. "And how is the patient now?" inquired the doctor, with a wry smile and an ominously exotic accent. Whereupon he answered himself, with dire satisfaction: "Our poor Miss Lucy seems very tired today." Naturally she was. The most sanguine person would lose weight and pep under the circumstances. The only thing to be surprised about was that poor Miss Lucy still lived, after what she had gone through. Imagine your own interne fluttering into your room, about midnight!—all dressed up, greatly animated; accompanied by a swarm of bats; producing hideous noises with his wings and claws and giggling in anticipation of a good drink of blood—your blood, if you please!

The audience shrieked with horror. We loved it. In fact, Count Dracula was admitted to the exclusive circle of our intimate legends —a sort of belated myth of our childhood. From now on, we would mumble, when separating at night: "My poor Miss Lucy looks very tired today." And when we saw each other again, the next morning, we wouldn't say good morning, but, in an eerie whisper, "And how is the patient now?"

Dracula was not to be equalled: even Eva Le Gallienne as Hilde Wangel, in Ibsen's "The Masterbuilder," fell short of his lurid charm. The most striking dramatic impression came from a Negro production of "Porgy," at the Theater Guild. It was the first show of colored actors I saw, and I thought them more accomplished and fascinating than the white Broadway stars.

The Negroes, I felt, possessed what the American stage was still lacking: a spontaneous and yet consciously developed artistic style. The Broadway theater, at the time, seemed still unaware of any post-naturalistic developments. There was less phony pretension and dislocation than in the European drama of the expressionistic period; but there also was less vision and a less passionate effort. The theater in this country seemed—even more obviously so than the theater in London or Paris—exclusively devoted to the entertainment of the audiences, in contrast to the higher aims of the German stage. The Negroes, however—and the Negroes alone!—surpassed the pattern of this drab routine and, thanks to their inherent artistic intuition, communicated a new rhythmic experience, a new histrionic style, a new melody.

We had plenty of time to explore the city with all the stimulating and puzzling aspects of its colossal, manifold life; for our own affairs stagnated and seemed to be quite in a deadlock. Our manager tried very hard to arrange a lecture tour for us, but somehow he did not succeed. We found his air increasingly perturbed and sorrowful when we dropped in at his office. "Our poor Miss Lucy!" we whispered to each other, full of sympathy. "She looks utterly tired again." The agent, of course, suspected that we had lost our minds, which made him feel even worse. He wiped the perspiration from his forehead, whereupon we asked, in Dracula's sonorous and sinister voice: "And how is the patient now?" It must have sounded very murderous. He shuddered.

Finally he got fed up with this nerve-wracking game and declared bluntly that, unfortunately, he did not have the right sort of contacts for our purposes. "If only your English were a little better!" he sighed. We must have pierced him with our at once pathetic and frightening looks; for he hastily added: "I realize, of course, that we have a contract and that you could sue me if I tried to violate it without cogent reason."

We mumbled something to the effect that, after all, among civilized people, one ought to come to some kind of a compromise.

He nodded. "Exactly," he said. "Among civilized people. A compromise, of course. I was on the point of suggesting it. What do you think of a thousand bucks?"

He wrote a check—melancholy but dignified and composed. His smile was plaintive but not without paternal sympathy as we shook hands with him. "When are you going to return to Europe?" he asked.

To Europe? We were half-amused, half-disgusted.

"Europe can wait!" we announced cheerfully. "We're off for California."

He was flabbergasted. He almost collapsed when we added: "And from there, we'll fix our own little lecture tour. For we do have the right contacts."

The trip was long, the country—huge and empty and bewildering. It was much bigger than we had anticipated. We had known its size; but no figure gives you an adequate notion of the overpowering reality. "Gee, how big it is!"—that was all we felt.

However, even this journey eventually reached its end—after four days and nights which seemed like four years to us. The scenery suddenly changed as if by magic: lush gardens and orange groves, in place of the barren plains. The promised land—there it was, glistening in the sun with its profusion of fruits and flowers, cypress and palm trees, picturesque paths and peaceful looking homes, a landscape blessed by the Lord.

The disappointment began in Los Angeles. How shapeless it was! How devoid of character! compared with the clear and vigorous beauty of New York. Los Angeles is no city, but a gigantic conglomeration of buildings and vehicles. It grows and spreads out like an exuberant creeper. It makes noise, is gluttonous and dynamic. But it is strangely lacking in substance and form, in life.

We were immediately struck by this obstreperous emptiness. Rather depressed and bewildered, we hired a yellow cab to Hollywood. The trip was long and did not make us feel better.

The curious thing about Hollywood is that it seems to be a provincial town which makes frantic efforts to imitate Hollywood. Everything is so amazingly Hollywood-like, so unreal and thoroughly arty. The palm trees which we had admired from the windows of the Pullman car; the magnificent apples and peaches; the window-displays, hotels, and movie theaters where "the stars see their own films": indeed, even the sunsets with their immoderate display of colors—the whole place with all its brilliancy seems to clamor: Don't I look precisely like Hollywood? Hollywood, the wish-dream of all pretty girls and ambitious men! The center of glamor! The legendary city! Visit the homes of our beloved stars in Beverly Hills! Our guide takes only $5 for pointing out to you the cozy mansion of Miss Lillian Gish . . .

The first cozy mansion to which our good fortune led us was that of Emil Jannings, the eminent actor, then at the zenith of his international fame. Nobody would have dared to foretell, at that time, that his mighty popularity was to wane so badly and abruptly—even before the gifted mime destroyed his reputation by running after the putrid laurels of the Third Reich. The silent film was the only adequate medium of expression for this actor, whose big and changeable face is so much more expressive than his voice, which sounds disappointingly feeble.

He received us in the most cordial fashion, a colossus of a man; fat and buoyant, beaming with success. He made $1000 a day and said he was homesick for Berlin. He had a sumptuous house; a butler who was so dignified that he could only whisper; a lion-headed chow dog with a blue-black tongue and nasty little eyes; a parrot who nonplussed the visitors by yelling obscenities; a good-natured daughter and an amusing wife. As Gussy Holl she had been a well-known actress herself, and one of the most refined and saucy "chansonettes" Germany ever produced. Her first husband was Conrad Veidt, who then was in Hollywood too, under contract with Universal. We saw him almost every day at the Jannings' and he took us out to "the lot" to admire his grisly make-up in "The Laughing Man." Veidt was as handsome and nonchalant and unassumingly intelligent in those faraway days as he is now. He looks as supple and demoniac as a tiger with sex-appeal, but really is a jolly, good-hearted chap—whereas Emil Jannings has the reassuring appearance of a big, loyal dog but is, indeed, callous and astute.

We had imagined life in Hollywood to be colorfully international—informal, mixed, and utterly amusing. What a naïve mistake! The truth is that the social ceremonial among movie people is of Chinese strictness and intricacy. The castes are rigidly divided according to the double discrimination of income and nationality. A social center like the Jannings home—which, at that time, was the "official" meeting place of the German colony—was more exclusive, indeed, than any aristocratic salon in Europe. To be admitted there one had to live up to a lengthy roster of requirements. Nobody was asked unless he could prove a certain minimum of income—$750 a week, or so. (We were treated in this respect as humorous exceptions—funny to have around but utterly unimportant.) Other essential conditions were these: Never ask the host any favor! He'll refuse it bluntly and won't see you again. Show your appreciation of heavy food and drinks! Enjoy a risqué joke when the host feels like telling one, but watch your step as to what you can risk yourself! Be sophisticated enough to grasp the subtle wit of Madame Jannings, but not so foolhardy as to vie with her in sophistication! Above all, speak German! None of this American blubber in the Jannings home. It's a German home, if you please!

Sometimes our little parties were joined by a remarkable young woman—deep-voiced, lion-maned, carelessly dressed, and astoundingly beautiful. She appeared after dinner, without any notice or formality, striding through the fragrant darkness of the garden, over the terrace, straight into the drawing room: a breath-taking apparition, saturnine and nonchalant; bare-headed, almost sloppy in a loose raincoat and heelless sandals. "I am so terribly tired," she complained in a ringing voice, and added, the corners of her mouth tragically lowered: "May I have a whiskey?"

She was the most attractive woman I had ever seen in my life: in fact, I have found none more attractive so far. Her face was pallid and sad and spacious—at once marble and sensitive: the face of a depressed goddess, with a defiant mouth and wide, tragic eyes full of golden shadows. She had large, delicate hands and the broad shoulders of an athletic Greek youth. Her voice sounded Pythia-like—savage and sonorous, when she discussed the weather or a book or the role she was working on. It was indescribably moving to see her smile, which occurred but rarely. Her gorgeous and inconsolable face brightened reluctantly. Then the smile lingered around the eyes and the wonderful arch of her lips—reluctant now, on its part, to separate from this lovable landscape. Finally it went out, a transitory flame, and the magnificent brow was again bathed in sorrow. Yet she declared, rather surprisingly, with an abrupt expression of grim merriment, that she was now feeling better. "Thank you," she said solemnly. "I was terribly tired; but now everything is fine. I had a dance and a drink. Thank you ever so much." And she withdrew into the fragrant darkness of the California night from which she had emerged.

Emil informed us that she had recently arrived from Germany but was Swedish by birth. A compatriot of hers, a very gifted director, had brought her to this country. He went back to Europe and died —leaving her alone in Hollywood: quite alone with her prodigious beauty and her future fame. "Sure enough," said Emil, "she'll be a colossal hit."

Her name was Greta Garbo.

Erika wrote letters to various organizations or individuals whom we expected to arrange lectures for us. I wrote articles. Erika refused to write articles: she said that there were plenty of writers in our family, and she wanted to be an actress. But I laughed at her and said, "Poor thing! You'll be a writer all right. Wait and see. It's a curse with us."

There were plenty of things to write about, even outside the realm of the animated shadows and fabulous salaries. I wrote about a big football game in Pasadena, Stanford vs. Pittsburgh, on January 1, 1928: how uproarious and thrilling it was; the colossal crowd, of course, and the whole gaudy set-up: not the game itself, which rather bored and confused me. My report of a prizefight in Los Angeles, Mushy Callahan vs. Jackie Fields, must have been deplorably unprofessional: I was bewildered by the brutality of the whole affair—especially by the bloodthirsty yells of the mob: "Go on, Blondy! Give it to him! . . . Send him home, Jack! Kick him in the pants . . ." In fact, I could not help feeling somewhat depressed in view of such obstreperous sadism.

Even more disconcerting was the performance of Miss Aimee Mc-Pherson at the Angelus Temple, with its fantastic mixture of authentic ecstasy and glaring humbug—the sweeping hysteria, the tremendous hoax. The priestess, I felt, looked like a blend of Mistinguette and an insane pastor. It was fascinating to watch her handle the microphone: she would never forget to shift, with a swift, jaunty motion, so that it could catch her voice when she changed her position. It seems that this kind of cold-blooded showmanship is compatible with a delirium that may be perfectly genuine. I was greatly impressed by Miss McPherson's bold and ingenious tricks. Several years afterwards, in Germany, I had a striking opportunity to remember her stunning show. It was another raving performer—the little man-of-destiny with his cute mustache—whose well-staged mesmerism reminded me so disturbingly of the California priestess. But the doctrines he preached were, alas, more dangerous than hers.

I wrote articles about Upton Sinclair, whom we met through mutual friends in Pasadena, and about a youngster by the name of Hickman, whose sinister case made huge headlines in the California press. As for Upton Sinclair, I was amazed by his youthful appearance—he was the author of forty books!—and impressed by the seriousness of his moral and political views. We found him passionately interested in everything that went on in Europe and remarkably well informed. He is the type of man who wants to amplify his own knowledge, rather than to display the scope of his erudition. That is why he chose European affairs as the subject of his conversation with us continental visitors. We might have learned a great deal if he had discussed American conditions. There were so many puzzles. That case of young Hickman, for instance . . .

I got very excited about this particular story, mainly because of the sensational way in which it was publicized by the press. It was my first introduction to the glaring methods employed by the sensational kind of American newspaper in playing up a big, hot murder story.

Hickman was suspected of having kidnapped and slain a young girl named Marion Parker. It was one of those grisly affairs—nothing extraordinary about it. Even the weird touch of hysteria or virtual insanity involved, was in keeping with the traditional pattern. The blackmail letters which Mr. Parker received when his girl disappeared were full of that boisterous eloquence strangely characteristic of murderers. The terrible correspondent signed his notes "The Fox" and headed them with enigmatic formulas like "Death and Destiny," or "The Poor Angels"—elaborately designed and adorned with flowers or stars. The father kept the rendezvous as suggested by the criminal, delivered the amount of money demanded, and received the maimed body of his murdered child.

A wave of horror, fear, and indignation swept Los Angeles. Innocent folk became the victims of man-hunters who frantically rummaged every spot between Pasadena and Santa Barbara in search of the assassin. One man was lynched in the street and later found hanged in his prison cell. He had nothing to do with the Marion Parker affair, as his family proved—after his death.

The article which I wrote on the Hickman case for a liberal weekly in Berlin was very grim and dramatic. However, I never found out or bothered to investigate, whether the presumptive murderer was actually electrocuted. Maybe I was afraid to learn that he had finally confessed, or that he was killed although he kept denying.

Hollywood does funny things to your sense of time. Is it the equable weather, the monotonous splendor of the California sky? However, you forget that time passes or, at any rate, do not realize how quickly it flies away. Who would think of Christmas in a climate that allows you to have your daily swim in the ocean, no matter whether it's December or July? And yet there it was, Hollywood's gaudy "Xmas" inundating the place with phony snow, red flowers, colorful garlands, and dreary caricatures of Santa Claus carrying huge posters along the uproarious Boulevard. Everybody was exceedingly busy, tossing about with attractive-looking parcels, huge bouquets, and nicely decorated Christmas trees which seemed strangely unreal in the midst of this glaring carnival.

As for ourselves, we were much too broke to buy any gifts or sentimental knickknacks. In fact, we could not even have afforded a Christmas cable to our dear ones in Munich, if Erika had not pawned one of her finest belongings—the fur cape of which I had once so foolishly disapproved. How happy I was now that we possessed so valuable an object! Yet, the amount of money it yielded was just sufficient to meet the most urgent needs. Not one cent was left for the hotel bill which assumed disquieting proportions. The manager—so utterly suave in the beginning—had already paid us a rather embarrassing visit. We tried to convince him with a great display of nervous eloquence that we were, indeed, the most popular and trustworthy creatures on earth. It was out of sheer eccentricity—we intimated—that we delayed that trifle of a payment. "You know how young people are," we said apologetically, as if the reluctant payers were not we ourselves but a couple of capricious millionaires in whose services we had got used to a lot of crazy things. "A silly bet, maybe," we suggested, all desperate merriment. "Or something. . . ." we added vaguely.

But the manager made it very clear that it made no difference, as far as he was concerned, whether it was a sophisticated whim or plain poverty that prevented us from meeting our obligations. We had to pay, or else . . . What a tiresome fellow!—utterly devoid of charm and imagination.

"And how does the patient feel now?" Erika asked, very somberly, as soon as he had left.

"My dear Miss Lucy," I replied, serious but composed, "there is only one thing to do. We have to sit down together and to make a plan."

"To draft some effective cables, I presume?" This idea obviously cheered her up.

"Exactly," I confirmed, and added gravely: "He who fails to send cables will receive no money."

"A fine old saying," Erika dreamily nodded. "But, of course, we'll have to wait until after the holidays."

"Naturally," I said. "Let's hope that nasty manager will be reasonable for a little longer."

"We have to be cautious and cunning," Erika admonished me—looking as hardboiled and astute as she possibly could. "Don't forget that the lobby is a danger zone, from now on!"

How could I forget it? The clerk peered at us most suspiciously when we passed by his throne-like desk. "Say! Mr. Mann!" he shouted. But we were absorbed in animated chat. "Merry Christmas to you!" we waved at him—gracious and absentminded.

Christmas Eve at the Jannings' was a great affair, opulent and hilarious. But we almost spoiled the party—or rather, it was Gilbert Adrian's unrestrained fancy which endangered the harmony of things. For we had begged that notably gifted young artist to improvise something nice and gay—a saucy cartoon or pretty flower piece, as a Christmas present for our attractive hostess. Our friend Adrian, always so sweet and helpful, said, O.K., we could count on him. Late in the afternoon, on December 24, we dropped by at his house on our way to the Jannings', all dressed up, very elated and joyful.

"Here you are, kids," said our friend Adrian, with a broad magnanimous grin; "this is the gift for Gussy."

It was so neatly packed up that we hesitated to open it and rushed away with our mysterious treasure, after having kissed friend Adrian most gratefully. It was in the taxicab, only two minutes from Emil's mansion, that we were overwhelmed by curiosity and decided that, after all, we ought to have a glimpse of the drawing. Hastily we removed the cover, and almost fainted with horror. For what we saw was delightful but indescribably naughty—the most daring caprice, just as cute and shocking as it could be. No doubt, a masterpiece in its way —Beardsley at his best: but impossible for a German mother on Christmas Eve.

That we had to appear empty-handed was bad enough; but even more perturbing was the question of where and how to hide the objectionable item. By no means did we want to throw it away: it was much too pretty. The only thing to do was to leave the scandalous product in the garden discreetly covered by the blooms and bushes.

Everything worked out very nicely. Gussy smiled forgivingly as we stammered our apologies for not having finished our little needlework in time: the slippers, the nightcap, the embroidered napkins—none of the useful surprises was ready . . .

A mood of perfect harmony, a true Christmas spirit, prevailed until Emil had the unfortunate, or rather disastrous idea of taking a little walk in the garden. And what was it he found, hidden behind his favorite rose-bush . . . ?

His question—"To whom belongs this dirt?"—was so intimidating that we blushed and confessed. Presently his face turned wolfish. "So that is the little gift you've been working on," he observed, in an ominously lowered voice. "A delightful surprise. Very tactful, too. A sophisticated joke, I suppose? We are highly amused—aren't we, Auguste?"

His calling her Auguste made the whole scene still more frightening. He never used this name, except on the most dramatic occasions.

"Exceedingly funny," he insisted with scathing sarcasm. "Particularly tasteful as there happens to be a young lady in this house. Ruth Maria, where are you?" he shouted—possessed, as it were, by an abrupt fear that his child might have disappeared, driven away by shame and in-dignation. But there she was—sprawling on the couch, smirkingly absorbed in the sight of Adrian's work.

"What's the matter, dad?" Her voice sounded pleased and drowsy. "It's a lovely picture. Kind of Christmas-like, too. I'll be glad to keep it, if mother thinks it isn't good enough for her."

The whole party guffawed: it was an Homeric laugh. Emil joined in with the most jovial bass. His abruptly adopted pose of jolly tolerance was even more hypocritical than his former wrath. Garbo's chuckle was guttural, like the sonorous cooing of a pigeon. Lya de Putti shrieked with merriment; Connie Veidt brayed, Murnau roared, Lubitsch giggled. The general mirth reached its turbulent climax when Mrs. Jannings snatched the picture from her daughter and declared she wouldn't give it away for the jewels of Mary Pickford.

It was the same evening, if I remember correctly, that I heard Gershwin's "Rhapsody in Blue" for the first time, and was crazy about it. The most thrilling music, I felt, since the early Strauss. I was spell-bound by its sweeping verve, its bold wit and dynamic sweetness. And I tremendously like what the young composer had allegedly said to an interviewer who asked him how he had got the idea of writing this particular piece. "Why, I was twenty-one years old and lived in New York City," Gershwin replied. "What kind of music would you expect me to write?"

And it was the same Christmas Eve of 1927 when our friend Raimund von Hofmannsthal almost killed us in his amazing little vehicle that almost looked like a car. He drove us up the hills: the route was narrow, serpentine, and dangerously steep, and we had quite a few drinks—champagne, and beer, and Scotch. The brakes of the age-old Ford hardly worked; but we didn't mind it. We sang the great tunes of the "Rhapsody," and raved about Greta Garbo, and laughed about Adrian's picture. And Los Angeles lay spread out down below—ablaze with its millions of lights.

Our cables proved effective as a set of magic spells broadcast into the world. Money poured in—enough of it to satisfy the awesome manager of the Hollywood Plaza and to pay for two Pullman reservations from Los Angeles to New York.

We arrived just in time for our first lecture, which was scheduled at Columbia University. It was much less painful than we had anticipated. Erika's introductory speech (she had memorized the English text, and, surprisingly enough, it sounded almost natural!) was followed by my German "causerie" on young European writers. Then Erika concluded the program with her recitals of new German poetry. The whole thing clicked rather nicely. We went to Harvard and Princeton. In both places we were the guests of the respective German departments. We were delighted by American college life: it was more civilized and yet less ceremonious than what we had seen at European universities.

We had a swell time traveling about. Our eagerness to go places and meet people was unabated, although we had already covered quite a bit of ground. It was exciting to see old cronies again, under unexpected circumstances: "You here, in Boston, old man. What a surprise! Last time I saw you was at the Odenwaldschule: it seems ages ago . . ." And sometimes a new face was striking. Curiously, I can hardly recall the features of many a celebrity we then met, but distinctly remember those who were yet anonymous, at the time, but destined to become somebody. That young chap, for instance—the seventeen-year-old son of our host, somewhere near Philadelphia. How could we know he had talent? Because there was an aura around him—a nervous vibration or a floating light, I don't know what it was: but I felt it. The physiognomy of our host, a certain Professor Prokosch, has long faded away in my mind. But when I came across a book by Frederic Prokosch, ten years after our visit with his family, I remembered promptly his boyish face as it was then—irritable and restive, at once brightened and burdened with the promise of future works. I also recollect the dogged attention with which he listened to our tales concerning the progress of our journey.

"So you're going to see Asia?" he asked, breathless with envy and delight. Yes, we said, probably we'd see a piece of it. "Asia . . . ," he repeated.

I went there and he didn't. Yet he saw more of it than I did.

We had long made up our minds that we would go back to California and from there embark for Honolulu and Japan. It was sheer madness on our part to defy the warning letters and imploring cables we received from our parents, publishers, and protectors: "Come back now. It's enough! You'll get yourselves into trouble." But we were stubborn. "Thanks for your excellent advice," we flashed back. "Highly interested in everything you say. Besides, we are off for Japan."

Meanwhile we counted our cash supplies. Just enough to finance the trip from Boston to Milwaukee where "the literary Mann Twins" were scheduled to address a German-American club.

"But, after all," Erika musingly observed, "we must not arrive completely penniless in Milwaukee."

"Why not?" I said. "The taxi driver can pay the Red-Cap, and the doorman of the hotel will be only too pleased to pay the driver."

"That's correct," said Erika, already comforted. "And then, of course, there always remains my fur cape."

In Milwaukee as well as Chicago we saw a great deal of the German-American crowd, which was a curious but not really gratifying experience. We found most of those people strangely out of touch both with American life and all progressive developments in "the old country." With obstinate sentimentality they clung to a Germany that had long ceased to exist: an ideal Fatherland full of cozy Ratskellers, dashing lieutenants, picturesque ruins, tasty sausages, prosperous business, and fair-haired maidens.

In Chicago we stayed several weeks, impressed by the roaring vitality and dynamic ugliness of that city. Everything seemed in the making, growing rapidly, assuming gigantic proportions. Everything was unfinished and exorbitant—planned on a colossal scale; carried out with savage energies. The new hospital with the most modern equipment, the new museum, the enormous spaces of the new Michigan Boulevard—it is all one scheme, one bold and ambitious experiment.

". . . But, after all, we cannot arrive quite penniless in Lawrence, Kansas . . ."

We could. It was a very interesting experience. We spent two days with one of the college fraternities. The young people in Lawrence were exceedingly fond of singing. They sang lengthy hymns before dinner, merry folk-songs between the courses. The "question period" following our lecture was particularly lively. The first speaker, an elderly lady, declared that she didn't really care for literature: her hobby was the harp. Would our European guests be good enough to tell her something about the recent developments of harp music in Europe?—There you've got us, Ma'am . . . And then, of course, people always asked those bewildering questions with regard to our father: "Does your father still write?"—as if writers, like pugilists, were in form only from their sixteenth to their thirtieth year, and then had to retire. Or: "Is your father working on something particular, just now?"—which sounded as if novelists were in the habit of trifling away their time but could pull themselves together, in exceptional cases, and accomplish something "particular" and worthwhile.

We left Lawrence for Tokyo, Japan, equipped with twelve dollars and fifty cents and the blessings of our new friends. The next stop was Wellington, Kansas. There we left the train, partly because our railway ticket didn't take us further; partly because we were avid to see a real, authentic, provincial little town in the Middle West. People had impressed and annoyed us by constantly telling us: "You must never forget—New York is not America. Hollywood is not America. Even Chicago is not the real thing . . ." And Wellington, Kansas? Was this bleak idyll—America?

What curious, nightmarish days we spent at The Antlers Hotel! The citizens of Wellington, peering at us from their rocking-chairs when we crossed the lobby, must have wondered what sort of business we had in their little town. Could they guess that we just dallied with composing cables to Europe and cruising between the railway station and Main Street? We tasted the messy "fancy" drinks at the drugstore bar. We took photos of the church, the bank, the restaurant called Café Hamburg (why?) and also of several farm houses with cows. We even hazarded an excursion to a neighboring village by the name of Oxford where we inspected the oil wells. When some money from home arrived, we continued our journey and arrived safely in Hollywood, after having visited that prodigious anomaly of nature, the Grand Canyon of Arizona.

It must have been an utterly ingenious guardian angel who arranged our appearance at the Friday Morning Club in Pasadena, where we got a $50 fee and met a wonderful lady who presented us with a $1000 bond. She did it casually, at a tea party in her home—with a gentle, oblivious smile. "I have something for you, children," the benefactress mildly observed, just when we were on the point of leaving her musical reception—depressed by our poverty and the elegiac songs recited by an aging opera star. And she handed over to us a mysterious looking document, nicely rolled and laced. Erika was so overwhelmed that she curtsied, which was the least she could do.

We transformed the bond into cash, and the cash into a boat ticket from San Francisco to Honolulu.

Frisco may be dangerous as an entrance to the United States; for all scenery and impressions the continent has in store must fall short of that extraordinary city. But no other place in the United States could be so apt to fill the heart of the departing traveler with the desire to come again. The Golden Gate, alluringly opened towards the mysteries of the Orient, also is the effulgent portal to the Western Hemisphere— the New World. With its double perspective and twofold promise, the harbor of San Francisco at once dismisses and retains the wanderer.

The days on the Pacific were long and lazy and full of dreams. We watched the waves and the flying fishes and the ever-changing tints of the vast horizon. There was plenty of time to think. We thought of America and Europe and ourselves. What did it mean to us—this first contact with the United States?

It meant something strange and overpowering—billow-like, dazingly great. New York was great. The desert, the Grand Canyon, the open spaces of the Middle West, the violent growth of Los Angeles and Chicago; the youth in the colleges, on the highways, in the vociferous stadiums; the mountains of New England, the Mississippi, the splendor of San Francisco, the madness of Hollywood; the boom, the confusion, the athletic strength; the effusive verve of the "Rhapsody in Blue," the rhythm of Negro dances; even the appalling scenes of the stockyards, the slums, and Aimee McPherson's circus—all this was great and wondrous and captivating, and it was a tremendous experience to see it.

But all this was not our world. It was a rich and dynamic world, pregnant with infinite potentialities: but it was not ours. It was a world we studied, admired, and criticized; it scared and enchanted and thrilled us. But we did not feel at home in this world. We remained Europeans.

We lingered two weeks in Honolulu—not only because we enjoyed ourselves in this lush and peaceful paradise, but also, or mainly, for want of means to continue our journey.

The situation, at once familiar and nerve-wracking, repeated itself at the Imperial Hotel in Tokyo, where we sojourned almost two months —not quite voluntarily. We were kept in that luxurious prison by the evil spell of our unpaid bill. The prices of the Imperial were almost as fantastic as its Moorish facades and the baroque arabesques of its furniture. It is, indeed, one of the weirdest and most spectacular places I have ever seen—"definitely influenced by Aida," as one of our jocose friends observed. We sometimes hoped a nice, effective earthquake would pulverize the whole thing—including all its fancy decorations and fancy bills. In fact, one of the shocks we witnessed during our stay was violent enough to throw us out of our beds and to adorn the walls with a capricious pattern of cracks and flaws. But the armored sanctum of the super-cashier, alas, remained undamaged.

Tokyo is the most tenacious and ugly capital in the world. Nature makes desperate efforts, time and again, to destroy the powerful and unpleasant city; but it emerges from all ordeals—strengthened rather than weakened or purified—a dynamic Phoenix: indestructible. After every tribulation Tokyo hurriedly reconstructs itself, like one of those mythic monsters whose hideous claws and fins grow again even faster than they can be cut off.

I disliked Fascist countries before I hated Fascism. The truth is that, as far back as 1925 or 1928, I enjoyed myself more in Amsterdam or Stockholm than in Rome or Tokyo, although the two former places have the reputation of being "dull" whereas the latter are vaunted as "interesting."

How curious—that a couple of callow vagabonds should be sensitive to symptoms and undercurrents which are neglected or overlooked by the bulk of professional observers—diplomats, correspondents, and the like. They send secret messages and detailed memoranda with respect to the political developments and economic trends. But they fail to notice or to understand the most obvious things. They don't grasp, for instance, that something must be wrong with a country where too many uniformed youngsters can be seen marching through the streets of the capital. The picture becomes even more disquieting when the pugnacious kids are in the habit of singing ugly songs. That is what happens in Tokyo all the time—an embittering nuisance. I am against marching kids; always was. Without understanding the words of their blaring anthems, I realize what it's all about. It means even bigger nuisance—Lebensraum, and the New Order, and national indignation . . . And finally it means war. That's what it boils down to—war.

I am irritated by people who begin to whisper as soon as foreigners are about. They either want to kill the foreigners, or they are afraid that they, on their part, might be murdered by their Gestapo because they have been seen plotting with foreign agents.

I am against countries where politics begin to overshadow all other interests and activities. Ambitious individuals can be fascinating: ambitious nations are a bore and a danger. Japan was tense with national ambition: one felt it everywhere—if one were able to see anything.

Is Tokyo an interesting city? True, the fortress-like palace of the Emperor, that invisible descendant of the Sun God, is impressive enough. Some of the spacious gardens are beautifully arranged. The theater street teems with gaudy life. It may be worthwhile to visit Tokyo just for the sake of that extraordinary district. The contrast between the rigid ceremonial of the classic drama and the bold experiments of the modern stage is one of the most striking and characteristic phenomena in Japanese life. No doubt, it is an unforgettable experience to see one of the great tragedians like the celebrated Ganjiro—a dynamic and disciplined artist on a classic scale. But even more bizarre than the odd, ritual apparatus of the Nipponese drama—which is, perhaps, the most conservative form of art still alive anywhere in the world—was a Japanese production of one of our favorite modern plays —Frank Wedekind's "The Awakening of Spring." The little vanguard theater where this stunning performance took place reminded us of all those familiar institutions in Hamburg, Berlin, and Munich, where we had ventured on similar extravaganzas ourselves. We were delighted and bewildered to hear Wedekind's familiar sentences pronounced in the exotic idiom, and it was a charming, queer experience to make friends with the actors who tried so hard and with so much talent to imitate the gestures and intonations of our own youth.

Our friends in Tokyo began to wonder about the unexpected length of our stay in that city. In the beginning we had been feted as colorful, if slightly eccentric visitors. A reception was given us at the German Embassy; we executed our literary program, and His Excellency, Ambassador von Solf, a pompous and sanguine gentleman, delivered a humorous speech flouting modern literature in general and "our dear young guests" in particular. But gradually people became somewhat puzzled and irritated. Maybe we were not "the literary Mann Twins," really, but a couple of dangerous impostors? Or we were literary and twins, all right, but in the service of a revolutionary Chinese organization? Or did we intend to write a satiric novel on the German colony in Japan?

We left, but only for Nikko, the famous sanctuary not far from Tokyo. For two days or so we enjoyed the colorful grandeur of this unique set-up—the gaudy pagodas, holy shrines, and wonder-working springs; the temples, turrets, and fountains lavishly adorned with lacquered and carved work—a sort of Oriental baroque, overflowing with arabesques, meaningful symbols, flowers, animals, tiny bells, and diabolic grimaces.

Excursions of this kind were refreshing; but we had always to return to our golden cage, the glamorous jail of the Imperial Hotel. We quailed before the disconcerting politeness of the manager, whose smile became more impenetrable every day our bill remained unpaid. It was this sealed, cruel smile of the Japanese people that almost got do down. They scurry, they dodge, they bustle; they make little bows and tell you flowery stuff; they prepare their wars, they exercise in the streets; they imitate everything, they dream of their future expansion and want to become the rulers of the East or the universe—always smiling: equipped with the inhuman, sweetish, merciless grin as with a murderous weapon.

Finally our guardian angel did his duty: the old cable-trick worked. This time it was the august publishing house, S. Fischer, in Berlin, which rescued us—under the condition that Erika and I jointly write a book on our journey. "There you are!" I teased my co-author. "Didn't I tell you so? You just have to write, and that's that."

We stopped at Kyoto, the old Imperial residence, crammed with temples and curiosities. Our sojourn there was particularly colorful and yet trying, as we stayed in an authentic Japanese inn, called Tawarary Hotel, where nobody understood a word of English and nothing was served but raw fish with brown spicy sauces, tea, and rice cooked in various ways. Nor were there any chairs or knives or forks or beds. Life was a Lafcadio Hearn-like idyll on straw mats—supervised and embellished by a giggling little army of geishas—dexterous and thoughtful creatures constantly amused about the gawky fashion in which we ate our rice and squatted on our cushions.

The last Japanese curiosity we inspected was the fishing in Gifu. It takes place at night, in the most picturesque surroundings, with a dozen cormorants as the main agents of the thrilling performance. They swim ahead of the boats which cover the river with colorful lamps and fluttering lanterns. The cormorants look very pretty and self-assured—dark feathered swans who draw the skiffs of many obstreperous Lohengrins. The whole set-up is pleasantly operatic: it has the character of a popular festival, with singing youth, picnicking families, drums, guitars, and decorated barques. Everybody watches the cormorants, who pounce with astounding alertness upon their victims. These are the little fishes—thousands of them, teeming about like insects, allured by the flickering lights. The gluttonous birds swallow

them—or rather, they catch them but cannot swallow them really. For the long necks of the cormorants are tied up with metallic rings which prevent them from actually consuming their prey: the fishes never reach the stomachs of their hunters but are retained in their narrow gullet. Yet the cormorants insatiably continue their murderous sport until their throats are filled with the fidgety victims and can be emptied by the jubilant fishermen.

We decided to take our way home over Korea and Russia, as Peking seemed almost inaccessible, after the collapse of the Northern Army. General Chang Tso Lin had just died; everybody treated us with gruesome accounts of the chaotic conditions that prevailed in the heart of China. Heedless tourists had to risk, ostensibly, not only the loss of all their possessions, but also of their noses and other indispensable parts. For those Asiatic soldiers once deprived of their leader turned rather beastly, indeed—so we were informed—and had surprisingly unpleasant methods of massacring unwished-for visitors.

We preferred to give credence to such horror stories—at least partly and with reservation. For they provided us with plausible, indeed, cogent reasons for choosing the shorter and less costly route. No doubt, we were a little exhausted by the constant strain of our financial jugglery and the abundance of ever-changing impressions. So we contented ourselves, without too much disappointment, with Mukden instead of Peking. In fact, the old Manchurian capital is impressive enough to let you forget what you have missed in China—especially if you don't know it. Mukden's Chinese city, separated from the international settlements and protected by a forbidding wall, gives you at least a foretaste and idea of what Peking may be like. The gaudy and busy life in the narrow streets, the massive grandeur of the Imperial Palace, and, above all, the simple beauty of the famous Pe-Ling graves, somewhat outside the town—the atmosphere and architecture of Mukden are suggestive enough to make you realize why China is stronger and more mysterious than her boastful little neighbor, Japan.

Chung-Chan, half Chinese, half Russian; Harbin, two thirds Russian, one third cosmopolitan cocktail; Krasnojarsk, Russian; Omsk, Irkutsk—Russian, Russian, Russian . . . Siberia was endless and incredibly hot, and the vodka was hot too but we didn't have enough money to buy as much of it as we would have liked to. Russia was vast and warm and expensive. The journey from Harbin to Moscow seemed five hundred times as long as the distance from Manhattan to the Hollywood Boulevard. A chicken in Omsk cost more than a sumptuous dinner in Beverly Hills. We ran out of money again, in the midst of Siberia. Our guardian angel was in excellent form—most efficient and imaginative. The unknown fellow-traveler to whom we addressed a desperate billet—"Dear stranger! . . . have lost our pocket book . . . Just ten dollars, dear Sir!—to be refunded in Moscow . . . otherwise we must starve to death . . . especially the thirst is so painful . . ."—turned out to be a German novelist, Bernhard Kellermann, author of a popular best-seller, "The Tunnel," and an old acquaintance of our father.

The last great sight of the journey was the Red Square—magnificent on an almost appalling scale, with the colossal walls of the Kremlin, the colored dome of the St. Basil Church, and the simple blocks of the Mausoleum where Lenin's well-preserved body—a brittle but powerful fetish—receives the homage of his people.

. . . "There you are, children! after all!"

This was the familiar cadence of Mielein's voice—jumping up and down, with a little flaw in the middle.

"Dear me!" she said. "I am afraid you look a little bit ridiculous. Not like a couple of grown-up globe-trotters, really."

Erika was rather offended. "Why," she said. "I am a very distinguished lady with a fur cape."

"You look all right," Father said, reassuringly. It was very impressive and touching that he had gone out of his way to meet us at the station, a most unusual gesture on his part.

The whole scene was utterly dreamlike. The two little ones, Elizabeth and Michael, paraded in their nicest clothes, with huge bunches of flowers. They had grown considerably since we saw them last. Of course they had: it was almost a full year we had been away.

"You look like an old lady to me," I said to Elizabeth. "Dignified but wrinkled. My dear Miss Lucy," I added mysteriously, "you seem unduly tired today."

Our parents exchanged sorrowful glances, while the two little ones giggled.

"Now, what was the most wonderful thing you've seen?" asked Elizabeth, five minutes later, when we had settled down in the car.

"Bernhard Kellermann!" declared Erika and I, in one voice.

The family smiled uncomfortably.

"And what else?" Michael insisted. "I mean, besides Herr Kellermann?"

"Nothing much," said I. And, with a grandiose and casual gesture: "Rien que la Terre . . ."

"Didn't I tell you?" whispered the kids to each other. "They have become very funny. Have you noticed? He already talks Japanese to us . . ."

CHAPTER SEVEN

Europe

(1928–1930)

WHAT is Europe? A minor extension of the Asiatic continent—a peninsula of complicated structure, named after a Phoenician princess. She was kidnapped by Zeus, who chose the disguise of a bull to please her. What wondrous spark did they carry along, the prodigious beast and his sweetheart, on their watery ride to the Isle of Crete? Their seed spread and multiplied. It was received by the chosen soil, the Hellenic. From this holy ground emerged the miracle, the birth of the Occident.

This is what happened on the shores of the Aegean Sea: A handful of philosophers and athletes challenged the immensity of Asia and Africa. They were proud and daring enough to conceive only their own way of life as human: the non-Hellenic world was tantamount to chaos. Beyond Hellas was nothing but barbarism: silence, darkness, stagnation. Outside, the dead land, the cactus land, motionless and barren under a torrid sun. Outside, boredom and cruelty; the worship of tyrants and animals, the withering wind from the desert. In Asia and Africa, the magic rites and bloody sacrifices, the bleak grandeur of the grave. But in Hellas, the nervous élan of life, the spirited endeavor of the individual.

In Hellas, the beginning of epos and tragedy; the establishment of the polis upon the agonistic principle and the pedagogical Eros. In Hellas, discipline and harmony and the dream of freedom. In Hellas, contradictions, laughter, the striving for truth, the serene and sensual intercourse between gods and men.

The barbaric world, monotonous and diffuse, abides in its dreamless coma: but the Occident changes, develops, absorbs new colors and rhythms, rejuvenates its substance. Hellas fuses with Rome; the new entity thus created receives and integrates the revelation of Christianity. Out of this marriage emerges the true vision of the Occident.

If Europe has been lovable and great, it is by virtue of this twofold heritage. Golgotha and the Acropolis are the tokens of her survival. She jeopardizes her glory when she distorts or disregards this double source of her substance. The diversity of Europe will inevitably fall into anarchy unless organized and illuminated from this innermost heart.

Western man often falsified or forgot his mission. He who ought to have come as the bringer of freedom and sympathy became the scourge of other continents, the exploiter of foreign races. The roster of his outrages is appallingly long; at home as well as abroad he played havoc among those whom he governed and exploited.

And yet, the criminal record of the Occident—the blood-stained chronicle of conquests and revolutions—paradoxically connotes the splendor of the European genius. In fact, all the afflictions and devastations Europe imposed on the world at the same time mark the vast accomplishments and promises of human history. If the restless ambition of the European soul was instrumental in corrupting five continents, the same energy has always been ingenious and potent enough to produce simultaneously the counter-poison and remedy.

The European drama proceeds dialectically: every force or action provokes its own opposition; every thesis is followed by its antithesis, and even the subsequent synthesis is but a new experiment, another transient conjunction in the play of competing forces. The unending strife and change within the microcosm of Europe often hampered or paralyzed the progress of civilization; but, Phoenix-like, the continent emerges from all its defeats and errors. The weariness or pollution of one of its elements could always be compensated. When Rome turns sterile or scandalous, there is always a Martin Luther. When the ancien régime is foul, there are the Cromwells and Robespierres. Bonaparte appears when the revolution has fulfilled its intrinsic purpose. The antagonism between the Papacy and the Imperial Crown throughout the Middle Ages; the struggle between Catholicism and Protestantism in the sixteenth and seventeenth centuries; the rivalries among the great national powers during the eighteenth and nineteenth—this perpetual flux of tension and reconciliation, this dialectic game of affinities and frictions is the true source of Europe's flexible tenacity.

The token of European power went to and fro, from the South to the North, from the East to the West. Every shift implied much more than just a new constellation in the balance-of-power game. The establishment of a new hegemony necessarily meant that a new style—a new philosophy and way of life—was to become predominant, for a while. Thus every shade in the kaleidoscope was once given its chance to determine the coloring of the entire system. But while one ingredient assumed temporary control over the whole complex, the others were by no means eliminated: under the surface they remained active and influential, waiting for their turn.

No doubt, the continent will, in the long run, be completely doomed when it allows one of its component parts to oppress the others. The permanent hegemony of one constituent would be tantamount to the disintegration of the organism. The harmony of Europe is based upon dissonances: uniformity means death, according to the intrinsic logic of Europe's structure and mission.

This is the double postulate Europe must fulfill or else perish: to maintain and develop the consciousness of its unity (Europe is indivisible) and at the same time not to violate or deny its diversity conditioned by history and nature (Europe—the delicate accord of incongruous components).

Europe seemed alarmingly small and brittle when I thought of her in Kansas or Korea. I loved her even more on account of her fragility; but at the same time my apprehension increased as regards her future. Up to that point I had been altogether entangled in specifically European problems, having never left the continent hitherto. The new impressions—however desultory they may have been—could not but affect my views. The vast spaces of America and Asia made me realize that Europe is not the world and cannot afford to waste its energies in nonsensical interior feuds. My new perspective enabled me to look through the basic fallacy of European nations. They still think themselves in a position to contend with each other for the rule of the universe, while the only relevant issue confronting the continent now is how it will hold its own among the colossal rivals surrounding it.

A journey around the world is an effective lesson to cure any European of complacency. The traveler learns to conceive his homeland—the continent of Europe—as one center of energy among others. By creating a universal civilization, Europe has forfeited, once and for all, the right, indeed, the possibility of governing the universe. The precariousness of her plight becomes evident in view of the stupendous growth of organized power all over a globe that has long made itself independent of the tutelage of its exploiter and educator.

Almost everything I wrote during the two years following my return from this voyage was devoted to the problematical status of Europe in its relation to the world. I tried to tackle the subject from various angles, but what stimulated and puzzled me chiefly were both the contrast and the affinity between American youth and my own European generation. Almost needless to say, I approached the issue in a highly emotional vein—no matter whether I treated it in the form of a comedy, a novelette, a book review, or a lecture. The idea was invariably to show the American as an embodiment of tonic naïveté—sturdy, inexperienced, almost shockingly wholesome and conspicuously fair (both as regards the coloring of his hair and his sporting principles). His trans-Atlantic partner, quite the contrary, appears erratic and delicate—versed in all kinds of sordid and somber secrets. According to Plato's erotic dialecticism, they inevitably attract each other—the effulgent athlete and his saturnine counterpart. "Les extrêmes se touchent," or they fervently seek each other. But usually their wistful flirtation turns out to be a failure involving a good deal of bitterness for both sides. At any rate, that was the melancholy conclusion of my comedy presenting the adventures of a European guest student in a Californian college. Of course, the girl "from the other side" is infinitely highbrow but at the same time a good sport: in the end she renounces her American boy friend for the sake of his previous sweetheart—one of those vigorous natives.

I am afraid it was rather flimsy stuff, my dramatic treatise on American youth. The satiric sidelights didn't amount to much, and the plot was clumsy. People were probably right when they reacted coolly on its opening night in a big Rhenish city. It may be, however, that this unfavorable reception was partly caused by a certain lack of understanding, indeed, elementary knowledge, in respect to American problems and conditions. How could a German audience appreciate the satire on college life in California or the bitter-sweet fondness of a sophisticated visitor for a blond-haired baseball champion? They would hardly have caught what it was all about, even if the presentation had been more effective. The average cultured German, though fairly well informed as to the economic and political importance of other continents, remained utterly unaware of any psychological or social developments, apart from the European.

After my return from the United States, in 1928, I tried whatever I could to communicate my newly acquired vistas. Not only did I plead for European solidarity, but I also warned against European arrogance and the potential danger of European nationalism. With ardent obstinacy I preached to my compatriots, who paid scarcely any attention, that it behooves a good German to be a good European and, furthermore, a good citizen of the world. To attain this goal it is vital to know what is going on outside our own narrow sphere. I reviewed and recommended books by American authors, even if they failed to impress me from a literary point of view: the factual material they offered made the reading worthwhile. Unflaggingly I praised Upton Sinclair, that eminent compiler of massive information; Sherwood Anderson and Ernest Hemingway, both of whom I greatly admired as artists; the poetry of Sandburg, whom nobody knew in Europe. I even attempted to propagate the work of young, unknown writers like Robert S. Carr, whose novel, "The Rampant Age," was available in a translation by W. E. Süskind. My article (in 1929) on that book concluded, after having contrasted its documentary merits with its artistic inadequacy:

"Why, then, do we like them—those young Americans so infinitely different from ourselves? It is their vigor that fascinates us, and we are moved by their striving for truth. . . . Their attitude towards life is more naïve and probably more fervent than ours, thanks to their lack of sophistication. No doubt, there are scores of adventures and experiences, both sensual and intellectual, they cannot share with us. That is why many of us are inclined to feel superior to our trans-Atlantic comrades. What a mistake! For our subtleties are attainable to them: it is a question of time. But we shall never regain what they still possess. It is our paradise lost."

Europe remained my real love and paramount concern. Our relation to other peoples and continents was but one aspect of the European problem. In fact, the potential evil of European nationalism seemed remote and rather academic, considering the immediateness of that other danger—the suicidal disunion of the continent. Anyone endowed with a modest amount of common sense and political knowledge could easily see that Europe was drifting towards disaster unless a workable scheme was agreed upon to prepare and establish its ultimate unification.

For a while I was considerably impressed by the intelligent and ardent appeal of Count Coudenhove-Kalergi, the founder and leader of the Pan-Europe movement. The chivalrous charm of his personality added to the attractiveness of his message. Of half-Japanese extraction and related to several European families of great distinction, he is a striking example in favor of racial fusions. This cosmopolitan nobleman is as handsome and resilient as could be. His mind is acute and candid. Accustomed by his personal background to think in international, indeed, intercontinental categories, he seemed particularly fit for his self-appointed mission.

The European scheme conceived by Coudenhove-Kalergi was strictly continental—excluding the British Isles and the Soviet Union, both of which figured as autonomous spaces in his reorganized universe. As for the British Empire, the Count was full of the most cordial feelings: he recommended close collaboration between Pan-Europe and the Commonwealth. In fact, his philosophy was definitely molded by British ideals and concepts. The type of the perfect gentleman—manly and gentle: at once urbane and heroic—was extolled in almost all his writings as the bearer and guarantor of an Occidental renaissance to come.

When speaking of Russia, however, the Pan-European became ominously reserved. He called her Asiatic, and he disapproved of

Communism. His own notions and propositions regarding a new social order were too beautiful to be true. Not that he thought the present system as good as it ought to be: he was keenly aware of its shortcomings and inherent dangers. But he did not expect much improvement from purely economic reforms. On the contrary, his primary concern was in the moral aspects of the evolutionary process. No violence would be necessary, according to Count Coudenhove-Kalergi, if all Europeans, employers and employees, accepted the code of gentlemanly conduct.

In the beginning the Pan-Europe movement attracted both the young and the intellectuals. Being a young intellectual, I was all in favor of it. It struck me as the most convincing scheme I had heard of. Besides, why should it not be feasible, after all? Aristide Briand was said to be graciously interested in Coudenhove's ideas. The Pan-Europe movement enjoyed considerable publicity all over the continent and found influential supporters in Geneva, Paris, Berlin, Rome, and other capitals. It was only by degrees, after the end of the Briand-Stresemann epoch, that the anti-Soviet angle became predominant and gradually determined the character of the organization. When big business began to flock to the herald of the gentleman-evolution, people of my stamp withdrew.

However, in 1928 and 1929 this particular implication of the Pan-Europe scheme was inconspicuous, or, at any rate, not obvious enough for me to notice it. Nor did I mind the polite omission of Great Britain in Coudenhove's hypothetic realm. The concept of a "continental policy," with a moderately anti-British tinge, was more or less accepted among German liberal intellectuals. Ever since the days of Rousseau and Voltaire France had been the admitted model and educator of the "good-Europeans" in Germany. The two most illustrious representatives of the species, Heinrich Heine and Friedrich Nietzsche, both were virtual French nationalists, while not concealing their almost hostile indifference towards England. Of course, this predilection for France was derived from aesthetic penchants, rather than from political considerations. Still it could not but have consequences in the political sphere, if only in the sphere of political thinking. Our liberal vanguard—the group of which I counted myself a part—not only was emphatically Francophile, but deemed the problem of Franco-German relations the pivotal issue for the pacification of Europe and the world.

When recommending and claiming the Franco-German alliance, we always took it for granted that the two nations would collaborate under the auspices of the League of Nations, in a truly democratic and progressive spirit. The personalities of Stresemann and Briand, those two champions of the rapprochement, seemed to guarantee its inherent moral meaning and tendency. The idea never struck us that the alliance might be brought about by men of very different stamp: namely, the big industrialists and their political agents. Out of naïveté and ignorance, we failed to grasp the possibility of a partnership between French and German big business, at the expense of labor and liberalism in both countries.

So positive and intense was my belief in the desirability of a Franco-German rapprochement at any price, that I was inclined to hail even the visit of Pierre Laval to Berlin. Unaware of his record, I was all in favor of him, simply because he came in his capacity as a French Premier and was accompanied by Briand. I remember the day when those two gentlemen—the foxy politician and the aging herald of European solidarity—called on the Wilhelmstrasse. The same afternoon I happened to have a date with a less formal French visitor, the Socialist writer Henri Barbusse. He had been kind enough to ask me for one of my books, which I handed over to him adorned with a personal dedication. His face seemed petrified with indignation and bewilderment when he read the text. I had made the howler of referring to the Laval-Briand visit as a promising and cheering event. Barbusse said nothing but turned rather icy. It was much later, in Paris, that he disclosed to me his painful astonishment in view of what he called "your praises for Monsieur Laval." I tried to explain and defend myself. It was not Laval I had praised but the improvement of Franco-German relations. "Improvement?" asked Henri Barbusse, Did I call it "improvement" when the exploiters of the German proletariat discussed a deal with their colleagues in France? "Don't you know what that scoundrel Laval stands for? Whose interests he represents?" I had to admit that my knowledge of Pierre Laval's affiliations was indeed rather vague: whereupon Barbusse gave me a gloomy look. "That's the way you are," he observed, sighingly. "You liberals and idealists. Always reveling in beautiful words and emotions; but no inkling as to what's going on in reality."

That is the way we were. Or rather—as I am disinclined to arraign anyone except myself: it was my own attitude that the French writer described. I was superficial, irresponsible.

In theory I recognized and stressed the political responsibility of the man of letters. I knew that literature, being the comprehensive expression of human experiences, must not disregard or belittle the essentials of human life, such as the problem of how to organize international relations or the distribution of vital goods. However, I found it tiresome and depressing to delve into these matters in a sober and detailed way. Instead of facing the issue squarely and tackling them realistically, I contented myself, in most of my political statements, with vague complaints and even vaguer suggestions.

When any one among my listeners got up to bother me with cumbersome questions, I presently turned lyrical and elusive. "My dear friend," I said, irritated but gentle, "the minor technicalities are really none of my business. After all, I am not a politician but a poet: which means that my foremost interest is in the mysterious essence of life, not in its practical organization."

I had worked out my little scheme convincingly and nicely. On the one side, I held, we have "the mysterious essence of life"; the pleasure, the drama, the dream, the sensual ecstasy. On the other side—and now you must try to be serious!—we have our political responsibility. It may be painfully dull; but there it is, we can't dodge it. So let's be sober and diligent and forget the ecstasies, as long as we have to deal with social-significance stuff. It behooves all of us to concentrate, once in a while, on those drab but meaningful topics.

You don't get away with it. Life is indivisible: you cannot split it into various departments, with limited responsibilities. The full stake is required, whatever you try to do. The price you have to pay for every valid thought or constructive deed is invariably the same: it is suffering and unflagging endeavor, a long tedious effort, and suffering again.

A writer who wants to integrate political subjects into the scope of his work must have suffered from politics, just as he must have suffered from love in order to write about it. He must have cruelly suffered: nothing less will do.

My fundamental error was that I ventured on those tremendous issues without having them in my heart and blood, without having suffered from them. I took it for granted that a writer can cope with any conceivable topic, no matter how involved and crucial it may be: if only he commands a sufficient amount of skillfulness and pluck. Out of a naïve sense of duty, rather than out of ambition, I devoted my "spare time" to the pivotal questions of our epoch. How could my contribution be solid and effective? It was not paid for with suffering.

Curiously enough, the period of 1929 and 1930 has, in my recollection, a savor of prosperity, rather than of open want and latent tension. True, I was informed of the appalling number of unemployed workers —two millions in 1929, three millions in the following year. But I trusted that the Government would take care of them. Besides, business seemed to improve, thanks to the official policy of stimulating private initiative. The results of these efforts were obvious and gratifying, especially in the cultural sphere. Notwithstanding the crisis, there evidently was a strong sector of the middle class willing and able to spend considerable sums for the purchase of theater tickets, books and magazines, paintings and phonograph records.

A Nazi gangster by the name of Frick ruled in Saxony; but in Berlin it was business as usual. The music halls and swanky restaurants were jammed, the Flechtheim Gallery sold Picassos, and the social elite raved about a new film by René Clair or the Monte Carlo Ballet.

A civil war seemed in preparation, with both camps mustering their formidable strength; the nationalistic Steel Helmet against the Social-Democratic Reich Flag. The Reichswehr, meanwhile, puzzled and fooled the public with its Sphinx-like, non-partisan pose, while secretly fostering the anti-Republican forces. But the Republic, with unabated optimism, trusted God, the Reichswehr generals, and the cunning stunts of Dr. Hjalmar Schacht.

The League of Nations was a hackneyed joke sneered at by the jingoistic mob; but the international crême de la crême met on Unter den Linden and on the Kurfürstendamm. While Dr. Göbbels cursed France at the Sportpalast, a little Frenchman by the name of André Germain would be treating a party of Germanic lads with Russian caviar and French champagne. Germain looked like a caricature of a character out of a novel by Proust. He was the heir of the potent Crédit Lyonnais and the author of a stimulating booklet called "Hitler ou Moscou?" The decision, almost needless to say, was in favor of Hitler. Monsieur Germain was wholeheartedly for the Führer: partly he thought Nazism might protect the interest of the Crédit Lyonnais; partly he felt an emotional penchant for muscular, fair-haired heroes in becoming black or brown uniforms. "Vive la jeunesse allemande!" crowed the little monster. He had the voice of a moribund mouse, the complexion of a mummy, and the eyes of a snake. His guests responded with a roaring "Heil Hitler!"

While criminal elements invaded the political scene, a drama called "The Criminals," by Ferdinand Bruckner, was the sweeping hit at the Deutsches Theater. The great attraction of the show was Gustaf Gründgens in the role of a morbid crook. The star of Hamburg had finally been discovered by the connoisseurs of the capital. Berlin was smitten with his dashing meanness. He made so much money that he could afford to be a Communist. When the performance at the highly capitalistic Deutsches Theater was over, his limousine carried him to the suburbs, where his appearance was scheduled at a meeting to celebrate Stalin's birthday and accuse the Social Democrats. Half Robespierre, half Brummel, he pranced in front of the flabbergasted proletariat—the cynical bon vivant disguised as herald of the revolution.

(Erika got her divorce just in time. She who had forgiven him for the vagaries of his struggling days, could not bear the affectations of his tawdry grandeur.)

No doubt, it was a great time for discoveries and rediscoveries. Big business discovered the "constructive forces" inherent in the Nazi Party. Erich Maria Remarque discovered the timely appeal of the Unknown Soldier. The unemployed discovered the demoralizing wretchedness of a beggar's life. The poet Bertold Brecht discovered "The Beggar's Opera." The mighty film company, UFA, as usual, topped all competitors by discovering the legs of Marlene Dietrich, for whom a masterpiece by Heinrich Mann, "Professor Unrat" (alias The Blue Angel) was just good enough as a vehicle.

A group of Swedish professors discovered "Buddenbrooks."

For a number of years the press kept irritating and fooling us with constant Nobel Prize talk: "Thomas Mann should get—is going to get —has already gotten the great award of the Swedish Academy." There were premature announcements followed by embarrassing congratulations. So when the long-anticipated event actually took place, the Magician just lifted his eyebrows.

It was indeed a turbulent affair. Mielein groaned because she had to buy herself a lot of superfluous things for the obligatory trip to Stockholm. The telephone kept ringing, and the mail assumed disquieting proportions. Colleagues vied with each other in flatteries. Eight letters out of ten ended with a request for money. It would have required six Nobel Prizes to fulfill one-half of these fantastic demands. The winner was urged to finance sanatoriums and bakeries, the cure of an epileptic and the world revolution. When he politely refused to invest seventy-five thousand marks in a traveling circus, the would-be Barnum snapped back, on a scrap of paper: "My only answer to Mr. Mann is Pfui!"

Of course, people overrated his income. In reality it was by no means considerable. The circulation of his major works increased on an international scale. In Germany proper the popular edition of "Buddenbrooks" was a sweeping success, while "The Magic Mountain" maintained its leading place on the best-seller lists. It was quite a boom, and our household took on a thriving aspect.

Not that the style of our domestic life fundamentally changed: it was always determined by my father's tastes and animosities. He had refused, obstinately and quietly, to accept, indeed, to acknowledge poverty during the meager years. Now he seemed scarcely impressed by the fact of his comparative wealth. Both his delicate stomach and his deep-rooted discretion prevented him from indulging in any kind of excess. His only luxuries consisted of fine phonograph records, two handsome cars, and a melancholy country house.

As for this new retreat—susperseding the one in Tölz—it was situated on the Baltic Sea, in a part of Lithuania near the German frontier. The place was called Nidden—famed for its desert-like dunes and a rare sort of elk that were wont to block the highway with their massive bodies. If I am not mistaken, those unusual elk were of the one-horned type. At any rate, they looked as though they had just escaped from a fairy-tale zoo—weighty and bewitched, with sad, fathomless eyes.

Another curiosity of Nidden was an extensive camp where young men underwent a thorough training in all kinds of semi-military sports, particularly in gliding. There must have been hundreds of lads; when the wind was good, we could hear them sing and roar from the German side of the frontier. Occasionally we would watch some of them strolling along the beach. Their sweaters and overalls were adorned with swastikas.

That was Nidden—gloomy and picturesque. I went there but once, for a couple of weeks or so. There were so many other places to go. Europe was alluringly small—an intimate landscape teeming with colorful figures.

I recall hotel rooms—dozens, hundreds of them, scattered all over the continent. I spent my life in hotel rooms. Home meant to me the hospitality of my parents, or a room, somewhere, in a squalid inn or a grand caravansary.

My life was not without a certain regularity, almost monotonous, for all its erratic scurry. Almost never did I discontinue my work. When I arrived in a new resort, it was my first occupation to unpack and arrange, with nervous pedantry, the well-assorted desk equipment that I carried along in my bag. If necessary, I traveled with a complete reference library. During the time I was engaged in writing "Alexander," a novel about the Macedonian conqueror, my luggage was burdened with Aristotle, Xenophon, and Homer. I perused Babylonian legends at the Grand Hotel in Stockholm; Persian chronicles, in a country house near Florence. However, the quest always ended in Paris.

A centrifugal force—irrational and irresistible—seemed to impel Alexander away from the heart of Europe, outward, into the vastness of Asia. Awe-struck and enchanted, I followed him on his maniac venture, while being directed, in my turn, by the reversed energy, a centripetal force that flung me toward the center of the continent. For Paris was the center.

It was the center, for all its hedonistic inertia and cynical corruption —the living heart of Europe, despite such scandalous affairs as those around Madame Hanau (in 1928) and M. Albert Oustric (in 1930). The sordid conspiracies between politicians and financiers; the wire-pulling, blackmailing double-crossing; the sinister intrigues involving cabinet ministers, gamblers, journalists, film magnates, courtesans, and, inevitably, M. Pierre Laval—all these were things one heard discussed on the café terraces and read about in radical magazines. But the Paris I knew had but little in common with this at once furtive and spectacular sphere—this underworld in full dress (with the great rosette of the Légion d'Honneur).

The Paris I knew was that of an intelligentsia that hardly partook of the machinations of the cheating and ruling gang. There were affinities between the artistic world and the aristocratic "monde," the "Faubourg St. Germain" dissected and immortalized by Proust. Moreover, there may have been certain threads connecting bohemians with the plain underworld of Montmartre, the realm of dope fiends, pimps, and petty prostitutes. But the writers, painters, actors and musicians kept clear of any contact with those piratic intriguers from the stock market and the right wing of the Chamber of Deputies.

It was a mixed crowd that gathered, say, at the salon of the Duchess of Clermont-Tonerre, a blue-blooded blue-stocking of considerable wit. Indian Princes or Russian Commissars, Dadaists or mustached ladies— deep voiced and cigar-smoking—were familiar characters in this open-minded milieu. But M. Pierre Etienne Flandin? Or M. Tardieu? It seemed out of the question.

Society is a highly complex organism full of tensions and contradictions—particularly the mellow, skeptical society of a very old, somewhat weary civilization. The French novelists have excelled in examining and dramatizing the competing interests and impulses that determine the fluctuations of the snobbish hierarchy. The salons I knew in Paris, in 1929, hardly differed in any essential way from those frequented and portrayed by Balzac, a hundred years before. The young men I met in the home of Madame Jacques Bousquet, at Charles de

Noailles', or at the Polignacs, were as slick and ambitious as are Stendhal's Julien Sorel or Balzac's dynamic dandies. However, a new shade seemed added to the repertoire of their gestures and intonations —a sort of problematical innocence and sensual playfulness; something childlike and yet depraved. The adventures of the nineteenth-century tradition were dashing and purposeful, even when displaying a Byronic weariness. Their more fragile successors of 1927, on the contrary, maintained a quality of disarming and perturbing helplessness, for all their overstressed cynicism.

Some of them had the grace of bewitched infants—easy to corrupt: easier to destroy—when they dallied with narcotics or the risky anomalies of sex. There was a tendency towards self-annihilation in all their playful adventures. Exclusively concerned with somatic problems and pleasures, they still appeared strangely lost and uprooted in this material world.

This pose and pathos, at once savage and subtle, saturnine and frivolous, were by no means reserved to any particular nation or social class. It was a type, an attitude to be found at any place from Oxford to Heidelberg, from Villefranche-sur-mer to Salzburg, Prague, and Warsaw. Just as a certain sector of a certain generation all over the world could be enthralled by the exuberant appeal of Goethe's "Werther," a certain sector of a certain generation—my own—responded unanimously to other images and persuasions. It was this strange community of an idiom and an emotional climate to which Jean Cocteau referred when addressing me, in a preface he contributed to the French edition of my Alexander novel, as one of his "compatriots": "je veux dire, d'un jeune homme qui habite mal sur la terre et qui parle sans niaiserie le dialecte du coeur."

I met Cocteau in 1926. His great friend, Raymond Radiguet, the young poet whose precocious genius he discovered and publicized, had died about one year before. Jean had just recovered from a nervous breakdown, a disintoxication cure (he temporarily stopped smoking opium), and his sensational conversion to Catholicism. He lived in his mother's apartment, rue d'Anjou, where I was received by Maurice Sachs, the journalist and lecturer, all dressed up in a becoming soutane.

Jean talked a good deal about the wickedness of big cities and the beauty of simple life.

Since then I have visited him in many a dwelling, but it always remained the same: only the young men and their costumes changed. Besides, Jean, while moving from one building to another, never did leave the district around the Madeleine, fixed, as it were, to the sight of the basilica.

He lives in a world of his own, a bedeviled sphere full of secret sigils and allusions at once glaringly artificial and of unquestionable authenticity. The magic apparatus with which he surrounds himself seems an integral part of his being. The sketches by Picasso and models of sailing boats, the plaster casts of male feet and female hands (the latter dressed with crimson rubber gloves); the canvases by Marie Laurencin and Giorgio de Chirico; the portraits of Sarah Bernhardt, Nijinsky, and Radiguet; the antique busts decorated with purple draperies; the Chinese pipes and yellowed sport magazines; the skeletons, mirrors, lamps, and diving bells—this whole inspired mess seems to grow out of his nervous, dexterous hands as the protoplasm emanates from the medium's body.

Cocteau, who looks troubled and bewildered when he has to walk from the Place de la Concorde to the Opéra, feels evidently at ease in the midst of his uncanny bric-a-brac. Nimble and brisk he capers among the gaudy atrocities with which his apartment is crammed. And how strangely relaxed and concentrated appears his lean, ageless face when he sprawls on the pillows to prepare another "petite pipette" for himself. A weird sort of peacefulness transfigures and hardens his features while he is occupied with sucking the spicy reed whose fragrance Picasso has called "less stupid" than all other odors on earth. "Liquor provokes paroxysms of folly," Cocteau is wont to say: "Opium provokes paroxysms of wisdom."

Undoubtedly, he is one of the most gifted beings I have ever known and, perhaps, the most nearly perfect one. That is not to say that I think him the greatest character or the greatest mind or the greatest poet. (He has written great poetry, though.) He may be a morbid clown, a treacherous freak, and what not. But he is not to be equaled as a phenomenon—something irresponsible and irrefutable as are rainbows, peacocks, or shooting stars. Can a rainbow lie? Is a peacock unreliable? The display of their grace is their truth. Can a rope-dancer betray principles? He has none. Neither has Jean Cocteau.

He is neither a moralist nor a liar but, primarily and essentially, a performer. His only principle is not to be a dilettante. Equally remote from the barricade and the ivory tower, he leads his risky life on the high trapeze, the most exacting and ingenious acrobat of his epoch.

You cannot afford to slouch or potter, up there, on the tight, vibrating rope. You have to be soulless and fearless to execute, year after year, with unabated alertness, the dazzling stunt of the "Grand Ecart." The acrobat, almost heroic in his dogged conscientiousness, summons no other alternatives to the one: succeed or break his neck. Cocteau always succeeds.

Whatever he performs or produces—it clicks. His nightmares and hallucinations are composed with crystalline accuracy, always strictly in keeping with the respective medium employed. His cartoons are as brilliant as is his poetry: in fact, he is the one writer able to illustrate his own works without blurring or dislocating his vision. His dramatic fantasies equal his novels in conciseness and suspense. The songs and sketches he wrote for the "vedettes" of the music hall are no less effective than his famous librettos for the opera or the ballet. I have watched him in the studio when he directed his remarkable film, "Le Sang d'un Poète": he commanded the same briskness and bravura he displays in his conversation.

The hours spent in his company assume in my recollection a savour both of burlesque show and magic ritual. I visualize Jean Cocteau—a jesting wizard and bewitched jester. His feline, weightless body seems to be withered and impelled by intoxicating siroccos. The same glowing breath has dried out his hair, distorted his lips and eyebrows, parched and shriveled his skin. He has the eyes of a hypnotist and the hands of a pickpocket. His smile is that of a cunning infant or an infantile murderer. He adorns himself with feathers, scarfs, and daggers as he impersonates birds, statues, and movie stars. He lies whenever he opens his mouth. All his aperçus are as deceitful and as revealing as is this cryptic "mot" he chose as motto for his autobiography: "Je suis un mensonge qui dit toujours la vérité."

Cocteau wants us to believe that there is a mystery hidden under his tinsel disguises. But perhaps there is no mystery? Maybe the masquerade is an aim in itself? He is, perhaps, Narcissus who pretends to be the Sphinx?

The real Sphinx does not indulge in arias and caprioles. She is discreetly demoniac.

It was Cocteau who observed that "the mystery begins only when all confessions are made": which is as truthful an aphorism as are all his lies. If Gide had coined this bon mot, it would have been truly true.

"I don't like your lips," Oscar Wilde said to André Gide. "They are straight like the lips of those who have never lied. I will teach you the art of lying to the end that your lips become beautiful and voluptuous as are the lips of an antique mask."

And yet the meticulous confessions of that tight-lipped Protestant, André Gide, are more puzzling and iridescent than the most sparkling stunts of either Jean or Oscar. How harmless appear their antics compared with Gide's unfathomable candor!

Cocteau, the embodiment of the lie, says always his whole truth when he lies. André Gide, on the contrary, always lies when he tells the truth; for he has too much truth: he can reveal but aspects of his complex, contradictory being. Yes, he lied when he truthfully said: "I am the Immoralist"; for he also is a passionate moralist. His Christian pathos is authentic beyond any doubt: but so is his pagan fervency. The structure of his mind has been molded by Protestant traditions: but Catholic moods have played an integral role in his life. He is the legitimate heir of Mediterranean lucidity—with a penchant for the violent confusions of the Germanic soul and the nebulous grandeur of the Russian.

All potentialities of the European genius are integrated in the amplitude of Gide's spirit. His intellectual biography is involved and dramatic, like a fugue by Johann Sebastian Bach (whom he admires most among all composers); whereas the experience of Jean Cocteau is essentially static, for all his quivering agility. Small wonder that the immutable "enfant terrible"—at once erratic and sterile—is fascinated by the wide scope which his older and greater brother embraces and dominates. "How I envied him his Protestant childhood!" Cocteau exclaims, in the preface to one of his early books, "Le Rappel à l'Ordre": "I visualized him skating with singular grace on the waters of Russia, with a Bible in his hands. In beautiful English style he wrote his name on the ice . . ."

I recall having asked André Gide how he liked the bizarre silhouette Cocteau presented of him. He produced a brief, nasal sound, rather a snuff than a laugh. "Ah! celui-là!" he said, with a sort of humorous exasperation as if complaining about a naughty child. And half-amused, half-irritated: "Quel blagueur! Toujours des chinoiseries!"

How distinctly I remember the most minute details of my first meeting with André Gide. He had asked me for luncheon; I stopped for him at his apartment, rue Vaneau, near the Boulevard St. Germain. The first picture of him that looms up is that of a quaint and haggard wanderer by my side, vigorously striding towards the Luxembourg Gardens. His face, nervous and weather-beaten, wears a half-mask of shadow falling from the brim of his slouch hat. At the first look, you might take him for a faintly eccentric professor—the type of man who would spend his days between his laboratory and outdoor exercises. In reality, Gide has an admitted animosity to gymnastics. "Pas de sport!" was his succinct reply when friends inquired of him the secret of his youthful appearance. I like to imagine the diabolic grimace he may have made when disclosing this anti-athletic credo. There can be an uncanny flash in his eyes—a momentary twinkle altering, for one startling moment, the placidness of his brow.

It amused me to watch him out of the corner of my eyes while he lingered in front of a fountain or a fine old building to elucidate its architectural merits. He talked with a scholarly elegance—his head bent slightly sideways, his eyes narrowed to two glimmering slits, the cigarette dangling from his lips. I expected him any moment to drop his cumbersome disguise and to appear in his true, or at least in a truer, form—as a faun-like shepherd, perhaps, or as one of those aging warriors whose lean and muscular thoraxes are presented in certain antique reliefs. But he remained the inconspicuous gentleman in a wide, colorless pelerine, a sensitive wanderer with slit eyes, narrow lips, and admirably shaped temples.

We had our meal in a modest brasserie, whose terrace faces the

Luxembourg. Gide talked mostly German literature, dwelling on the particulars of certain things by Goethe, in whose works he seemed greatly interested at the time. His features brightened with an almost sensual joy when he praised "Clavigo" or "Die Wahlverwandtschaften." "C'est très, très curieux!" he kept saying, as though discussing something utterly mysterious and a trifle risqué. "C'est prodigieux!" And he sniffed briefly, which was a nervous habit with him.

He smoked almost incessantly, but after the meal apparently forgot to light another cigarette. When I offered him one, he refused. "It's a terrible vice," he said, with an ambiguous grin.

"Usually I am too weak to resist." And he added, while his eyes stared into space, for a thoughtful moment: "I suppose I am fairly strong in wanting things and getting whatever I want. But when it comes to rejecting a temptation, to resisting evil . . . alors ça, c'est une autre histoire . . ."

There is one other moment which jumps to my mind whenever I think of this luncheon. A young boy passed by and tried to sell us a bunch of lilacs, withered, odorless stuff. He was ten or eleven years old, an ugly little creature with large, intelligent eyes in a sallow face. Gide gave him a handful of change but renounced the flowers—a gesture which obviously impressed the lad but at the same time somehow hurt his feelings. Gide seemed exceedingly intrigued and stimulated by this double reaction: "Did you notice that wry glance he gave me? He was very offended. Did you ever pay a prostitute and then spurn her services? She'll give you the same look—precisely the same puzzled, disapproving glimpse. The really amusing thing about it is that the boy would much rather steal the money than accept it as a charity . . . C'est bien curieux, ça! C'est prodigieux . . ."

It was the same accent of delight and curiosity he had had when raving about Goethe.

There were quite a few French writers I made friends with during that period. Naturally enough, I saw a good deal of those specializing, so to speak, in Franco-German relations. The poet-diplomat Jean Giraudoux, for instance, had just come out with a sturdy play, "Siegfried," dramatizing the tension and affinity between our two nations.

Giraudoux has a definite penchant for the Germanic soul, and I always had a weakness for Giraudoux, despite his somewhat noncommittal suavity. He gives the impression of a Swedish tennis champion who has a French mother (hence his elegant manners and eloquence); was educated in Oxford (hence his nonchalant haughtiness); and is in love with a Teutonic poetess (hence the bluish dream in his eyes).

Others who tried to promote the rapprochement were Paul Morand, the assiduous student of international sex habits, and Maurice Rostand, the slightly eccentric scion of the French classic, Edmond Rostand. As for Paul Morand, I was amused by his early books: "Fermé la Nuit" and "L'Europe Galante" are masterpieces of the semi-pornographic genre, infinitely more saucy than Dekobra or Pitigrilli. Morand might have become a real writer, if it had not been for his inordinate vanity and lack of intellectual backbone.

Maurice Rostand, on the other hand, is handicapped by his too-beautiful heart and his much-too-beautiful hair. He looks like Sarah Bernhardt in the role of a remorseful courtesan who has become an abbess. "Tout Paris" smiled about poor Maurice; but I didn't. I did not laugh at his melodrama, "L'Homme qui a tué"—presenting a French poilu who ventures on a pilgrimage to the home of a German soldier whom he killed in the war: for I knew that Maurice actually meant all his fine and noble rhetoric. He just happens to be fine and noble. Nor did I chuckle at all when Maurice—the man could never kill—whispered to me, during a performance of "La Dame aux Camélias," at the Odéon: "Excuse me for crying. Seems kind of silly: but my emotional life is precisely like that of Camille." I knew it was the truth and nothing to be funny about.

There were many others: their faces and voices come back as I recall the jolly luncheon parties and gregarious evenings of 1928 and 1929. These are the vigorous and ambitious features of Jules Romains; this animated chat comes from Léon Pierre-Quint, who treats me with delightful, if somewhat lurid, anecdotes as to the manias and mannerisms of his late friend, Marcel Proust. I recognize the suave eloquence of M. André Maurois—Membre de l'Académie Française in every smile and gesture, long long before he was really admitted to that august institution. Paul Valéry's profile looms up, elegantly shaped, the perfect embodiment of Gallic esprit and intellectual dignity. I visualize the studio of Eugene McCown, the American painter, whose artistic and social career was started and flourished under the auspices of our mutual friends Gide, Cocteau, and Crevel; and the studio of Pavel Tchelitchew, the most Parisian Russian I have ever seen. And that of Marc Chagall, the most Russian of all Parisians; to visit his workshop means to intrude into a sorcerer's kitchen. The uncanny host, mercurial and relentless, is occupied with bewitching violet horses, blue roses, and unsuspecting salesmen from Odessa. His flowers have the phosphorescence of exploding stars; the skies of his imagination are inhabited by hovering lambs and the embraces of bedeviled lovers. Watch your head! It may fly off, as happened to the bearded peasant on Chagall's canvas, and to these hilarious dancers who apparently fail to realize how deplorably headless they are, and also to Claire and Ivan Goll, the poetic couple of Auteuil, whose bewildered smiles hang high up, at the flowering top of the Eiffel Tower: Chagall, in drawing their likeness, has captured their equilibrium.

Saint-Exupéry, to whom André Gide introduced me, raved about risky flights he was planning while the literary public raved about his arresting novel, "Vol de Nuit." Julien Green, another friend of Gide's whom I would like to call a friend of mine, seems unable to produce a loud word or a mean thought. When I first met him I suspected it was Julien Green, Jr., I had been presented to—the son of the man who wrote "Adrienne Mesurat" and "Léviathan." For I had imagined the author of these masterly novels to be an elderly gentleman who had spent many a monotonous year in the stifling confines of a provincial little town. But the Julien Green I shook hands with, was young, handsome, alert. One might have taken him for an elegant globetrotter and civilized nobody, if it had not been for a strange sadness and somber glow in his eyes, a distrait intensity which one discovers only after a while. But even this absent-minded intensity of his gaze hardly explains his uncanny insight into the petty desires and appalling crimes of a sinister world so remote from his own background. What mysterious power is it that forces him mercilessly to transform his own experience into the macabre images of this dusty inferno? I shall never forget the musing casualness with which Julien Green once observed to me: "It's not I who produce my novels. Somebody else moves my hand . . ." I am positive that he did not lie.

It was René Crevel who introduced me to the circle of Surrealists, with which I was connected from its foundation, in 1922. It was the period when the radical movements launched shortly before or during the War—Futurism, Expressionism, Constructivism, and the like—gradually lost momentum. So did Dada, an artistic venture started in Cologne, in 1916, by an enterprising young painter, Max Ernst. Subsequently Ernst joined a set of French artists and writers, whose spiritual leader was the poet and essayist André Breton. Others who belonged to this initial group of Surrealist Founding Fathers were the poets Paul Eluard and Robert Desnos, and the novelist Philippe Soupault and Louis Aragon. There was also a founding mother, or rather a founding Muse, called Gala, a woman of extraordinary punch and imagination; faithfully devoted to the Surrealist movement, first in her capacity as Madame Paul Eluard, later as an assiduous promoter of Max Ernst's talents, and finally as Madame Salvador Dali. The dashing Catalan visionary was Breton's latest discovery at the time of my first contact with the Surrealists.

They were pleasant enough fellows, most of them. As for the high priest of the cult, André Breton himself, I knew him but very slightly. I am easily frightened by a high priest—especially if he happens to have an unduly big head to boot. But Max Ernst is good company, a handsomely gray-feathered bird with cunning eyes and a disarming smile. Louis Aragon, who was considered by many the coming novelist of his country, had the laughter of a bloodthirsty child and the elegant verve of a bull-fighter who is out to seduce a rich American heiress. Paul Eluard looked like a pensive warrior, while Salvador Dali, ambitious and agile, seemed all too ready to pick up Breton's hallucinatory gibberish—the muddled and boisterous blend of Freud and the Apocalypse, Marxism, music hall and paranoia.

No doubt, they were provocative, ingenious, sparkling with irreverent wit, those intense young men gathering around their pugnacious oracle, M. Breton. Yet I could not help feeling somehow embarrassed, indeed, alarmed, to see René so completely under the spell of their rampant paradoxes. He was by far the most delicate and most lovable one of them all. How could he fail to notice that there was something sterile and insipid about the showy ecstasies and rabid arrogance of his pals? How doggedly they tried to appear daring and dangerous! But, at bottom, their blatant gags and eccentricities were just so many contrivances to catch the public attention.

Nothing on earth could be more tiresome than the clichés of madness. The Venus of Milo may be a bore when presented as the obligatory norm of Beauty. It is the privilege and natural function of youth to debunk ideals and smash idols. But the iconoclasts should beware of indulging in a new form of academicism while they amuse themselves with arraigning and ridiculing the academicians. Jean Cocteau was right when he warned the habitual breakers of taboos and statues that "en cassant des statues on risque d'en devenir une."

The Surrealists, petrified in their seditious pose, promptly established a new formalism, after having done away with the code of traditional evaluations. The debunked goddess of Beauty was superseded by a grisly Venus with fish tail, her eyes teeming lice, and a pianoforte in place of her bosom—another stereotype, a new bit of bunk. Whoever dared to convey any doubts or objections was defamed by the coterie. In many instances the truculent heralds of the Surrealist creed were not content with mere tongue-lashing. The Surrealists were realistic enough to realize that the efficacy of violent words can be considerably increased by the addition of violent actions. To antagonize André Breton and his clique was a dangerous thing to do. They developed a brilliant technique in nightly "holdups" and similar "practical jokes." Cocteau was one of those to suffer from their gruesome sense of humor. When his one act drama, "La Voix Humaine," was first produced at the Comédie Française, his Surrealist colleagues interrupted and almost ruined the show by launching a violent riot. Even worse was what they did to him when his mother was seriously ill. In the middle of the night Jean was dismayed by a telephone message to the effect that "Madame votre mère est morte." All in tears, the loving son rushed to the rue d'Anjou only to be received by the guffaws of those frolicsome terrorists.

"Are you mad?" I asked René when he told me this rather sickening story. "Or what is wrong with you?"

Presently I felt sorry for having uttered my question. For I knew that the problem of insanity was a veritable obsession with my friend René. His father had been in a state of mental disorder during the last years of his life, which he ended in Madame Crevel's drawing-room. Small wonder that the son was haunted by misgivings. He often dwelt on the likelihood or inevitability of hereditary taint, especially in the case of syphilitic diseases. Was this erratic temper a symptom of future madness? Who is mad?—René kept questioning: He who accepts, indeed, relishes the fetid corruption of our life? Or the one who suffers from and protests against it?

"Maybe it's you who are mad," he said, with an ominous grin. "Or Monsieur Cocteau. Or, perhaps, the whole world."

It was this helpless and furious question, Are you mad? If not ...? which he chose as a title for his new novel, "Etes-vous fous?", published in 1929. It may be inaccurate, if not unfair, to label this romantic diatribe as a novel. Its logic and suspense are those of a feverish dream. The leading character, Vagualame, alias René Crevel, roves aimlessly through a world that seems half-brothel, half-bedlam. Racked by the hypocrisy and boredom of modern civilization, the iconoclastic vagabond keeps roaming from city to city, from one "cultural center" to the next, terrifying the scientists and society ladies, the priests and politicians, the exploiters and exploited ones, with his terrified question: "Etes-vous fous? Si non ..." The wrath and wit of Vagualame-Crevel are directed against the Pope and Madame Cosima Wagner, the French grammar, D'Annunzio, the Good Lord, Henrik Ibsen, and the Prince of Wales. He sneers at Count Coudenhove-Kalergi and his Pan-Europe Movement, at the Swiss sanatoriums, Hollywood, the Catholic writer Mauriac, and the Czech industrialist Bata. Neither the lesbians nor the Emperor Franz Joseph are spared. The frantic traveler lashes the House of Lords in London, the Académie Française in Paris, and the Institute of Sexual Science in Berlin. The founder and leader of that Institute, Professor Magnus Hirschfeld, happened to be an old acquaintance of mine. In reality a nice enough old chap, he appeared in René's hallucinatory prose as a weird charlatan called Dr. Optimus Cerf-Mayer, ravenous and perverse, full of fiendish devices.

"What a thing to do!" I scolded that wide-eyed flagellator, Vagualame. "To present old man Hirschfeld as a sort of Moloch clamoring for the sacrifice of at least one hermaphrodite every other day. That's the way you exaggerate and distort even the most innocuous characters. If your canvas had any resemblance to reality, it would mean that the universe is populated by idiots and murderers."

"Which is the truth and nothing but the truth," said René, with a merry chuckle.

"Are there no exceptions?" I asked, a trifle offended.

And he, with a golden flash of tenderness in his eyes: "Why, of course. There is my little Yolande."

Yolande—the comrade and guardian angel, to whom Vagualame clings in distress and devotion. Yolande—the wondrous bloom in the midst of frenzy and filth. She, nobody else, is exempted from Vagualame's defiant inquiry. How could he ask her whether she is mad? She protects him from madness.

"Etes-vous fous?"—the alarmed and alarming question came from many lips and disquieted many hearts. I heard it pronounced in many languages and contexts, cried out in anger, dropped in flippant contempt, whispered in sorrow and dread: "Are you mad? If not . . . ?

"Total übergeschnappt!" This is Yolande's voice, raucous but sonorous and full of cheering cordiality. Vagualame's angelic companion is in reality Fräulein Thea Sternheim, my great friend Mops, the daughter of that demoniac playwright who married my fiancée. Pamela, consequently, is the stepmother of Mops, who is two or three years older than she is. But how am I akin to Mops' mother, popular Madame Stoisy Sternheim? She is the divorced wife of the man who married the stepmother of René's guardian angel. Consequently . . . Nuts.

"That serves you right," Mops chuckles when I tell her that I am on the point of leaving for Baden-Baden, where her daddy and my ex-fiancée enjoy their honeymoon. "The old man is completely pixilated. Total übergeschnappt." Do you know what he wrote me the other day? That he had made up his mind to become as handsome as General von Seekt. Sounds kind of bad, doesn't it?"

At the Stephanie, in Baden-Baden, Mr. and Mrs. Sternheim receive me in the dining room, all dressed up for dinner. I haven't seen either of them since I left for the journey around the world.

"You look fine," I say to Pamela.

"Not half as attractive as does his Excellency," snaps Carl Sternheim.

The General, former chief of the Reichswehr, occupies the table next to ours. He is an elegant old boy, all right, all monocle and dashing mustache.

"Voilà un homme!" Sternheim crows. Napoleon's succinct verdict in reference to Johann Wolfgang von Goethe is the only adequate formula to express the playwright's feelings towards his Excellency.

"He is indeed remarkably well-built," confirms Pamela, motionless and erect; her face with the majestic aquiline nose and the shiny eyes, mask-like and taut above a fancy collar of black lace. "But now you ought to eat your soup," she adds, in that glassy, hypnotizing voice of hers.

Her husband, bumptious and aggressive, dwells on a comparison between the martial charm of Herr von Seekt, on the one hand, and the dreary sloppiness of "certain callow scribblers," on the other. "His Excellency and I," he exclaims, "we belong to the family of the Eagles. Whereas you young fellows are just a bunch of lame ducks. That's what you are, lame ducks."

"Your soup!" admonishes Mrs. Sternheim, née Wedekind.

The General, who cannot help catching some fragments of Sternheim's talk, seems amused as well as irritated. Now he whispers a few words to his lady, while looking askance at our perplexing party. I know only too well what he says. "Don't laugh now, Friederike!" says his Excellency. "Herr Sternheim just called me an eagle."

"Did he really?" chuckles the Baroness. "Total übergeschnappt!"

I writhe and perspire with embarrassment, while the dramatist keeps leering at our arrogant neighbor. And is he not right, the monocled warrior, to contemn an intellectual who makes an ass of himself by worshiping and wooing the saber and the mustache? What a triumph for the General!—considering the reputation of Carl Sternheim as the most mordant satirist, the relentless debunker of patriotic and heroic trash. Some debunker, indeed! Smitten with a monocle: fawning upon a pair of handsome epaulets.

"That's why we'll lose the war," I feel, with a sudden pang. What war is it I am thinking of? "Our war," of course, the age-old struggle of the civilized people against the warriors.

. . . . The same night I returned to Berlin.

The next news regarding Sternheim came from a sanatorium, where the playwright gradually recovered from what his physicians euphemistically called a "complete nervous breakdown."

"Sei pazzo?"

This is Venice, its iridescent twilight, the Moorish dream of its architecture, the wistful song from the Grand Canal.

Two young men and two girls sprawling in a gondola.

Erika and I, and a friend of mine, and our "Swiss child," Annemarie, the eccentric scion of a patrician house. She is delicate and ambitious and looks like a pensive page.

"Annemarie!" I admonish her. "Don't make your Inconsolable Angelface!"

We keep teasing her in the most tactless fashion on account of a dedication we recently found in a book given to her by the French novelist Roger Martin du Gard. "Pour Annemarie," wrote the author of "Les Thibaults," "en la remerciant de promener sur cette terre son beau visage d'ange inconsolable . . ."

"What's wrong with you, anyhow?" I ask her.

"Many things," she says, with that slightly guttural Swiss intonation. "There are so many sad things to think of."

"For instance?"

"Mother is mad at me again."

"So what?"

There is a stillness; only the soft, splashing sound the gondola produces gliding through the water, the stale, fetid, bewitched water of Venice.

Annemarie, after a pause: "When I talked to her on the phone this morning, she was kind of upset because Fair-Enough didn't make the race. So, of course, she said I am morally unbalanced. It's always the same thing. As soon as something is wrong with the horses, she remembers how bad I am."

After another silence: "And then I thought of Toscanini too."

"Arturo? Did he, too, tell you funny stuff on the telephone?"

And Annemarie, the Swiss child—suddenly erect, with a hardened face and a dark, angry flash in her eyes: "How could they dare to slap his face? Those dirty Fascists, I mean. Toscanini's face! Think of it! And why? Because he didn't feel like conducting their lousy anthem. Oh! it's outrageous! Sickening, that's what it is."

The gondolier darts a radiant look at her, just to make the strange lady feel better and for the sake of his tip. But Annemarie shows him a forbidding grimace. "To slap his face!" she grumbles. "The one great man you've got!"

"Sei pazzo?" grins the gondolier.

"Están locos?"

... The Easter Sunday bull fight in Sevilla: a gala affair, in the presence of the King.

The gaudy ceremonial unrolls under a glowing sky. Intoxicated with vanity, the toreros caper in front of the torpid bull, murderous dancers in their short boleros. But the animal remains motionless in its coma, no matter how jauntily they swing their scarlet capes and scarfs.

The mob, already impatient, begins to trample and whistle. His Majesty yawns—hiding his gaping mouth behind a gloved, languid hand.

The tattered habitués, jammed to the torrid roof of the amphitheater, heckle and incite the fighters. "What's wrong?" they bellow, and their voices are hoarse with sadism and liquor. "What are you waiting for? Why don't you give it to him?"

At this critical moment a new toreador enters the arena, graceful and pugnacious on his prancing horse. His gesture is brisk and chivalrous as he salutes the King. His Majesty yawns again. He yawns while the horse bows to him. He continues to yawn when the toreador throws his lance at the lethargic bull. The bull groans, bleeding from a wound on his side. But he does not move. He defies both the toreador and the King. The bull is the only one in this huge arena who refuses to pay homage to His Majesty.

This time the ruler fails to cover his mouth as it gapes in another spasm of yawning. His impoliteness is the signal to the stately doña who shares the box with her royal lover. All of a sudden she rises, a towering specter in black satin, and darts a crimson flower straight into the arena. Is it the toreador she is aiming at? But she is blind, her face being hidden behind a magnificent shawl of black lace. The flower lands precisely between the bull's gentle, reproachful eyes.

This dainty projectile proves more dynamic than all spears and arrows. The bull jerks, trembles and jumps. In that moment of excitement, blurred by dust, he tumbles while thousands rise from their seats, not knowing how the toreador has made his long awaited kill. Even the King wakes up. Only his somber mistress remains motionless —her right arm still stretched out, her head bent slightly backwards. No doubt, the same sinister power that transformed a rose into a deadly weapon, touched her heart and petrified her veiled features, her ebony hair, her delicate, murderous hands.

The mob bursts into delirious applause. What fun and triumph!—to see him fall who was the only proud and peaceful being among them. The bull ends his life without having fought, without having bowed to the King. His last roar curses, implores, asks the exuberant crowd:

"Están locos?"

"Are you mad?"

. . . Munich, summer 1929.

The scene: a gigantic tent on the Theresia Meadow, a vast field situated at the periphery of the city. The tent is jammed with people, twenty thousand, thirty thousand of them. It is dark; only the platform glares, singled out by the spotlight. And from there, from the illuminated rostrum, comes the voice, the ghastly howl of a mad dog.

"The Jews!" hurls the barking voice, in a monotonous paroxysm of fury. "Those filthy Jews have done it, who else?"

A young chap not far from our place, screams abruptly, as if bitten by a snake and unable to repress his outcry: "Hang the Jews!" Whereupon the voice, with slimy banter: "Patience! Patience, my friend! They'll hang, all right."

The crowd snickers and guffaws.

"Dear me!" whispers our English friend who was so eager to attend this lurid affair. "He is a paranoiac."

"Who dominates this so-called Republic?" bellows the voice. And the chorus responds: "The Jews!"

"How extraordinary!" whispers the English friend. "He is positively demented. Don't they notice it? Or are they crazy themselves?" He looks aghast with surprise.

The voice, panting now, breathless with hatred: "Who dominates the so-called League of Nations? The international trusts? The newspapers? The Kremlin? The so-called Catholic Church?" And, following each question, the stereotypic roar: "The Jews! the Jewish rats! Hang the Jews!"

"Are they mad? Or what?" our friend keeps asking. He repeats his question in various idioms, finally in German. "Sind Sie toll, mein Fräulein?" he inquires politely of a buxom Hitler maiden sitting next to him.

Happily, she is too excited even to hear his question. She flutters, tramples, perspires, all beside herself, in a quasi-sexual trance.

But the British observer insists, with merciless courtesy: "I beg your pardon, Madam. Did you ever consult a really good psychiatrist?"

How much like him that is! That's the way Brian is, Brian Howard, a young writer from London, with whom we spend the summer in a funny little hotel on the Walchensee. He doesn't care a straw about people hissing at him and piercing him with their looks. One of those husky fellows might rise and knock him out with his little finger. Brian doesn't care. Frail but plucky, he wouldn't mind a scrap with great big Göring himself.

"We may as well beat it," I suggest. "He's a bore, that's all there is to it. Nobody takes him seriously, anyhow."

The murmur of indignation around us grows ominously as we withdraw from our seats. "They must be foreigners," I hear one Hitler youth whisper. And another, rather angrily: "To hell with them. They've made dirty cracks about our Führer." Whereupon a third one, with a superior grin: "Never mind. They're nuts."

While we struggle our way towards the exit, the hideous voice, dispersed and amplified by the microphones, follows us throughout the hall. "Versailles . . ." hoots the voice. ". . . disgrace of our nation . . . I promise you, German mothers! . . . heads will roll . . . the Bolshevists . . . I promise you, German peasants! . . . the national upheaval . . . the Nordic race, those exorbitant milk prices . . . And who profits by it? Our arch enemy, those parasites and scoundrels—those swarthy, greasy hook-nosed, stinking . . ."

Where to escape from this hideous voice? Is Lapland far enough? Or the harbor of Cadiz, at the southern tip of Spain?

Erika is an excellent driver. Her little Ford car looked shaky and shabby but was more trustworthy than many a Mercedes limousine. We zigzagged Europe together, in an unending flight, as it were. In Petsamo, at the northern end of Finland, we dreamed of escapades into the Polar zones. From Cadiz it's just a stone's throw to Morocco. Morocco is far enough.

The city of Fez is enchanting. But the Arabian guide insisted we could never grasp the real spell of the Orient, unless we tasted the Oriental drug, the magic herb called hashish.

It didn't look appetizing—a sort of greenish-black dust. The guide said it was the finest hashish there is. "It's even better than the one I use at home," he assured us. "My wife thinks it's too good and too expensive for us. It's a quality for princes."

"He is a liar," Erika complained. "I don't feel the faintest effect. The 'qualité des princes' consists of chocolate powder mixed with sugar and cinnamon."

"Isn't it too bad?" I said. "Let's have another spoonful, anyway. It couldn't do any harm."

We had already consumed three times the quantity suggested by our guide. Now we swallowed another substantial dose, regardless of his warnings.

After a little while we grew exceedingly gay. Everything made us giggle—the shape of the carafe or the tassels on Erika's slippers, the name of the hotel whose furniture was so funny, or the name of the Arabian town to which our laughable little car had carried us and in whose humorous center this comical caravansery was situated. "Fez!" we chuckled, with nonsensical merriment. "What a name! Visitez Fez, la Mystérieuse! Why don't you visit Fez, la reine de Morocco, where every man wears a fez, even the guiding gazelle of Fez: our guileful guide beguiling us with his fez with the tassel . . . Why don't you visit the gazelle with the mystery tassel, the tasseled prince of the qualified guides: "Mes princes et mes princesses!—visitez donc—et plus vite que ça!—le mystère de la qualité—les guides Feziens aux principes Hashishaux—le Hashish Marocain aux qualités mystérieuses . . ."

We shrieked with laughter about the most preposterous puns and had an excellent time, for an hour or so. Then we fell abruptly asleep.

Erika lay on the bed; I sprawled on an armchair, in the midst of the messy room. Her outcry penetrated my trance-like sleep. "Oh! my Lord! Oh!" she groaned—flinging through the apartment, her eyes fixed and widened in a white, horrified face. "I'm young to die! I am through!" she lamented—pacing desperately between bed and window.

"What is wrong?" I asked, helplessly.

Never before had I seen her in such a state. I was indescribably worried.

"That devilish stuff!" she moaned. "That hashish! We're poisoned— both of us . . . Oh! my Lord . . ."

"I am all right, so far," I said, and began to tremble.

"Well, I am not," she cried, and resumed her tormented running.

Something had happened to her in her sleep—something weird and overpowering, an inconceivable shock. "I've been too deep," she kept mumbling—constantly pacing the room: "Much too deep below . . . It was almost death . . . What devilish stuff! We're going to die . . ."

I wanted to call a doctor but Erika decided: "Let's go!"

In slippers and dressing-gowns? I hesitated, but she pulled me towards the door, out into the sultry darkness of the African night.

We had to cross the whole width of the garden to reach the central part of the extensive hotel. There were no lights, except the dim shimmer from our rooms and the distant shine from the main lobby, where the night clerk slumbered behind the switchboard. The many odors of the plants and blooms were alarmingly sweet and strong in the humid, velvety air. Even more intoxicating than the scent of roses and jessamine was the monotonous concert produced by the crickets and frogs. Their unending lament almost drowned the familiar noises wafted into the park from behind the stone wall, from the Arabian city. These sounds were always the same: the guttural cries with which the half-grown lads communicate from one hiding place to another; the saturnine bells announcing the approach of a leprosy-stricken outcast; the bleak song of a drunkard. The bewitched city, Fez la Mystérieuse, sent every night its immutable invocations to a starless and motionless sky.

"Say something!" Erika begged, in a strangled voice, while we stumbled side by side through the maze of flower-beds and bushes. "If you don't talk," she whimpered, "I'll fall again . . . oh! into the bottomless . . . into the big, black hole . . . Why don't you say something?"

"It may sound funny to you," I said. "But I don't feel my right arm any more. It must have disappeared. And now the left one . . . how strange!"

"What's wrong with your arms?" She shook my shoulders while she shouted at me: "Oh! that devilish stuff!"

Never shall I be able to describe what it actually was like. It was worse than anything words could define. It was insanity. It was hell.

First my arms flew away; then the legs; then my neck, my head, my body. I burst literally asunder. I exploded, dissolved; I broke into a thousand pieces. My identity cracked: the fragments of my organism fluttered throughout the park. Oh! my hair!—entangled in thorny thicket . . . My estranged, terrible mouth, blabbing from the top of a cypress tree. My feet, aimless and derelict, ran through the flower-beds: while my heart—a lump of throbbing disconnected nerves—fell into the abyss of a black, fathomless night.

The statement that "my identity cracked" may be somewhat misleading. Indeed, it is euphemistic, considering the infernal lucidity with which I realized and observed the unspeakable spook. This was the most horrid thing about the ghastly experience: that I remained aware of what I was passing through, watching with infinite dismay and disgust the process of my own disintegration. My brain, isolated but by no means darkened or paralyzed, hovered somewhere in the midst of the schizophrenic mess.

"This is an extremely serious incident," observed my lonely brain. "Possibly my legs and lips will never find the way back to me. At any rate, it will take considerable time—forty-eight hours, perhaps, or four thousand and eight hundred years. . . ."

I heard Erika's voice: it came, surprisingly, from the roof of the central building. "Why do you jump all the time?" she asked. "Why do you dance? Stop dancing!"

I answered, from the fountain: "I don't dance at all: you must be seeing things. If I did dance, however, it would not be I who did it. How can I stop dancing, since it is not I who would dance, if I dance?" . . .

"Etes-vous fous?"

First the sleepy concierge asked us the inevitable question, then the driver who had happily been rescued at an Arabian house of evil reputation. He was tipsy and kept scolding us during our ride to the hospital.

The car swam through clouds. Erika sang and I danced. The driver said we should be ashamed of ourselves. I yelled with fear as my head daringly hopped about, up there, at the roof of the big mosque. "Don't yell!" said the driver. "I'll beat you if you do it again."

Erika wrung her hands so violently that one could hear the joints crack. Throughout the whole trip she sang and wrung her hands— maybe in order to stay awake.

It must have been about three o'clock in the morning when the chauffeur delivered us at the entrance of the Hôpital Militaire. The air had abruptly chilled or, perhaps, was always cooler here than in the maze of the Arabian town. It was still fairly dark, but the darkness was not black and velvety any more. A gray, creeping glimmer around the tops of the palm trees already announced the coming of the dawn.

The soldiers heckled and teased us, while our driver reported to an older man in white linen coat. "An overdose of hashish," I heard the old man say, from immeasurable distance. "Silly kids they are. Well, we'll give them something to make them sleep. They'll overcome the shock. Good thing you brought them here."

His voice sounded jovial and soothing. I rather liked the man.

"No, we are not gypsies," Erika assured the soldiers, who were greatly amused by the colorful rags we wore.

"Just nuts, that's what they are," guffawed one of the fellows.

But the elderly officer smiled at us, "Never mind!" said his forgiving heartening smile—the smile of an old scholar and soldier who has witnessed and experienced many things in many continents. "Never mind their calling you crazy. Evidently, you are a bit out of order, just now. But in a day or two you'll be all fixed up again. Wait and see! Sanity will be quite an adventure, now that you've had your little escapade into the vestibule of madness."

CHAPTER EIGHT

Olympus

THE worship of masters and martyrs is the finest privilege of youth. It may have been an unreliable friend, a reluctant fighter, all too self-ish and desultory. But I certainly was, and, for that matter, still am, a loyal follower, fervently devoted to those, living or dead, who molded and enriched my intellectual life. It is from the example of my saints and heroes that I drew the strength for my own endeavors.

There are various patterns of admiration. It is one thing to be in-trigued and inspired by those close to us in our actual life; another, to honor the genius whom one has never seen. The pure feeling of rever-ence cannot but be affected as soon as emotional elements are involved: it may be obfuscated or intensified, at any rate, it somehow changes its nature. This goes in particular for so complex and delicate a relation as that between father and son. Resentment and respect, protest and gratitude are insolubly intermingled. Fame and authority of the father become a stimulus, a thorn, an obsession to the striving son. Inevitably he will try to imitate the paternal model and at the same time to under-line his own originality.

I prided myself on being disorderly and eccentric, as my father is punctual and disciplined. I reveled in mysticism, for I thought him a skeptic (which is, incidentally, only half-correct). He is by instinct and tradition a Protestant: I was attracted by Catholicism. With the one exception of Nietzsche, most of the great men in whose works and characters he took particular interest left me rather cool: Richard Wag-ner and Frederic of Prussia (both of whom I disliked), Goethe (whose cosmic serenity is hardly apt to seize youthful imagination), Henrik Ibsen (whom I thought a bore), August von Platen, the poet, and

Theodor Fontane, the novelist (neither of whom was especially appealing to me). However, while I dissented from most of his specific opinions, I could not help accepting—half-subconsciously—the complete scale of his general evaluations. The very vocabulary I employed was imbued with the savor of his intellectual personality. His psychology of the artist—this enthralling mythology of death-bound romanticism counterbalanced by the ironic tenderness for life—has essentially influenced my own views of the artistic mission and conflict. It is useless to offer resistance to this gentle persuasion: I had his terminology in my fingertips, his images in my blood. The contradictions of my feeling could not prevent me from seeing through his eyes the great developments of cultural history. How could I avoid thinking in his categories, taking over the concepts he had coined or elucidated? I was too intimately familiar, in the fullest sense of the term, with the fugue of his musical dialectics.

So profound was the entanglement that it even affected my attitude towards other writers. No doubt, my admiration for Heinrich Mann was fundamentally genuine. I was truly impressed by the dynamic élan of his essayistic prose; enchanted by the colorful grandeur of his vision. Yet it is undeniable that I overemphasized this enthusiasm— not to annoy my father (he hardly disagreed with me in respect to Heinrich Mann's stature), but in order to prove my emancipation. As everybody expected me to think Thomas Mann the most eminent writer, I insisted on the greatness of his brotherly competitor. I remember that I once stirred up a minor storm in the literary tea cups when I declared André Gide to be the most important contemporary author. This statement, coming from me, was considered viciously tactless.

I don't want to decide to whom I owe the more profound and lasting stimulus, to my father or André Gide. For, if the former's intellectual cosmos is the basis and starting point of my own thinking and striving, Gide's work has accompanied me throughout the years as an older brother, a beloved friend. Yes, he is to my generation what the prodigal son is to his younger brother when he comes home, matured and deeply experienced. Gide invokes their dialogue in one of the most unforgettable scenes he has ever written, "Le Retour de l'Enfant Prodigue," the masterwork of his youth. The admired brother confirms what the child has already divined in his reveries: that there are other kingdoms to discover, outside the familiar hierarchy, and also lands without a king. The traveler, weary but still glowing with the seduction of foreign zones, offers his brother the fruit of adventure and restlessness: not the apple of wisdom which quenches the thirst, but the savage pomegranate whose bitter-sweet aroma makes for even more thirst—and makes you love your longing.

Gide—an inspired comrade rather than a leader—has never pretended to possess the solution of our doubts, but anticipated, echoed, and infinitely deepened our questioning. We recognized our own uncertainties in the continual monologue of his writings. His advice was all the more helpful as he never assumed the attitude of a teacher. He was not infallible, not doctrinaire, not sublime. He was problematic but great; haunted, erratic, complicated—but very great. His example did not suggest that I change the very substance of my character: how could I? On the contrary, he urged and encouraged me to become myself in a purer, more conscious and uncompromising way. He did not want me to be different but to improve, according to my inherent law and pattern. The great self-analyst helped me to discover myself. He guided me through the labyrinth of my own nature and sanctioned whatever I found, the desires, the qualms, the oppressed impulses. Not that he made me complacent; if I am, he is not to blame (there is no complacency in his heart); but he gave me self-assurance and the fortitude to endure life and to accept my own being with all its potentialities, dangers, and dilemmas. I enjoyed being myself and tried very hard to intensify and better my own character; for I thought, naïvely and fervently: If you try very hard to transpose your intrinsic being to a higher plane; if you are faithful to your innermost designs and make the best out of them—really, truly, seriously the best—then you must have a slim chance to become—gradually! after many set-backs! if you are very lucky!—almost like André Gide.

Was he one of my "gods"? Did he belong to my Olympus? Yes and no. In a sense, his figure occupied a central place in my Pantheon. But, again, I was somehow hesitant to admit contemporaries, or rather, any contemporaries whom I happened to know. There is a difference, after all, between a man and a legend, although a legend can be very human and a man can be very legendary. Yet the symbols of our faith, the temple of immortality, should be remote from the vicissitudes, the emotional haze, the ambiguities of our daily life.

I keep speaking of my Pantheon and Olympus as if they were a well-known institution—a sort of fellowship, nicely endowed and recognized in official circles. In reality, however, there is nothing but a childish phantasmagoria, something vague and baroque I made up for the purpose of organizing the profusion of images and ideas reeling in my head.

I dallied many hours of many days with a kind of blueprint indicating the various centers of energy, the danger points, the peaks, gulfs, and sources of my inward landscape. This curious map probably was almost as muddled as the state of my thoughts. Yet I greatly regret that the document is not available any more. An honest and thorough account of my intellectual credo as it used to be, may prove rather revealing, indeed—not only with respect to my own background but also, or above all, as a résumé of the moods and tendencies I shared with my generation. The highly emotional philosophy to which I then adhered undoubtedly involves elements inimical to progress and civilization. But it also contains the counter-poison and remedy. If some of my heroes bear and propagate the bacillus which now corrodes our world, the last genius whose holy name I invoke and whose message struck my heart, is utterly incompatible with barbarism and retrogression.

I shall try to reconstruct my Olympus. It may be possible to juggle the lost entity; but the result cannot but be dubious and fragmentary. For how could I help mixing the quintessence of recent experiences with the mistakes and divinations of my past? Since then, many an idol has tarnished or completely faded away. The topography of my celestial scene has undergone significant modifications. Nevertheless, the center is still intact, still fresh and valid and acceptable.

I close my eyes. I recall the pantheon of my youth. They come back: I recognize, with infinite gratitude, the smile, the gaze, the silence of my gods.

My Olympus is divided into one "official" and one "private" part. All recognized masters and national heroes are placed in the official pantheon—nicely adorned with laurels and oblations. All august genii of our civilization, from Caesar to Washington, from Euripides to Victor Hugo, gather in the marble hall of immortality. The atmosphere is chilly. A solemn silence prevails. The demigods exchange frozen smiles and only from time to time drop one of their axiomatic bon mots. A bearded Father-God, Jupiter-Jehovah supervises the ceremonials. Even those among the participants who used to be gay or passionate when they still walked below have long adapted themselves to the lofty style of the classical Olympus. They have all forgotten what it means to laugh, to weep, or to love. They are petrified, sacred statues.

My own "private" Olympus, the "romantic" one, is, of course, definitely less respectable. While in the classical sphere everything stands motionless in a cold, equable light, the horizons of my Olympus seem to phosphoresce—sometimes beaming with serenity; sometimes darkened by shadows falling from unknown spaces.

The two pantheons are strictly separate from each other. They do not overlap; but some heroes are simultaneously present in both spheres. Just as certain capricious grands seigneurs lead a double life between the royal boredom of their residence and a more hilarious underworld, some of the immortals have a twofold existence, exhibiting their official greatness in the classical realm, while disclosing very different qualities—tragic and humorous features—in the more informal sanctum. Rembrandt, Bach, and Dürer; Dante, Milton, Beethoven, and Goethe parade in the niches of their official glory. But once admitted to the romantic group, they begin to move, to suffer, to live. Michelangelo, tormented by his exorbitant creative power, resembles one of his magnificent slaves as he groans and writhes, the painful image of human genius: Prometheus bound to the rock. Leonardo, next to the raving Titan, appears more composed and placid. But such is the penetration of the Olympic light that the elaborate surface of his canvases becomes translucent, and we are allowed to perceive the tremendous drama behind the smiling tranquillity. If Michelangelo is Prometheus, this one, his gentle brother, is Daedalus, the builder of the Cretan labyrinth, who challenged the gods and tried to escape their fury by means of wings made from feathers. But he flew too near the sun: the wax of his wings melted, he fell, and now has plenty of time to brood over his sacrilegious inventions. For he now is imprisoned in the very labyrinth he constructed with so much daring acuteness. There he ponders on never-heard-of machines—deadly weapons and fantastic conveniences. Surrounded by solitude as by an impenetrable wall, his features become rigid, and gradually he learns the unspeakable smile of the Mona Lisa; the sweet and murderous mask of a Medusa numbed by her magic insight, loneliness, and insatiable ambition.

How many of the classical monuments and holy monsters I witnessed on their way from the official temple to my more problematic sanctum! When I was young and callow, however, even such human masters as Mozart or Molière had not yet revealed to me the tragic and romantic aspects of their genius. Even now I would hesitate to admit Aristotle, Martin Luther, or Racine to my intimate circle. Rafael, Rubens, Victor Hugo, and Richard Wagner are bluntly refused; Brahms and Ibsen received with frosty politeness. On the other hand, it is undeniable that many of my private gods possess neither the stature nor the dignity indispensable for membership in a really exclusive club. It is, indeed, a rather motley crowd gathering around a mysterious center, which incessantly moves and fluctuates and suddenly bursts into flames. Is this a volcano? A fiery whirl of energies? Behold, it is a throne, and out of the throne proceed lightnings and thunderings and voices.

Next to the gyrating focus stand the archangels, four of them, or rather, five! for the one who wears an antique garment has two faces —Plato's pensive and impersonal features and the appalling mask of Socrates, the ugliest and most attractive man who has ever lived. Oh, the incorrigible old satyr and cunning lover! How he leers and chuckles! Whom does he try to seduce? Where is Alcibiades? Or has Socrates found another victim for his cross-examination? His technique of confusing and refuting the partner through insidious questions is rather annoying. And how ambiguous is the wisdom of Socrates! First he employs a considerable amount of wit to demonstrate that the awareness of evil is virtually tantamount to avoiding it. Knowledge, says Socrates, is the source of morality. Only he who knows can be good. But, with a stunning somersault, the paradoxical moralist concludes: "As for myself, I know only one thing—that I know nothing."

Is Eros nothing? Is Socrates an agent of the nirvana? For he admits himself that he is an agent of Eros. How often, and with what sagacity, has he praised and analyzed the peculiar character of that demon!—his roguish whims and cunning strategy; his cruelty, his sweetness, his almost infinite power. So fervently devoted to Eros is this teacher and lover that he offends the other gods by denying or belittling their existence, an outrage for which the people of Athens send him to prison and death. The sage, before he empties the cup of hemlock juice, startles the crowd, once more, with one of his unfathomable mots. He advises his friends to sacrifice a cock to Asclepius, the God of Medicine: "For I have been sick very long," says the parting philosopher.

Is to die—to recover from a long disease? Oh, Socrates! But what, then, is Eros? . . .

Plato adds a new element to the cult of Eros, the "Idea." Eros is the messenger of the Idea, a dexterous courier between the Absolute and a perishable reality which contains and slowly develops an inherent pattern—its own potential perfection. The Idea allures and animates reality as the lover tempts the beloved. With beauty as its weapon and bait, the Idea woos the heart of man, most delicate spot of the universe: the vulnerable point where the material world gains consciousness and becomes sensible to the appeal of Perfection.

Plato's program of the "Republic" is neither utopian nor materialistic, but a fervent attempt to specify and elucidate the innermost design that must be fulfilled by man. The ideal social order and "Civitas Dei" claims and promises the salvation of man in the sphere of his own empirical reality.

The human race—with these words another cherub joins in the Hellenic duet—is no goal in itself. Man is but a pretext and device for higher purposes, conceived and created to prepare the coming superman.

His voice—at once shrill and flickering—does not make a very good impression. This angel looks frightful as well as pathetic, with his huge moustache and his sloping forehead. His nearsighted eyes burn as two tragic flames under the bushy brows. An indefatigable invalid, he proudly suppresses his groaning as he keeps climbing the steep path up to the icy peaks of bewitched mountains. Breathless, haunted, maniacal, he ascends the heights of glacial solitude, hankering for the enormous views of far distances and beyond, of blessed beauties.

Torn by stomachaches and mental disturbances, he extols the Will for Power and the magnificence of ruthless vitality. Life is wonderful, cries Nietzsche; I enjoy every minute of it. So utterly pleasant is life, according to his hectic declamation, that he wants it to continue forever. One life is not enough: he insists on its eternal return. The whole performance "da capo!" clamors the tormented invalid.

His hymns add a curious note to the mighty repertoire of the Choir Invisible. Nietzsche's songs of praise always sound like violent polemics. He distrusts what he loves as he distrusts himself. His blasphemies are reversed prayers, homage in disguise. So ardent is his desire to overcome his own problematic nature, that he must defy where he would like to worship. With desperate perspicacity he discerns the rotten spots in all ideals of modern civilization. His paradoxical humanism seems to question the very basis of human morality. The most penetrating and most immoderate psychologist of all times, he not only debunks the hollow slogans and hypocrisies of a decadent society, but also hazards to attack the ultimate, unquestionable truth. His iconoclastic furor spares nothing, not even himself. In fact, it is on his own vulnerable heart that he inflicts the most cruel pains. The innermost design of his aggressive frenzy is self-crucifixion.

He is very great, for all the embarrassing dislocations of his style and thought. He is even greater than he realizes, or great in a different way. It is not in his pompous masquerade as Zarathustra that he appears most impressive, but in the painful reality of his human drama.

His impatient genius attempts to push man forward on his uncertain and hesitant march towards the ultimate goal—the fulfillment of the Idea. "Life wants to rise," he proclaims, "and rising, conquer itself." He too flies too high, so near to the sun that he scorches his wings and falls, like Daedalus. Whose is the lacerated carcass? The woeful face polluted with blood and tears, whose is it? Is he the superman the mob clamors for? How he totters and stammers! His tongue, already numb in the beginning of his paralytic decay, toilsomely forms his wail, his confession and testament: "Ecce Homo . . ."

"Ecce Homo! Voilà l'Homme! Hail to you, my lover, my brother, my comrade! You are welcome—whoever, wherever you are!"

This is a different voice—the sonorous organ of the third archangel. His heartening bass addresses and exalts man not as an idea and potentiality but as a collective organism, Man—among all creatures the most problematical, most frightening, most deplorable, and by far the most lovable one. He loves Man who is descended from the ape (he believes in Darwin). He loves Man who is God's problem child and favorite creation (he believes in God).

The armies of those I love engirth me, and I engirth them;
They will not let me off till I go with them, respond to them,
And discorrupt them, and charge them full with the charge of the Soul.

He is less delicate and saturnine than his fellow-cherubim. With exuberant pride he announces his identity:

Walt Whitman am I, a Kosmos, of mighty Manhattan the son,
Turbulent, fleshy, and sensual, eating, drinking, and breeding . . .

He is satisfied; he sees, dances, laughs, and sings; he is self-assured and generous: "And what I assume you shall assume; for every atom belonging to me, as good belongs to you." He enumerates, with indefatigable enthusiasm, the splendors of the universe—the rivers, the mountains, the grass, the animals, the cities, the achievements of modern technique and the ancient rituals, the natural grandeur of all human beings, the dignity of all races, the beauty of all literatures, the truth of all religions. He is the poet of the Body and the poet of the Soul, the cosmic cataloguist, rhapsodic as well as conscientious. The Mystic Trumpeter he is, embracing, glorifying, describing all things created.

There is no morbid excess in his "most jubilant song." He is sound, full of common sense and overflowing kindness. His vision of the future is at once bold and feasible. In his concept of universal democracy, as in Plato's vision of the ideal "Republic," reason and divination, pragmatic and metaphysic elements are integrated. What he calls the "Eternal Progress" becomes an essential part and stage of a vast cosmic process—"unceasing, unbeginning," surpassing, but not refuting or eliminating, the capacities of human reason, the efforts of our good will. The postulate to organize the world, to promote justice and peace, to abolish slavery, to increase the ever-threatened dignity of man—the entire code of social responsibilities thus appears to be mysteriously interwoven with an even wider program and transcendental scheme, conceived and planned beyond this world but applied to it.

Eros, the double-faced demon and mediator between the visible world and the invisible, connects the progressive, yes, the scientific enthusiasm of Walt Whitman with the darker, more mysterious ingredients of his work. Indeed, his heartening speech carries undertones, hardly audible sometimes and yet always powerful, echoing the tune of a secret message that has reached him—from where? Oh, the whisper of heavenly death; the touch of mystical breezes, wafted soft and low; that music always around him, caressing him like a phantom; the melodies of unseen rivers: "or is it the splashing of tears? the measureless waters of human tears?"

Do we still recognize him—the sturdy bard of an "athletic Democracy"? There he stands, "pensive and faltering," as he writes down the words, "the dead":

> For living are the Dead;
> (Haply the only living, only real,
> And I the apparition—I the spectre.)

These words are the cue for the fourth cherub—a sickly youth, bland and yet passionate. Friedrich von Hardenberg, alias Novalis, is a disciple of St. Francis of Assisi, a spiritual cousin of Shelley, and the most original mind in the brotherhood of German romanticists. The hectic flush of his cheeks indicates the phthisical disposition. He has the look of a somnambulist—at once penetrating and introvert—and the bland, oblivious smile characteristic of infants, madmen, and angels. With a wistful sigh he responds, distrait and understanding, to the appeal of the "heavenly whisper," and then withdraws to the shady realm of his own reveries. Jaunty and clairvoyant, he roves through the floating darkness as a diver through the maze of a submarine landscape.

"We dream of voyages through the cosmos," says Novalis. "But is not the cosmos in us? We do not know the depths of our spirits. Inward goes the mysterious road. Eternity is in us or nowhere . . ."

In his daring vision the concepts of Death and Future, salvation and dissolution, merge in a vast and meaningful identity. His cult of death is not nihilistic but a profound and paradoxical glorification of life. "Life is the beginning of death. Life exists for the sake of death. Death is ending and beginning at the same time. Separation and nearer self-union at the same time." The substance of our world cannot be destroyed but must undergo the mystic transformation from shadow into light. "Now, to be sure, it seems internally so dark, so lonely, and formless. But how completely different will it seem to us, when this tenebration is finished, and the shadow body has been removed. We shall enjoy it more than ever, for our spirit has missed it."

What a beatific day it will be!—the day of the glorious reintegration. God and man, man and nature, substance and idea imbue, penetrate, embrace each other. It is only then, when this vast marriage takes place, that the curse of individuation—the evil privilege of isolated existence will be lifted from us. Words, names, and figures are replaced by harmonies; the tedious monotony of our mechanized civilization fades away: a new collective rhythm sweeps throughout the world.

The child and the artist—long considered the immature or anomalous types of the human species—are the heralds and initiators of the coming miracle. For only those two, the child and the poet, possess what most other men have forfeited: faith and intuition. "The artist," says Novalis, "is thoroughly transcendental." Therefore: "Only an artist can divine the intrinsic meaning of life." "The true poet is omniscient—a miniature cosmos." The artistic experience not only reaches back to the early stages of the human development but also anticipates our future elevation. The double perspective of prophecy embraces beginning and end as an entity. Life has been dreamlike: it will become dreamlike again—a magic ceremonial, innocent and serene as the plays of children: logical and transparent as a crystal or a mathematical formula. "The life of the gods is mathematics," as Novalis tells us.

This eschatological process is of an at once chemical and, metaphysical nature. It affects not only the relationship between God and man but also the unconscious, or inarticulate, drama of the animals, trees, rocks, and waters. "Since the deity condescended to become man," Novalis says in one of his most suggestive aphorisms, "he may become stone, plant, beast, or element as well. There is, perhaps, a constant process of salvation going on in the realm of nature."

What mostly attracted me is the organic fusion of pagan and Christian elements in his philosophy. His erotic mysticism has a definitely Hellenic savor. On the other hand, our phthisical rhapsodist is Christian enough to accept the notion of sin, if in a rather unconventional way. "Sin," he says, "is the great attraction for the love of God. The more sinful you feel yourself, the more Christian you are. Absolute unification with the deity is the purpose of Sin and Love."

The voices of my four archangels find each other in the pathos of this metaphysical sensuality. Their prophecies amalgamate through the connecting power of Eros. The Greek philosopher of the Idea and the American Camerado; the Christian visionary and the iconoclastic psychologist who called himself "the Anti-Christ"—they are akin to each other as all four of them adhere to the same basic concept of transcendental humanism. Their vision is both tragic and optimistic. Human beauty and grace, the somatic splendor of youth mirrors and confirms an extramundane harmony, the eternal pattern and stimulus of our own endeavor. The youthful impulse to reorganize the world, the revolutionary élan of every new generation is religious in its essence and roots—no matter how "materialistic" or "atheistic" in its extraneous forms.

"To the young, the Republic is the natural way of life. Wherever there is youth, there also is Republic."

From which one of the great Four comes this statement? It might be by Plato or Nietzsche, Whitman or Novalis.

These four, then, are the most prominent figures in my romantic Olympus. Around this nucleus gather the minor spirits.

It is unfair to speak of minor or major Olympians: such clumsy differentiations are devoid of relevancy in these sacred halls. The Pantheon is a democracy of kings. The hierarchy which is maintained with serene precision is a choreographic arrangement rather than an order of rank. Some of the angels next to the cherubim almost match their stature and radiancy.

This small one, for instance, is very great. At the first look, he seems just a sickly little Jew, rather meek and pathetic. But what eyes in his haggard, spiritual face, lustrous, eloquent, full of magnetic power! I recognize his tender and skeptical smile. He is Heinrich Heine.

The Heine of my Olympus is by no means the popular author of the "Book of Songs," but the wretched invalid of his last years in Paris, stricken with disease and poverty; writhing, shrinking, rotting in his bed; pinched and shaken by most hideous pains but still quiveringly alive, still alert and sagacious, in the midst of his agonies. While his organism decays, his mental power uncannily increases. His poetic journalism and journalistic poetry assume a new dimension of authentic grandeur. Illuminated by suffering, he discerns and analyzes the most delicate trends and potentialities of our civilization. The versatile go-between and interpreter between French and Germanic culture, Jewish and Christian philosophies, becomes a prophet—forecasting with striking insight the scope and impact of developments subterranean, invisible at that time, but which have meanwhile revealed their devastating dynamics. His warnings to the French to beware of the Teutonic danger anticipate not only the disasters of 1871 and 1914 but, moreover, the calamity we now witness. His prophecies concerning Russia, the meaning of Socialism, the latent crisis of Occidental culture, the plight of the Jews in Europe, the future of Christianity—all his mordant exposures and suggestive hints are, indeed, more revealing as to the roots and implications of our present emergency than anything written since Nietzsche.

The genius of Heinrich Heine is ample and sensitive: it embraces all aspects of the European soul. Sometimes he seems flippant and superficial; but in other moments his mind soars to the heights of true inspiration. He too dreams of the ultimate marriage of Jewish-Christian ethics and Hellenic beauty. In his most confident hours he visualizes the final balance between liberty and equality, aristocratic and socialistic principles, spiritual and somatic values.

From such lofty flights he falls back into the dismal reality of his invalidism—incarcerated, once again, in his squalid hole in the rue d'Amsterdam. From his grave-like cell the pain-stricken poet argues with his merciless God: "Whom do you want me to blame? Is our Lord not omnipotent? Is it he, then, who causes the disorder himself? What wantonness! What obnoxious mischief! . . . Thus we keep asking questions, until they close our mouth with a handful of earth. But is that an answer?"

"Yes, I know," he says to a friend who seems bewildered by the sacrilegious boldness of his poetry, "It is beautiful. Terribly beautiful . . ." And he adds, with a pallid, distracted smile: "A corpse is singing, or the grave itself . . ."

How much he experienced and understood!—the clairvoyant cripple in the loneliness of his agony. A romantic revolutionary and rebellious romanticist, he was able to grasp the promises and dangers inherent in either tendency—mechanized progress and its dialectic counterpart, the "conservative revolution." The inspired heir of Voltaire and the humanitarian Enlightenment also anticipated the gesture with which future poets would turn away from our polluted civilization. He was not lacking in insights and forebodings, certainly not. But his common sense prevented him from condemning the problematical world to which he belonged himself.

As the disintegration of cultural values proceeded, the tragic audacity of the creative spirits ominously increased. Nietzsche's tremendous example initiated the open rebellion. The challenge of his work and tragedy inspired other protests. Half a century after Heine's death, a new generation of Europeans ventured to spurn and deny their solidarity with this striving and erring epoch. Their daring disapproval manifested itself in various patterns and poses.

Another impressive cherub—the German poet Stefan George—demonstrates his detachment from our vulgarity by looking like Dante with a touch of Caesar and a Hellenistic priest of the decadent period. With matchless dignity he wears his ornate garment and the crown of laurels. At once elated and peevish, he stands apart from the motley crowd. How fervently I have admired him!—the idol of my youth.

It is hard, if not impossible, to describe his unique position to any one unfamiliar with the particularities of intellectual life in Germany. Only in a country where the cult of the "great man" is a veritable mania both with the masses and the cultural vanguard, could a poet assume such exorbitant moral and artistic authority. To scores of the most fastidious young men George's word and gesture was absolute law.

A scion of Rhenish wine-growers, he came from the German region most akin to Latin culture and the Mediterranean world. His genius was molded by Hellas, Rome, and the universal message of the Catholic Church. At first his exclusiveness was of a purely aesthetic nature: his career began under the auspices of Mallarmé and his Parisian Parnassus. Gradually, however, this aristocratic refinement— very much in keeping with the moods and trends of the fin de siècle —assumed the character of sacerdotal arrogance. An aesthetic style, maintained with admirable consistency, was offered and accepted as a spectacular challenge directed against the entire apparatus and terminology of a decadent civilization. The poet thus became the idolized center of an esoteric circle devoted to the work of Stefan George and his concepts of beauty and morality. The holy wrath of the mystagogue spurned everything he deemed vulgar, slouching, and nebulous. According to his disciples, only his work and figure possessed greatness and purity in the midst of so much blare and bustle. His tyrannic caprice compelled "the circle" to join him in the worship of an effulgent youth, Maximin, whom he glorified as a sort of bacchantic saint— half-Krishnamurti, half-Alcibiades. The magnificent carols celebrating the chosen juvenile and lamenting his death, are the heart and climax of George's poetic message. What might have seemed a hazardous, indeed, provocative whim—the virtual deification of a handsome boy— assumes true persuasiveness, thanks to the emotional and artistic fervency with which the feat is performed. Just as Whitman's democratic appeal owes its essential efficacy to its amative gist, the aristocratic hierarchy of Stefan George's vision is organized and animated from this pulsating kernel. It is from this fiery source that his protest against contemporary triteness and inertia derives its stringent grandeur.

The angel whom I find in the neighborhood of Novalis, is less dominating. If George serves the image and memory of a deified male, Rainer Maria Rilke is initiated into the gentle mysteries of trees and flowers, children, women in love, flowing water, very old men, music, the rain, the moon, and the autumn—everything that is floating, bland, irisdescent.

The French and Slavic elements prevail in the delicate organism of his genius. His stanzas resound the elegiac rhythm of Russian litanies and at the same time are full of those mellow pastels and subtle undertones he studied and loved in Paris.

He too is pained and alarmed by the exuberant ugliness and moral disintegration of our life in this century. But instead of cursing our ways and efforts, he withdraws into a magic realm of his own, striving with meek persistence for an ever closer understanding of the real thing, the pure stuff of which leaves and angels are made. Is it an escape, his unending exploration of secret landscapes, the nameless gardens of love? But what propitious escape that yields such abundance of wisdom and tenderness! His vision widens and becomes comprehensive: the "Sonnets to Orpheus" and "Duinese Elegies"—the lyric output of his later years—embrace the whole panorama, the entire repertoire of rhythms and melodies; the complete palette of colors, shades, and twilights. Orpheus, the singing god, equally at home in both spheres, the underworld and the realm of light, grasps and praises the "whole laudable tissue"; the unspeakable meaning of all images—pain, lust, darkness, blood, evening, wind, love, flower, tears, poem, death.

Oh, my forlorn angels! Fugitive cherubim! Those I have loved the most are the most saddened ones. Stefan George transmutes his suffering into the immaculate structure of his brocade verse. Rilke, offended by the jangling machines, seeks to decipher again the sigils of nature and dream, the primeval secrets inherent in the frantic whisper of lovers, the gestures of agony and embrace.

My Olympus swarms with erratic spirits. All of them apparently look for something—roving through the paradisiac scenery in an endless and hopeless quest. This one was for years my favorite, a dim and fidgety apparition: Herman Bang, the Danish novelist.

The position granted to him by the Olympian management may seem unduly prominent: the international public hardly remembers his name, which speaks only against the international public. I insist that his works—nine or ten novels, most of them rather slim, and some volumes of short stories—are one of the inconspicuous but imperishable jewels of modern literature.

Bang is a master of subtle understatement: he excels in suggestive connotations and revealing silences. His technique is purest impressionism, akin to what Debussy achieved through the medium of music; Monet, with the palette. The essential drama takes place between the lines—concealed rather than vocalized in rugged dialogues and casual allusions. There is no plot—only atmosphere; a nervous kaleidoscope of flitting shapes and motions. Most of his stories deal with very old people—prodigious remnants of sunken epochs: numb and petrified—or with meek, frustrated women who wither for want of love as flowers do without sunshine. Or his heroes are virtuosi, acrobats, waiters in international hotels—uprooted folks, people without a country. Bang has a morbid penchant for all sorts of vagabonds: in fact, he is something like a refined vagrant himself—a Nordic nobleman with the looks of an effeminate gypsy. His life ended in an American Pullman car, not far from Ogden, Utah. This appalling scene—the lonely agony in a vast, foreign land—might be the melancholy acme of one of his own novels. "Oh, Lord! grant his own death to every man!" prayed Rainer Maria Rilke.

And I enjoy watching this other wanderer, frail and restless, as he hovers from cloud to cloud—lingering here and there to light a cigarette or exchange hasty signs with other errant immortals. What a bizarre figure!—the one, I mean, who now waves at Bang with cordial nonchalance. He looks indeed fantastic, with one side of his body dressed in the striped uniform of a convict, while the other half is beautifully adorned with heavy silk and velvet, glittering jewelry, and a black carnation. His face, too, is divided into two uneven parts: one—tragic and worn under the shaven hair; the other, smooth and gluttonous, with sybaritic lips and a silky lock caressing the ivory arch of the forehead. Oscar Wilde, fleshy and alert, saunters along the heavenly boulevards, a stunning hybrid and embodied paradox. Prayers and

puns gush simultaneously from his lips. The prayers are as genuine as
the cracks are cynical and risqué. What a feat!—to cry "De Profundis,"
while at the same time smiling the corrupt and radiant smile of Dorian
Gray. Thus the ingenious Oscar shocks society twice, in his double
appearance as Prince Charming and penitent. His challenge is more
spectacular and effective than the saturnine unrest of his fellow-cherub
from Copenhagen. Still they agree with each other, united in the
pathos of a capricious and yet deadly serious protest.

A third traveler savagely interrupts their gossip. A truculent youth
rushes down the fluffy promenade as if chased by a pack of hounds.
His hair disheveled, panting, sweating, glowing, he flings himself
through the Olympic spaces.

"He smells like a panther, doesn't he?" whispers Bang.

Wilde giggles and shrugs. "No, like a drunken sailor," he observes
dryly.

"Don't you know who he is?" asks Bang, awe-stricken.

"Do I know him?" Wilde seems highly amused. "But everybody
knows him. Everybody knows Shakespeare Enfant . . ."

That is what the literati called him, with mock admiration and
genuine jealousy—Shakespeare Enfant . . . There he was a desperate
demon, his curls and eyelashes scorched by infernal flames; exhausted
by his Season in Hell; illuminated, haunted, bellowing with vitality
and distress: Arthur Rimbaud, the most dynamic escapist of all times.

Small wonder that he carried an aura of jungle odors as a comet
carries its tail. He returns from murderous escapades to the deserts and
forests of Africa, where he tried to purify his organism from the poison
of civilization. His exorbitant motions are those of a fugitive frantically engaged in stripping off his shackles. His starlike eyes widened
as in constant agony, he flies from his fame, his madness, the sugared
lies of those in love with him. He is the criminal tramp who has
raped a woman and now runs away, frightened by the police and her
awakening tenderness.

The woman he violated and hypnotized is the French language. She
had become too flowery and subtle: he embraced and shattered and
blessed her. He toyed with the vowels of the alphabet as a child does
with marbles. An inspired infant, he murmured his magic spell:

> A noir, E blanc, I rouge, U vert, O bleu, voyelles
> Je dirai quelque jour vos naissances latentes . . .

Fed up with his own tricks and triumphs; hankering for new rhythms and colors, never-heard-of forms of suffering and love, he embarked on the boat of rapture, his wondrous vehicle, "Le Bateau Ivre," light as cork, dancing high on the waves; blessed by the tempests, guided by the black sea horses, persecuted by gigantic serpents; the Drunken Boat gliding through the azures and greens of treacherous seas; entangled in the reeds of enormous weirs and marshes; the cursed—the enthralling vessel errant from pole to pole, accompanied by the golden and singing fishes, through the feverish nights of the tropics; freezing under the glacial skies of the polar zones; stranded on shores where panther eyes, flowers, and human skin mingle with metallic rainbows; haunted by evil currents and the mystic horrors of dusk and dawn; the delirious skiff finally emerging from the violet mists, hurricane-tossed into the birdless ether; rising, hovering, flying, a meteor, free and smoking, surrounded by electric moons; piercing heaven like a fiery wall; rapidly approaching the unspeakable horizon of flames: mortally attracted by the purple abyss, the vortex of ecstasy.

Generations have been under the spell of this prodigious image: Rimbaud's vision and tragedy became the most seductive stimulus in European letters, equalled only by the spectacle of Nietzsche's flight and fall. Among all my saints he is the most brutal and most beautiful. How willingly I followed him in his frantic escapades! How ardently my heart echoed his defiant and nostalgic farewell:

> Mais, vrai, j'ai trop pleuré. Les aubes sont navrantes.
> Toute lune est atroce et tout soleil amer.
> L'âcre amour m'a gonflé de torpeurs enivrantes.
> Oh! que ma quille éclate! Oh! que j'aille à la mer!
>
> Si je désire une eau d'Europe, c'est la flache
> Noire et froide où vers le crepuscule embaumé
> Un enfant accroupi, plein de tristesse, lâche
> Un bateau frêle comme un papillon de mai.

A cold, black pool, infinitely gloomy in the dusk; a saturnine child toying with a tiny ship: both so frail—the infant and the boat: both so wan and pathetic in the chilly twilight . . . Is this dismal scene everything he remembers of his homeland, Europe? Is there nothing to draw him back? Has even the tender eloquence of Paul Verlaine lost its persuasive power?

Poor Verlaine! He stretches his trembling hands out to the unfaithful companion. Look! his faun-like face is all wet with tears. What a woeful wreck!—depraved, slouching, polluted. Obviously, he is in a state of utter intoxication. It's absinthe again: the sharp smell of anise is only too conspicuous. Rather distasteful conduct, I must say, on the part of an elderly poet in heaven. But nobody seems to mind it. Placidly and not without benevolence, the other angels watch their slovenly colleague. Only Rimbaud apparently disapproves of his pitiful crony. He cruelly overlooks the drunkard, who keeps beckoning and leering at him. How unfair of young Rimbaud to be so reserved and chilly! After all, who would remember his name, if it were not for Verlaine's unflagging propaganda? Who fed and clad the tatterdemalion when he appeared in Paris, bare of cash and contacts? "Shakespeare Enfant" is violent and ungrateful. But his aging lover neither complains nor resigns. He seems at once rueful and coquettish—a weeping Satyr intoxicated with repentance and concentrated liquor. His sighs are poetry; his tears mingle with the absinthe in his glass, adding a salty flavor to its sweetish aroma.

Somebody sitting next to Verlaine casts his shadow over the milky fluid. The pale concoction of alcohol, anise, and wails begins to heave, to vibrate, to produce opalescent bubbles. Baudelaire, playful and diabolic, strews tiny paper flowers into the beverage. The effect is stupendous. The bubbles rise, phosphoresce, become shining billows, while the paper flowers, on their part, come up and bloom, like certain Chinese toy blossoms when thrown into the water. It is terrible and delightful to watch the exuberant growing of the "Fleurs du Mal," the hectic flowers of evil. They dance and radiate and constantly change their forms, assuming ever new and ever more baroque appearances. The inside of the glass seems transformed into a labyrinth of exotic vices and beauties. A black Venus emerges from the greenish foam—Baudelaire's beloved Venus Noire, an effulgent vampire—and executes her stunning Danse Macabre. Dexterous and satanic, she juggles with death's heads and bleeding hearts, always frightful, always beautiful; now, a glittering serpent: then, a tiger, an orchid, a dainty and dangerous cat. Yes, she is the subtle animal so often invoked and praised by Baudelaire. Hers is the glacial and bottomless look of the jewel-like, dagger-like eyes, the murderous grace and flexibility.

What an animal!—remarkably large and fine, indeed, and sagacious to an astonishing degree. A perfect sample of a black cat, one might say if it were not for the one lacking eye and the mark of white hair disturbingly conspicuous in the darkness of her silky fur. This mark, surprisingly, has the shape of a ghastly thing—of the Gallows!—O, mournful and terrible engine of Horror and of Crime, of Agony and Death . . .

No doubt, the caprices of the swelling "Fleurs du Mal" turn increasingly lurid. Baudelaire's artificial paradise merges with the authentic hell of Edgar Allan Poe. Ligeia's prodigious features loom up in the milky floods: the attractive ghost, all erudition and disquieting loveliness, embraces Roderick, last scion of the decaying Usher tribe. A gigantic gold bug creeps along swaying pendulum, while the intoxicated poet—dreaming dreams no mortal ever dared to dream before—broods over the nightmarish mathematics of his uncanny mystery stories.

The bubbles in Verlaine's tear-and-anise cocktail become more and more suggestive. Now they reveal the voluptuous scene of a masked ball swarming with jaunty ballerinas and harlequins. What a startling pellmell of colors, costumes, and melodies! This royal suite must be Prince Prospero's: only he can afford to entertain on so lavish a scale, while the hideous pestilence keeps devastating the country. Only he commands the wealth and imagination to surprise his guests with such staggering glare and glitter. There is, indeed, an abundance of the beautiful, much of the wanton, much of the bizarre, something of the terrible, and not a little of that which might have excited disgust. A multitude of dreams stalks to and fro in the seven chambers where the magnificent fête takes place.

All idioms and tastes commingle in a stunning olla-podrida. On one stage the bajazzos of the Commedia dell'Arte perform their inspired feats, while in the next room the feverish ballet of E. T. A. Hoffmann displays its baroque personnel of quaint professors, giggling sorcerers, and sagacious mice. Peter Schlemihl, the interesting freak with magic boots and no shadow, waltzes with the Black Venus, while the Flemish jester, Till Eulenspiegel, tries to amuse Prince Hamlet—unsuccessfully, though. The Dane remains sad and inaccessible. Motionless and without a smile he watches Till's frolicsome capers and faces, and when he finally opens his mouth it is only to begin his famous monologue, once again. But before he has had a chance to pronounce the initial line, the German romanticists interfere. What obstreperous clowns! Dexterously and swiftly they translate the text into German and now lilt it in unison: "To be or not to be . . ." swinging through the hell in the rhythm of Offenbach's Barcarole.

"Not to be, of course!" decides the peremptory voice of Arthur Schopenhauer. While the bleak oracle of his voice indicts the viciousness and emptiness of all things, the irresponsible poets continue to have a good time. Coleridge has joined them, poisoned by opium and German metaphysics. What a hoax! Goethe himself appears in the oriental disguise of Hafiz and mistakes a Persian bus boy for Gretchen. Faust meets Hamlet: the result is Manfred, an operatic mongrel. Lord Byron is not yet satisfied and hazards competing with his German master and admirer in the solemn mask of Tasso. But the audience thinks his performance falls short of what he did at Sardanapalus and, above all, in his most thrilling role—that of Don Juan.

The romantic Don Juan is intoxicated with Weltschmerz and his own sex appeal. First he bewitches the Ophelias, Gretchens, and Donna Annas with the suave melancholy of his speech and the lascivious grace of his gestures. As soon, however, as his idol and victim begins to respond to his charm—as soon as Don Juan is loved, he turns chaste and elusive. Look at him! he is Joseph, the dreamy interpreter of royal dreams, who first seduces, then disappoints the grand lady of Egypt. He escapes, he dances, he flies, saturnine, nimble, irresistible; an evasive Narcissus fluttering and sparkling in front of his spellbound admirers.

He raves and radiates and burns. He is a torch kindled and brandished by divine energies. He is a white horse that thinks himself a peacock. No, a mad bird who believes he is Nijinsky. But the Russian dancer, on his part, is haunted by the idea that he is a horse and that horses are birds and can fly, a minor misconception from which he had to be cured in a sanatorium. However, the fixed idea proved more powerful and tenacious than the skill of the psychiatrists. Evidently, the obstinate genius managed to dupe his guardians and to sneak into Prospero's palace. There he is—incorrigible, in brilliant shape, more bird-like and horse-like than ever. In a veritable delirium of grace he keeps whirling on the toes of one foot, inspired by the tunes of Debussy and Stravinsky; magically transformed into Petrushka, who is at the same time the Faun celebrating his usual afternoon sacrifice, the traditional matinée orgy, "Le Sacre du Printemps." A group of awe-stricken ballerinas, invented by Degas, gaze at their stunning colleague —the weightless maniac, the frenzied demon of dance.

Poor girls! They gain weight visibly while they stand absorbed in the spectacle of Nijinsky's ecstasy. He gyrates and blazes, consuming himself in his paroxysm of motion, while those unfortunate females gradually assume colossal dimensions. Their breasts, hands, and necks; their saddened foreheads and lazy feet—everything grows as if swollen by a mysterious grief, disfigured by a tragic elephantiasis. No doubt, these massive goddesses—drowsy mountains of flesh—belong to the species of large women as Picasso was wont to paint them during his classical period. Oblivious and supine, they rest and dream in august tranquillity, undisturbed by the uproarious goings-on around them.

Prince Prospero, as I notice now, has decorated his seven chambers according to the main periods of Picasso's artistic work—an exquisite gesture of reverence on the part of the capricious monarch. The first room mirrors the pallid tints and affected melancholies of the Blue Period. Lurid beggars, most of them blind to boot, are guided by emaciated youngsters through the floating dusk where they exchange inconsolable smiles with weary prostitutes. The gloomy set-up of this nether world invokes memories of a bewitched aquarium of which I frequently dreamt, a weird idyll swarming with wan amphibia who really were royalties and poets transformed by an evil spell.

In the next room the coloring is brighter, bathed in mellow, sensual tones. This is the rendezvous of the guitar-playing harlequins with their triangular hats—the spirits of the Pink Period, wistful and attractive. Their family life seems cozy enough, though their wives look rather phthisical. As for the children, they appear almost as frail as are the blue kids in the neighboring chamber; however, the pink ones are definitely more jaunty and dexterous. Some of them are earnestly occupied with odd physical exercises—dancing on a ball or on pointed fragments of glass. The mothers, dainty but merciless, watch their little boys capering in the rose, hazy twilight.

The third gallery is a horror. The wayward genius, Pablo Picasso of Spain, has allowed the jungle to invade the realm of his creation. The scene is crammed with diabolic masks and other monstrous tokens. Everything is distorted, dislocated, defaced. Nude women of appalling ugliness desperately stretch their angular arms and legs. From the walls comes the ghastly grin of colossal grimaces—the essence of sadness and insanity skillfully carved in wood.

Chamber Three is open to Chamber Four: the Negro Period and the Cubist overlap. The primitive idiom of the African solitudes explodes and at once becomes articulate in the cerebral violence of the Cubist constructions. Everything human and emotional is relentlessly exterminated for the sake of a new pattern of a heartless dynamic beauty. Chamber Four is, in its own way, more terrifying than even the Jungle Room. The human being that finds himself surrounded by those furious abstractions—the gyrating spirals, ravenous cubes, and bloodthirsty triangle—cannot but shudder, overwhelmed by a feeling of utter helplessness.

The gaudy mess in Chamber Five is more cheerful. We are in the room devoted to large still lifes and the ballet décors—a rather gay place, indeed. Flying guitars fraternize with fragments of wine bottles and newspaper clippings. Disconnected ciphers plunge into a whirlpool of green, gray, and pink; the apples of Cézanne hover against the background of an open window: outside floats the shining blue of the Mediterranean.

Thanks to Prospero's inexhaustible funds and ingenuity, this classical scenery has been most effectively staged at the other side of the window. One single step suffices to carry us, as by magic, from the merry pellmell of the semi-abstract still lifes into a landscape of mythic lofti-ness. Athletic juveniles play with dragons and panthers, while colossal ladies stride toward even more voluminous rocks and pillars. Every-thing is exceedingly large, very sad, and beautifully measured. No doubt, the snaky-haired monster, Medusa, whose regard turns the be-holder to stone, must have had a glimpse at these heroes, monsters, and matrons. Or whence comes the blight palling over the Sixth Room of Prince Prospero's suite?

Is there a murderous secret hidden behind the seventh door? What sinister gag may our witty host have made up for this chamber, which lies most eastwardly of the seven? None of the maskers venture to enter the Black Apartment; it remains deserted—watched by the paralyzed goddesses with the deformed limbs.

Beware! Don't touch the forbidden door! It may fly open and re-veal what no mortal eye ought to see. Who is foolhardy enough to unleash the tribulations of the Seventh Period? Don't you know what awaits you in Prospero-Picasso's terrible "chambre séparée"? Don't you recognize the appalling mummer, with his vesture dabbled in blood, his face besprinkled with the scarlet horror? Can you gauge the devastat-ing impact of this blasphemous mockery?

This is the Seventh Chamber—the boudoir of disintegration. The in-fernal landscape of total war and madness: the triumph of the Red Death. The seven periods merge into one fiery entity—melted and mixed by the Wrath of God. The seven trumpets blow the Marche Funèbre; the seven plagues rave throughout the world; the seven vials inundate the scene with the deadly splendor of indescribable tints. Dies Irae, Dies Illa . . . This is the apocalyptic hour when every-thing cracks and totters. The pale horse of Guernica—this is the end of the seven periods and the seven blasphemies. The last thing we see is a tumbling animal—tormented, defaced, its mouth wide open as if it wanted to cry out the helpless protest of all martyred creatures.

How annoying they are, these romanticists! I seriously resent their habit of turning things upside down and making a mess out of them. Nothing is spared by their anarchic wit. It is, indeed, embarrassing to watch their utter lack of discipline and logic. They admit characters out of books, plays, and paintings to this sanctum, where only the creators should enjoy their unending holiday. Small wonder that the more earnest ones among the Olympians seem disturbed by such obstreperous mischief. Father Freud looks remarkably worried as he saunters with his flock over the heavenly pastures. What an idyllic picture! His bleating sheep are the tamed and analyzed complexes, the wicked demons of the unconscious depth. How cute and harmless they seem!—crowding behind their kindly shepherd: funny little Oedipus complex, good old parricidal obsession, masturbation trauma, the familiar I-have-to-slaughter-my-aunt complex—particularly easy to cure. Father Freud pigeonholes and dominates the whole motley lot. Or doesn't he, really?

"How do you do, Herr Colleague?" This is the sonorous voice of Father Marx who enjoys the morning sun, resting in a deck chair, not far from the cave of the titanic novelists.

"So so," mumbles Freud. "I had naughty dreams last night, which always makes me feel pretty low. The romantic bedlam has haunted me, once again. Too many complexes and traumatic hallucinations, Herr Colleague!—too much monkey-business, even for a hardboiled old hunter like me."

Marx shakes his head and giggles. "How funny you are, Doc!" he says. "Don't you realize that the little eccentricities of our romantic friends are the inevitable result of labor conditions in Jena and Birmingham? According to the scientific theory of the surplus value . . ."

Freud raises a long, skinny forefinger. "Sex!" he exclaims as if it were a merry battle cry he darted against his colleague. "You seem to forget, once again, that sex is the sole motor of life—the source of all trouble and inspiration. The sublimation of the incestuous impulse . . ."

"Nonsense!" shouts the author of "Das Kapital." "Your fallacious doctrines are apt to divert the attention of the working people from the one issue that really matters—the class struggle. You are an agent of the exploiting class—unconsciously so, perhaps . . ."

"I am pleased to hear you employ my own terminology," smirks the psychiatrist—whereupon the sociologist murmurs something not to be repeated.

Freud—although keenly interested in this revealing symptom of Marx's repressed desires—prefers to change the subject. With a jaunty motion he draws his colleague to the entrance of the cave from which a hollow grumbling has punctuated their conversation. "Look at them!" says Freud, moved with pity: agitated with professional interest. "Rather nightmarish, aren't they?"

The imprisoned giants—but why don't they try to escape?—are engaged in all sorts of futile and tiresome labors. Small wonder that Tolstoi groans: he carries huge pieces of stone from one corner of the dingy room to the other, to punish himself, as it were, for having hitherto wasted his time with the production of masterpieces. Sometimes he falters and stands motionless for a minute, absorbed in prayers; looking like a very old Russian peasant, or a weather-worn piece of rock. "Let me be simple, my Lord!" mumbles the illustrious old man. "I abominate my fame, my talent, my work. I loathe literature. I disapprove of Anna Karenina. I don't want to be Homer. I want to be a peasant. Oh, Lord! let me do a peasant's useful, primitive work!" And he continues to carry the heavy stones—uselessly, stubbornly, heroically.

His brother Balzac, too, sweats and moans: but under a different sort of strain. He does not wear a peasant's smock-frock but a sumptuous mantle. Pompous and massive in the draperies, precisely as Rodin has presented him, he is occupied with adding the last touches to a vast mural fresco. "Completeness!" he growls, his face moist with genius and perspiration. "Money, and sex, never heard-of intrigues, amazing crimes: the whole tragedy, the entire farce . . . My picture has no value, unless it is comprehensive. Everything must be included: the sordid plots, the noble impulses, the strategy of love, the manias, the jealousies, the boundless aspirations—the full scope of human comedy.— I am God!" bellows the novelist. "I re-create the creation!"

But nobody listens. They are all deafened, blinded, dazed by their own obsessions. "Perfection!" cries Flaubert, bent over a fragment of marble, a minikin bit of the most delicate substance. For ages he has been carving and smoothing it but is not yet satisfied. "Only the form matters: only the perfect style has validity," he muses. "Programs are a swindle; faith is an illusion; progress—a hobby of the Philistines.

Emotions might ruin my prose. One comma is more real than God. Creation stinks. I have to purify it: to filter the chaos through the sieve of my immaculate style."

They are all hankering for one thing or another. Huysmans, a neurotic monk and student of Satanism, celebrates his Black Mass and seeks God in the maze of ceremonious obscenities. Herman Melville chases a white phantom gliding along the wall, the pallid shadow of an elusive fish: it fades away as soon as he tries to catch it. D. H. Lawrence rummages the ruins of Mexican temples for the traces and tokens of a new, healthy life.

Then darkness palls the scene. A sulphurous spectre looms up: Dostoievski has just crept out of an overcoat like a jinn in the Oriental fairy tale emerging from the magic bottle into which he was banished by a superior spell. The overcoat is Gogol's, neatly rolled and folded in the form of an egg. The Russian demon has expressly admitted himself, in a shockingly casual way, that he was born in this unusual and rather abhorrent fashion. "All of us come out of Gogol's Overcoat," he observed, referring to the masterly tale with this title. However, there he is, and he casts the dismal shadow of his genius over two or three generations. The macabre mannerism of his style sweeps the continent as a contagious disease. No matter whether you read him or not you cannot escape his influence: he is in the air. The unchained jinn from the east inundates Europe with his blatant revelations, apocalyptic jocularities, and the ghastly exuberance of his vision.

The milky clouds reverberate his cry. He shivers, his shoulders jerk, his face is torn by spasmodic grimaces, his mouth is covered by foam. No doubt, these are the symptoms of an epileptic fit. Both Marx and Freud are seriously perturbed.

"An intricate case," whispers Freud. "Difficult to treat: fascinating to analyze."

"Obviously the victim of economic conditions," murmurs Karl Marx. "The feudal system of Czarist Russia . . ."

"Do you really think, Herr Doctor, that the knowledge of your theories would suffice to heal his neurosis?" asks Professor Freud.

Marx replies, self-assured: "Why not? An injection of historic materialism should cure him."

"And how about this one? The reading of your stuff didn't make him very happy . . ."

The giant Sigmund Freud is pointing at looks very gloomy, indeed. Almost as colossal as Balzac but much less inspired, he broods over piles of pamphlets, rosters, compendiums, and sample pieces of various commodities—fruits, women's clothes, dried-out bread, bottles of wine and liquor. He has also a miniature model of an express engine and a microscope through which he examines a human heart.

"Emile Zola . . . ," whispers Karl Marx, at once awe-stricken and a little bit embarrassed.

"Your novelist!" Freud observes. "He is scientific enough, isn't he? Always aware of the dialectic process; thoroughly realistic . . ."

"He is an excellent writer," Marx angrily interrupts him. "I am certainly proud of this disciple."

"I don't deny his greatness," says Freud. "But I still don't think he looks happy. His whole being is as ponderous and opaque as his work. No lightness, no élan, no sublimation . . ."

"In any case, I like him better than this dreary rat," Dr. Marx snaps back. "He is of your ilk, I suppose—that tiresome snob, Marcel Proust. Quite a connoisseur of the unconscious, if I am not mistaken, and reactionary as hell. No inkling of the class struggle: nothing but decadent subtleties."

"I am satisfied with this pupil, if he is a pupil of mine," Freud replies, very simply. "He is a hero, don't you see that, Marx? He has explored and conquered new land, the unknown terrain of the soul. His psychology of childhood memories . . ."

"The memories of the rich," sneers Marx. "He happens to be a millionaire."

"He happens to be a genius."

"So am I," Marx declares.

Whereupon Freud, with a roguish smirk: "Undoubtedly, Herr Colleague. Only a genius can afford to be so stubbornly one-sided as you are."

Marx parries the hit: "So you possess at least one quality typical of the genius. For nobody will deny that your vision is limited, that you are narrow-minded."

While they heckle and irritate each other, Marcel Proust is frantically absorbed in the remembrance of things past. An asthmatic sorcerer, cloistered in his room, he tries to reconstruct what is sunken—to stop the merciless passage of time. Ingenious and obsessed, he employs smells, colors, tastes, and bits of music as divining rods to trace the lost paradise of reminiscences.

"I don't find it!" he whines. "Where is the forgotten perfume to guide me back to the promenade I used to walk with my grandmother? What sort of sherry wine was served at the dinner party of the Duchesse de Guermantes? Of what color was the gown Odette wore at the Verdrins' reception? I must go to the Ritz: maybe I'll find there the grande cocotte whom I want to portray. How can I succeed, unless I know the color of her gown and gloves? I have to investigate the appearance of her escort as well. How does the Prince de Sagan wear his monocle? What sort of flowers does Odette prefer as table decoration? The smell will make me sick: my asthma will get worse—I may have to stay in bed for weeks. What's the difference? The fragrance of those flowers might help me to rediscover the promenade where grandmamma used to take me . . ."

"How he suffers!" says Freud.

And Marx: "All of us suffer. Don't you?"

"I do," Freud admits. "That means that both of us have failed to disclose the universal remedy."

"Are we liars, then—both of us?"

"No. What we teach is true. But it is not the whole truth. We lie when we claim to possess the clue to ultimate wisdom."

There is a stillness: it seems to last forever. The sporadic yells of the giants fall into the silence like heavy pebbles into a bottomless well.

Is this the mountain of glory and happiness? It rather looks like an inferno to me. I see nothing but madmen and suicides. I see Jonathan Swift tormented by a brain tumor and too much insight into the brains of his fellowmen. I see August Strindberg haunted by his persecution mania as by evil ghosts. I see William Blake, inspired by God and confused by Swedenborg, hunting the precious specters of chimerical cherubim. I see Georg Büchner, the revolutionary genius of Germany, raving against and destroyed by the obtuseness of his time and countrymen. I see Vincent Van Gogh, his face taut with vision and agony. He achieves before a mirror the dire feat of cutting off his ear and at the same time finishing his self-portrait. Why just your ear, Vincent? The Holy Bible advises you to tear out your eye when it becomes a scandal. You mix up everything. You are mad.

Hölderlin is mad: his clairvoyant eyes transform the idyll of the Neckar valley into the heroic scenery of a mythic Hellas.

Franz Kafka sees the narrow streets of Prague swarming with demons and hieroglyphs. Hypnotized by the problem of the Original Sin, he searches all hiding places and dingy corners of the Ghetto for the name of the crime that he committed. What is my guilt? Who is my Judge? Where will the Trial take place? Why does the doorman of the Castle sneer at me? Why don't they tell him that he is already doomed and will be executed?

"What is our guilt?" moans the dismal chorus. "Who is our Judge? Where will the Trial take place? My God, my God, why hast thou forsaken me?"

The holy mountain shakes with their wolfish screams. Their distress rises like the Flood. They clamor for the redeemer. They urge and challenge and implore the highest Being. The boldest and most desolate one among them confounds himself, in blasphemous ecstasy, with the martyred god. "I am he!" yells Friedrich Nietzsche. "I am Dionysus whom they crucified!"

Every word you pronounce is a magic spell. Whoever the spirit you invoke—he appears.

He appears, and sheds his blessing, his smile upon the assembly of sinners and lunatics, rebels and invalids, drunkards, saints, somnambulists, and reformers. He knows all their errors and efforts; for he is their brother. The Son of Man is friendly and experienced, intimately versed in all our sorrows, pleasures, and endeavors: there is no quest or adventure he did not pass through, no emotion he could not share.

His message echoes the exuberance of Dionysus and also the cries of his martyrdom. The myths of sacrifice and resurrection came from Egypt and Asia Minor to the shores of Hellas: Dionysus, the god of drunkenness and tragedy, is the forerunner, indeed, the preincarna-

tion of the Messiah himself: Not only the Jews have forecast his arrival, nor are they the only ones who underrate his revelation.

His own priests have twisted and abused, throughout the centuries,
the innermost heart of his gospel. He has been presented as a zealot
who arraigns the weakness of human nature, He whose very appearance among us sanctifies the appetites of our mortal flesh. For, why
should the Spirit condescend to bear the humble disguise of the human
body, if the very stuff we are made of were sinful and doomed?

The dogmatizers and hypocrites have tried to truncate his testament,
indeed, to reverse its intrinsic meaning. By relating his prophecy to
"another world," they attempt to depreciate this universe and to divert
our attention from these earthly affairs. The vast significance of his legend is by no means that it grants us insight into other-worldly spheres
(Jesus is remarkably cautious not to betray cosmic secrets: I sometimes
suspect that he had a good gulp of the Lethean water before descend-
ing to our planet, as he did not wish to remember what no mortal
being must know); what he teaches us is, above all, the essential validity of our own experience. His Passion proves beyond any doubt that
here, in our midst, the decisive drama takes place. This Now is eternity. Now is the immortal life.

Futile to discuss whether the agony of his flesh actually is or only
symbolizes the authentic tragedy. We have no means nor right to perceive the drama, except through the medium of this symbolic creation:
the perishable image and the transcendental reality it embodies are
identical. Golgotha is the symbol and the truth. The crown of thorns,
the guffaw of the hangmen, Mary's mute complaint, the thirst he suffered from, the sponge with vinegar, the wounds on his hands and
feet—all this is the reality of our life, our own agony, our thirst, our
tears, our death.

The mystery is inherent in this world. His Passion confirms the
metaphysic impact of our drama: his resurrection guarantees the
salvation.

He suffered: it behooves us to accept suffering.

He rose from the dead: so we are not doomed.

He transformed the water into wine: nature will obey us, we don't
need to starve if we only follow his reasonable advice.

There is nothing unlikely or uncanny about the elegant gestures known as his Miracles. Why should he not heal the sick or transmute the substance of things? The metamorphosis of the divine vision into earthly stuff is infinitely more amazing than his casual experiments. The phenomenon of life is essentially magic: the primary wonder is that we move and die and are endowed with a soul. The miracles are natural as nature is miraculous. What strikes me as astonishing and depressing is only that no human being since the days of Christ has had the energy of faith to repeat the suggestive parables in action the Son of Man performed to instruct and entertain his brethren. How dreary are all of us, compared with his bold and colorful wit! He is the herald of Joy—the genius of unprecedented spectacles and motions.

He is dynamic, revolutionary. Behold, he makes all things new. The driving motor behind all rebellions, he provokes social changes, stimulates progress. His magnanimous message hails and demonstrates the solidarity of all human races. He has no prejudices: the outcasts, the adulteress are welcome to his heart. It may be that he is faintly biased against the rich, whom he compared to ungainly camels. The undue accumulation of wealth angers the Son of Man. The kingdom of heaven is revolutionary. Complacency and stagnation are more loathsome to him than even crime and transgression. The sinners are comforted by his smile, but the Pharisees quail before his fury. Forgiveness is granted to the prodigal son: lukewarm decency is unforgivable.

He is the Sword, the Tempest, the Fanfare—Rex tremendae majestatis. His appearance among us is not only the sweetest grace but also a challenge and an obligation.

What naïve and selfish fallacy!—to presume that His sacrifice automatically implies the end of our own woe and struggle. He is the redeemer, not because he liberates us from suffering, but because he reaffirms the goal of our toilsome pilgrimage.

The salvation is not a fait accompli but a pending process; not a finished action but a development—a tremendous promise. The Gospel of Jesus Christ is pregnant with future. It integrates and surpasses the boldest dreams ever dreamt—the most seditious programs and postulates. What other vision could be more daring than that of the Kingdom that will be granted to us when the Father's will is done on earth as it is in heaven?

He shines and thunders. My problematical heroes gathering around the Throne are struck by his exorbitant radiancy. They fall down before the phosphorescent Lamb. But the compelling charm of his smile and gesture soothes and encourages them. When they finally dare to look at him again, they find him indescribably handsome—with azure eyes and his face and hair white as wool, indeed, as white as the purest snow.

Says the Lamb: "Fear not! I am Alpha and Omega, the first and the last." And the chorus replies, swelling now, billow-like and at last united: "Sanctus, Sanctus, Sanctus!"

His ringing voice cools and blesses their brows and is like the water of many rivers; clear as crystal, proceeding out of the Throne. Behold, it is the pure water of life.

"Sanctus, Sanctus," repeat the sinners and prophets. "To him be glory and dominion forever and ever. Amen."

CHAPTER NINE

The Writing on the Wall

(1930-1932)

"This is a terrible loss . . ." I can still hear the saddened voice of our friend Bruno Frank when we discussed the news of Gustav Stresemann's death. "It's the beginning of the end," he concluded.

The meaning of his words may have been somewhat vague; yet none of us asked or argued. For we knew only too well what he tried to say: our own dismay confirmed his prophecy. No doubt, an epoch of German and European history, an interlude of delusive prosperity, well-intended efforts, and naïve illusions, was reaching its final stage. What would happen next? The atmosphere was charged with dangerous electricity: we could feel it in our fingertips.

Our world was menaced—by whom? What was the name of this challenge? We still refused to admit that a minor political party, a gang of fanatics and adventurers who called themselves "National Socialists," could threaten the entire code of Occidental values and traditions. We rummaged history in search of analogies that might express and explain our apprehension. Bruno Frank was among the first to formulate and to dramatize the yet half-latent crisis. In his novelette, "The Persians Are Coming," he condensed the complexities of our situation to the plainness of a didactic parable. Two statesmen—one French, one German—are burdened with the weight of the European tragedy. We witness their meeting somewhere by the Mediterranean, their fervent dialogues, their hopes and trepidation. One of them, the German, is already doomed: we see him stagger and fall. Will the survivor—Aristide Briand—be strong and faithful enough to meet the enemy singlehanded? Will he resist? Can he conquer? The Persians are powerful, well equipped . . .

The image of "the Persians," in the context of this suggestive tale, represents everything fundamentally hostile to our concept of human dignity. The author followed the antique pattern: his model was the symbolic duel of Salamis.

But myth never reproduces itself: history is its variation and development, not its repetition. The threat confronting the Hellenic communities seems almost mild compared with the peril we were to gauge and to meet. For this time the enemy did not attempt to storm the Acropolis from without: the evil forces gnawed and undermined it from within. The diabolic sow grew fat and mighty in our midst, while we stood paralyzed, watching the nauseous process. In fact, many of us fed and pampered the swelling monster, wittingly or not. The malignant weakness and complacency in our ranks were the most powerful allies of the enemy.

The blight of obscurantism and retrogression not only corrupted the political life but even infiltrated the views of the so-called liberal intelligentsia. The idolatry of "blood and soil," brutal force and poor style; the primacy of "instinct" and the mistrust of the intellect; the disparagement of both individual pride and social progress: the whole roster of fascist, or pre-fascist, moods and tendencies contaminated the jargon of professors, journalists, and playwrights—in short of everybody who wished to be in keeping with the Zeitgeist, to remain up-to-date. It was profoundly irritating to see Jewish book reviewers all in raptures, say, about the sinister autobiography of a certain Ernst von Salomon—one of the dashing young men, incidentally, who participated in the assassination of a truly great German Jew, Walther Rathenau. Out of "objectivity" and masochism, those perverse intellectuals politely analyzed and heartily encouraged their own murderers.

The "Frankfurter Zeitung," abused by Hitler as a "Jewish whore," praised the Nazi philosopher Ernst Jünger and defamed Bruno Frank's novelette. The left-wing literati, devoid of instinct and dignity, vilified each other, while Dr. Göbbels grinned.

I was not a moralist, nor was I bribed by the Weimar Republic (which saved its money for generals, industrialists, and the like) but this unworthy attitude gradually got on my nerves. I thought it cheap and obnoxious and altogether unworthy of a writer to jump on the band wagon of mystic retrogression. The French philosopher Julien Benda described this abject behavior most appropriately as "La Trahison des Clercs." It is bad and sad enough when Evil allures the laymen, the ignorant masses; but infinitely more shocking is the flirtation between the archenemy and the priests. And this is precisely what happened in Germany during those last years preceding the outbreak of the Third Reich. The clericals (i.e., the intellectuals)—not all of them but the majority—volunteered as the stooges of the anti-Christ (i.e., the anti-intellectual barbarians). One of them, the poet Gottfried Benn, whom I greatly admired, went so far as to call the idea of progress "the grossest vulgarity of human history."

Not much better than the actual traitors and deserters were those among my literary friends who watched the precipitation of the German drama with playful curiosity, thrilled and puzzled as by a well-staged mystery plot. Old Hindenburg appoints Dr. Heinrich Brüning, the Catholic leader, to form a new government (March, 1930). Isn't it exciting? How will Hitler react? And will the conservative bloc, now in power, take decisive measures against the rising flood of Nazism? Is the new Chancellor to apply the famous Article 48 of the Constitution? And if so, against whom? Brüning, an astute politician and at the same time a man of unquestionable integrity, tries to stem the catastrophe by placing additional burdens upon the workers and the lower middle class. Wages are cut, social insurances restricted. How is labor going to take it? No doubt, the faithful Catholic and servitor of big business hates and fears the "enemy to the left" much more than the Hitler gangs. They are a problem child that might be eventually tamed and educated, whereas the Marxists are really wicked. The left and liberal parties, on their part, begin to distrust the Chancellor. His unscrupulous application of the "emergency decrees" becomes unbearable: many experts deem it a violation of the Constitution. The Reichstag demands their immediate abrogation (July, 1930). What is going to happen? Brüning dissolves the Reichstag.

What next? The Republic, under the leadership of the Prussian Marshal and the priest-like politician, has shown itself alarmingly weak, boggling along without inspiration and self-assurance. It hardly seems in good shape to face the pivotal showdown.

The outcome of the Reichstag elections (September 14, 1930) was much more devastating than even the fiercest pessimists had anticipated. The Nazis produced 6,500,000 votes—5,700,000 more than they had obtained in the last election, an increase from twelve seats to 107, out of a total of 577. It was a terrific blow. Everybody, including the Nazis themselves, seemed bewildered by the magnitude of this triumph. It was a glaring vote of non-confidence against the Republic—announcing, strikingly and clearly, the popular disapproval of its hesitant, reactionary policy, its appalling lack of courage and imagination.

The lesson was cruel enough to arouse at last the slumbering energies of the liberal groups—or, on the contrary, to paralyze even the modest remnant of democratic initiative. The latter was the reaction: Hitler's first sweeping success utterly discouraged and confused the anti-totalitarian elements in Germany, rather than intensified their will and strength of resistance. The staggering figures of pro-Nazi votes were accepted as an ordeal, an act of God against which no opposition is possible. Most of the intellectual leaders in our camp turned despondent and jittery. Success is a convincing argument, especially to the Germans.

In literary circles—in my own milieu—defeatism and uncertainty prevailed. More and more of my friends began to wonder if the spirit of youth and revolution was not, perhaps, after all, with the other side. Even the official bards of democracy, men like Gerhart Hauptmann, the poet laureate of the Weimar Republic, became muddled and wavering. I remember one evening about that time—it was in the house of Hauptmann's publisher, S. Fischer—when the author of "The Weavers" seemed considerably puzzled as to the rightness or falsehood of Nazi doctrines. With many fumbling gestures and expressive grimaces he suggested that "Hitler . . . after all, . . . My dear friends! . . . no hard feelings! . . . Let's try to be . . . No, if you please, allow me . . . objective . . . May I refill my glass? This champagne . . . Very remarkable, indeed—that man Hitler, I mean . . . The champagne too, for that matter . . . Most extraordinary development . . . German youth . . . Almost seven million votes . . . As I so often said to my Jewish friends ... Those Germans ... incalculable nation ... very mysterious, indeed ... cosmic impulses ... Goethe ... Nibelungen Saga ... Hitler in a sense, expresses ... As I tried to explain to my Jewish friends ... dynamic tendencies ... elementary, irresistible ... This champagne! extraordinary flavor! Dionysian. ... German youth in its overflowing enthusiasm ... Well, to you, Frau Fischer!"

What he really tried to explain to his Jewish friends, in that baroque and indistinct manner of his, was his determination to come to terms with the Hitler régime, if and when it would be necessary.

Ambiguous slogans such as "the Conservative Revolution"—originally coined by Hugo von Hofmannsthal in a different sense and context—were employed as contrivances to establish a dubious link between the world of letters and the world of the brown shirts. This readiness to excuse and to understand, if not actually join, the Nazi movement did not necessarily spring from opportunism or cowardice. In many cases this fatal acquiescence had more profound and honorable reasons. No writer likes to dissent fundamentally from the bulk of his compatriots, particularly not from the youth. Pedagogues and poets pride themselves on their sensibility to the inarticulate voice of the younger generation. Was it not narrow-minded and reactionary to oppose the very tendencies to which youth adhered so enthusiastically?

Even so mature a thinker as Stefan Zweig, whose true devotion to peace and freedom is beyond any doubt, seemed impressed and confused. Whose fault is it, he asked shortly after the September elections, if millions manifest their disappointment with democracy? His answer was: Our fault, evidently enough; the fault of the democrats. Whereupon he explained the Hitler victory as "a perhaps unwise but fundamentally sound and approvable revolt of youth against the slowness and irresolution of 'high politics.' "

I find among my papers an open letter, entitled "Youth and Radicalism," in which I attempted to refute the argument of the great Austrian writer. "Not everything youth does and thinks, is a priori good and pregnant with future," I told him. "It may seem paradoxical that I should remind you of this; for I am young myself. However, many of my contemporaries—let alone the even younger ones!—are now engaged in propagating retrogression and barbarism with all that élan and determination that ought to be reserved for finer purposes. The revolt of youth can be in the service and interest of noble and ignoble forces. If German youth now turns radical should we not ask, above all, for the sake of which cause it rebels? What do the Nazis want? Which process do they try to accelerate? Are they eager to bring about, as quickly as possible, a peaceful, united Europe? I am afraid they want the contrary. Their radicalism, then, does not spring from frustrated hopes. They are disappointed and turn radical, not because progress comes too slowly, but because anarchy and reaction don't spread fast enough. Those 'radical' youngsters think that the caution of the older generation unduly delays the approach of the catastrophe. They are avid for their beloved apocalypse . . . As for myself, I want to have nothing, nothing to do with this perverse kind of 'radicalism.' I cannot help preferring the slowness and uncertainty of the democratic process to the devastating swiftness of those dashing counterrevolutionaries. I don't want to understand this kind of radicalism: I disapprove of it."

This I wrote in the year of 1931. (The statement is included in a volume of essays which was published under the title "Looking for a Way," Berlin, 1931.)

It is a question whether I was really entitled to pose as a representative of progressive, anti-fascist youth. What was my call to sermonize anyone genuinely concerned with the plight and future of democracy? What did I myself contribute to its defense, its improvement?

One thing that speaks in my favor is that I always loathed and despised the Nazis. My most ingenious enemy will not succeed in tracing a single feature in my character, a single phrase in my writings, that has any Nazi-like connotation. That is something. But it is not enough.

It may even be that this utter lack of any contact with the Nazi spirit hampered my ability to fight it. Some sort of affinity to your antagonist seems indispensable to put on a good struggle. A plague or a stink is hardly apt to incite your combative impulses.

Hitler was only a stinker in those days; to admire him, a dreary form of insanity. I thought him something to spit at—not worthy of any more chivalrous gesture.

It was at the beginning of 1932 that I spent half-an-hour or so watching him at a table just a few feet from mine. The Carlton Tea Room in Munich was one of his favorite places, which I didn't know when I dropped in there for a cup of coffee. My main reason for going there was that the Café Luitpold, on the other side of the street, was crammed with SA men. Hitler seemed to share my animosity for his storm troopers. He too preferred the more exclusive coziness of the smart little tea room.

The pastry was fairly good at the Carlton. He stuffed himself with strawberry tartlets, which I am rather fond of myself but couldn't touch for months after having seen him swallowing three of them. I found him surprisingly ugly, much more vulgar than I had anticipated. There were only two things that puzzled me while I studied, with cold, disgusted curiosity, his unappetizing features: first, what was the secret of his fascination? Why and how did he manage to make people lose their minds? And, secondly: Of whom did he remind me? He resembled someone whose picture I must have frequently seen. It was not Charlie Chaplin. Chaplin is engagingly attractive. No, the great comedian does not have Hitler's fleshy, nasty nose. Chaplin looks like an artist, whereas that gluttonous rat over there looked—like a gluttonous rat. He was flabby and foul and without any marks of greatness, a frustrated, hysterical petty bourgeois. It was a most unpleasant experience to have him so close to me, but at the same time it meant something like a relief. For I was positive that he had no chance to conquer Germany. "He is not to be our dictator," I felt with a sort of malignant satisfaction. "You have no chance, silly little mustache. Don't fool yourself, Schicklgruber: you are a washout. Five years from now, nobody will remember your name . . ."

Was there no bloody aura around his head to warn me? No writing on the wall of the Carlton Tea Room? There was nothing but dim, rosy light, soft music, and heaps of cookies; and in the midst of this sugary idyll, a mustached little man with veiled eyes and a stubborn forehead, chatting with some colorless henchmen. I caught fragments of their conversation. They discussed the cast of a musical farce scheduled for the same evening at the Kammerspiele. A great friend of ours, Therese Giehse, had the leading part. The Führer declared that he was looking forward to seeing this production: "I rather like Frau Giehse," he announced, with a weird sort of politeness, very much as if a madman tried to behave in a nice, civilized way, just to fool his guardians. One of his companions objected that Giehse had Jewish blood, "just a little bit of it, if I am not mistaken," he suggested. But his boss dismissed this remark with a vague and irritated gesture. "Nasty gossip!" he grumbled. "After all, I know the difference between a German artist and a Semitic clown."

I was shaking with inward laughter. If Giehse could only have listened! She is so proud of her pure Jewish extraction . . .

"He will not rule this country," I thought again, deeply amused and cheered. While I called the waitress to pay for my cup of coffee, I suddenly remembered whom Mr. Hitler resembled. It was that sex-murderer in Hanover, whose case had made huge headlines several years before. His name was Haarmann. He was in the habit of killing young boys whom he lured to his flat. Forty or fifty disappeared in his hospitable bedroom—quite a record, considering that Haarmann lived in an apartment house, surrounded by vigilant neighbors. A sort of homosexual Bluebeard, on an impressive scale. Very remarkable case. All psychiatrists and students of criminology were pretty excited about him, at the time. The likeness between him and Hitler was striking. The sightless eyes, the mustache, the brutal and nervous mouth, even the unspeakable vulgarity of the fleshy nose: it was, indeed, precisely the same physiognomy.

"You won't rule Germany, Schicklgruber," I thought, while rising from my chair.

No bloody aura? No writing?

It's not Hitler who is mysterious—he is just a louse with a bit of magnetism; but the Germans are. My mistake was not that I underrated Schicklgruber but that I overrated the Germans. They were smitten with his grammatical howlers and brassy lies, his slimy humor, his illiteracy, his bullying, his whining, his nervous fits, his half-crazed megalomania. Everything that made him revolting to me beguiled and inspired them. What is wrong with the Germans?

They are mangled by resentments and foiled ambitions; constantly obsessed with the idea of being persecuted, cheated, and attacked by all other peoples. They took the economic depression for an international conspiracy against the Fatherland. Everybody, they thought, envied and at the same time despised the Teutonic super-race. English bankers, French lawyers and Russian terrorists kept pondering over dire schemes to steal our Lebensraum. Profoundly muddled by their arrogance and guilty conscience, they suspected encroachments on German honor and interest in all developments of modern civilization: the trade unions and the stock market, abstract painting and the League of Nations, the Catholic Church, jazz music, and Freemasonry—they were all invented with the diabolic design of insulting and impoverishing the valiant folk between Breslau and Düsseldorf, Munich and Stettin.

I might have been a more efficient fighter if I had bothered to scrutinize the depth of the German psychosis. My illusions sprang from inadequate knowledge. I failed to understand their swagger and suffering, their latent madness, their painful inferiority complex. I was not familiar with their frame of mind. Their rodomontades and complaints sounded to me like the roaring of savage beasts. I was bored and disgusted by them but not frightened enough. I saw swollen Philistines, neurotic demagogues, hardboiled intriguers, boastful ruffians and gawky women. But I did not perceive the tremendous challenge all those pitiful characters collectively represented. I did not recognize the Persians: they were not before the gates but within the walls—right here, in Munich, Berlin and Hamburg; sitting next to me in the street car; peering at me from around the corner; smirking, grinning, and bustling; beaming with the thought of future victims and victories.

I traveled about, lecturing on European culture; amusing myself (and sometimes, perhaps, my hearers) with saucy flippancies ridiculing the Nazis; still isolated, irresponsible, erratic; dallying with subtle jokes and wistful reveries. I never addressed or attended any political meeting. I failed to join any liberal, anti-fascist organization. I spent more time in Paris or Villefranche than in Germany. I refused to have anything to do with the whole sordid mess.

No voices and signs to make me aware of what was actually going on around me? How could I miss the ominous traces disfiguring the foreheads of certain friends of mine? I mingled with the Persians and was blind to their murderous secret. Their faces seemed so innocent, and sometimes they were handsome.

No doubt, a lad like my friend Willi L. was a potential Persian, notwithstanding his smooth manners and tonic gaiety. We had fun together: he was a nice enough chap; good-natured, lazy, naïve. His vitality refreshed me, and I was amused by his amazing ignorance. Sometimes I would quiz him with insidious questions: "You know, of course, that Johann Wolfgang von Goethe was a mighty general fighting the Chinese, in the war of 1870?"

"O.K.," said Willi. "So what?"

He knew absolutely nothing—except the weight of all pugilists and the salaries of all movie stars. Descended from an impoverished family of the lower middle class, he had no job, no home, no ambition. He was penniless, thoughtless and faithless. You could make him believe anything, as he believed in nothing. He had discounted all philosophies and ideals before knowing them. Notions like "culture," "liberty," "human dignity," "peace," were to him just so many silly tricks to jeer at. He seemed cynical, bored, irreverent. Secretly, however, or subconsciously, he was craving for some sort of faith and discipline—something that would help him to overcome the utter emptiness of his life. What easy prey was a youth of his type to any blatant impostor!

I often wondered, musing over his face: What is going to happen to you, poor kid? His brow was so smooth and blank: anything might be written on this vacuous forehead. Could he ever be fooled by the rampant humbug of Nazism? He seemed immune from the intoxicating effect of boisterous words and gestures.

He wasn't. Nobody is immune: certainly not a derelict youth who possesses nothing to counterbalance the swindle. The Devil got his soul because the angels didn't bother to catch it.

I was saddened rather than surprised when I found him all dressed up in the becoming black uniform of Hitler's elite regiment.

"What's wrong with you?" I asked him, with hypocritical merriment. "What are you wearing those monkey clothes for? Have you gone nuts, or something?"

He made a peevish grimace; shrugged his shoulders. "To hell with it," he grumbled. "Do you think it's for the fun of it? A guy has to live, after all . . ."

"There you've got something, Willi," said I. "But why the hell does he have to live in this filthy masquerade?"

"Skip it!" he said. "It's good enough for the German people: so why should it not be good enough for me?" And he added, with a rather disquieting flash in his pale, gentle eyes: "We're going to be the bosses. Yessir."

"You won't," I said to him. "Not you, silly creature that you are." And after a pause I asked: "Do you believe in all that trash, Willi? Do you actually believe in it?"

He grinned at me; shook his head and tapped his forehead with the tip of his middle finger. "Now it's you who sounds nuts," he observed.

"So you don't believe in it?" I insisted.

He turned rather impatient. "I don't give a damn," he said. "Besides, nobody does. Nobody cares what I believe in or what I don't believe. They are just going to be the bosses, and that's all there is to it. Is that clear enough?"

Indeed, it was clear enough. He dropped me and our friendship and everything I stood for, simply because "the others" were going to be the bosses, and nobody cared whether he believed or disbelieved anything, anyhow.

"Good-bye, then, Willi," I said.

"So long, Klaus," said he. "Look after yourself. And if you ever need an influential friend in the party—well, you know where to reach me."

Was he among those brutes who invaded the lecture hall where Erika was reciting a poem by Victor Hugo? a poem for peace and reconciliation . . . The hideous incident took place during a pacifist meeting, arranged by a women's anti-war organization. Erika appeared in her capacity as an actress, not as a political speaker. The main attraction of the evening was a delegate from Paris: she delivered, eloquently and passionately, the greetings of French womanhood and their solemn vow that they would not allow their husbands, brothers, and sons to go to war against the German people once more.

The gang of Nazi troopers came some minutes too late to disturb the speech of the French emissary. However, they arrived just in time for Erika's performance. She stood on the platform, frail, erect, all passion and faith and glow. First she seemed not to notice the battle that developed in the background between the watchmen and the invaders. The recital continued but presently her voice was drowned by the beastly howl of the brown and black-shirted lads. "Enough!" they clamored. "Stop her! We protest in the name of the German nation! It's a disgrace! High treason!"

The people who had paid for their seats protested on their part; in vain. The heroic storm troopers, brandishing clubs and guns, advanced against the peace-loving ladies. The riot assumed disconcerting proportions. I didn't like the whole scene: not so much because I was afraid the dashing warriors might hit me (curiously enough, I didn't seem to expect they would), but rather because of Erika, who obviously failed to realize the actual danger confronting her. She did not withdraw from the platform but watched, with a sort of detached and yet ardent interest, the turmoil going on at her feet. I don't know, nor do I like to imagine, what the patriotic rowdies would have done to her if they had fought their way to the platform before the police interfered. Happily, the cops arrived at the last moment, whereupon the gallant anti-pacifists disappeared with astounding swiftness.

I must admit that I was rather dazed when I read the following headline in the next morning's issue of "Der Völkische Beobachter": "Terroristic police maltreat our boys who commit the 'crime' of attending public meeting." What an ingenious trick!—just the reverse of the truth. Nothing can be simpler, nothing more effective. Every thief knows that his best chance to get away with a stolen pocketbook is to yell: "Catch the thief! That guy over there has just robbed me!" "Jewish salesman bites German dog!" This exquisite piece of news which ostensibly appeared in a Nazi sheet had seemed hitherto nothing but a joke. The experience with the pacifist meeting and "the terroristic police" taught me that it was impossible to exaggerate the Nazi outrages: they matched, indeed, surpassed the boldest parody.

The abusive outbursts against Erika by which the witty heading was followed were no less absurd, but more dangerous. To be denounced in Hitler's official paper as a "flat-footed peace hyena" was no joke, in the Germany of 1931. Pacifists and "peace-mongers" were then almost as unpopular with the Nazi ilk as are the "war-mongers" nowadays . . .

The sordid piece in Adolf Hitler's gazette meant quite a blow to Erika's theatrical career. Promptly after its publication her summer engagement was canceled. This was only the first reaction of the spirited theater managers. Overnight she had become something untouchable, an outcast.

"Who would have thought it?" she wondered. "I hadn't the faintest idea that I would bring myself into such a mess when I agreed to recite that stuff by bearded old Hugo. Well, it's all right with me. If they want a fight—they can have a good one. I may be a peace hyena, but certainly I am no sissy."

Göbbels declared war against the Mann family. We got on his nerves, the whole tribe of us. Erika was their pet enemy. How could she dare to propagate peace and then call the "terroristic cops!" And then she even went so far as to sue the "Völkische Beobachter" for libel: she was fresh enough to feel offended by the statement that she had "no human physiognomy" but only something that looks "remotely face-like." The judge claimed several portraits of her as evidence: Erika's features were officially declared as "human" in the legal sense of the term. The Hitler paper had to pay—a matter it resented even more than a pacifist demonstration.

As for myself, I was not in the good graces of the awakening Germany, either. What I did to annoy the Nazis was all too little and inadequate, considering what I could and ought to have done. However, it apparently sufficed to irritate those touchy gentlemen. They were mad at me. "Wait and see, little man!" they threatened. "You'll pay for this, when the day comes!"

Heinrich Mann was a more serious and dangerous foe. His output of political prose, copious and articulate, meant a constant challenge to the self-styled messiah from Brunau. Along with Carl von Ossietzki and a very few others, the author of "The Subject" was the outstanding critic and commentator of the Weimar Republic, from its turbulent beginning to its wretched end. During those last years preceding the collapse, he had tried more passionately and effectively than any other political writer to reconcile the conflicting left-wing parties—to bring about the anti-fascist coalition, the People's Front against Hitler. The German Republic was doomed because this broad defense alliance failed to materialize. A clearsighted and devoted servitor of democracy such as Heinrich Mann knew, as far back as 1931, that the Third Reich had become inevitable, thanks to so many blunders and transgressions. But he already visualized the Fourth Reich looming behind the Third. Hitler's bloody régime—so Heinrich Mann prophesies ten years ago—will not last. It may cause bloodshed and misery, calamities unprecedented: but it will not last. Then comes the new Republic—"no longer the incomplete democracy of the past, but the true one desired by the people."

If there was anyone whom the Nazis loathed more intensely than even the undaunted republican, Heinrich Mann, then it was his brother. They considered him an apostate, which is worse than an enemy. Because he had opened his political career with an anti-political treatise on Culture and Protestantism, music, Schopenhauer, and the German sympathy with death, they clamored that he ought to sympathize with Hitler—or else he was a traitor and venal opportunist.

Indeed, he was "opportunistic" enough to challenge, twice within two decades, the ruling intellectual tastes and tendencies. For, when he came out, in 1918, against the bard of Western civilization, it was precisely that type who then dominated the literary scene. In 1930, however, he attacked the new fashionable idol, the "blood-and-soil" snob and nationalistic mystic, the Nazi, the opportunist. What did he gain from this tedious strife except loads of insults? No particular favors from the republican government, to be sure! The Weimar Republic was completely indifferent to the efforts of its literary supporters. The Catholic and Social-Democratic dignitaries—no less snooty, in their own way, than the Prussian Junker—ignored the contributions of the outstanding writers. It so happened, for instance, that Dr. Brüning and Thomas Mann attended a solemn meeting in Weimar to celebrate the hundredth anniversary of Goethe's death. My father was among the main speakers. The ceremony was concluded with a banquet, over which Dr. Brüning presided. Unbelievable as it may sound, the Chancellor of the Reich did not even condescend to meet the only winner of the Nobel Prize for Literature Germany had produced since 1914. It is impossible to imagine the same kind of thing happening in any other country but Germany. Only there—only among Germans—the gap between the sphere of actual power and the realm of the idea seems, indeed, insurmountable.

No writer could hope to earn gold or glory by sticking out his neck for the German Republic. It was an utterly thankless job. A man like my father was counted by the Nazis among the "November criminals" (although he had been opposed, at the same time, to the revolution), whereas the republican officialdom considered him just a writer (which always meant, and will probably always mean, something highly suspicious to Prussian generals, bureaucrats, and the like). There can be no doubt that the author of "The Magic Mountain" would have had a better time in his homeland if he had either yielded to the mighty neo-nationalistic wave, or else renounced political activities altogether. As things were, he lived not only under a constant and painful strain but also in real danger. The enraged fanatics of the radical right threatened him with assassination; in fact, my mother often feared that some truculent youth might actually attempt to carry out the threat. The list of their victims was long . . .

The famous "Address to the Germans," which he delivered at the Beethoven-Saal in Berlin, almost exactly one month after the Reichstag elections (on October 17, 1930), was the dramatic climax of a long, bitter strife. The scandal started when he appealed to the German middle class to make its peace with labor and socialism in order to avoid the Nazi calamity. At this point the insulted German honor rose from its seat and bellowed with indignation. The German honor wore blue spectacles (as did General von Ludendorff when he escaped to Holland): yet one could easily recognize the well-known physiognomy of Arnolt Bronnen, the writer. He had made himself a reputation as the author of dashing pornography, a prosperous field to which he remained faithful in his new capacity as Nazi prophet. The biography of Horst Wessel, as presented by Mr. Bronnen, certainly yields a lot of first-rate material to any one specializing in pornographic topics. The colorful saga of the murdered pimp might have been a sweeping success, if a bunch of nasty competitors had not launched the rumor that Bronnen's real name was Bronner and that he was a Jew. The affair looked pretty nasty, indeed; but fortunately, the German honor is cunning. Mr. Bronnen came out with a streamlined statement admitting that he was actually named Bronner and that Bronner was a non-Aryan name, but insisting on his own immaculate racial extraction. The ingenious son publicly accused his late mother (a pure Aryan) of having cheated the late Mr. Bronner with an unknown gentleman of guaranteed non-Jewish blood. Who gave a damn whether Frau Bronner was faithful to the Jew who happened to be her husband or not? Nobody cared about the disgrace of one anonymous woman—her ambitious son less than anybody else. Having slandered his mother, he was entitled again to speak—or rather, to shout—as the guardian and representative of the national honor. He had the privilege, indeed, the duty of calling Thomas Mann a "liar," a "traitor," an "enemy of the people." Thus he fulfilled, promptly and efficiently, Dr. Göbbels' order to start "a little something" at the Beethovensaal.

These were our enemies—the scum. These were the future bosses.

Could we fool ourselves as to the outcome of the struggle on which we had now embarked? Of course not, rationally and consciously. Hitler's final victory—Germany's doom—became from day to day more unavoidable, just as in the case of certain diseases the lethal conclusion is certain, unless a tonic crisis suddenly alters the clinical picture. Curiously enough, however, the invalid, and even more so those devoted to him, never ceased to hope for precisely this sort of crisis— the miraculous change and improvement. It is one thing to say, "I shall have to die"; another to believe it in deadly earnest. Eagerly and naïvely, we clung to any encouraging sign.

Hindenburg has been re-elected? A very promising fact! True, he is a senile Junker and surrounded by scoundrels to boot. But what took place in March and April, 1932, was nothing short of an open contest between the Weimar Republic on the one hand and Hitler and his gang on the other. The two candidates for the Presidency became the symbols of two incompatible ways of life. The would-be dictator represented everything we abominated, whereas his competitor. . . . But did the Marshal represent anything we were fond of? Was not he as well inimical? Utterly opposed to our tastes and tenets? True enough. But, again, in this particular constellation he was the champion of democracy—paradoxical as it may sound . . . Would Dr. Brüning support him—and how fervently!—if he were not the guarantor, indeed, the savior of freedom?

At this point one might object that Brüning, after all, was not really our man, either. But who would be so choosy, with Hitler almost in power? The policy of the minor evil seems convincing enough when the major evil is overwhelmingly big. So we accepted the cynical and reasonable slogan of the Social Democratic party: "Drink a schnapps—and vote for Hindenburg!" It was not just one schnapps we swallowed. After having consumed quite a few of them, our minds were stimulated enough to fancy the obtuse general as a sturdy paladin of all republican virtues.

However, I must not present us as more deluded and unsuspecting than we actually were. In general, a mood of bitter readiness prevailed in our midst. My mother, who had been so notably clearsighted during the war, again proved her perspicacious realism. I distinctly recall many a conversation anticipating the hardships and adventures of exile. Will it be very bad? we kept asking each other—and our flesh began to creep, in a half-apprehensive, half-pleasant fashion. Then one of us would add, hastily, as if to reject in advance any possible opposition: "For, of course, we don't want to stay here when . . . I mean, if. . . ."

All of us understood.

My diary confirms what I so clearly remember. Just to quote two samples at random: "May 25, 1931. Serious talk about the necessity of leaving Germany. Appalling triumph of madness." And, under the date of the following day: "Again long conversation with Mielein concerning exile. Is it inevitable?"

But even if my memory were blotted out and my personal notes had vanished, my literary output during these last years in Germany testifies to the same misgivings. I do not refer to political articles, most of which are rhetorical and ephemeral, but to the authentic expression of what I suffered and knew. The two major things I produced in that period (from 1930–1932), one novel and a play, foreshadow the grief of future homelessness. Never in my life have I been so despondent, so helplessly uprooted as then, in that estranged country of mine.

This has nothing to do with literary failure or success. True, my last theatrical venture, an adaptation of Cocteau's novel "Les Enfants Terribles" was rather a flop, and a pretty noisy one, too. Nor can I pretend that the novel, "Treffpunkt im Unendlichen" ("Meeting Point in the Infinite Space") was anything like a sweeping hit. But it was not this absence of popular approval that depressed or surprised me. Both my dramatic version of Jean's uncanny tour de force, and my attempt to survey in an extensive tale the complexities of the modern bohemia, were received with that insidious sort of curiosity to which I was long accustomed. Why, then, did the usual insults and misunderstandings hurt and baffle me this time? I must have discerned certain ominous undertones in the familiar chorus. That the critics jeered at my novel and the audiences at my play may have been somewhat disturbing, but I hardly took it seriously. What struck and saddened me, really, was something else—far more frightening and mysterious, a mortal chill in the air, a shadow creeping over faces, an evil spell, a doom.

There was nothing I could reasonably complain about. If my play provoked scandal—wasn't that precisely what I was aiming at? And was it my aspiration to produce a popular novel? Obviously not. The book could not but displease: it was conceived as a protest against the prevailing mode of neo-primitivism. In fact, I was fairly well off, considering my luxurious proclivity to challenge the public taste. I made money contributing to leading magazines, broadcasting, selling a movie script, and so forth. But in the midst of all these prosperous activities I sensed the innermost lack of substance and truth in everything I accomplished. Behind the specious façade loomed the hieroglyphs of a secret warning.

MENE, MENE, TEKEL, UPHARSIN . . .

Who understands this weird idiom of our indignant God?

He who neglects or misinterprets its meaning, must die.

He who grasps it but is lacking in fortitude, will be doomed as well.

Only he who understands and is strong enough to bear, indeed, to forget his knowledge—only he will survive.

I have lost more friends through suicide (including the less direct patterns of self-destruction) than through diseases, crimes, or accidents.

Several suicide waves occurred in my immediate environment. The first of them took place during the last years preceding the establishment of the Third Reich.

I don't know, nor do I want to check, who started the macabre vogue. Was it the ghastly example of Pascin, the Parisian painter, whom so many of us had known? He actually slaughtered himself, in the most complicated and hideous manner—opening his arteries and at the same time strangling himself at the latch of his door. With the blood oozing from his wounds, he wrote a farewell on the wall, the last homage to his woman: "Ne m'oublie pas, ma chérie! Je t'adore . . ."

The writing!—the bloody writing written on the wall . . .

There must have been a mortal blight in the air.

The daughter of Arthur Schnitzler, the Viennese poet, killed herself in Austria. It was a sad and romantic story—not without a flavor of sombre elegance, well in keeping with the Schnitzler style. Yet the father who had made up so many plots of that pattern, shook his head and murmured, "My child, my child . . . This is the first time I am really angry at you . . ."

It is no easy job to be the child of a genius. Hofmannsthal's oldest son, Franz, killed himself. The night before the funeral, the father had a horrid dream about an evasive silk hat that he had tried to catch. But the hat was hanging high up, on the wall—so high, indeed, that he could not manage to reach it. He stretched his arms, hopped, jumped, tried all sorts of tricks—but in vain: the hat remained inaccessible. It was the most painful nightmare. The next morning, walking behind the coffin of his son, it so happened that he dropped his hat. He stooped to pick it up but could not reach it nor could he rise any more. He tumbled, groaned, collapsed. It was a stroke—so they said. It was a tragedy on the great, antique scale. Hugo von Hofmannsthal was killed by his dreams and grief. Maybe he died because he had seen something behind the hat—a writing written on the wall . . .

MENE, MENE, TEKEL . . .

In Paris, one winter afternoon, a young man entered my room—a stranger: I had never seen him before. He said that he was a painter;

he came from Switzerland, and didn't know many people in Paris. Did I mind his staying with me for half an hour or so?

We talked books and it turned out that he shared many of my animosities and views. I remember that he found on my desk a recent publication by a friend of mine, the young Frenchman Jean Desbordes, a protégé of Cocteau, at the time. He seemed attracted by that particular volume. It was called "J'Adore," and consisted of rhapsodic invocations praising the lust and grandeur of life.

"Yes, life can be adorable," the young stranger said, and added with a strange, unfocused look into space: "If one is strong enough to bear it . . ."

He was strikingly handsome—tall and vigorous, with nostalgic eyes of a radiant, steel blue. His name was Walser. He promised me to bring some of his paintings along, the next time we would meet.

I punctually turned up at our rendezvous the next evening at the Café du Dôme. But he didn't come. That's just like him, I thought, faintly irritated. An irresponsible creature, a bohemian without discipline. Probably fell in love with a statue in the Luxembourg Garden or a colored prostitute on the Boulevard Clichy. "Tant pis pour lui, ou tant mieux . . ."

"Tant pis pour lui, ou tant mieux": he was dead. Shot himself, the day after his visit to me, just a few hours after he told me that life can be adorable: provided that one has the strength and fortitude to bear it.

Most people think life dreary but bearable, whereas a delicate minority is smitten with life but cannot endure it. Ricki, for instance, enjoyed life tremendously and yet talked a great deal about suicide. "It's a pity I'll have to do it," he would say, with an oblivious smile. "Just now when I'm having such fun with my little house and Wolfram."

Wolfram was a long-haired terrier, silky and gentle eyed. He wore a tiny silver bell on his collar, which produced an angelic little noise announcing his arrival and that of Ricki. Every other day or so, Ricki drove from Utting by the Ammersee where his little house was situated to Munich for a chat with friends, a visit to an art gallery, or some other business. He wasted much time that way, but that couldn't be helped: he insisted that he had to live in the country but, on the other hand, couldn't stand the loneliness, not in the long run and without occasional interludes. After a while the solitude of his studio became oppressive to him. Then he clamored for encouragement. "Tell me that I am a good painter!" he would request, with jocular urgency. "Kind of Rembrandt-like?" he lamented. "Or don't you think I am?"

Too proud to admit the gravity of his doubts, he deliberately exaggerated his worries and restlessness. He suffered from women, and made mordant cracks about his masochism. He abominated the social set from which he was descended—the highly cultured Jewish bourgeoisie—and sometimes whined in front of a mirror: "Today I look again precisely like my brother! What a shame! Don't you notice it, children? Of course, you do. Pretty agonizing, isn't it? I am a hideous old creature . . ." Whereupon he amused us with a quivering performance aping his brother, mother, grandmamma—the entire family including uncles, nephews, aunts, asthmatical pet dogs, and gouty but faithful old servants. After having exhausted himself with uncanny caprioles, he would conclude with a flash of fearful bitterness in his beautiful, gold-brown eyes: "And I am just one of them! Just one of the nauseous bunch . . ."

Sometimes he would launch out, all of a sudden, into a rampant diatribe over the political situation in Germany and the weird events that might be in the offing. "Don't you realize it?" he kept asking us, with painful obstinacy. "Everything is lost. We are doomed—you and I and my jolly cousins in Frankfort; doomed, the whole lot of us, including Offi and Ofey and Hindenburg and Cardinal Faulhaber and W. E. Süskind and the labor unions. The Nazis will come and swallow my little dog Wolfram and Erika's car, and your books, Klaus, yes, and my pictures too." Then he imitated Hitler—the way he shouts and prances—until all of us shrieked with laughter. Finally he would join in our mirth and end his show with the casual remark: "You're right, I suppose. That pompous ham! It is not worthwhile to die on his account."

We did not want him to die. He was our dearest friend, our brother. We could not afford to lose him. Out of selfishness and love we tried our very best to prevent him from doing what he was so terribly eager to do.

The project of our Persian journey was just one of our devices to cheat Ricki out of his suicide. We persuaded him to embark with us on an expedition in two cars through the Balkans and Asia Minor, into the vast spaces of Persia. Annemarie, "the Swiss child," would join us. Wasn't it a grand, exciting idea? To get rid, for a while, of the whole mess here at home!

We plunged into preparations. Ten thousand things had to be taken care of: visas, financial arrangements, newspaper contracts, the equipment of the cars; tents and clothes, thermos flasks, water-proof overalls, and hats for the tropics had to be purchased. Ricki thought of everything. He bought himself a pair of shoes that were supposed to last for at least fifteen years, and even a gun to protect all of us against the Persian robbers. It was lots of fun. We tossed about with maps, piles of Baedeker guides, unpaid bills, and farewell letters to our many friends. Ricki seemed as cheerful and thrilled as the rest of us. Only sometimes—not very frequently, though —he turned somewhat peevish; not sorrowful, really, but sullen. In such moments he surprised and even frightened me by a queer twinkle, a weird flash in his eyes, something wry and dangerous I had never noticed in him before. Nor did I like the insidious nonchalance with which he asked certain puzzling questions or submitted, very casually, minor propositions that failed to make any sense. He would inquire, for instance—glancing at me askance, with furtive aggressiveness—whether I was interested in money: "If you could get, say, ten thousand or fifteen thousand marks, all of a sudden: without any effort on your part—would you enjoy that, old scoundrel?" It sounded as if he intended to steal the money for me. I laughed, but a little uncomfortably.

Another time he suggested, rather abruptly, that we start the journey without him—just the three of us. "Bucharest seems an excellent meeting point," he asserted, and added with that weird, oblivious smile of his: "I could follow you, in a week or so . . . It would give me time to settle my affairs with Uncle Sigmund in Frankfort."

But as we seemed surprised and hesitant, he dropped the idea at once. "You're right, I suppose," he said quickly. "It's an idiotic scheme. Poor old halfwit that I am. Incidentally, what is your shoe number, Klaus?"

What did he want to know my shoe number for?

"I just wonder," he chuckled. "I hope your feet aren't bigger than mine. Otherwise my wonderful new shoes may hurt you . . ."

The departure was scheduled for May 5, 1932. The preceding day we drove out to the grounds of the leading Bavarian film company, the "Emelka," where pictures were to be taken of us for the newsreel. We were all dressed up in our overalls, quivering with pride and expectation. Our two new cars, gaudily lacquered, streamlined, "dernier cri," sparkled in the sun. It was a glorious day.

Ricki seemed to enjoy himself tremendously. While the camera men kept us waiting, he entertained the technicians and extras with beer and clowning. Everybody liked him. We had to wait an hour or so until the director was ready to shoot. He wanted Erika and Annemarie to sit inside the car, while Ricki and I were supposed to squat side by side—occupied as it were, with repairing some imaginary damage on the wheel. Ricki kept joking as long as the camera man was busy with preparations. I remember his teasing me about my clumsiness in all matters technical, which was a traditional banter.

"I'd like to see you," he grinned, "fixing a wheel, out there in Persia . . ." The very moment, however, when the "all clear sign" was given, his face altered in a terrible way. An indescribable expression of grief—of painful fury at once numbed and distorted his features. His eyes—wide open and blind with anguish—stared into space. I heard him gnash his teeth, a most nerve-wracking little noise. It was as if he dropped, for one dreadful moment, the mask of cheerfulness, so that the camera could register and preserve what he concealed from us, the grimace of his agony.

We spent the rest of the day together. It was after midnight when we separated. Ricki had to drive to his country place to pick up his things. We were to meet the following afternoon, about three o'clock.

The next morning while we were busy packing, he called twice from Utting; the first time, to give us some advice concerning the brand of gasoline we should buy; the second time, shortly after eleven, he dwelt on a minor problem with respect to the route from Prague to Bucharest.

For luncheon we had Annemarie and a girl who had been close to Ricki, during the last five years. It was a Sunday, the meal ceremonious and opulent—a farewell feast, with all of us in high spirits. We discussed the trip and my mother admonished me not to drive too fast. "Let Ricki do the job as soon as the road isn't good or you begin to feel tired," she said. "You're such a poor driver. Ricki is much more efficient."

The phone rang while we were sitting in the lobby, after lunch, each of us with his cigarette and his demi-tasse. My mother got up, but I insisted that it was my privilege to answer the phone: so we rushed to the drawing room, both of us. I was faster but politely gave precedence to her.

"Hello," she said, still a little breathless from our race and still laughing. "Hello . . . yes, this is Mrs. Mann . . . in person, yes . . . Who is speaking? . . . I don't get your name . . . Who? the police? . . . the police station in Utting?"

It is as if it happened yesterday. I can see my mother, petrified. I hear her voice, very low, a shaky whisper, but correct and respectful, the way one talks to the authorities. "Yes, officer . . . I get what you say . . . Are there no letters? Nothing? . . . I see . . . So I have to inform the mother . . . Very well . . . No use to send a doctor . . . I see . . . Thank you. Yes."

He had shot himself in the heart, about noon. Before doing so, he had charged his maid to fix something in the garden, where she was near enough to hear the detonation but too remote to interfere at the decisive moment. His last word consisted of four brief words, neatly displayed on his desk: "Please inform Mrs. Mann."

There were two chatting groups in the lobby, one gathering around the coffee-maker; the other next to the phonograph. My mother and I had to keep our appalling secret until somebody stopped the gramophone and we finally caught the attention of those laughing, ignorant people. But who knows the suitable method of breaking news of such an unspeakable sort? You can only stammer and fumble and let the others guess what you don't dare to pronounce. "Something awful has happened . . . Ricki. . . ."

This was sufficient. Somebody yelled: "Is he dead?"

What a nightmarish, unforgettable scene! There are things—gestures, screams, and expressions—which may seem trivial and melodramatic when one reads about them in books. "Her face turned white as the ceiling . . . She sank into a chair . . . She burst into tears . . ." It sounds like familiar clichés. But how frightening is the traditional pantomime of dismay when it actually happens! Yes, Annemarie's face —the bold and lovely face of a tragic page—did turn white as the ceiling; the other girl sank into a chair—groaning as if suddenly hit by almost unbearable pain; Erika burst, indeed, exploded into tears.

"What insanity!" she whimpered. "What a mad thing to do!" And I see my father caressing her hair—which suddenly looked disheveled— and drying up his tears with his big handkerchief which always smells so strongly and refreshingly of eau de cologne.

"Come, come, come . . ." he said. "You have still many friends and all of them love you. Come, come now . . ." She looked so terribly young as she wept and shuddered—a pain-stricken little girl, with that wild hair of hers and a reddish, distorted face—woeful, childish, in-finitely touching.

I rushed upstairs aimlessly, almost mad myself. But my room, on the second floor, was empty—only the half-packed bags; no Ricki. And I rushed back to the lobby, only to find the same group in the same positions numbed by grief; transformed into an assembly of pallid statues, with Erika's tears and hair as the only things alive in the midst of a ghastly silence.

Then, the mournful bustle of the following hours and days! The black coffee, the sighs, the cigarettes, the mourning gossip, the gregari-ous tears. How we stuck together, all his friends; warmly and sadly, to discuss the details of the tragedy, to move each other with heart-breaking anecdotes. So many of his enigmatic gestures and utterances now became painfully clear. All the schemes he had tried to work out in these last weeks and days revealed the sinister evidence of his in-tention. Of course, he wanted us to leave Munich and to start on the journey so that he might have more leisure to carry out his diabolic

project. As this contrivance failed, he decided to fool us up to the bitter end. But why? Who on earth forced him to make this trip if he
didn't feel like it? Why should he lie to us and pretend that he was
crazy about Persia, while in reality the idea of going there frightened
and tormented him? Or did he actually wish and intend to go? Did
he not just double-cross us when he seemed so happily excited about
every detail that had to do with the venture? Was he split within
himself, genuinely engaged in preparing both journeys—the one to
Persia, and the other one? Was it not just a maneuver when he praised
the solidity of his new shoes? Fifteen years they would last. . . . But
what did he have in mind when he asked my shoe number? And
how about that remark concerning the ten thousand marks that I
might suddenly get, "without any effort on my part"? If his little
estate was to be distributed among his five or six most intimate friends
as he had been planning, it would yield an amount of about ten thousand for each of us . . .

The following day Erika and I drove out to Utting. We wanted no
one to accompany us on this journey. It was a delightful morning; the
beloved scenery of lush meadows, wooded hills, and old peasant houses
lay in a silvery mist; all serene beauty and peace. It was gorgeous to
watch the faint silhouettes of the mountains gradually emerge from
the floating haze, radiant blue of the midday sky.

Ricki's house lay in eerie stillness. The lower part of the garden,
near the lake, was swampy, and there always was that queer, disquieting smell of stale water and decaying plants. So this was the idyll to
which he withdrew from his hectic pleasures and intricate romances.
What a ghastly "Sans-Souci!" A bewitched background, indeed, for his
deadly reveries . . .

A very soft, silvery ringing received us when we entered the house.
It was the tiny bell on Wolfram's leather collar.

We faltered at the foot of the stairs, scared as children are by darkness. A whisper guided us: "Go upstairs! Don't be afraid young lady!
We have laid him out in his little bedroom."

It was only then that we noticed the two old women standing side
by side in the middle of the narrow lobby, two massive figures, bleak
and quiet, with their hands complacently crossed across their swollen

stomachs. "Go straight up!" they repeated, as if in one toneless but penetrating voice.

Instead of answering the two ghost-like women, Erika and I began to weep—at once and simultaneously. Through a veil of tears I saw Erika approaching the staircase, taking toilsome and stiff little steps as though walking over nails or on glowing stones. Hand in hand, two scared, desolate youngsters, we climbed through the dingy twilight up to the terrible room where our brother lay shot.

The old ones kept nodding and mumbling behind us. I realized— and was at once embarrassed and strangely comforted by this thought —that both were greatly satisfied, indeed, pleased with our behavior; our tears and stooping attitude perfectly corresponded with their idea of two decent young people who come by car to inspect the body of their deceased cousin, schoolmate, or business friend. During all my life—I could not help feeling—I have hardly performed a gesture that would have been comprehensible or gratifying to those dreary old things. But now, in this hour of suffering, I act according to what they deem comme il faut.

Finally we reached the little corridor at the top of the stairs. Erika opened the door—and there it was, surprisingly bright in the sunlight, sober and horrible: the chamber of crime, the cursed cell of agony and fear and unbearable visions.

But who was this uncanny doll over there, on the bed? He appeared at once cute and forbidding—a brittle little something made of wax-like, delicate material. How strange and haughty was this unknown face!—the mouth slightly screwed up in a faint, unfathomable grin. This could not be Ricki.

Neither of us had seen a corpse since that legendary visit to the morgue in Tölz, so many years ago. Now we remembered the drowned baker's immaculate, icy brow: in Ricki's unspeakably altered face we recognized the same hostile transfiguration. The dead resemble each other. But the baker's mouth was mercifully covered by a neat, white bandage hiding the evil smile . . .

"How small he is!" Erika finally managed to say, infinitely surprised rather than terrified.

He was incredibly small, all shriveled up and withered, already mummified. I suddenly understood that to die simply means to dry out. The essential difference between the living flesh and the dead is by no means that between motion and stillness. A living man can be very quiet—and why should a dead man not beckon or walk or caper, under particular circumstances? But the dead man is dry. All fluidity has evaporated: not one moist spot is left. Death is crisp, clean, and barren.

"How clean his hands are!" I heard Erika's broken voice. "I've never seen them so clean . . . Look at his fingernails!"

Then she produced an oppressed little scream: "What is that?" And she pointed at the wall behind the bed. It was freckled with blood. He had spread the last traces of his moist, perishable existence all over the chalky wall of his bedroom.

We stood close together, clinging to each other—paralyzed by horror. My own words sounded meaningless, almost shocking to me: "He must have hit an artery . . . his heart, probably. . . . He didn't feel it, though—I suppose . . ."

The blood stains looked like the scattered fragments of a mysterious pattern—a last message, a warning, the writing on the wall.

MENE, MENE, TEKEL, UPHARSIN . . .

What is the sense of this lurid formula? Who knows how to juggle the purple spots of the torn hieroglyph? What terrible secret did our departing brother try to communicate with the blood of his heart? We could not decipher the message. Our eyes were blinded by tears.

MENE, MENE, TEKEL . . .

Do these words forecast the ignoble farce in store for our distracted country? The coup d'état carried out by Herr von Papen against the Prussian Government in the summer of 1932, was, indeed, an embarrassing affair—most revealing as to the complete fatuity of our political life in general, the appalling weakness of our so-called left parties in particular. The legal administration headed by the Social Democrats yielded to an adventurous baron and a handful of disloyal cops. The immortal hoax of Köpenick repeated itself, on a larger scale and with tragic consequences. When everything was over and the dashing reactionaries had seized the power over Prussia, Messrs. Braun and

Severing, the thrown-out ministers, shook their heads and sighed: "Our conscience is clean. Resistance would have meant bloodshed."

A scornful laughter echoes from other spheres. "Your fussiness is delightful, Mr. Severing! I adore your delicacy, Mr. Braun! Among ourselves, your Excellencies, there will be quite a bit of bloodshed, not too long from now, thanks to your wisdom and caution. Streams of blood, your Excellencies! nice, fat, purple cataracts. The chronicle of coming disasters has already been written on the walls, with authentic blood, gentlemen! . . . Are you blind, Mr. Severing? Are you illiterate, Mr. Braun? Can neither of you read?". . . .

The Hero of Tannenberg, boss of the German Republic, publicly boasted of his illiteracy. "Since my early boyhood," he announced, with stunning shamelessness, "I haven't read a single book." How could he be receptive to blurred hieroglyphs? His was the sturdy health and the callous conscience typical of half-wits—and crooks. Without any moral scruples he fired Dr. Brüning, to whom he owed his power. Intrigues flourished around and against the Chancellor, General von Schleicher. Cunning Herr von Papen and the President's criminal son, Major von Hindenburg, easily convinced the old man that Herr von Schleicher, a "rapacious Bolshevist," intended to rob the Hindenburg clan of their lovely estate, Neudeck, in Prussia. The Marshal raved, Franz von Papen smirked, and the Major became wealthy. The camarilla sold Germany, not for a pottage of lentils, but for a piece of land and the vows of Mr. Adolf Hitler. Von Papen whispered into the hairy ear of the old general that everything might work out very nicely and that a new Cabinet of "national unity" could be formed, if only Schleicher were sacrificed and Hitler made Chancellor. Hindenburg—senile and dishonest—understood nothing of the plot except that Papen guaranteed him the maintainance of Neudeck: in fact, an additional bit of Prussian soil was beckoning as reward when that "damned Bohemian corporal"—Schicklgruber Adolf—got his appointment to the Chancellery. "Why don't you sign the harmless document, sweet old dad?" whispered Hindenburg Jr.

"What is your Excellency waiting for?" urged Herr von Papen. "It's just a formality. That man Hitler is our obedient tool. We, the friends of your Excellency and the pillars of order, will actually rule the country."

The corrupt old landlord gazed at the document, a white piece of paper covered with letters and signs. "I can't read any more," he mumbled. "Damned printed stuff. Always annoyed me. Old soldier doesn't bother. Only for the sake of German Fatherland. Hurrah. Bohemian corporal—no discipline. It's all right, I suppose. Only for the sake of the Almighty God, hurrah. Neudeck—Prussian soil, my old bones will rest under oak trees, hurrah, hurrah, the family tradition. Where is my pen, Baron? . . ."

Happy the dead who were spared the ghastly comedy! It was surely no fun to watch the whole personnel of European democracy beaming and bustling—all in raptures about the prospect of double-crossing each other with the help of that boisterous parvenu from Brunau, Austria. M. François Poncet, the Ambassador of the French Republic to Berlin, rushes to and fro between the wealthy semi-Fascists in Paris and their pals in Germany—a distinguished procurer, "bien soigné, bien pensant, bien payé," quivering with hope to bring about a good, solid alliance of heavy industry and Nazism directed against labor strikes, high taxes for the rich, and the Soviet Union. The industrialists in Lyons, Birmingham, Detroit, and Düsseldorf are smitten with the scheme. The Kremlin, meanwhile, makes its own cunning policy, based upon the axiom that everything that's bad for the Social Democrats must be good for the Communists. The World Revolution—they say—can only profit by chaos.

While Germany was all but boiling into civil war, the British amused themselves with their dusty intrigues: "Balance of power, gentlemen! Don't forget the lofty tradition of our Empire!" . . . His Holiness in Rome is full of paternal hope: the totalitarian movement may at last do away with atheism. Only Mussolini seems a trifle disturbed: the new competition annoys him. But, then, what has he to fear from that little man Hitler. After all, the German would-be dictator is his ape and creature . . .

Nobody understands the apocalyptic signs: The continent seems tickled by its own inevitable doom—literally tickled to death. The bankers, cardinals, and foreign secretaries take the howling challenge of the Horst-Wessel song for a joke—the writing on the wall for a funny paper.

MENE, MENE . . .? How funny!

TEKEL . . . ? That's a good one!

UPHARSIN . . . ?

What a scream!

Smirking, giggling, guffawing, they stagger into the abyss.

On January 30, 1933, I left Berlin early in the morning, as if driven away by evil forebodings. The streets were calm, clean and empty, when I rode to the station. I looked at them, but not carefully enough. I did not realize that it was for the last time.

I was going to Munich but planned to interrupt the trip at Leipzig, where I had a date with the leading director of the City Theater, who was interested in a play of mine. He looked pale and troubled when he greeted me at the station. "What's wrong?" I asked him.

He seemed surprised. "Don't you know? The old gentleman has appointed him."

"The old gentleman? . . . Whom?"

"Hitler," he said. "He is Chancellor."

And this is the writing that was written, Mene, Mene, Tekel, Upharsin. This is the interpretation of the thing: *Mene:* God hath numbered thy kingdom and finished it. *Tekel:* thou art weighed in the balance, and art found wanting. *Peres:* thy kingdom is divided, and given to the Medes and Persians.

The Persians. . . . The Persians are coming! . . .

CHAPTER TEN

Exile

(1933-1936)

Exile began in Munich. When the Nazi terror had already swept Prussia and other parts of the Reich, Bavaria still defied the new masters. In February, 1933, after the Reichstag Fire, or even before that date, many a liberal journalist or cautious Jew thought it wiser to move from the banks of the Spree to the Isar River.

In Munich, there was no Gestapo as yet, but just some good-natured cops supervised by an upright Major, Herr Scharrnagel, and Premier Held, a Catholic. People who might already have been arrested if they had stayed in Berlin were free, in Munich, to attend masked balls or go skiing in the Bavarian Alps or applaud an anti-Nazi show, "The Peppermill," which drew enthusiastic crowds to the handsome and intimate little theater, "the Bonbonnière."

"The Peppermill" was Erika's newest venture: she organized the troupe, wrote the songs and sketches, and acted as master of ceremonies. The members of the cast were all young, some of them highly gifted, especially our friend Giehse, the star of the Kammerspiele, a stout and sanguine person. Even the Nazi critics were in the habit of praising her as the "embodiment of sturdy Germanic humor," ignoring the fact that she was Jewish and a passionate anti-Fascist to boot.

This last month in Germany assumes in my recollection a savor of grim and feverish merriment. Everybody kept drinking and dancing, having decided as it were to forget the sinister reality with the help of intoxicating noises, liquids and embraces. The tangos and waltzes were punctuated by the grisly news and rumors pouring in from Berlin. We danced at the Regina Palast Hotel when the Reichstag burned in the capital. We danced at the Hotel Vier Jahreszeiten when the incendiaries accused innocent men of their own wanton crime. I don't know where we may have danced when the anarchist Erich Mühsam, the pacifist Carl von Ossietzky, and the Communist Ernst Thälmann were arrested by the Gestapo. But I shall not forget the Peppermill Ball, which took place in our house and was a considerable success, although some of the most important guests happened to come very late. This lack of politeness was all the more astonishing as the gentlemen in question were all descended from old aristocratic families and, therefore, should have been well-bred. But the excuses they offered were cogent and at the same time depressing. They had just conferred, for a number of hours, with Prince Rupprecht von Wittelsbach, the legitimate pretender to the Bavarian throne. But his Highness, an aging man, rather sluggish and barren of adventurous spirit, stubbornly refused to follow the appeal of his monarchistic friends. He liked life in the country, hunting and mountain climbing, and did not care to be King.

"The Peppermill" did so well that the little troupe intended to move from the Bonbonnière to a more spacious theater. Erika came to a quick agreement with the owner of a popular night club in Schwabing. She was supposed to reopen her show on April 1, which gave her sufficient time for a rest in Switzerland. A friend of ours had asked us to stay with her, in the mountains. The air was tonic, up there, and the snow hills glittered gorgeously in the sunshine. But when we turned on the radio, the dazzling panorama presently palled on us. The goings-on in the Reich seemed increasingly disconcerting. Hadn't those in the know assured us, again and again, that Hitler would hold no real power, but was used by big business and the general staff of the Reichswehr as their puppet and window dressing? The initiated are usually wrong, which does not prevent them from being exceedingly positive. Germany, they explained to us, rather haughtily—was to be ruled by the I. G. Farben, the United Steel, and Privy Councillor Dr. Hugenberg—not by an anti-Semitic brawler named Adolf Schicklgruber. But maybe the puppet would turn out to be more astute than even the wire-pullers? It was, perhaps, Herr von Papen's turn to be duped for a change?

However, we decided to take a chance and to return to Munich, as planned originally. Schicklgruber or I. G. Farben, Erika had to start rehearsals. And as for myself, I was in the midst of very promising negotiations concerning a new play of mine.

In Munich, we arrived just in time to witness the triumphant entrance of General Ritter von Epp, Hitler's Gauleiter and representative in the Bavarian province. The very man who had once "liberated" us from the Bolshevist terror, now appeared as the plenipotentiary of the brown-shirted terrorists.

At once we realized that conditions had changed fundamentally, in an appalling way. Even the traditional obstinacy of our compatriots proved inadequate to cope with the Nazi challenge. The clerical politicians, who had formerly boasted they would arrest Hitler's man at the Bavarian frontier, were compelled to give in, and were subsequently arrested themselves.

As usual, our chauffeur Hans showed up to meet us at the train. But his attitude seemed ominously altered. He looked pale and troubled. "Be careful!" he warned us, with strange urgency, "both of you, but especially Miss Erika! The Nazis are after you. Don't go out! Don't tell anyone you're here! Don't let them catch you! Or else . . ." The grimace with which he ended his speech, was more suggestive than any words could have been.

It was only later that we found out what made him act in such a peculiar fashion. He was a traitor with a twofold guilty conscience, our chauffeur Hans, whom we had always taken for a nice enough fellow. He had been a Nazi spy throughout the four or five years he lived with us—a stool pigeon appointed by the Brown House to report on all goings-on in our family. But this time he had failed in his duty, out of sympathy, I suppose. For he knew what would happen to us if he informed his Nazi employers of our arrival in town. By sparing us he may have endangered himself. Small wonder that he panted and gesticulated, torn as he was by misgivings, qualms and contradictory impulses.

These were hectic and gloomy hours—the last hours we spent at home. Following Hans's advice, we kept in hiding in our rooms: not even the maids were supposed to discover us. But the telephone functioned. We could make a long distance call to Arosa, Switzerland, where Mielein and the Magician rested after a lecture tour to Brussels, The Hague, Amsterdam, and Paris. It was good to hear their voices. The conversation was painful, though. For they did not want to understand what we had to make plain to them but did not dare to say plainly: that they must not come home, at this point, but should remain where they were. Why? the Magician insisted. Why did we think his return inadvisable? We stammered something about the weather, and that the most disturbing kind of spring-cleaning was going on in his studio. But he said the weather could hardly be worse in Munich than it happened to be in Arosa. As for the cleaning about which we made such a fuss, it could not last for ever, after all. It took a long time for him to grasp the saddening state of affairs.

Several of our friends were already under arrest, while others had thought it wiser to leave the town or the country—for the time being at least. We agreed with those who preferred a hasty departure to any possible collision with the truculent visitors. It took us just a few hours to wind up some current matters, whereupon Erika joined our bewildered parents in Switzerland. I left the following night. Destination: Paris.

How distinctly I recall the hours preceding that pivotal trip! Although without an inkling as to the moment's inherent gravity, I was suddenly struck by what I then considered an irrational apprehension and disproportionate melancholy. For luncheon a friend of mine kept me company, and as he happened to be a gay, pleasant fellow, everything seemed all right as long as he was around. Left alone, however, that overpowering, dazing sadness caught and paralyzed me again. I didn't know what to do, all by myself in the big, empty house. There was nothing but a hostile, oppressive stillness. I didn't dare to call up anybody, as Hans had warned me again to inform as few persons as possible of my being in town.

Hans, the good-natured scoundrel and twofold double-crosser, was the last person I talked with in Germany. We had a drink together before he drove me to the station. When he opened the door of our nice old limousine, he observed with a roguish, embarrassed grin: "Well, I guess that's the last time that I'll have to drive a member of the Mann family. Tomorrow morning your car will be in the garage of the Brown House. Major Klötschke thinks it's a swell car. He'll use it as his private vehicle."

After a pause he added, driving the car along the familiar alley and over the bridge across the Isar River: "You must understand my position, Herr Klaus. A fellow wants to live, after all. No ill feelings, I hope?"

"No ill feelings," I said.

I walked the short distance from the parking place to the train. Hans followed me at a respectful distance. It was the last time I set foot on German ground.

The date was March 13, 1933.

My luggage consisted of two suitcases, a typewriter, a topcoat, and a bunch of magazines and books. I had packed a few things, as though it were just for another journey. In fact, I hardly expected to stay away for more than a couple of months. Not that I ever considered returning to a Germany dominated by Hitler—certainly not. But I took it for granted that the Nazi farce wouldn't last. No doubt, the powerful democracies would know how to cope with those primitive rascals. It could hardly be difficult for France, Great Britain, and the United States to do away with a handful of morbid impostors. All that seemed necessary was one stern and impressive gesture on the part of those governments, the recall of their diplomatic representatives or the severance of trade relations with a Nazified Reich. The German people would inevitably come to their senses, once they had been made to understand that one doesn't get away with arson, forgery, murder, in a civilized world.

I recall two incidents that occurred during those initial weeks of exile. Trifles in themselves, they were, nevertheless, revealing shocks to me.

The first incident took place in a Paris restaurant where I was having dinner with some German friends. It was the time when anti-Nazi periodicals, founded by refugees, sprang into existence everywhere. By means of glaring cartoons and flamboyant manifestoes these well-intended sheets tried very hard, and unsuccessfully, to incite public opinion abroad against the German tyranny. The paper whose layout and text we were studying carried a huge swastika on its front page, a polemic swastika, to be sure; probably dripping with blood, or with a diabolic grimace in its center. But the American lady sitting next to us failed to notice these accessories, nor did she perceive that several of my friends looked Jewish. All she saw was the swastika: all she heard was our German talk. So she got up—a portly woman, middle-aged, well-preserved—and, striding by our table, pierced us with scathing looks. "You should be ashamed of yourselves," said the lady, "instead of gloating over the symbol of your disgrace." It was the swastika she referred to, as her dramatic motion clearly indicated. And she strode away—not without having spit at us. It was the first time in my life I saw an august female spit with the violence and trained technique of an infuriated truck-driver.

There we sat—flabbergasted. None of us had been swift and plucky enough to inform the lady of her fatuous slip. How absurd! to confound us with our most implacable enemies. Maybe we ought to wear conspicuous signs announcing our status as refugees? But this idea was dropped shortly. It involved too many disadvantages.

For we were to find out before long that the upright matron from the other side of the ocean was indeed an honorable exception. The majority of people looked askance at us—not because we were Germans, but because we were refugees. There was no reason, they thought, for any decent and orderly citizen to run away from his country, no matter what kind of government happened to be in power. They took the Nazi régime for "just another government." They didn't understand.

And this was the second revealing shock, not much of an incident, really; no dramatic affair; just a conversation.

It chanced on a café terrace that I met a Swiss fellow whom I had known for years. A suave, intelligent chap: I was certainly pleased to see him. But the harmony ended as we began to talk politics. My civilized friend from Zurich or Lucerne was surprised, indeed, almost disgusted when I told him that I did not intend to return as long as Germany was ruled by the Hitler gang.

"I don't mean to be rude," he said, "but I think you're foolish. What is so terrifying about your famous Hitler? An astute politician, but there are dozens of them. Don't you realize what an awful blunder you make? To give up your home, your friends, your career—everything! On account of what? Because you have an animosity to Herr Hitler's nose. It's too silly for words."

They didn't understand.

Some of our friends, back home, didn't either. Letters reached me from Munich, Berlin, and other places repeating, almost literally, the admonitions of my Swiss acquaintance. W. E. Süskind, for instance, told me in a nicely couched epistle that he was indeed disappointed in me. Had I lost all my curiosity, my open-mindedness, my adventurous spirit? Had I become a political doctrinaire? An obtuse fanatic of republican virtue? Why not have a look at what was actually going on in our good old city? Life under Hitler was thrilling and colorful—full of suspense and promise, according to W. E. Süskind. "Come back! Better today than tomorrow!" he urged me. "If it were dishonorable to be in Germany now, do you think I would stay? Don't you know me—don't you trust me any more?" Prejudice and resentment, he said, had confused my mind and corroded my loyalty. He, on his part, was clear-headed and loyal enough to take over the editorship of a literary monthly now coordinated to the "cultural policy" of Dr. Paul Göbbels.

I wrote him: "I shall not come back. I do not distrust you. I feel sorry for you. There are things which nobody can touch without polluting, indeed, poisoning himself."

I have never heard from him since.

Every refugee had his own W. E. Süskind—his own tempter and warner. I suppose they were prompted by genuine concern, our cousins and cronies in Germany, when they tried to explain to us why we were altogether mistaken and ought to correct our pernicious fallacy. They did not mean to corrupt us, nor was it their purpose to lure us into a trap. They just didn't understand.

The essential reason for exile, in our case, was irrefutably simple. It had nothing to do with the fact that my mother is of partly Jewish extraction. (She would have been recognized as a "second-rate Aryan," according to the fantastic racial arithmetic adhered to by the Nazis. As for ourselves, my sisters, brothers, and me, we could have enjoyed all privileges reserved to the "Aryan.") Nor was it on account of our political record that we had to leave our country. The Nazis might have been only too pleased to forgive us for trespasses as they had done in many another instance. The truth is that we left voluntarily, or rather, that we were forced away by our own disgust, our horror, our forebodings.

We left because we could not breathe the air in Nazi Germany. The fear of suffocation is a plain, cogent reason for any preventive action—no matter what its consequences may be. Anyone endowed with a normally functioning mind could perceive what we grasped from the very beginning: that no understanding or compromise is possible with Hitler and his ilk. You might as well suggest that a reasonable man ought to adapt himself to syphilis, or that he should overcome his prejudice against poison. For Hitler is not a problem: he is a plague. There is nothing to discuss about his "principles": he has none. He can't be appeased or refuted. What is the method of appeasing a mad dog? There are phenomena you cannot cope with, except by stamping them out, or else by avoiding them until they are stamped out. So that we did: we avoided the plague, and at the same time we tried our best to expose its devastating impact and accelerate its termination.

It was a tedious, ungrateful job, to warn a world that wished, rather, to be fooled. They dismissed our admonitions as they dismissed Hitler's glaring self-arraignment, "Mein Kampf." Aghast and horrified, we watched the international diplomats and intelligentsia being duped by blatant lies and transparent devices. What a nauseous, alarming spectacle! The Nazi régime wallowed in blood and filth: but the British Ambassador was smitten with the sanguine personality of Field Marshal Hermann Göring and with the sophisticated charm of Dr. Paul Joseph Göbbels. The Teutonic hooligans burned the masterpieces of world literature on public squares in the Reich and persecuted the outstanding German writers: but the great Norwegian novelist, Knut Hamsun, and the American jester, Ezra Pound, thought Hitler an eminent promoter, not only of "Kultur," but also of culture at large.

The Führer never revoked the insults he hurled against France in his book. But French politicians and industrialists kept flirting with Hitler agents, while French writers did not shrink back from visiting the Reich upon invitation of the very man who offended their nation.

The German labor unions were dissolved and their leaders arrested: but the Labor Party in Britain warned against any measures that could provoke Mr. Hitler.

American and English pacifists went on pilgrimage to Berlin and Berchtesgaden while the German champions of peace and internationalism suffered and perished in concentration camps.

Catholic priests were tortured and defamed by the Gestapo: the Vatican signed a Concordat with Berlin.

How could they make agreements with a gang of sadists and impostors? How could the gentlemen from London, Washington and Paris shake hands with those responsible for the atrocities of Dachau and Oranienburg? Did the sinister spectacle of the Reichstag Fire Trial not suffice to enlighten and repulse the appeasers? And the sickening obscenities with which Julius Streicher—Hitler's intimate friend—submerged the Reich from his headquarters in Nürnberg? And the disgrace of the Day of Boycott designed to ruin and to humiliate the Jewish citizens? And the secret rearmament? The falsification of Hindenburg's last will? The inordinate boasts and provocations with which every Hitler speech bristled?

Evidently, it was not enough. Only a few reacted. The majority, including the ruling clique, remained aloof, apathetic. The British Tories and Laborites, the French bureaucrats and professors, the powerful men from Wall Street and Detroit—they were no less obtuse and cynical than our Papens and Hindenburgs, Hugenbergs and Thyssens.

The same fools and climbers who acquiesced in Hitler's crimes and distortions kept denouncing the refugees. They fawned upon the tyrant, and sneered at his victims to boot. The refugees—they said—are tactless, noisy, and hysterical. They try to talk the world into an anti-Hitler crusade, because Hitler threw them out of Germany—not without sound reasons, perhaps. How dull and dreary are the refugees! The poor among them are indeed shockingly wretched, whereas the rich display unsuitable luxury. Nobody likes to have people around who actually look like martyrs—shabby and emaciated; nor does anyone care for those who pretend to be martyrs while feasting on caviar and champagne.

Hitler may be a danger but at least he is not a bore: quite a few "democrats" of high standing thought him vastly stimulating. As for the refugees—those onerous Cassandras—they were mostly considered a pain in the neck.

It does not make sense to speak indiscriminately of "the refugees."

The German emigration never formed a social or political unity. Consisting mostly of Jews, it is to be regarded as a primarily unpolitical body. For there can be no doubt that the vast majority of German Jews would have remained in the Reich, if only the Nazis had allowed them to stay. There is nothing derogatory or malicious about this statement. I just do not believe that the reactions and insights of the shopkeeper Moritz Cohn differ basically from those of his neighbor, the shopkeeper Friedrich Müller. Why should the Jewish sector of the German bourgeoisie have protested against a government that was hailed, or at least accepted, by millions of their non-Jewish countrymen?

The predominantly non-political attitude of the German Jews inevitably hampered the formation of an effective anti-Hitler front. Moreover, such an effort was complicated by the discrepancies among the political émigrés. There were a multitude of cliques and factions with almost nothing in common except their hatred of Nazism. The Catholics did not trust the Social Democrats, who, in their turn, refused to collaborate with the Communists. The monarchists had their own objectives and intrigues. As for the ex-Nazis, men like Hermann Rauschning and Otto Strasser, who had but recently joined the opposition, they were considered by many as the most competent leaders in our struggle, on account of their insight into Nazi tactics and purposes.

Within this motley vanguard of the political emigration, there was one homogeneous group and representative minority—the writers. While many of the outstanding German painters, scholars, actors, and musicians had tried to make their peace with the régime and still worked in Germany proper, the exodus of German literature was almost complete. Apart from a few sad exceptions, the German men of letters did not give a bad performance in those critical weeks and months of 1933. Not only the Jews among them tried to arouse the conscience of the world against the Nazi disgrace. No less undaunted and spirited were their non-Jewish comrades—Fritz von Unruh and

Leonhard Frank, Berthold Brecht and Oscar Maria Graf, Oedön Horvath and Werner Hegemann, René Schickele and Annette Kolb, to mention just some of them. The alternative confronting those so-called "Aryans," was dishonor and security at home, or honorable insecurity and possible wretchedness abroad. I do not believe that any of us regrets the decision made.

Our function and task were clear and significant. There was a double function, to be more precise, and the task was twofold. We had to warn an unaware and drowsy world, to begin with, and also to provide the German underground movement with information and encouragement: this was the political aspect of our mission. At the same time it behooved us to preserve and develop those literary values and traditions now suppressed in the land of poets and thinkers.

It is, perhaps, typical of the German mentality that the cultural front against Hitler functioned much more smoothly and effectively than the political opposition. In fact, the German writers, publishers, and editors in exile did a remarkable job, especially during the initial period from 1933 to 1936. No detached and knowing critic can examine their output without recognizing its intellectual scope and literary value. Many a German novelist or poet did his best work as a refugee in Amsterdam or Nice, Paris or Copenhagen. Almost all of them maintained their former standards.

Among us writers a natural feeling of solidarity prevailed, notwithstanding the differences of our respective tastes and tenets. The Communist partisan and the religious visionary, if both were genuine men of letters, could find each other on a plane inaccessible to the quarrelsome politicians. While the former deputies of the Reichstag and the would-be leaders of a future German republic doggedly abided by their obsolete antagonisms and selfish aspirations, the men of literature fully realized that we were all in the same boat and that all depended on each other's help and comradeship.

It was a gregarious and gossipy world, the world of German literati in exile. The less contact we had with our readers, the more we stuck to each other. After a few months of common homelessness, we began to form something like a wandering family, an erratic clan scattered all over Europe. Only a few of us had a permanent residence. But even without knowing anybody's address, one could easily find everybody. There were certain meeting places in most of the major cities. Amsterdam—where our two leading publishing houses had their offices—Paris, Prague, and Zurich became soon the centers of a diffuse but lusty literary life.

They had their own hierarchy and code—this roving tribe of sophisticated pariahs. They had taboos and sorrows of their own, their special prejudices, hobbies, and fixations. We also had our Legion of Honor: paradoxically, it was the Nazi régime that appointed its membership. What the gentlemen in Berlin considered the most humiliating punishment, the so-called "expatriation" implying the loss of one's German citizenship, was regarded by us as the supreme mark of honor. I am proud to state that the name of my own family appeared in each of the four initial "black lists" issued by Dr. Göbbels.

Heinrich Mann was the first to receive the enviable distinction. He had left Berlin soon after the Reichstag Fire and, once in France, he lost no time in raising his voice to arraign and ridicule the brown canaille. Grief and indignation, combined with a total change of all external circumstances, may either break a man or, on the contrary, have a rejuvenating effect on his mind and organism. Heinrich Mann —a man in his early sixties at the beginning of his exile—experienced something like a second youth. Once again he commanded the incisive wit and forceful eloquence to which the charm and the validity of his earlier work are due. His epic evocation of Henri IV—the main product of these troubled years—does not fall short of his most brilliant achievements like "Der Untertan" (The Subject) or "The Little Town." As for the political manifestoes he composed about the same time, they live up to the great tradition of Voltaire, Hugo, and Zola, whom this German writer in France recognized and extolled as his masters. The wrathful and inspired "J'accuse" which Heinrich Mann sent from a modest apartment house in Nice reverberated throughout Germany. It was heard in the fortresses and castles of the Nazi chieftains, and it was also heard by the underground. The man who couched those poignant and winged indictments surely deserved the honor of being outlawed by the Third Reich.

My own name was included in the second list, published on November 6, 1934. Among my fellow-expatriates were the playwright and novelist Leonhard Frank, the stage director Erwin Piscator, and Hitler's former collaborator, Dr. Otto Strasser. All of us were found guilty of high treason as we had endorsed an anti-Nazi declaration addressed to the Germans of the Saar zone. The plebiscite concerning the future status of the Saarland was imminent, at the time, and we did whatever possible to gear up the campaign.

Of course, the Saar manifesto was just one reason among others that prompted the Nazis to excommunicate me from the "Volksgemeinschaft." I irritated them in many ways—particularly by means of a political and literary monthly, "Die Sammlung" (The Collection), that I founded and edited in Amsterdam. The magazine, under the sponsorship of André Gide, Heinrich Mann and Aldous Huxley, was designed to focus the scattered energies of our exiled intelligentsia and a congenial European vanguard. For I published not only the output of German writers, but also presented translations from French, Italian, English, Czech, Russian, or Spanish texts. Among those who contributed to "Die Sammlung" were—besides the whole plethora of exiled celebrities—Wickham Steed and Stephen Spender, Ignazio Silone and Count Carlo Sforza, André Gide and Philippe Soupault, André Maurois and Jean-Richard Bloch, René Crevel and Jean Cocteau, Benedetto Croce and Ernest Hemingway, Ilya Ehrenburg, and Boris Pasternack. I tried to introduce to my German-reading audience the writings of young Swedes, Czechs, and Dutchmen; I featured reports on cultural conditions in the United States and Brazil, China, Palestine, and Soviet Russia. But an integral part of each issue was devoted to anti-Nazi exposures, anti-Nazi satires, anti-Nazi statistics.

The third "expatriation" list carried Erika's name, along with some flattering remarks as to her treacherous activities. She had reopened "The Peppermill" in Zurich, on January 1, 1934, and the attraction of her satiric show proved even stronger in Switzerland, Czechoslovakia, the Netherlands, and other countries than it had originally been in Munich. "The Peppermill" had over a thousand performances all over Europe, from 1933 to 1936. The lyrics and one-act plays were still mostly Erika's work, although some others—including myself—contributed to the program. At once acrid and graceful, not without poetic and nostalgic undertones, the intimate and unassuming play created something like a new polemic style.

So lasting and lively was the continental success of "The Peppermill" that the Nazis thought it necessary to stage a riot when Erika opened her second season, at the Zurich "Kursaal." Hitler's stooges in Switzerland, the boys of the so-called Swiss Front, disturbed the performance by means of their usual devices, whistling, howling, and singing. This time they threw stench bombs—an appropriate novelty. The police (happily, controlled by the Social Democrats) had to intervene, whereupon new bands of Frontists invaded the theater. A regular battle developed. It was a tremendous scandal, resulting in official disputes among the appointed representatives of the Canton Zurich. Some of those gentlemen conveyed the opinion that "The Peppermill," being a cultural proposition of unusual standard and, moreover, inspired by liberal principles, deserved governmental protection, whereas others insisted that no alien, however high-minded and talented, should be allowed to incite uproarious demonstrations in their peaceful city. As usual, the democratic body decided in favor of a compromise: "The Peppermill" was permitted to carry on; the Frontists were mildly warned not to throw bombs any more, and as for Erika's license to reopen her show next year. . . . Well, the Canton Council would consider her application in due time.

The Nazis, meanwhile, publicized the Kursaal incident as a spontaneous outburst of Helvetian anger over Erika's gross misbehavior. In order to stress their solidarity with the Frontists, who had acted in this affair as trustworthy Nazi tools, the officials in Berlin deprived Erika of her citizenship. In her case, the pompous anathema was particularly futile and ridiculous; for she had just married the English poet, W. H. Auden, and had thus become a British subject.

As for our father, the Nazis were more reluctant—still a trifle afraid of public opinion abroad. At this point, his works were not officially banned; although, as far back as 1933, to ask openly for a book by Thomas Mann in a German book store was a risky thing to do. For his feelings towards Nazism were generally known, and were emphasized, furthermore, by his refusal to return to Munich. His house, his cars, his library—all his belongings had been confiscated; his name was abused and slandered by every Nazi scribbler.

The inevitable clash was caused by a literary polemic, inconsequential in itself, between a refugee periodical in Paris and the leading Swiss newspaper, "Neue Züricher Zeitung." My father, drawn into the argument, made remarks which were obviously unpardonable from the Nazi point of view. The almost immediate, if somewhat indirect, consequence of his statement was a letter from the Dean of Bonn University—a blunt and clumsy note to the effect that the title of honorary doctor, which my father held from that institution, had been taken from him. From this dreary piece of information resulted one of the classic documents of anti-Fascist literature, known as "A Letter to the Dean of the Philosophical Faculty of the University of Bonn," by Thomas Mann.

Now the Nazis abandoned their diplomatic restraint and declared the author of "Buddenbrooks" not to be a German citizen any more. My mother and my four younger brothers and sisters were simultaneously excommunicated.

Those who do not know life in exile may be inclined to overrate and overdramatize the suspense and martyrdom it involves. No pattern of reality is romantic or unbearable in the long run. Man is capable of adapting himself to all kinds of conditions, however unusual or trying they may first seem to him. It is life's intrinsic mystery and its main characteristic that it remains always life—quite independent from the accessory circumstances which may determine its respective shape.

So when I say that I spent the three initial years of exile mostly in Amsterdam, Zurich, Paris, and the South of France, I do not want to emphasize unduly the word "exile." To live in Amsterdam means, first of all, to live in Amsterdam—no matter whether you stay there in your capacity as a student of Dutch art or as an enemy of the Nazi régime. I stayed there in my capacity as an enemy of the Nazi régime; but still I enjoyed looking at the superb canvases by Rembrandt, Frans Hals, and Vermeer van Delft; I was elated by the great symphonic concerts at the famous "Concertgebouw," and used to take pleasant walks through the Vondel Park or along those picturesque canals which always enchanted me with their Venetian smells and perspectives. They also scared me a little, as I was told that their stale, slimy water was teeming with fat, poisonous rats. To live in Amsterdam is tantamount to spending one's days surrounded by tulips, bicycles, and portraits of Queen Wilhelmina. Amsterdam—that means sitting in front of the Hotel Américain, reading a neatly printed newspaper called "Telegraaf" or "Het Volk," while sipping a glass of the colorless and aromatic Bols liquor. In Amsterdam there are huge barrel-organs, prosperous-looking gentlemen who seem to derive from a Dickens novel, and ungainly, bright-haired lads in heavy wooden slippers. Everything is big and nourishing and a trifle quaint in that fine old city of Amsterdam.

All this has nothing to do with exile. Nor is the splendor of the Lake of Zurich affected by my status as a refugee. The hue of the water is blue, or gray, or blackish-violet, whether I stroll along these shores with a brand-new German passport in my pocket, or furnished with just a provisional document which the Dutch Government, most generously, put at my disposal. The sailing boats on the Zurich Lake are white phantoms hovering in a mist of rose and silver shades. The streets of Zurich are clean; too spotless, indeed, to be really attractive. Zurich is almost alarmingly hygienic; the whole place has a tinge of vegetarian restaurants and expensive boarding schools. I am fond of Zurich. It has almost matchless pâtisseries: only Gerbaud in Budapest can compete with Sprüngli and Huguenin. There are surprisingly many psychoanalysts, excellent book stores, skillful dentists, relatively few criminals, gorgeous views, and good people. This is the main thing: that there are good people in Zurich. They cherish their good Swiss money but also their good Swiss liberty. They are proud and stubborn, and don't trust anybody—especially a German. There is a curious sensitivity hidden behind their sedateness. They are less robust and more irritable than they may seem at first, those dignified and sturdy citizens of Switzerland. To provoke their wrath is inadvisable: they are fierce and tenacious fighters. To compliment them seems superfluous; for they are fully aware of their value: in fact, they deem themselves and their republic irreplaceable. The odd thing about it is that they happen to be right.

My parents settled in Küsnacht near Zurich, after some experimental stays in the Italian-speaking part of Switzerland and on the French Riviera. Both Mielein and the Magician were completely taken with Zurich. It offered precisely what he needed for his work and health, and therefore she liked it too. The at once idyllic and highly civilized atmosphere fitted his tastes and habits perfectly. In Küsnacht there was country life with its tonic quietness and magnificent promenades, yet it took scarcely half-an-hour to drive to the heart of the city, where there would be the most appetizing shops, a German theater, and a few friendly familiar faces. In many respects Zurich seemed even preferable to Munich: the new home at Küsnacht had advantages in which the lost one, in the Poschingerstrasse, was lacking. The Joseph saga grew, slowly but steadily. Time and again, we would sit together for an evening in the Magician's studio and listen to a new chapter.

There was the familiar aroma of cigar smoke, leather volumes, and eau de cologne. There was the traditional bric-à-brac, pedantically arranged on the desk; and Mielein hastily distributing ash-trays among the audience before the reading begins. And here, evoked by the sonorous voice, appeared Joseph, that graceful and clever youth, so intimately known to all of us for so many years. He still has the dark, dreamy eyes of his beautiful mother, Rachel. He is as slick and dapper as ever, our brotherly friend; and yet he has meanwhile passed through adventures and tribulations, has been down below, in the pit, and conversed with sullen cherubim; but in the end he was sold to African merchants. He was only a half-grown lad when we saw him the last time, in Munich. While we were occupied elsewhere, altogether absorbed in our endeavors, Jacob's favorite son also grew and matured.

What a queer and moving reunion, on the shores of the Zurich Lake! The mystic playboy has not fundamentally changed in exile. His eloquence is intact, his wiles and pleasantries have not tarnished by any means: his individual spell is as effective in the palace of Potiphar as it was in Jacob's tent, back home. Does Potiphar's wife despise him as a refugee and foreign-born nobody? Quite the contrary, the elegant priestess and sacerdotal grande dame is smitten completely by his evasive charm. She woos the exotic slave: she loses her mind; she suffers. How she glows and struggles! How she writhes in bitter-sweet ecstasy! She strips off her stateliness like a cumbersome mask. Love breaks her pride and ruins her complexion; love degrades and bedevils her, as it degraded Gustav Aschenbach on the Venetian Lido. Love holds her in derision, makes her tragic and ridiculous and human. She jeopardizes her home and dignity for her terrible love. Love is her inferno, her fever, her exile.

We settled down in exile as in a strange, empty house that seemed bleak and forbidding at first. Not that it could ever become a cozy dwelling place: it remains uncomfortable and a trifle weird. But then you begin to forget, after a while, that there are more convenient and lovable homes. The security and joy that may be in the world cease to be real in our consciousness once we have realized that they are not for us.

There were still enough things to be grateful for. There were friends, to begin with, old friends and a few ones too; fellow-émigrés and sympathetic natives in all those countries where we stayed for some time. I knew men and women who were born in France, Switzerland, or Holland, but associated so intimately with us refugees that they almost became estranged from their own milieus. Annemarie—the "Swiss child" with the face of an inconsolable angel—was one of these peculiar sham-émigrés. Her loyalty to certain ideas and persons induced her to abandon temporarily her own sphere of life and to partake in our uprooted, problematic existence. A little house she owned in Sils Baselgia—the most magnificent spot of the magnificent Engadin valley —became one of our meeting- and resting-places.

Zurich was full of friends. A Swiss publishing firm, Oprecht & Helbing, and the City Theater were the double focus of all social and literary activities involving the refugees. Besides, my youngest brother and sister, Michael and Elizabeth, went to school in Zurich, and subsequently attended the music conservatory. As for Elizabeth, her speech soon adapted itself to the typical Swiss intonation—that at once gauche and vigorous cadence the German language assumes in the Helvetian zone. While she looked, talked, and almost felt like a Swiss girl, Michael fell in love with an authentic daughter of Switzerland: which is probably the male way of recognizing an adopted country.

To the two youngsters exile meant not much of a tribulation; indeed, exile hardly existed. Nor was it bitter to my second sister, Monika, who spent her time in Florence playing the piano and relishing the splendors of Italian landscape, painting, and architecture. It was in Florence that she met a young art student of Hungarian extraction, Jenö Lanyi, whose wife she was to become.

Golo's situation was more difficult. In 1933, he had just concluded his studies in Heidelberg and attained his doctor's degrees. The young historian and philosopher seemed at the beginning of a brilliant academic career when the dire whims of history upset his plans and prospects. He found new fields of activity in France, where he was connected first with the École Normale of St. Cloud, near Paris; subsequently with the University of Rennes as a lecturer on German letters. He also tried his luck in Czechoslovakia. But all these provisional solutions could by no means make up for what he had forfeited when leaving Germany.

Did this uprooted young scholar dream of Tübingen or the lovely banks of the Neckar, in his dreary hotel at Rennes or in front of the Hradshin in Prague? I don't think he did. We were not given to nostalgic reveries. The present state of Germany was too sickening to foster any kind of homesickness. Besides we were taken up with the immediate and palpable problems our delicate plight involved. There was no time for sentimental reminiscences or futile dreams of return and "a better future."

The faces and landscapes we had left behind began to pale, to lose all relevance to our own lives and feelings. Germany lay under a pall of darkness, blood and guilt—immeasurably distant, inaccessible. The country of our birth became the forbidden zone, the cursed land of madness and outrages. The frontiers of the Reich were fiery barriers: whoever crossed them was doomed.

Curiously enough, there were people who took a chance. It seemed so odd that our two women servants—Mary and Maria—spent their vacations in Bavaria. Maria—a foolhardy thing—had even inspected our house on the Isar River. Incredible as it may sound, she hazarded a chat with the brown-shirted guard who patrolled in front of our stolen home, to protect it—from whom? It was he, the vigilant S.A.

man, who confided to our Maria that the former dwelling of a well-known traitor and novelist was destined to become a sanatorium for unmarried German mothers.

This sounded promising for Maria's colleague, Fräulein Mary, who could pride herself on an illegitimate boy. Time and again, she brought him along to Zurich, to let him enjoy a few nourishing holidays in our Küsnacht villa. He was a cute enough little chap—very bright and observant. What he had to report as to conditions at school and in the Hitler Youth sounded grisly enough. While relishing the whipped cream of which the Führer had deprived his nation, the tiny superman, in his turn, treated us with uncanny recitals. What bloodthirsty songs they learned in Munich, nowadays! Most of those dire ballads dealt with Jews or other objectionable beings who would be exterminated by the legitimate or illegitimate sons of Germania as soon as they were big enough to handle a gun or dagger.

There was something weird and yet comical about this piping little voice, pronouncing, in a very perfunctory fashion, such an abundance of threats, boasts, and invectives. Evidently, the lad had no inkling of the ghastliness of his repertoire. To him, a Jew meant precisely what the big, bad wolf may mean to a normal child. With unabashed naïveté he praised himself a "fair Germanic youth" (in a song called "The Future of our Reich"), although he happened to be more on the swarthy side. In fact, he looked rather Jewish. Could it be that Mary had polluted the "Aryans" by mingling with a pariah of non-Aryan stock? She giggled when we asked her this ticklish question. Said Fräulein Mary: "There you've got me, Herr Klaus. It all happened so quickly, on the train between Augsburg and Munich. Really, I hadn't time enough to investigate his racial purity."

As we exchanged surprised and apprehensive glances, she added hastily: "Of course, my boy is an Aryan, though. It's a principle with our government that all healthy boys whose fathers can't be located are counted as regular Aryans. The Nazi big-shots just take it for granted that an honorable woman like me wouldn't have any dealings with a dirty Jew."

They had stunning stories to tell, the travelers who returned from that bewitched and frightful land. Strangely enough, Offi and Ofey, fabulously old, at this point, belonged to the daring group of go-betweens who helped maintain a last, threadbare contact between the refugees and their former home. The venerable couple, still comparatively brisk and enterprising, had made up their minds to ignore the Nazis. Callow people like us always exaggerated things, according to Offi and Ofey. They were compelled to give up the house in which they had lived for half a century. Situated near the Nazi headquarters on the Brienner Strasse, the Pringsheim mansion disturbed the Führer's architectural designs. At shortest notice, the two old people had to quit their home, which was presently pulled down by the arbitrary master-builder. Thus Hitler destroyed another token of our youth—a focus of memories.

Ofey and Offi, however, failed to understand this obvious hint of destiny. With that queer obstinacy typical of the aged, they abided by their decision not to leave the country, but to stay in Munich until the end of their lives. Along with all their treasures, our grandparents moved into a new apartment just around the corner from their former home.

Of course, there was nothing really exceptional about their attitude. Life continued in Germany, after all; and most people participated in it as long as they were allowed to do so. Some of our former intimates even profited considerably by the new state of affairs. Gustaf Gründgens, for instance, hitherto a flamboyant champion of Communism, made a staggering career under the auspices of Field Marshal Hermann Göring. This mighty mountain of bedizened fat has a fervent penchant for the stage, as he proved by marrying a provincial heroine, Emmy Sonnemann. It was thanks to the fair-haired prima donna that Gustaf, already half in disgrace because of his naughty past, was given another chance. He chose the role of Mephistopheles in Faust for his come-back and, on occasion of the opening night, surpassed himself in sparkling charm and saucy wickedness. Göring, completely bedeviled by such a breathtaking display of bold depravity, presently forgave him for all his former slips, including his objectionable marriage. Before long Gustaf was appointed manager of the State Theater and thus became the leader, not to say the Führer, of theatrical life in the Third Reich.

I visualize my ex-brother-in-law as the traitor par excellence, the macabre embodiment of corruption and cynicism. So intense was the fascination of his shameful glory that I decided to portray Mephisto-Gründgens in a satirical novel. I thought it pertinent, indeed, necessary to expose and analyze the abject type of the treacherous intellectual who prostitutes his talent for the sake of some tawdry fame and transitory wealth.

Gustaf was just one among others—in reality as well as in the composition of my narrative. He served me as a focus around which I could make gyrate the pathetic and nauseous crowd of petty climbers and crooks. There were quite a few old acquaintances I had to include in this disgraceful procession. Emil Jannings, for instance, the dynamic mime with the unctuous voice of a "père noble" and a slimy lump instead of a human heart; André Germain, the vicious and ludicrous freak who sang Hitler's praises in French; the frustrated poet laureate, Hanns Johst; many an ambitious little comedian or powerful, blood-stained adventurer—I let them all march past, the opportunistic jesters and pretentious stooges, the glib intriguers and facetious fawners.

Maybe it was unfair on my part to present Pamela in the midst of this sordid lot. She had abandoned Sternheim, soon after the outbreak of the Hitler calamity, and subsequently joined the cast of the Berlin State Theater, under Gustaf's management. Such conduct could not but strike me as a betrayal of our mutual past. But maybe our grief and anger rendered us unduly severe. In cases such as Pamela's there was, perhaps, more tragedy involved than we could grasp, under the circumstances. We just perceived the spectacle of moral aberration, failing to realize from how many baffled efforts and from what desperate struggle such a fiasco may have been the result.

"Mephisto, The Story of a Career," published in Amsterdam in 1936, was the third book I brought out in exile. The polemic chronicle of corruption was preceded by two novels of a more lyric type—"Journey into Freedom," 1934 and "Pathetic Symphony, A Tchaikovsky Novel," 1935. Both experiments deal with the drama of uprooting which, in a sense, always was, and now admittedly became, the crux of my own experience.

I wrote on Peter Ilych because I love his music. Not that I overrate his rank as a composer: obviously, the author of such all-too-pleasing hits as the Nut-Cracker Suite or 1812 is no Beethoven. But then a Beethoven novel would almost inevitably turn out to be a pompous bore. The flawless, authentic genius may be praised and scrutinized in an essay's discussion; but it does not require, indeed, it virtually excludes the imaginative approach of a novelist. What attracted and enthralled me in Tchaikovsky's work and personality was just his problematical grandeur, the disputable validity of his inspiration.

I wrote his story because I know all about him. Only too intimately versed in his neurasthenic fixations, I could describe his aimless wanderings, the transient bliss of his elations, the unending anguish of his solitude. All I had to do was to articulate his own melodious confession—the gloomy message of his "adagios," the frantic tempo of his "prestos" and his "allegros."

He was uprooted, disconnected: that's why I could write his story. In Russia, they disparaged him as an imitator of Western patterns: the Asiatic exuberance of Moussorgsky's scores was played off by the critics against Peter Ilych's urbane melancholy. The Germans scolded him for aping the French, whereas the Paris press disapproved of the German influence perceivable in his music.

He led the haunted life of a fugitive, notwithstanding his worldwide successes culminating, paradoxically, in a sort of official and perfunctory fame as Russia's foremost composer.

He died the lonely and furtive death of a man who feels he can't bear life any more, but is ashamed of his weakness. I love his music for the sake of his lonely death, to which it is the sweet and powerful prelude.

The journey evoked in the other novel is an escape from Nazi Germany. The heroine is an at once valiant and sensitive girl—eager to fight, ready to sacrifice her private life, if necessary, in the interest of the Cause. A country house in Finland where she finds a temporary shelter becomes the setting for her emotional crisis. The young squire with whom she falls in love is endowed with arresting qualities but is deplorably lacking in political consciousness. The issue thus confronting the bewitched traveler is the classical alternative between love and duty. Should she indulge in this bitter-sweet, aimless adventure? Or does it behoove her to follow the appeal from her friends of the Underground movement? Has she a right to relish the savage grandeur of Nordic solitudes, the wondrous frenzy of her rampant romance? Torn by qualms and remorses, she might be disabled for both the political work and the kisses.

The dilemma I tried to define, but hardly succeeded in solving, is typical of my own state at that time, indeed, of the problem besetting my generation. For we were all perturbed by the discrepancy between our natural tastes and traditional preoccupations and the responsibilities imposed upon us by the political situation. This moral and intellectual crisis was by no means reserved to the refugees, although it manifested itself most clearly and violently, perhaps, among those deprived of their homes and habitual affiliations. But the young French and English writers, the literary vanguard of the Low Countries and Scandinavia were affected as well. The relentless strain of those days compelled the sensitive and creative minds everywhere to revise a philosophy of laissez-faire and individualism to which all of us had adhered more or less openly, in various ways and degrees.

A vogue of social consciousness swept the intellectual élite of a generation hitherto preoccupied, almost exclusively, with sexual and psychological issues. Not that this ethical awakening assumed necessarily the form of militantly political activism. In the case of Aldous Huxley, for instance, the reaction against flippancy and faithless sophistication from the beginning tended towards that philosophy of quietism and passive absorption in God, which the author of "Point Counter Point" later embraced without stint. But more characteristic of the predominant tendency is the example of André Gide, whose force and genius it is to anticipate and define new moods and postulates yet inarticulate but already imbuing the air with their coming persuasion.

Gide's much-discussed conversion to Communism, which took place at this time, was the extreme, spectacular manifestation of these general trends—the high-minded and naïve attempt of an aristocratic intelligence to coördinate his views and divinations to the scheme of an organized and collective effort. The aging individualist tried fervently, and vainly, to conceive the Soviet experiment as the guarantee of man's coming greatness and intrinsic perfectibility. His new credo had but little to do with Marxism, but was admittedly derived from Christian tenets and promises.

In fact, the whole vogue of left-wing enthusiasms I am referring to can hardly be described as a triumph of Marxian doctrines. True, some of my friends and contemporaries may have been close, at that particular point, to communistic vistas. A poet like Stephen Spender—to cite one individual case at random—probably was what the political jargon calls "a fellow-traveler." But as for W. H. Auden and Christopher Isherwood—both militantly left throughout the early Thirties—there are scarcely any traces of Marxian philosophy noticeable in their political writings. The motive power behind Auden's poetic-revolutionary appeal—*But to-day the struggle*—is at once simpler and more complex than the scientific eschatology of the materialistic gospel.

Never was I more intensely pained and puzzled by the inadequacies and errors inherent in the Marxian creed than during my stay in Moscow. I went there in July, 1934, to attend the First Congress of Soviet Writers. It was a large-scale affair remarkably staged and highly interesting. Many of the things I observed were indeed apt to impress on me not only the splendid efficacy of Soviet organization, but also the dynamic faith impelling this apparatus. It was fascinating—indeed, elating—to witness the joyful élan with which the plain people participated in the collective effort of building the Socialistic society. Literature, being recognized and propagated as an integral part of this vast, comprehensive scheme, evidently appealed no less to the public imagination and general interest than did the great economic or strategic issues. The Writers' Congress was a fine demonstration of this national concern in literary matters. All sessions were profusely attended by workers, soldiers and peasants, who partook with intelligent zeal in the discussions on modern poetry or the function of the theater under Socialism.

There was something touching and encouraging about the genuine enthusiasm with which the masses hailed the appearance of Maxim Gorki. The grand old man of Russian letters seemed the most popular man in the Union, next to little Father Stalin himself. It was chiefly to Gorki's presence and presidency that the Congress owed its attractiveness. There were, to be sure, more brilliant speakers than the venerable

Chairman, who whispered patriarchal platitudes in a piping, pitiful voice. At once timid and stuffy, his stage-personality could by no means cope with the irresistible violence of André Malraux's rhetoric or the arresting sagacity of Ilya Ehrenburg's speech. Louis Aragon is an elegant and effective orator. Bucharin's elaborate lecture was illuminative, if only with regard to flaws and limitations of Marxian literary criticism. The delicate and pensive poet Boris Pasternak, the sanguine novelist Count Alexei Tolstoi, even the red-bearded opportunist Karl Radek—they all seemed more stimulating to me than the illustrious old man whom the Soviet people worshipped as the undisputed pope of Socialistic letters. Whenever Gorki rose, the vast audience seemed awe-struck—petrified with attention. A grand reception in his country house, a palatial mansion kept on an opulent scale, was definitely the climax of the Writers' Congress. The international poets feasted on vodka and caviar; Gorki, an irritable oracle, answered questions, and the Kremlin was represented by Molotov, Kaganovich, and Voroshilov.

I stayed a fortnight or so at the Hotel Metropole in Moscow, and saw as much or as little as our guides were supposed to show us. The impressions I was allowed to gather sufficed to confirm and deepen my respect for certain basic objectives and accomplishments of the Soviet régime. But my qualms and objections were confirmed and deepened as well. An account, "Notes in Moscow," which I ran in "Die Sammlung" (August, 1934) echoes both my enthusiasm and my apprehension.

What intrigued me most was not so much the cult of official heroes, the nationalistic complacency, the rampant militarism: I had anticipated those features and tried to understand them as both inevitable and extraneous. From its very beginning the Soviet régime had to cope with such unique and perilous conditions that many of its shortcomings and transgressions may be explainable and pardonable. Nevertheless there were perturbing elements in the innermost structure of the Communist philosophy—fallacious, unacceptable tenets that had little to do with the danger of encirclement or the need of electrification. The essential triviality of orthodox Marxism is more difficult to bear than its explosive and brutal impact. It is not the revolutionary guillotine, indeed, not even the merciless apparatus of the GPU which frightens me most profoundly: it is the shallow and erroneous doctrine of dialectic materialism.

Assuming that the means of production have to be socialized, I could never embrace a gospel that promises salvation of the human race by virtue of an economic measure. I reject a philosophy which banishes and defames all metaphysical thought as a capitalistic contrivance to distract the proletarian attention from the only matter that counts, namely the class struggle. I do not believe that religion is the opium of the people (although I realize that religious ideas have been often abused to paralyze the human will to progress). To betray and slander the Mystery is no less pernicious than to sabotage Progress.

To dodge the tragic is not tantamount to bringing about the golden age of Socialistic prosperity and general happiness. To deny the unfathomable does not imply that absolute truth has been found. The literature of "heroic realism" disregards as many essential realities of human life as does any apocalyptic mysticism. The central enigmas of Sex and Death remain insoluble—quite apart from the potential solubility of the social problem by means of Five- or Ten-Year Plans. (This does not speak against the Five-Year Plan, to be sure; but it speaks indeed against its propagandists. Appointed to claim and to explain feasible and overdue reforms, they indulged in disparaging the unreformable.)

Yes, the antithesis between social discipline and individual freedom remains relevant and often disconcerting—no matter whether the Soviet party line acknowledges or dismisses this antagonism.

Only he who has experienced the devastating impact of these problems and alternatives is in a position to gauge their magnitude and their validity. The tempting simplifications of the Marxian dogma are sometimes dangerous to those striving and candid minds impervious to the glaring grossness of Fascist fatuities and of Nazi nonsense. I have seen many an irreplaceable intelligence hopelessly entangled in the immanent contradictions of rigid materialism. The case of René Crevel is the most tragic and most obvious example to illustrate what I try to point out.

He committed suicide in the summer of 1935, immediately before the opening of an anti-Fascist congress he had been instrumental in organizing. I shall never forget the morning when I learned that René was dead. The heat was stifling in my narrow room. The man who called me up was a German poet and devout Communist. He had collaborated with René in preparing the Congress against War and Fascism. René's speech was scheduled for one of the opening sessions, along with the appearance of André Gide, Heinrich Mann, E. M. Forster, André Malraux, and so forth. According to the German poet's report, René had spent his last evening with a group of colleagues, in a café on the Boul Mich.

"He seemed entirely normal," said the Communist. "Not depressed, or anything. Only sometimes he had such a curious way of staring into space—as if looking for something. But he couldn't find it—whatever it may have been."

Then he went home and swallowed his deadly tablets—the same drug, incidentally, which had killed the hero of his early tale, "La Mort Difficile." The only note he left on his chaotic desk consisted of five words: "Je suis dégoûté de tout," his cruel farewell to the Communist Party, his Surrealist and non-Surrealist friends, the world of Fascist crimes and anti-Fascist phrases.

"Leicht zerstörbar sind die Zärtlichen." "Easily destructible are the tender ones": It was another friend of mine, the poet Wolfgang Hellmert, who chose this line of Friedrich Hölderlin as the theme for the only story he wrote before he destroyed himself. Bland and civilized as he was, he avoided the rash and spectacular gesture of suicide. But the mortal balm of morphine to which he had recourse instead, produced the same effect, if only by degrees.

"To-morrow, perhaps the future," promised W. H. Auden—never a Marxist, but a one-time revolutionary.

> To-morrow the rediscovery of romantic love,
> The photographing of ravens; all the fun under
>   Liberty's masterful shadow;
> To-morrow the hour of the pageant-master and the musician,

The beautiful roar of the chorus under the dome;
To-morrow the exchanging of tips on the breeding of terriers,
    The eager election of chairmen
By the sudden forest of hands. But to-day the struggle.

Today, the incredible and yet truthful accounts of atrocities committed in concentration camps; today, the staggering stories of anti-Nazi writers kidnapped by Nazi agents (yes, I knew that fellow Wesemann, who narcotized the journalist Berthold Jacob in Basle, Switzerland, and drove him over the German frontier). Today, the inordinate bunk of Hitler proclamations mystifying five continents. Today, the brown propaganda covering the globe with its slimy network. The extermination of the tender ones, the martyrdom of vulnerable hearts, the suicide of our friends, distress and madness, rampant agony —today.

Today, that is February, 1934: the civil war in Vienna. A man by the name of Fey—a trusted collaborator of Chancellor Engelbert Dollfuss—uses a brief absence of his boss to play with the lives and homes of Viennese working men. Major Fey thus seals the doom of Austria. A few months later, the same gentleman will be involved in the assassination of Dr. Dollfuss.

"Voici le temps des assassins!" Rimbaud's terrible augury will be fulfilled, today.

June, 1934: Hitler purges the ranks of his intimate friends and initial followers.

"Traitor!" the Führer shouts at his beloved pal, the homosexual Captain.

"Who is a traitor?" bellows Captain Röhm, in his turn. "You, Adolf! You!"

Adolf's response is a massacre of unprecedented dimensions; an avalanche of horror sweeping the Reich from one end to the other; a well organized and yet elementary slaughter on a grand, epic scale.

October, 1934: the crime of Marseilles. A Fascist terrorist schooled in Berlin "liquidates" the King of Yugoslavia and the French Minister of Foreign Affairs, Louis Barthou—the one statesman of vision and integrity France has produced since Aristide Briand.

"Voici le temps. . . ." It's today. Today is 1935—another year to witness the growth of evil, the triumph of lies and hatred.

1935: Hitler, thanks to the support of the Vatican and the French Republic, comes out victorious in the Saarland. It's a landslide in favor of Nazism. Everybody seems pleased. The Führer has declared that he will have no further territorial claims, once the Saar is German. Everybody believes in the Führer's word.

About two months afterward, the same Führer startles the world by proclaiming compulsory military service for all able-bodied young Nazis. The other countries desperately try to match the Third Reich's formidable preparations. In vain: Hitler keeps leading the race.

Today, it is Abyssinia. The black-shirted bandits have the time of their lives dropping high explosive bombs on loam-huts. His Majesty's Government in London considers sanctions against the open aggressor. But Mr. Eden, who meant to stop Signor Mussolini, is stopped, in his turn, by Monsieur Laval. The French Republic sabotages the sanctions against Fascist Italy. The aggressor wins. Mr. Eden resigns.

Today, it is Spain: a new hateful grimace, the grimace of General Franco; a new crime—the crime of Spanish officers, priests, and squires leading Moorish troops and Italian mercenaries against those loyal to the legitimate Spanish Government; a new upheaval—the first stern reaction against Fascist oppression.

Tomorrow, perhaps, the future. But today, the sickening smell of cadavers, the monotonous flood of lies, the grin of treachery, and the groan of the victims.

Today, our futile protest, our exile. Tomorrow, perhaps, the struggle.

CHAPTER ELEVEN

The Volcano

(1936-1939)

THE Dutch liner "Statendam" is a fine, portly vessel, if not very rapid. She takes a full week from Rotterdam to the docks of Hoboken.

The skies were genial over a placid sea when Erika and I crossed the Atlantic, in September, 1936—once again together, and again unaware of what might be in store for us on the other side. Ages seemed to have passed since we had last made the trip. What infinite promises had the sea winds carried in those faraway days! We were foolish and vigorous—invulnerable in our resilient naïveté—when we ventured on our merry expedition around the globe. Nine years can be an almost immeasurable amount of time, if they are crammed with experiences and losses, bitter surprises, frantic efforts, the vicissitudes of a long and fatiguing quest.

No doubt, we were wise and weary in 1936, compared with the callow adventurers we had been in 1927. But we remained responsive to the tonic message of the salty breeze. The curly foam of the waves, so fleet and yet immutable, was as delightful as ever. Thank God, the grandeur of this unending panorama, the wondrous shades and formations of the billows and clouds, had not yet lost their comforting power.

Not that we tried to forget the Europe we left behind—the beloved continent laden with guilt, torn by self-inflicted wounds, convulsed with hatred and fear. How could we hope, how could we wish to escape from the problems which formed so integral a part of our own plight and future? But the gravity of this plight, the darkness of this future seemed brightened and mitigated when visualized in a vein of oceanic detachment.

Relaxing in our deck chairs, we were at leisure to reconsider and evaluate our endeavors and accomplishments of the past three years. No doubt we might have done better. Maybe we could have done worse. Erika, in particular, had no reason to be worried or dissatisfied. For she had succeeded in building up what seemed the most pertinent medium for unfolding her talents and promoting her cause. "The Peppermill" was something more important than just a successful theatrical enterprise. It was the valid and complete expression of Erika's artistic personality and political faith. Why then did she not continue to tour Europe with her well-geared vehicle? Disturbed by misgivings rather than by actual incidents, she renounced what still appeared a prosperous and effective venture. With the air in Europe becoming more sticky and more oppressive from season to season, even from month to month, she thought it advisable or, better, necessary to seek new openings, to take daring chances. So she had decided to try her luck and that of her little troupe on the slippery ground of Broadway.

As for myself I had as little reason for discontent as she had. From a professional point of view the period from 1933 to 1936 had been the most prolific and most gratifying one in my life. It was my good chance to find a publisher who is also my friend, a rare and valuable coincidence. It was under the auspices of his firm, the Querido Verlag in Amsterdam, that "Die Sammlung" could appear for two years—a fairly respectable lifetime for any literary review, let alone a magazine without a country. While editing "Die Sammlung," I somehow managed to produce three novels, and still had plenty of time for making lecture tours and contributing to scores of other periodicals.

All this might have gone on for another year, or even a little longer. But at bottom I sensed that my position was precarious, if not untenable. A liberal German writer had no chance in Europe, considering the present state and obvious trend of affairs. Would I find conditions more propitious on the other side? What was in store for me over there seemed even more uncertain than what I left behind. But there was nothing to lose, while a lot might be gained if this reconnaissance trip proved successful.

The New York we rediscovered in 1936 was the same city we had known and loved so many years before. What had happened to New York during the decade of our absence had nothing to do with changes. Quite the contrary, the beautiful and powerful metropolis had developed and intensified her own intrinsic rhythm.

How could New York have been really and fully herself without Rockefeller Center? This most arresting novelty, which we at once admired, means not only an additional asset to the scenery of New York: it is the dynamic expression of New York's innermost being. The first reaction in front of this glorious building is hardly that of surprise. You are not surprised when you see the very substance of a great city—its immanent Idea, to use this term in its Platonic sense— materialized in a towering symphony of steel, concrete, glass, and stone. It is only later, when you have looked at it dozens or hundreds of times, that you begin to marvel.

The New York of the Twenties was a roaring promise—its features twisted by prohibition and prosperity; its potency controlled by boot- leggers and big business. In a sense, it was yet an inarticulate city. The poets, instead of speaking out what their nation suffered and felt, with- drew to the speakeasies or to the Parisian Boulevards. Furtive and iso- lated, they concealed their images from the people. One of America's greatest poets in this century, T. S. Eliot, lived in London and wrote enigmatic poetry—some of it in French. To the American masses his message was incomprehensible: he was mute.

The American myths were speechless. The fidgety pantomime of the silent films was the pallid and blurred reflection of the American dream. The flitting shadows of Chaplin and Valentino, the taciturn antics of Buster Keaton and Harold Lloyd, the sweetness of Lillian Gish—these were the aphonic clichés in which the people recognized their own secret experiences and desires.

When the speakeasies vanished, New York found her voice again. It was high time for the creation of a new American idiom. If prosperity does not need explanation, depression certainly does.

The economic crisis aroused the social consciousness of the "lost gen- eration." While silence began to dispirit Europe, the United States became eloquent. The rugged and seditious protest of the hunger marches was superseded by the New Deal action and discussion.

The abominable conduct of the old world was instrumental in curing the new one of its nostalgia and its inferiority complex. The American vanguard ceased to leer at Europe. The prestige of that continent dwindled, thanks to Hitler, or rather, on account of the appalling weariness displayed by the Führer's victims. Who would admire or imitate a civilization that could so easily fall prey to a handful of brutes and swindlers? American youth, once again, clung to the American way; the European way had so disgracefully failed.

Of course this development involves not only enormous chances but also ominous potentialities. For it is apt to foster American Isolationism which, in its turn, is partly responsible for the European débâcle. In 1936, American national self-assurance outweighed American consciousness of international solidarity. With Europe in a seemingly hopeless mess, it was tempting not to mind "other people's affairs." Only some weak-minded dupes or malignant sympathizers were impressed by the blatant distortions of Nazi propaganda in the United States. But if it is true that next to nobody fell for the Hitler lies, it is also true that only a very few shared our grief and anger over the Hitler crimes. Almost exclusively those more or less directly affected by the European happenings seemed sincerely concerned. The Communists were almost the only ones who really cared about Spain, as Moscow happened to be involved. The Jews continued to enlighten the country with anti-Nazi material, as the Nazis continued to maltreat the impoverished, beaten, powerless "non-Aryans" in Germany. But as for the average people, they just thought themselves mighty lucky to be citizens of this peaceful and prosperous country (which was a right and approvable thought). The safest way, they felt, of preserving this trans-Atlantic oasis was to avoid all meddling in non-American matters (which was a fallacious and even dangerous feeling).

The intelligentsia were intent on scrutinizing and reaffirming the roots and rules of American aesthetics and philosophy, or .else they seemed absorbed in the various aspects of the New Deal experiment. The same people who, ten years before, would have discussed the particularities of Picasso's style or the images of James Joyce, and Proust, now tossed about with the names of union leaders, intricate statistics and cryptic abbrevations—CIO, WPA, CCC, SEC, AAA. During the weeks and months preceding the Presidential elections in 1936, the White House was more than ever the focus of public attention. The objectives and accomplishments of the Roosevelt Administration were the predominant issue in every American's mind.

There was something encouraging and refreshing about this general keen concern with the problems of social progress. To newcomers like us, the American preoccupation with labor questions, housing programs, farm reforms and so forth, opened a world of stimulating and instructive vistas. At the same time I could not help feeling that those fervent New Dealers as well as their dogged antagonists were somehow on a wrong track. Or rather, the track was right but it might end in a deadlock if the wanderers stubbornly disregarded the magnetic influences and disturbances emanating from distant centers of energy. Many of my liberal American friends seemed to believe that the New Deal could succeed even if Europe went Fascist. They were as mistaken as their opponents, the promoters of the economic laissez faire philosophy. Both the reformers and the conservatives signally underrated the relevance of international developments to the American dream. The illusion prevailed that the United States, for some shadowy reason, was absolutely immune to the germ of Fascism and disintegration. The Americans overestimated the width of the Atlantic, just as the French indulged in wishful thinking about the impregnability of the Maginot Line.

Moreover, the majority of the American people harbored fallacious ideas with regard to the essential reasons for Europe's decline and crisis. They blamed the quarrelsome character of "all those little nations," and particularly the traditional German wickedness, for a calamity which is really derived from much more complex and universal sources. Out of this double mistake—the overestimation of the geographical distance and the underestimation of Nazism as a manifestation of international evils—sprang the naïve belief that "it can't happen here."

Sinclair Lewis's novel was a timely, impressive warning. I had read the book in a good German translation, published in Amsterdam. Now my English had improved sufficiently for me to enjoy the English original. Moreover, I saw the WPA production of the play Sinclair Lewis had based on his dire prophecy. The stage version of "It Can't Happen Here" came out simultaneously in English, German, Yiddish, and Italian. Although the drama fell short of the poignant tale, I thought it a good idea and gratifying symptom that a government-supported theatrical enterprise did its utmost to popularize this meaningful parable written in deep concern by one of America's outstanding novelists.

I recall a rather sumptuous reception following the opening night, at the home of Mrs. Sinclair Lewis, Dorothy Thompson. The brisk and attractive American correspondent whom we had known years before in Munich, Berlin, and Vienna, was now at the point of becoming a national figure. Equally opposed to Hitlerism and to the New Deal, she was the mouthpiece and champion of that conservative liberalism represented, in the most dignified manner, by such papers as "The Herald Tribune." Miss Thompson's spirited punch meant a powerful asset to the cause of an enlightened bourgeoisie engaged in a twofold struggle against Fascist retrogression and what they considered devastating reforms. The illustrious columnist began to assume the appearance of a Roman Empress, whose ambitious and nervous grandeur we can still recognize, with respectful apprehension, in certain busts of the decadent period.

Many of our old American friends had increased in stateliness since we had seen them last. George Davis, for instance, whom I knew in Paris when he was frail and young and composed his first novel, had meanwhile become a well-to-do editor. Selden Rodman—once a handsome, savage-looking vagabond who roved through the streets of Munich and somehow found our house—settled down, discovered his common sense, and founded a magazine by this name, together with Alfred M. Bingham. Joseph Brewer whose lively publishing firm had once ventured on the American version of my "Alexander" novel, was now doing an excellent job as President of Olivet College.

Others had scarcely changed. Frederic Prokosch maintained the pensive grace he had commanded as a boy in his father's house. His first literary attempts lived up beautifully to the arresting promise his child-like gaze seemed to convey, at the time.

Ernest Boyd was as red-bearded, sparkling, and provocative as ever, obstinately sticking to his own original mode, in which the eccentric style of a legendary bohemian is curiously interfused with the quaint "savoir vivre" of a former Consul General of Great Britain.

Virgil Thompson managed to live in a New York hotel exactly as though it were situated somewhere in the Latin Quarter. Eugene Mc-Cown, too, carried a Parisian flavor along with his canvases and souvenirs when he moved his studio from the banks of the Seine to a building near Fifth Avenue.

As for Glenway Wescott, he now appeared almost as conspicuously European in America as he used to be conspicuously American in Europe. As a writer and a character he is just as suave and subtle. Being fond of highly civilized people, I always relished his company. The perfect elegance of his manners appears all the more impressive if considered as the result of constant and conscious efforts, rather than of a natural disposition. Wescott's urbanity is so elaborate that it becomes at times almost frightening, like the unduly prolonged performance of a risky acrobatic feat. I have experienced in his company moments of anxious suspense. More often than not I feared that my dapper and dignified friend might abruptly strip off his glossy mask and do something shockingly rude.

In the presence of men who deliberately stress their asperity I am inclined to expect the opposite transformation. I recall one evening, for instance, when Selden Rodman had me to dinner, together with Theodore Dreiser. Needless to say, I was impressed by meeting one of the most potent narrators of modern American letters—not one of my favorites, but undoubtedly a figure of great dimensions. His personality testifies to the authenticity of his writings. The at once rough and inspired man to whom I was introduced obviously commanded the relentless vitality and the earthy insights necessary to produce such valid, if somewhat ponderous, documents as "An American Tragedy," "The Titan," and "Sister Carrie." His features, as they appear in my memory, are constantly darkened and twisted by minor spasms of fury. It seems, mistakenly, perhaps, that he was angry all evening about one thing or another. Most of the time it was the Catholic Church that annoyed him—particularly as I dared to defend that fallible but meritorious institution. The argument about the Vatican must have dragged very long: I am under the impression that we discussed nothing else. While the dispute went on I indulged in the secret hope that the great novelist might abruptly perform a startling and lovely gesture—an unexpected motion of quaint, almost baroque gallantry, like kissing Mrs. Rodman's fingertips and saying, a little hoarse with emotion, "I am ever so happy to look at you, my adorable lady." But nothing of the kind occurred, alas. Dreiser remained intransigently bilious, just as Wescott stuck to his polished and flawless manner.

It is perhaps only the genius who can afford to live without a label. Instinctively assured of his identity, he is in a position to dismiss all traditional patterns and poses. He repeats or transforms himself according to his unpredictable and inescapable vagaries. No real genius is afraid of being underrated or misunderstood. He improvises his own idiom whether it is intelligible or not to his listeners. He delivers his message—that is all that matters.

There is at least one American genius I knew, namely the novelist Thomas Wolfe. Maybe he was not a mature, fully developed genius. The idiom he created may have been rugged and redundant. But it is his idiom, strikingly and compellingly so. It bears the marks of valid and authentic intuition.

I did not know him well: in fact, I saw him just once. But I shall never forget the hour in his modest flat on First Avenue. The view from his window was strangely in keeping with the mood inherent in his books. The hazy panorama of river, bridges, and gliding boats might have been one of the bleak and yet enchanting visions in which his prose is so rich.

He talked the way he wrote—rushing reminiscences, poetic images and boisterous clichés. A visionary colossus, he kept pacing the room as if haunted by an irrational fear that his huge, massive body might collapse before he had completed his message. His streaming eloquence was violent, muddled, erratic, and fascinating—no matter whether he imitated with inspired malice the mannerisms of a literary critic, or whether he dwelt on an anecdote about a sad little Jew he had watched on a train somewhere in Germany.

His recent trip to our former homeland was the predominant topic of conversation. Maybe Wolfe believed that our main reason for calling on him was to obtain news about Germany. He knew plenty of stories —stories about the chieftains and the little fellows, about old generals, new buildings, beggars, Jews, the sex life of Adolf Hitler, the streets of Berlin, and the family of Ambassador Dodd.

But the "finest surprise" he had in store for us was his elderly woman servant, a native of Bavaria. He wanted us by all means to meet her. We had to wait quite some time until she showed up. She had an enormous goiter and spoke the most hideous German-American gibberish I have ever heard. Wolfe watched us with fervent interest as we exchanged some embarrassed phrases. He thought perhaps that our nostalgia for Munich equaled his own longing for the lost myth of his home town. His maid's Yorkville slang, he supposed, might connote for our ears "the great forgotten language," that irretrievable tune that kept haunting him throughout his bitter, inspired life.

"The best of luck to you," he said to Erika and me when we left him. "I hope you'll like it here. You may find it a little different in the beginning. But I guess you'll like it."

He turned out to be right in both respects. We were going to find things somewhat different in the beginning, and we were going to like them the way they are.

Almost inevitably newcomers slip at first. They take it for granted that everything that was good enough for Europe will go over in a big way on this side of the Atlantic. The failure of "The Peppermill" in New York is just one of innumerable incidents to refute this axiom.

I suppose that "failure" is an unduly harsh word to describe what happened to Erika's show when it opened somewhat hastily on December 29, 1936, at the Chanin auditorium, atop the Chanin Building. It was not one of those downright, merciless flops as Broadway witnesses them once or twice each month. The critics as well as the audiences sensed that there was something fresh and promising in that informal sequence of sketches, songs and dances. But somehow it didn't quite click. The response was thin, compared to what it used to be in a dozen European countries. Maybe Erika made a mistake when presenting her show more or less in its original shape, but not in its original language. It was too outlandish and not exotic enough. The vigorous talent of Therese Giehse was hampered by the foreign idiom as by an inflexible corset, while John T. Latouche, the most dynamic personality among the Americans in the cast, seemed impatient to cry out his own message, his American Ballad.

However, the experiment was worthwhile—perhaps from the American point of view, and certainly from Erika's. This initial contact with American audiences could not but teach her a great many things helpful for her further career in this country. Her show had already improved and somewhat Americanized itself when it moved from the Chanin roof downtown to the New School for Social Research. In these more congenial surroundings the venture picked up and notably gained momentum. But when the interest of the theatrical agents and powerful impresarios awakened it was already too late. Some of the indispensable members of the troupe were on the point of embarking for Cherbourg or Rotterdam.

So did I, early in February, 1937—without being quite positive, at bottom, whether my "reconnaissance trip" had succeeded or failed. I had delivered some lectures, addressing mostly the liberal German groups in New York City and vicinity, but also a few American audiences, including the young ladies of Smith and Sarah Lawrence Colleges. Also, I had duly mailed my reports on American conditions to a number of periodicals in Prague, Basle, Paris and Amsterdam, and had contributed, or made arrangements for future contributions, to "The Nation," "Common Sense," "The Saturday Review of Literature," the "Washington Post," and some other American papers. The main result, however, was a contract with the well-established lecture agent, William B. Feakins, who guaranteed me an extensive tour, a regular "coast-to-coast" expedition, for the coming season. That meant the promise of return—new prospects, exciting chances.

When I returned to Europe I noticed that I felt more buoyant and confident than before my trip. So I lost no time in composing a lengthy, rhapsodic speech, "America—Token of Hope"—surveying my impressions and rationalizing my enthusiasm. Before long I delivered the address in Holland, Luxembourg, and Switzerland.

A group in Vienna also wanted to learn what rendered me so hopeful. But I am afraid my optimistic oratory may have sounded a trifle forced in the dreary surroundings of Schuschnigg's lusterless capital. The Vienna of 1937 was paralyzed by fear, abuzz with dire rumors, poisoned by treachery. The splendid monuments of its past cruelly emphasized the murky aspect of its present state. One promenade through the streets of Vienna sufficed to convince any clear-sighted person of Austria's doom and imminent disaster.

During my last stay in Vienna—I knew it would be my last one, even while staying there—I realized, more definitely than ever, the baleful gravity of Dollfuss's and Schuschnigg's errors. How could those clerical politicians ever hope to save the independence of their country by depending on Hitler's mentor, stooge, and predestined partner in Rome? Obviously, the Austrian Government had no chance to cope with the Nazi peril—within or without the frontiers—while affronting and persecuting the only powerful and active anti-Nazi block available, the Social Democratic Party. No doubt the blunderers of Vienna will be counted among the main culprits when it comes to scrutinizing the responsibilities involved in the drama of Europe. And this goes not only for the plain Fascists like Prince Stahremberg and Major Fey. It is also true, alas, in the more tragic and more complex cases of Dollfuss and Schuschnigg themselves. Neither their personal integrity nor their martyrdom can ever erase the story of their guilt.

Prague, too, was endangered when I went there in 1937—no less, actually, than was Vienna. And yet what a refreshing contrast! While in Vienna everything stagnated and waned, Prague appeared self-assured and productive. Not that the Czechs were inclined to underrate the challenge confronting them—quite the contrary. But they trusted their Western allies, and above all they relied on their own vigor and the righteousness of their cause.

They are fine people, the Czechs—imaginative, brave, and liberal. I make this statement unafraid of being called a Czech nationalist, although it happens that I am not only an admirer of Czechoslovakia but also a citizen of that country. Thanks to the generous gesture on President Benes's part, my whole family—excepting Erika, who is a British subject—was granted the citizenship of Czechoslovakia. I was entitled, therefore, to feel at home for a change while sojourning on Czecho-slovakian ground.

I stayed longer in Prague than my lecture engagements necessitated. The complex, iridescent charm of that city greatly appeals to me. I am responsive to all ascepts of its multiform splendor, of which the shape and flavor integrate so many elements and traditions. Not only Slavic and Germanic influences are interfused in the structure of that extraor-dinary place: there is a savor of French civilization intermingled with Russian moods. The proud serenity of the Italian-Austrian baroque assumes a somber grandeur in the narrow streets of Prague's ancient districts.

Prague has many faces. One of these faces is age-old, marked by struggle and suffering, burdened with sinister memories and eerie legends. But there is also another Prague—a youthful city, all sprightli-ness and ambition. The Czechs, as a people, believe that the best of their life is still ahead of them. Among all European nations except Russia, the Czechs are perhaps those most decidedly oriented towards the future. A long and tragic history has had a hardening and strength-ening effect on this tenacious race. Far from being worn-out and de-pleted, the Czechs emerge from all their tribulations with unabated hopes and energies. It may be that the true source of this resilient vitality is an inborn faith and a natural disposition through which the Czechs differ, again, from all other European peoples east of France. The Czech people are democrats by nature and tradition.

A genuine, living democracy always finds the representatives and leaders she deserves and needs. The Czechs had Thomas G. Masaryk, the Liberator-President, one of the few truly great and admirable statesmen Europe has brought forth in this century.

Before the grand old man withdrew from the public scene, it was his last act of wisdom and statesmanship to recommend his trusted friend and collaborator, Dr. Edward Benes, as second President of Czechoslovakia. The heir of Masaryk's power was also the most faithful herald and promoter of those lofty and basic tenets in which his venerable predecessor so ardently believed.

When I was received by President Benes, at the Hradshin, Masaryk was still alive but already invisible to the people—a distant oracle cloistered in the solitude of his country seat. I remember the momentary cloud of anxiety and sorrow that darkened Benes's face when I asked him a conventional question concerning Masaryk's state of health.

"His constitution is strong," Benes said, somewhat hastily. "Indestructible, one would like to believe . . ."

His absent-minded smile, affectionate and musing, told what a bitter blow the death of Thomas G. Masaryk would mean to his successor.

The patriarch of Czechoslovakia passed away about four months after my visit to Dr. Benes.

The hour of informal, animated conversation I spent with President Benes belongs to my most cherished memories. He is affable, without being patronizing; eloquent, alert, of keen and ready perception. His speech and attitude are gratifyingly devoid of all pomposity. In contrast to most of his European colleagues, he commands a hearty sense of humor. I recall the swift and roguish twinkle in his eyes when he observed—in reply to a compliment I had paid him: "Well, you see, the chief of a big, powerful nation can afford, perhaps, to be heedless and sluggish. I can't. One must not be drowsy if one has to run the affairs of a little country. I don't know—or rather, I don't like to imagine—the consequences of any slip or negligence for which I might be to blame."

He is vigilant and versatile, an astute expert in international affairs. Too experienced to be duped by the most cunning trickster, he is also too faithful to lose confidence—not even in view of the most discouraging odds. From both his idealism and his intelligence springs his unshaken belief that the cause of progress and democracy will come out victorious in the end. The triumphs of retrogression and brutality cannot but turn out to be specious and ephemeral.

The main part of my interview was devoted to a thorough review of the political scene as it appeared in the spring of 1937. It looked grim enough. I may have hinted at my apprehensive feelings. Dr. Benes's smile was at once knowing and reassuring.

"Don't be afraid," he said. "Bad things may happen—in Spain, here, everywhere. The evil may become mighty strong: but the good is stronger. Wait and see, my young friend! Our side is much stronger."

If there are two sides, Budapest is situated on the other side of the fence. Hungary is Fascistic. Not quite openly and seriously so, to be sure. Nothing in Hungary is done in full earnest. There always remains an overtone of gipsy music, a tinge of cheap, melodramatic farce. It is perhaps this fundamental lack of gravity which prevented Budapest from becoming as mortally dull as are the capitals of other Fascist countries.

It is the most corrupt and frivolous city imaginable, and undoubtedly one of the most amusing places on earth. If once the night life of Berlin surpassed and superseded the traditional wickedness of Montmartre, subsequently Budapest outdid the Babel on the Spree as far as tawdry elegance and sexy fun is concerned. Horthy and Gömbösch, the tyrants of Hungary, maltreated their political antagonists as relentlessly as any Hitler or Mussolini. Social conditions, especially in the villages, resembled those in France before 1789. But the night clubs of Budapest radiated and blared. The picturesque promenade along the Danube River resounded with the laughter of saucy dames and dashing gigolos. Young British globe-trotters and bon vivants loitered in the lobbies of the big hotels or in the corridors of the Turkish Bath establishments famed all over Europe for their salubrious wells and their loose morals.

Of course there was another Budapest, besides the lethargic wretchedness of the Hungarian masses and the pleasure-seeking bustle displayed by the ruling clique and a handful of wealthy foreigners. There was an intellectual Budapest: restive, oppositional, leading a furtive, almost illegal life in clandestine conventicles. That refractory vanguard—mostly but not exclusively of Jewish stock—formed something like an inner emigration within a motley, cynical community.

The elegant mansion where I enjoyed hospitality during my repeated stays in Budapest was one of the centers of this curious sphere. My host, Baron Louis Hatvany, belongs to the school of Western European liberalism that follows Voltaire's example, not only as far as humanitarian principles are concerned, but also regarding the serene and civilized way of life. Hatvany is a fervent democrat and, moreover, a literary connoisseur, an unflagging promoter of belles lettres and an accomplished novelist in his own right, a man of the world, an aristocratic champion of progress and liberty.

He became almost a martyr, thanks to his indomitable love of Hungary. Having been a member of the democratic government established in Budapest soon after World War I, he was compelled to flee twice—the first time, since he was a Baron and wealthy, from the Bolshevist Bela Kun; the second time, as a liberal, when the Horthy clique came to power.

His exile in Paris, Berlin and Vienna, must have been relatively comfortable. Yet he could not endure it. Torn by nostalgia—an incurable romanticist, for all his Voltairean skepticism—he returned to Hungary, trusting to the governmental pardon granted to him after a number of years. Almost needless to say, he was promptly arrested. Thanks to the protests of his many influential friends abroad, the devastating sentence passed against him was revised after a year or so.

"Never go home!" he warned me. "Believe a veteran émigré! The Fascists do not forgive—no matter what they may tell you." And, after a little pause, with a bland smile full of self-irony and affection: "Yet even in jail it was better than out there where people don't speak Hungarian . . ."

That was about one year before he had to leave Hungary for his third exile, which has not yet come to an end.

In 1937 his large, stately house still was a meeting place of the political and literary vanguard in Budapest. I owe to the Hatvanys a great many stimulating contacts, some of which resulted in valuable and lasting friendships.

The best meeting of that European spring was the one with a young American, Thomas Quinn Curtiss, introduced to me by the Baron. He had studied the cinematographic and theatrical developments in Vienna and—more extensively—in Moscow, where he worked as a pupil of Sergey Eisenstein. His dream was to produce a film in Budapest, a

Hungarian Rhapsody, something grim and daringly humorous, in the Erich von Stroheim line.

There was something in his ways and looks reminding me of René Crevel. Maybe it was just an accidental, physical resemblance— the curve of the eyebrows, high and restive, over wide and bewildered eyes. But I think it is more than that. I recognized in my new friend the aimless fury and the desperate jocularity I had known in René's spoken or written outbursts. If Curtiss had had a chance to make his fantastic film it might have turned out as rampantly sad and playful as were René's romantic diatribes.

We traveled together for the rest of the spring and summer. I showed Curtiss the places to which I had always returned throughout those last restless years—Annemarie's peasant house in Sils Baselgia, our Küsnacht home, Amsterdam, Paris, and the lovable spots near Toulon—Bandol, Sanary-sur-mer. I was happy. I could work again.

It was only a slim tale, though, which I produced, somewhere between the Netherlands and the Côte d'Azur. My hero, this time, was a royal martyr and madman, King Ludwig II of Bavaria, whose sombre glamor had seized my imagination when I was still a child. I remembered what the nurses and cooks had told us about his tragedy, rather than what I had subsequently read in historic reports and treatises. His prodigious castles—monumental whims scattered all over Bavaria—belonged to the mythic landscape of my childhood.

The opinion prevailed in Bavaria that the King was not insane at all, but became the victim of a sordid conspiracy initiated by his successor, the Prince-Regent Luitpold. Moreover, there were obstinate rumors to the effect that Ludwig had not been really drowned in the waves of the Lake of Starnberg, but was still alive, hiding somewhere in the solitude, a sort of neurotic Lohengrin endowed with eternal youth.

Be this as it may, he remained alive in my heart. The iridescent twilight in which his drama is bathed never ceased to captivate my fancy. In fact, it meant quite a relief to delve into the poetic ambiguities of King Ludwig's legend—that wondrous piece of genuine folklore with its stimulatingly psychopathic touch.

Literary vagaries such as that, however, are pardonable only as a vacation pastime. As soon as I returned to the United States, in September, I had to forget all about the inspired melancholia of drowned or immortal kings. Hitler was neither drowned nor immortal. He had to be done away with or he would drown the world, in his turn, with cataracts of blood and with the filthy flood of his lies. It was not my job, under the circumstances, to indulge in reveries about morbid fairy-tale princes, but rather to do my bit in fighting a very prosaic tyrant.

So I did my bit—haranguing the Elks in Buffalo, the liberal intelligentsia in Boston, the Rotarians in Des Moines, the Friends in Philadelphia; I spoke at the Book Fair in Detroit, to the students at Cornell University, to Jews in Chicago, to the ladies in Richmond and Kalamazoo, the highbrows of San Francisco, the teachers in San Diego; I don't know to whom I lectured in Los Angeles; but I know only too well in the case of Hollywood, California.

It was a long tour William B. Feakins's office had arranged for me, for the season 1937–38, and I rather enjoyed it. To make a lecture tour through the United States means to come in touch with multitudes of different milieus, and to meet many people. It implies not only a good deal of talking on your part, but it provides you also with the opportunity to listen, to look around. I listened and looked. I had a tough but stimulating time. I was pleased that Feakins offered me a contract for the coming year.

Another assignment I took along when embarking again for Europe was a book to be written for Houghton Mifflin. The Boston publishers wanted Erika and me to compile the characters and the experiences of our fellow refugees in a comprehensive and yet dramatic account. The volume thus produced was supposed to become a kind of analytical and anecdotal "Who's Who" reviewing the personnel and the accomplishments of the German anti-Hitler emigration. The somewhat euphemistic title agreed upon was "Escape to Life."

Before we had even started to compose our melancholy pantheon of exile, the field we had to cover was considerably enlarged. A new wave of refugees came from Vienna.

The end of Austria, although long predicted and anticipated, still came as a stunning shock. Our reaction to such "inevitable" and disastrous events is very much like what we feel when a beloved person, whom we know to be stricken with an incurable disease, finally comes to die. Not only does the loss—long expected or not—remain bitter and hard to bear: the verification of our misgivings is incredible in itself. The fact that we feared and foretold a certain pernicious occurrence renders us all the more sensible of the blow when it actually falls. For our prophecies were not only designed to caution the unexpecting world against an imminent danger: the main purpose of our calling the calamity "inevitable" may have been to prevent it from taking place. At the bottom of our hearts we never believe ourselves to be right when forecasting unpleasant developments. Secretly we take it for granted that Providence will give us the lie. What dismay and disappointment when the upsetting thing occurs in spite of our having predicted it!

It is one thing to know that Austria is doomed: another, to read, in the ship's-paper of the "Ile de France," that Dr. Schuschnigg has just arrived in Berchtesgaden to receive his orders from Hitler. This was evidently the end; yet we would not be spared more weeks of tormenting suspense. Will the Austrian Chancellor resist, after all? What will be the outcome of the plebiscite—that desperate last-minute maneuver of the Austrian Government? Can Schuschnigg depend on labor? Are the Social Democrats likely to forget the massacre of 1934? How strongly Nazified is Austria outside of Vienna?

While we still indulged in conjectures and calculations, Hitler's armies already moved towards the Austrian frontier. And there it was—the inevitable, incredible event.

This is the night from March 10, to March 11, and this is the Boulevard St. Germain in Paris. Our table at the Café de Flore is piled with newspapers. I am with a crowd of English friends—Brian Howard, Nancy Cunard, Sybil Bedford, James Stern, and three or four others. Brian is all flurry and agitation. He loathes Hitler much more than do most Englishmen—I mean, than most Englishmen used to do at that early point. For Brian had lived in Munich and Salzburg and Vienna: he knows what it is all about.

"Now, really!" he snapped at Nancy Cunard. "It makes me rather nervous, my dear, to watch you eat this horrible welsh rabbit, while our friends in Vienna . . ." And, as if suddenly struck by a weird and irrefutable intuition: "This means war, my dear!"

My friend Brian was wrong. It was not yet the hour. Our hopes and shudders were premature. The fall of Austria meant bloodshed, but it did not mean war. It meant suicides, firing squads, more concentration camps, more fugitives, a hundredfold increase of anguish and distress. But peace was saved, once again.

Of course it may seem questionable whether life on the edge of a volcano can be aptly called "peaceful." I have had a great many friends who chose to plunge themselves straight into the fiery depth of the crater, rather than to endure any longer the anguish of waiting for the next explosion. Naturally, the individual reactions to the approaching disaster differ greatly from each other. There are those who remain motionless, in a stupor of dread. Others become fidgety and keep hopping about, impelled by a somewhat hysterical sprightliness. Others, again, take to weeping and praying. A foolhardy minority wants to fight the volcano. They clamor for action, and are generally considered quite mad.

My personal behavior in such a critical situation may be defined as a compromise between resistance and escapism. That is to say, I abandon myself to work as if it were a solution or a narcotic. The very act of writing has a soothing effect on my nervous system. Besides it gives me the feeling, mistakenly, perhaps, that after all I am doing whatever I can to meet and master the emergency.

But it is difficult to concentrate on the written word, with the volcano smoldering and grumbling. Even the type of literary endeavor directly related to current events seems remote and irrelevant in view of rough, imperative realities which require action, not analysis.

In the spring and summer of 1938 I worked on two books about exiles—the documentary survey, "Escape to Life," and a novel, "The Volcano," in which I tried to tackle similar issues and characters from a more detached and more imaginative angle. Neither effort, however, was adequate to resuscitate one of Hitler's victims; nor could my prose save anybody from the claws of the Gestapo or melt the callous heart of democratic consuls. A consul is a much more important man than a novelist. For the novelist can only immortalize the suffering of his fellowmen, while the consul is in a position to shorten it by means of a stamp in a passport. In fact, many a famous Austrian novelist would have kissed the boots of the Swiss Consul General in Vienna for the sake of a visa. As soon as they were in Zurich, the fugitives began to beleaguer the American Consulate. Those happy few who obtained the permit to enter the United States had first to woo the French Consul to grant them a transit visa. All this took painfully long and, more often than not, involved a good deal of superfluous humiliation.

The fiery mountain has many devastating qualities. Not only does it smolder and thunder; it also contaminates the air with its evil reeks. The volcano stinks.

The real thing, the explosion—so I thought at times—might be preferable to the calamitous dragging expectancy. That is why I went to Spain. Some newspapers had asked me to go there as correspondent and I accepted. Or rather, we accepted; for Erika had been approached with similar requests. We both wanted to see the apocalyptic actuality of a volcanic outburst. Moreover, we realized that what was happening in Spain was but a bloody prologue, a sort of mortally serious rehearsal of what might be in store for the world at large. The Civil War in Spain not only foreshadowed but actually prefigured and anticipated the universal conflicts to come. It was on Spanish soil that the moral fronts were set, the issues at stake disclosed. Significantly, one of the crucial notions of the present struggle, the concept of the Fifth Column, was coined in Madrid, then the heart and the citadel of anti-Fascist resistance.

It was a great experience to witness the resilient fortitude displayed by the people of Barcelona; to watch the fight at the Ebro front; to see Valencia—full of attractive life, even under the shower of German-made high explosives. But one must have been in the besieged city of Madrid to grasp the elating grandeur of the Spanish example. The epic endurance of Madrid's men and women will forever be not only an inspiring model but also an imperative obligation. The Fascist mercenaries who were repelled from the Ciudad Universitaria must not be allowed to conquer elsewhere.

The University City where the onslaught was stopped is situated at the periphery of Madrid proper. The foe was actually within the capital. Madrid seemed torn into two camps, one already occupied by General Franco's troops, the other doggedly defended by the inhabitants and their friends from the International Brigades. The defenders proved stronger than the Italians, Germans, and Moors, marshaled by the treacherous general. Yet the Loyalists never succeeded in driving the enemy further back than from the very heart of Madrid. Throughout the siege, which lasted for more than two years, the army of the rebels remained within sight, just in front of the martyred city. The artillery bombardment never ceased completely. We heard the hollow detonations, even while sauntering through the streets of the fortress-capital.

The general mood in the Madrid of that heroic epoch was one of grim, composed determination. The city appeared at once numbed and transfigured in its bleak, stringent glory. Life was monotonous and austere. There was no laughter, no wailing. The awareness of continuous danger marked and hardened all faces. The tragic and indomitable city seemed to echo the battle-cry of the Republican cause: NO PASARAN!

We found the same spirit everywhere, throughout the zone held by the Loyalists. The Fifth Column—dangerously active as it may have been—remained entirely invisible. Stealthily, against the interests of the people, the reactionary saboteurs did their corrosive work. We came in touch with a great many types of men, during our stays in Barcelona, Valencia, Madrid, and at the Ebro Front, near the ruined place that formerly was Tortosa. I don't think that anybody watched us. The censorship was strict, but only as regards the information we mailed or wired abroad. Besides we were free to do whatever we pleased. And wherever we went we met with that calm and adamant resolution: NO PASARAN!

From Juan Negrin and Alvarez del Vayo down to the last soldier, everybody was unshakably convinced, not only of the righteousness of the Loyalist fight, but also of its victorious outcome. The rank and file as well as the Republican leaders were gratefully responsive to moral support and encouragement, but they did not need any comfort. Del Vayo's broad and hearty smile was not that of a man who lives under the shadow of imminent disaster. His face—placid, almost serene—reflected the courageous confidence with which he tackled his grave and precarious task. Without agitation or weariness he faced and discussed the future. Like Benes of Czechoslovakia, Alvarez del Vayo believed that a good cause and sound intelligence have more of a fighting chance than an evil cause and morbid stupidity, even if the evil and stupid side happens to be more formidably equipped, for the time being.

The boys of the International Brigades felt the same way—all those anonymous young workers and intellectuals who flocked to the ranks of Democracy, from Paris and Birmingham, Prague, Leningrad, or Chicago. There may have been professional ruffians among them, fanatics, good-for-nothings, flotsam. But the general atmosphere of faith and seriousness touched and transformed even those who originally joined the Brigades as a reckless adventurer would join the Foreign Legion.

We made friends with soldiers, officers, political instructors. We interviewed working women, poets, homeless children, nurses, governmental officials, mothers whose sons had been killed, fugitives from Guernica (Catholic priests among them), truck drivers, invalids, pilots. We listened to the experiences of such unbiased and trained observers as Matthews of the "New York Times." We saw ghastly, tragic things— hunger, wretchedness, and exhaustion. Life is not cheerful when civilization collapses. I depend on civilization; I abominate war. I didn't have a good time in Spain, naturally. The air raids did not scare me. (I am not afraid of death.) But the sight of ruined houses is frightening: there is something so indescribably doleful and embarrassing about the way their gaping wounds reveal the maimed intimacy of their former lives. I hate to look at undernourished children. It depressed me to see grown men argue over the end of a cigarette that I happened to drop, forgetting that it represented a rare and valuable item. Such things are grisly to witness. They indicate or foreshadow the disintegration of our civilized world. They announce the jungle. (I am afraid of the jungle. We live much closer to it than we realize.)

But we did not see one ugly thing in the beleaguered cities of the Spanish Republic. I mean "ugly" in a moral sense, not aesthetically. Meanness and ugliness may have been there; but we failed to see them.

Yes, we did see them—once. That was when we interviewed two Nazi prisoners. They were pilots; their machines had been shot down by the Loyalist anti-aircraft.

The fellows came from Saxony—a region of Germany where people speak the most unattractive German dialect and are supposed to be very sly. Frankly, we felt a bit apprehensive when we entered their cell. For we expected them to be violent and defiant. What if they spat at us and called us terrible names? "Rats! Traitors!" they might shout. "To gloat on the misfortunes of your compatriots! What a dirty, dastardly thing to do!"

But the two did nothing of the kind. They grinned and fawned. They were slimy and diplomatic. How glibly they lied in their unattractive dialect! How shamelessly they betrayed their Führer! How they vied with each other in assuring us of their peaceful principles!

"If we had only known that there are women and children in Spain!" the man from Leipzig exclaimed. "We surely wouldn't have dropped those bombs. But our officer told us that there are only Bolshevist hordes in Madrid and in Barcelona."

And the fellow from Dresden added: "They also told us that the Loyalists have no anti-aircraft to speak of. And we dopes believed them! Well, there we are, in a fine fix. Aren't we, Fritz?"

They exchanged quick glances. Both smiled. Their smiles were wry and hypocritical—the most dishonest smiles I have ever seen.

This interview with the two Saxon pilots was the one ugly experience I had in Republican Spain.

When we visited Madrid and Barcelona—in July, 1938—the doom of the Loyalist cause was already decided upon, not only in Berlin and Rome but also in London and Paris. The only ally the legitimate Spanish Government could depend on—namely the Soviet Union—was hardly in a strategic position to furnish adequate help. The Russian support, not effective enough to save the Spanish Republic, was instrumental in discrediting the Negrin Administration. It was thanks to

Stalin's insufficient assistance that the liberal men of Barcelona were denounced as rabid Bolshevists.

The Kremlin was not popular at that point outside the Soviet Union and the political realm of the Comintern. The trials staged by the Stalin régime had sapped Moscow's prestige abroad. The People's Front showed disquieting flaws; in fact, it was on the point of cracking.

This dismal development could not but affect the tactics and attitudes, not only of the professional politicians, but also the anti-Fascist intelligentsia. In German refugee circles the controversies were especially bitter and venomous. Immoderate and tactless in all political matters, the fugitives from the Reich smeared each other with gross and fatuous accusations. The leading German weekly in Paris, "Das Neue Tage-Buch," transformed itself from an anti-Hitler organ into a Red-baiting scandal sheet specializing in denouncements to the effect that Stalin was at least as bad as Hitler, even a little worse. Whoever hesitated to convey such a declaration was slandered as a venal agent of the Third International.

The Communists, in their turn no less mendacious and unscrupulous, suspected German influence and German bribery wherever any criticism of Stalin's supreme wisdom dared to raise its ugly head. It was the time when the anti-Trotsky obsession took on truly clinical forms with all loyal agents of the Comintern. Their policy was based on the double axiom that Trotsky was the Devil, and that everybody who was not a hundred percent for Stalin must be somehow tied up with Trotsky. Consequently, all deviations from the Party line were inevitably and essentially devilish.

My own position in this sad and violent feud was ambivalent and delicate. Like most of the liberal intellectuals, I had hoped for and believed in the feasibility of a United Front against Fascism. At the same time I was fully aware of the deficiencies and perversions inherent in the Soviet State and, more particularly, in the tactics of the Comintern. These mistakes and transgressions were glaringly recognizable to any detached, clear-sighted observer. But no upright, intelligent person could acquiesce in the libelous maneuvers of the Red-baiting mob. If the practices of Russian courts were shrouded in ominous darkness, the methods and the objectives of the anti-Russian crusade were only too obvious.

Yet the only time that I meddled with one of those depressing controversies I came out against the Communists, or rather, in favor of André Gide—not that I thought his sensational anti-Soviet pamphlet, "Retour de L'U.R.S.S.," a masterpiece from any point of view. In my opinion, Gide's account of his Russian experience is entirely lacking in both the clearness and profundity characteristic of his style and vision. His communistic adventure was ill-starred from the very beginning. He mistook his newly developed social consciousness for a categorical imperative to mingle with party politics. This basic misconception could not but result in disappointment and embarrassment for both parties involved.

For, of course, the Communists must have been angered and bewildered, on their part, about Gide's cool reaction to the Fatherland of all Proletarians. When he went to Moscow in 1936, clumsy and obstreperous flatteries were lavishly showered on him. But the visitor—vexed rather than pleased by such a turbulent welcome—failed to respond in the expected and appropriate fashion. He remained vigilant and detached.

The Bolshevists thought him ungrateful as he repaid their bountiful hospitality with loveless criticism. Of course he was as candid as ever when he stated, in the Preface to his famous pamphlet, that the lie, "if only the lie of concealment," may seem opportune under circumstances, but in reality always plays the enemy's game. Politically untrained, he forgot that in the dubious sphere of partisan polemics every acknowledgement of weakness or corruption in our own camp is likely to be exploited by a reckless and cunning foe.

It was painful to see Gide's frank but one-sided statements quoted and extolled in the Fascist and semi-Fascist press. All anti-Soviet papers from the august "Temps" down to the cheap "Matin" and the abject "Gringoire" devoted enthusiastic editorials to Gide's newest "conversion." In fact, some particularly juicy spots out of "Retour de L'U.R.S.S." found their way into the slimy mire of Nazi journalism.

But even more shameful and disconcerting was the campaign against

Gide subsequently launched by the Comintern. The very man whom the Marxist critics had praised only yesterday as a paragon of revolutionary virtue was now denounced as a decadent fool, an insidious trickster, deceitful agent of the capitalistic system, in short, as a Trotskyite. Once again, the Party zealots revealed their complete lack of respect and objectivity towards spiritual values and accomplishments.

My extensive apology and panegyric for André Gide was featured in a semi-Communistic magazine. I deemed it appropriate to reaffirm my unshaken faith in his integrity and his genius, in spite of a tactical mistake he may have made on unknown, slippery ground. It was a matter of chivalry and natural gratitude to pay homage to one of the most admirable men of our epoch, at a point when his name was being abused by the Marxian fanatics and misused by the Fascist criminals.

"I didn't anticipate such a tiresome hullabaloo," Gide told me when the controversy was at its peak. "What's the whole fuss about, after all? I just described, as precisely as possible, what I've seen in Russia. It seems that we have either to lie, or else to have the scandal provoked by the truth."

"Le Scandale de la Vérité" was the title another great and incorruptible Frenchman—the conservative writer Georges Bernanos—gave to a political manifesto: a farewell message to his weary, misguided people. He had been among the valiant French Catholics who came out against General Franco in favor of the Loyalists, when the Vatican vied with the Bank of England in supporting and encouraging the rebels. This time Bernanos spoke on behalf of his own country, indicting the politicians who sold out the honor and future of France like a supply of over-aged champagne.

For the hour of disgrace approached, the "Dies Ater" of Munich when France betrayed her ally and therewith betrayed herself.

The weeks preceding the dismal and fatal event were charged with gloom and misgivings. In my personal life, this period from the middle of August until the middle of September 1938 has a particularly sad significance. The last time I saw Europe. . . .

The dissolution of our ménage in Küsnacht could not but increase this feeling of gravity and irretrievable loss. My parents had come back from the United States to supervise the removal of our household. Most of our belongings had fallen prey to the Nazis. Whatever had remained—and what had been acquired since—was to be shipped overseas to form the nucleus of a new home in Princeton, New Jersey, U. S. A.

The last piece of furniture we would release for the packers was the radio apparatus. Formerly the transmitter of profuse harmonies—connecting us with the Salzburg Festivals, the Paris Opera, the Scala of Milan—the machine now became a doleful oracle gushing sinister news. While the candelabra from Lübeck—saved by I don't know what kind of propitious chance—followed Father's desk and library into grim-looking boxes, the family would gather in the empty hall to listen to the weird and muddled reports on Lord Runciman's mission in Prague, Hitler's rampant demands, the "grave views" taken by Mr. Chamberlain and M. Daladier. We heard the undisguised apprehension in President Benes's manly, familiar voice. We grasped the utter gravity of the situation. No doubt, the crisis over Czechoslovakia was more dangerous than any of the previous tensions had been. Would Hitler get away, once more, with what the "usually well-informed" Parisian Cassandra, Geneviève Tabouis, was wont to call his "chantage à la guerre"? Blackmailing by means of apocalyptic threats—that was the simple formula, the very essence of his policy. Could he forever succeed in terrorizing the world by exploiting the natural pacifism of the civilized peoples?

In Paris, where I spent the pivotal week from September 10 until September 17, war was generally expected. There was no enthusiasm in view of the imminent conflict; but there was no panic, either. The disaster seemed inevitable, considering Hitler's brassy determination to violate and rob Czechoslovakia no matter what the consequences might be. With Paris bound to Prague by solemn vows and treaties, Hitler's attack would automatically constitute a "casus belli" to the French Republic.

Mr. Chamberlain's flight to Berchtesgaden was a well-staged, effective coup. But I did not have the impression that this spectacular gesture was hailed by the French as a wise and heroic deed. Besides, the Prime Minister's "peace mission" was apparently destined to fail. The

British visitor left Bavaria as abruptly as he had arrived. Evidently, no accord had been reached.

It was on board the "Ile de France" that I was struck by the first news of Austria's agony; it was from the liner "Champlain" that I followed the second act of the Czech drama. I must have been about midway between Southampton and New York when Chamberlain flew to Godesberg and returned empty-handed, once more. When I landed, on September 25, all odds were definitely on the side of war. There were rumors about skirmishes at the German-Czech frontier. Benes seemed inclined to accept Soviet Russian support. Hitler ranted and raved. London and Paris were nervous.

The first afternoon in New York I attended a monster meeting on behalf of Czechoslovakia. Dorothy Thompson and my father were among the speakers. I shall never forget the thundering cheers responding my father's promise and demand: "Hitler must fall!" Madison Square Garden resounded with the roaring approval of ten thousand men and women. But Mr. Chamberlain disapproved.

The conspiracy of Munich was the most devastating blow to the cause of peace and democracy. It implied either the complete, definitive surrender to the Nazi juggernaut, or else the postponement of the conflict to a date when the auspices, morally as well as strategically, would be much less propitious. The cynical betrayal of Czechoslovakia, the last outpost of democracy in Central and Eastern Europe, could not but weaken and hurt our side, irreparably perhaps. Chamberlain's "Peace with Honor" was a dishonorable defeat.

At the time we believed that the policy of the British Tories and the Bonnet clique in France was prompted by positive pro-Nazi feelings. Most European liberals doubted the semi-official version, explaining the surrender of the democracies as a result of sheer weakness and pacifism. Today I realize that the situation was more complex—a dreary muddle, rather than a diabolic plot. But, then, in cases such as that various tendencies and motives overlap. Of course, the immediate reason for Chamberlain's and Daladier's compliance, in 1938, was their technical inability to resist. This inability, in its turn, however, was partly derived from their latent or open desire to collaborate with Nazi Germany against Soviet Russia. If the disaster of Munich was inevitable, under the circumstances, the policy which resulted in those cir-cumstances was not dictated by inescapable necessities. It was dictated by human cowardice, short-sightedness and ignorance.

The winter 1938–39 appears strangely vapid and meaningless in my memory. The political depression made everything pall on us. The disgrace of Munich was followed by the collapse of the Spanish Re-public, another triumph of evil caused by democratic inefficiency and stupid selfishness. It was the complete blackout of our hopes. All our doings and interests tarnished under the blight of bitterness and dis-illusionment.

Not that we were constantly grieved and abandoned ourselves to idle brooding. As long as life keeps going, it never is dominated ex-clusively by one sorrow or fixed idea. However black our mood, there always are bright occasions—pleasant diversions, sudden flashes of joy.

Our new home in Princeton hardly looked like a mourning house. It was a stately and spacious affair—quaint and dignified; just what a house in Princeton should be like. The evenings were pleasant and long, in a living room of unduly grand dimensions. We would sit around the fireside and listen to Raymond Gram Swing and to Wagner records, or else the Magician would treat us to a bit of cerebral sorcery: that is to say, he would read to us a new portion out of his Goethe story, with the concluding chapters of which he was occupied at the time. I recall the Christmas Eve of 1938 when we listened to the curious evocation of Goethe's matin reveries—an uncanny tour de force of psychological prose, tracing and illuminating the stream of conscious-ness as it floated and wove, a hundred and thirty years ago, in Ger-many's most powerful mind. The present faded away, blotted out by virtue of serene, kindly witchcraft. There was no Princeton University, no New York City, no treacherous peace, no imminent war, no Vol-cano. There was nothing but the monologue of an astonishing old gentleman waking up in Weimar, contemplating, planning and dream-ing in the sober and solemn light of a new working day.

The Magician, a conscientious craftsman in his enthralling domain, remained unflaggingly diligent. So did Mielein in her own less spec-tacular fashion. Genial and energetic, without fuss and bustle, she continued to perform those minor miracles which are the secret and the privilege of mellow and unselfish womanhood. No poet has adequately praised as yet the beauty and helpfulness of an ideal wife; nor has any creative man ever paid the valid and commensurate kind of homage to his mother.

Our indebtedness becomes unspeakable when it is too ample and too profound. How could we formulate our gratitude to the very being without whom we would not even be in a position to formulate anything? She who has not only given me life as such, but has also preserved and ennobled it by virtue of her love—what kind of exaltation would she expect or accept? The only thanks she cares for is that the life for whose sake she suffered remain unpolluted, and that it be lived out according to its immanent destination.

The life of a family is like the life of a tree—complex and manifold, with different developments on every branch and twig; yet connate and consolidated. So involved and delicate an organism would tarnish or disintegrate if it were not organized and animated from a dynamic center. In the case of our family this discreet but powerful focus is the woman to whom I refer in these pages with an affectionate nickname. It is thanks to Mielein's fortitude and ingenuity that this particular tribe could carry on as a unity and do its bit in behalf of the general cause. Not only does she concern herself with the affairs and worries of those members of the clan who happen to be around, she also looks to the troubles of absent relatives and friends. Her desk seems always submerged with SOS messages from five continents. All sorts of requests poured in, throughout the season 1938-39, as before and afterwards: two cousins in London need affidavits; Uncle Peter cables from Brussels, while Uncle Klaus, the musician (Mielein's twin), has complicated wishes, somewhere in Indo-China. What could be done on behalf of old Dr. X in Jerusalem? Y's case in Shanghai seems comparatively simple: he just wants a little money.

Naturally, Offi and Ofey caused considerable anxiety—wayward and cranky as they more and more became. Now, all at once, they made up their minds to leave Germany. If they had made their decision three or four years before, when we urged them to do so, they could have spent the rest of their lives in easy circumstances. As things stood now, it was next to nothing that they could take along when moving to Switzerland. It was preferable, however, to be poor in Zurich than to occupy a palace around the corner from Hitler's.

Happily, we six children were doing more or less all right, for the time being. Golo was active in Zurich as the editor of a literary bimonthly. Monika, now Mrs. Lanyi, wrote joyful letters from London, where her young husband hoped to obtain an appointment as a teacher of art history.

As for Elizabeth and Michael—"the little ones," "the kids"—they came of age by stealth and behind our backs, as it were. It was quite a sensation when Elizabeth disclosed that she was engaged to be married. Everybody was startled, moved, overjoyed. "To be married?" we exclaimed, foolishly. "The child? The cute one? The dainty creature?" But the man of her choice, G. A. Borgese, the Italian-American scholar, poet and novelist insisted that she was not only more lovely but also more mature and more efficient than any girl between eighteen and eighty he had ever seen, and that he was positive she would prove an excellent wife and mother. Curiously enough, he turned out to be right.

Let the volcano grumble! Life continues and proceeds with unabated vigor. That was the way my young brother Michael felt, and his Swiss girl friend too. If the classic pair of lovers, Hero and Leander, did not permit the Hellespont to disrupt their romance. Fräulein Gret from Zurich, Switzerland, defied the whole Atlantic and rushed over to join Michael. There she was: in no time they got married. It didn't take quite a year until the stammer and whimper of the most handsome baby boy accompanied the song of Michael's violin.

Weddings were celebrated. Children were born. The volcano smoldered. The air remained imbued with ominous signs and sounds. A subterranean tremor forecast of the coming explosion.

The proximity of disaster was tangible everywhere. I sensed it when I traveled about—with Erika or alone—to address groups in Ohio or California, in Oregon or New York, Canada or Kansas. Erika had made a considerable career as a lecturer in this country. Audiences were particularly interested in what she had to say regarding the educational system of Nazi Germany. Her book, "School for Barbarians," had established her reputation as an expert in this dismal but crucial matter.

Most of our topics were of a saddening nature. We talked about Madrid and Munich, about treachery and wretchedness and unending persecution. When our book, "Escape to Life," was released (in the spring of 1939) we were frequently asked to discuss the plight and the works of the refugees from Germany and German-occupied zones. In March, a new group was added to the army of fugitives. Hitler invaded Prague.

But this event, the second violation of Czechoslovakia within one year, had other repercussions of a more pivotal kind. Suddenly, over-night, so to speak—it became evident that public opinion in Britain awakened to the enormity of the Nazi challenge. The invasion of Prague marked the end of appeasement, the fiasco of Chamberlain's scheme.

It took painfully long, however, for this decisive change to result in palpable consequences. No international front against Hitler seemed attainable, for the time being. While the United States abided by her absolute neutrality, the negotiations between London, Paris and Mos-cow kept ominously dragging. What was it that slowed down and baffled those vital conversations? Why did the democracies hesitate to concede to the Soviet Union a strategic position in the Baltic countries? Was it true—was it conceivable—that the Kremlin had a secret flirta-tion with the Brown House? There were dire rumors to that effect. They increased alarmingly in view of Litvinov's sudden resignation. He was the initiator and most effective promoter of Moscow's collec-tive security policy. His withdrawal could not but indicate evil things in the making.

Was there anybody who really knew what was going to happen? Could any mortal man instruct and reassure us?

I felt like asking the President of the United States when I was pre-sented to him, on May 11, 1939. The reception at the White House formed the solemn climax of an international writers' congress ar-ranged by the PEN Club on occasion of the New York World's Fair.

Mrs. Roosevelt is one of the rare hostesses who manage to give a touch of intimacy even to a mass meeting. A heartening appeal emanates from her smile and look. She seems particularly interested in the affairs and opinions of every individual with whom she just happens to chat. Only a woman of so aristocratic a background and with so democratic a heart can afford the exquisite simplicity typical of all her words and ways.

The First Lady excused the President, who was too busy to join our luncheon party. He wanted to welcome his guests, however. The little army of poets, essayists and novelists, moving slowly in line, passed by his armchair which he had turned away from the desk. Each writer was introduced to the President, who shook hands with every visitor. His smile was genial, if somewhat oblivious. But the look that accompanied it was forceful and penetrating. There is something arresting about the way his eyes are shaped and colored. Their radiant blue is all the more impressive through the contrast with the shadowy tints surrounding them. But while the darkness of his eye-sockets is a familiar feature of Mr. Roosevelt's face, the limpid energy of the eyes cannot be reproduced photographically. The effect is unexpectedly striking. "Isn't that amazing?" I thought, while receiving his hand-shake. "I hadn't the slightest inkling that his eyes are so powerful and so bright."

Yes. I definitely felt like asking him a few questions concerning the things to come. Why not use the opportunity? I could hardly find another man with equal insight and influence.

But it would have been unsuitable to bother the President. So I just made a bow and withdrew, while the next man approached our obliviously smiling, bright-eyed, initiated host.

The next man was perhaps a representative of Chinese literature, or a delegate from Paraguay. Or maybe it was Ernst Toller's turn. In fact, most probably Toller stood just behind me. We stuck together throughout the whole festive, fatiguing day.

It was the last time I saw him. He killed himself, eleven days afterwards. I might have caught one more glimpse of his face, though. For he lay behind me in an open bier, when I delivered a brief obituary address. But I avoided looking at him. He had hanged himself. I dreaded to find his face and neck disfigured by the marks of the strangulation. Besides I would hardly have seen much, anyway. My eyes were blinded by tears.

In June our parents and Erika embarked for Europe. As for myself, I hazarded a trip across the United States in a fantastic vehicle that scarcely deserved the proud name of an automobile. Nor do I deserve to be called a driver. The friend with whom I traveled was not a very accomplished motorist, either. We had a good deal of fun and trouble. It was the first time I crossed the continent by car. The experience was as compelling and as unforgettable as that of my first trip from coast to coast by train, twelve years before. To travel slowly, in a shaky, worn-out car, is the best way to grasp this country's vastness and grandeur. The flitting views caught from the platform of a Pullman train are but inadequate fragments of a reality which is infinitely more powerful and astounding.

The generous dimensions of the American landscape produce a soothing effect on the minds of those who have been harassed too long by the petty maze of European thought and European geography. The very bigness of American rivers, mountains, highways, forests and lakes becomes meaningful and reassuring. For in view of this bountiful land we recognize, once again, what immeasurable resources of space and energy still are at the disposal, not only of this country, but also of man at large.

Riding across the plains, over the dizzy passes, through the deserts, parks, and forests; moving along the open roads, the long brown paths of America, I forgot, for the first time in years, the European volcano. How could the whims and spasms of a distant monster endanger or affect this massive magnanimous country? In Utah and Nevada the concept of Isolationism becomes plausible. In California, however, it loses its relevance. In front of the Pacific one senses, once again, the inescapable grip of world-wide problems and perils.

My little house in Santa Monica resounded with the dramatic accents of Mr. Kaltenborn's voice. His tense gravity always suggested the worst. I had a good laugh when I read Saroyan's crack about Kaltenborn, whose "excitement" he calls "so official that my young nephews were under the impression that he was the cause of the war."

My amusement was a bit uncomfortable, however. Ignorant, like Mr. Saroyan's nephews, I hankered for information. Was there to be a war? Would the Danzig affair turn out to be the pivot? And if so, what would be Russia's stand?

Dazed by the bombshell of the Nazi-Soviet Pact, I tried doggedly to concentrate on a book whose publication was scheduled for the fall. My co-author—Erika—labored somewhere in Switzerland or in Sweden, while I struggled in California with our intriguing topic, "The Other Germany." It was a ticklish, not to say painful job to analyze, at that crucial point, the famous Two Souls which, alas, dwell together in the breast, not only of Goethe's Faust, but also of Goethe's nation. But is there any double soul inherent in that prodigious phenomenon called the Third Reich? Definitely not. It is the gross and glaring manifestation of Germany's evil side—absorbing or polluting the nobler features of a dangerously complex national character. Once again I delved into the abysmal labyrinth of German guilt and German inspiration. While Hitler's armies were already being brought in formation for the march into Poland, I searched the writings of German classics for an explanation of the German enigma. How deeply and bitterly they all suffered from Germany! What a sorrowful concern behind the neatness of Goethe's sedate but scathing criticism! Hölderlin's auguries echo the distress and protest of a noble and wounded heart. How can the Germans endure the vulgar trickery of their present leaders, since it was unmasked in advance by Heinrich Heine's illuminated flippancies and by the hallucinatory diatribes of Friedrich Nietzsche? It was he, the most formidable intellectual energy Germany ever produced, who hurled this terrific arraignment against his compatriots:

"I feel a desire, indeed, a duty, to tell the Germans for once how much they already have on their conscience. They have all the great cultural crimes of four centuries on their conscience—and all for the same reason, because of their innermost cowardice in face of reality, which is at the same time cowardice in face of truth; because of their untruthfulness which has become distinctive; because of their 'idealism'!"

Nietzsche's wrathful indictments were punctuated by the dire messages broadcast from London, Warsaw, Paris, Berlin, and Washington to my idyllic dwelling on the Pacific coast. The suspense increased. The breaking point was near.

This was the predestined hour of the ordeal. There it was, the out-burst of the volcano—brought about, rendered inevitable, not only by the utter wickedness of a felonious clique; not exclusively through our inertia and smugness, our lack of energy, pride, and vision. Thanks to our lethargy and to his own viciousness Hitler got what he was driving at—an apocalyptic turmoil. In consequence of his petty and fallacious policy, Mr. Chamberlain was now compelled to face and to admit what he had tried to dodge at any price. Hitler's revolting bark and Cham-berlain's dignified proclamation informed us that, on September 3, 1939, our world had been set afire.

I thought of the bloody sword, whose appearance on the glowing sky the Magician had forecast, in the mythic days of August, 1914. Were there any martial tokens perceptible, at this juncture, in the Sep-tember skies of a convulsed, feverish Europe?

The message I received from my parents and Erika, the morning after the declaration of war, was dated from Stockholm, and read:

"Safe and confident. Looking forward to witnessing together with you the twilight of the false gods. Love."

CHAPTER TWELVE

Decision

(1 9 4 0 – 1 9 4 2)

Time present and time past
Are both perhaps present in time future,
And time future contained in time past.
If all time is eternally present
All time is unredeemable.

T. S. ELIOT

Fragments of a Diary

JUNE *14, 1940, New York:* The Nazis in Paris. Our nightmares materialize.

June 18, 1940: The defeat of France, although a disastrous blow to the cause and future of democracy, might be reparable and, therefore, bearable. It is the humiliation of France, the treachery of her ruling clique, which is so obnoxious and discouraging. The military fiasco was to be expected: all of us knew the inadequacies of French morale and organization. But how could anybody foresee the abysmal cynicism and stupidity of those venal politicians and generals? Marshal Pétain is as hideous as was Marshal Hindenburg. In fact, the hero of Verdun may be even more dangerous than the hero of Tannenberg. Beware of heroes! Distrust those decorated Frankensteins! Don't let them delude you with their silver mustaches and gouty legs! They can be surprisingly nimble and alert, those venerable tricksters, when it comes to selling out their beloved country to Fascism.

The same day, later: The only comfort in black days like these is a vague and general faith in the future. Happily, things don't stand

327

still: they move, change, develop—perpetually, swiftly. Hitler's parade in the Champs-Elysées is by no means the last word of history.

June 19, 1940: If this country allows Hitler to win the war—that is to say, if the U.S. abides by her "neutrality" and witnesses the fall of Britain without making the utmost effort to save her: how, in such a case, would matters develop here, in America proper? Will it be possible to stay here if the Fascist currents increase as they undoubtedly would under those circumstances? But where could one go from here? What refuge would remain intact and accessible if the enemy conquers or corrupts this hemisphere? In what language shall we have to formulate our protests and hopes? In Chinese? I am told that's a tricky idiom to learn . . .

June 26, 1940: The strain and balm of work without which all this would be entirely unbearable.

Notes for an article on Thomas Masaryk. What a man—great and wise and gentle: lovable, even in his mistakes. Realistic enough to succeed as an organizer and ruler: pure and idealistic enough to make his authority acceptable even to the most dogged individualists. Exceedingly interested in his dispute with Tolstoi concerning "absolute" and "conditional" pacifism. The grand old man who once created the epic panorama of "War and Peace" insists that war is evil, indeed, unpardonable—no matter under what conditions or for what purpose it may have been waged. Masaryk asserts, on the other hand, that war—although hateable in itself—can be instrumental in promoting certain causes and objectives that could not be attained otherwise. (But, according to Tolstoi, even the noblest cause will be corrupted when accomplished by ignoble means.)

What vast profusion of vital topics! How many essential problems to think and write about! Now more than ever it is imperative to test and clarify the basic notions of our philosophy.

The same day, later: More and more taken up with the project of a new literary review. I have a hunch that it is precisely this I ought to venture on, at this crucial point: the foundation of a truly cosmopolitan magazine devoted to creative writing and the discussion of all great, timely issues. Something on a much larger scale and infinitely more exciting than "Die Sammlung" used to be. I cannot help feeling that an international forum of this particular type could have a significant function, here and now.

"Solidarity" may be an appropriate name for the kind of periodical I would like to see established—or rather, that I would like to establish.

June 28, 1940: Anxiety because of Golo, Uncle Heinrich, and others, somewhere in France. The complete lack of first-hand information fosters the circulation of appalling rumors. Franz Werfel is said to be dead; Lion Feuchtwanger and Heinrich Mann, caught by the Gestapo (together, allegedly: which would make the event even more gruesome, from many points of view . . .). All this may be fabricated— malignantly or naïvely. But, perhaps, there are other atrocities—even worse than those made up. What may have happened to Gide? To Cocteau? What is the attitude of the French Communists concerning a débâcle for which they, too, are responsible? It would be interesting to have a chat, just now, with people like Malraux or Aragon.

June 29, 1940: No, it is hardly worth while—indeed, it has become quite impossible, to talk politics with any loyal member of the Third International. Their essential fallacy is to confound the cause of progress with the political interests of a great power, namely the Soviet Union. This hazardous identification renders them disloyal to the cause of progress. The dubious axiom, "Right or wrong, my country," does not sound more convincing in its Marxist version, "Right or wrong, my party line." We anti-Fascist, non-partisan liberals could rely on the comrades as long as the party line happened to make sense, during the honeymoon of the People's Front. But matters have changed since.

The Stalin-Hitler Pact may have been inevitable, thanks to the policy of Mr. Chamberlain. But was it necessary to betray the anti-Fascist cause just because the Kremlin chose, or was forced into, a risky and cynical diplomatic game? It is not Stalin's action but the attitude of the Comintern which strikes me as revealing and revolting. Literally overnight they dropped the slogans of the People's Front epoch and presently adopted a brand-new set of principles and phrases. The same men who had hitherto sneered at our pacifist ideals suddenly discovered that war is an ugly thing and that Hitlerism should not be licked but appeased. Moreover, they suddenly discovered that British Imperialism is at least as rotten as is the Nazi régime; that there are reactionary elements in the New Deal, while Hitler's gospel contains revolutionary potentialities, and so forth. With amazing agility and shamelessness they performed their somersaults according to Moscow's orders. Or does Stalin not even bother to issue orders for his international stooges? I am inclined to believe that the Little Father is but faintly interested in the doings of the Comintern.

The same day, later: The only argument speaking in favor of the Reds, at this point, is the Red-baiters. If the party line is apt to corrupt and confuse the mind, the anti-party line is even more obnoxious. To follow Stalin, even when he errs and transgresses, is certainly not an attitude becoming an upright, intelligent man. But to slander him, even when he is right—to abuse him where he deserves to be praised— is equally stupid, and may be still more dangerous.

July 3, 1940; Washington, D.C.: Worn out and somewhat depressed, after a long, busy day in this torrid city. Came here to discuss the magazine project with various people whose moral support could be of decisive value for my enterprise. But did I really succeed in arousing their interest?

Interviewed Archibald MacLeish, at the Library of Congress; Michael Huxley, at the British Embassy; Major Hurban, Minister of Czechoslovakia; and a few others . . . Maybe it is the "official" atmosphere of the capital that renders even the poets so diplomatic and noncommittal.

July 5, 1940; on the train (between Kansas City and Los Angeles): Joined my parents and Erika at Chicago. Crossing the continent en famille.

Reading, among other things, "The Heart is a Lonely Hunter"—the melancholy novel by that strange girl, Carson McCullers, who came to see us the other day. Very arresting, in parts. An abysmal sadness, but remarkably devoid of sentimentality. Rather grim and concise. What astounding insight into the ultimate inconsolability and incurability of the human soul! Her style and vision remind me somehow of Julien Green's. Wonder if she may know him. . . . I hope she'll write that story about the Negro and the refugee, to which she referred as one of her next projects. Uncannily versed in the secrets of all freaks and pariahs, she should be able to compose a revealing tale of exile.

. . . Took several new German books along, with the intention of reading them during the trip. Something by Alfred Döblin, whose talent I greatly respect. But an odd inhibition prevents me from concentrating on anything written in the idiom of which I know every shade and potentiality. Can it be that Hitler has polluted the language of Nietzsche and Hölderlin?

July 12, 1940; Brentwood (Los Angeles): Now the news from "our people" in France pours in—only too much of it. Desperate cries for help: that is to say, for visas to the United States. They cable from everywhere—from Nice, Marseilles, Vichy, Perpignan, Casablanca. Others are already in comparative safety, in Portugal. Others, in the absolute security of death. New wave of suicides.

July 14, 1940: No doubt, something like a miracle has occurred in Britain since the terrible days of Dunkirk. For the first time the moral determination of a united people confronts and checks the assault of Hitlerism. Gradually one realizes, awe-struck, the incalculable magnitude and impact of this event.

July 15, 1940: Long conversation with C. I. this afternoon. Everything he is, thinks, and writes is so familiar and lovable to me. And still I find it difficult to follow him in his new development—the absolute pacifism to which he now adheres together with, or under the influence of, Aldous Huxley and Gerald Heard. His horror of war is not only understandable but indeed the only decent reaction towards the devastating boredom which is warfare in the twentieth century. The only question is whether we were last fall—or, for that matter, are now—in a position to choose between war and peace. Needless to recapitulate the depressing list of errors and transgressions to which the inevitability of this war is fundamentally due. Since the disaster of Munich and the fall of the Spanish republic, the issue—War or Peace? —has no relevance any more. The democracies forfeited peace when they tried to collaborate with Hitlerism, which is the essence of war. What began in September, 1939, is by no means another martial adventure but a desperate effort to prevent the spirit of war from conquering the world. How can a genuine pacifist disapprove of a struggle designed and destined to save pacifism? How can he recommend a "negotiated peace," which would be tantamount to the endless and hopeless continuation of war?

The same day, later: . . . Not as if I were unfamiliar with those moods of discouragement and disgust. Why not admit it to myself? Sometimes I cannot help wondering whether the outcome of this war is actually going to have such a decisive bearing on the future of our civilization. Could it be that the inevitability of the struggle implies in itself an irreparable moral and political fiasco of all parties involved?

August 19, 1940: Erika off for London. She isn't the kind of person just to stand by and watch. Duff Cooper's invitation was a welcome signal. It gives her the desired opportunity to participate actively in the war effort, by broadcasting to the German people and collaborating in other ways with the British Ministry of Information. With how much envy and anxiety did I witness her departure from the air field of Los Angeles!

August 21, 1940: Tea with Huxleys. Aldous in brilliant shape. Much less timid and intimidating than he used to be. His delightful malice, now banished from his philosophy, still animates his conversation. It pops out, most amusingly, when he describes his experiences in the film studios. Anita Loos, who seems the most intimate friend of the Huxley ménage, assists him. The Hollywood flapper whom Aldous presents as the last love of the aging millionaire is drawn with a saucy realism that reminds me of "Gentlemen Prefer Blondes," rather than of "Point Counter Point."

The only allusion to the war comes from Mrs. Huxley when she speaks of the hardships and dangers to which her relatives in Belgium are exposed. Besides, we avoid any reference to the political situation, as though according to an unspoken agreement.

August 25, 1940: Cable from Erika. She is in Lisbon. Describes her flight over the ocean as most enjoyable, uneventful, and "cozy."

September 6, 1940: A new issue of the English magazine "Horizon"—founded during the war, run by young people on a remarkable literary and moral level. Their attitude towards the war—somewhat reserved and skeptical in the beginning—becomes increasingly positive and constructive, thus mirroring and confirming the crucial change of British morale.

The reading of "Horizon" strengthens my determination to go ahead with my own project. If a venture of this type has a fighting chance in war torn, beleaguered England, why should it not succeed in this yet neutral country? (I may call my magazine "Zero Hour," which I feel to be a more suggestive name than all the others previously considered.)

September 7, 1940: Erika in London. Her first cable sounds confident, enthusiastic. But she sent it several days ago: it may be dated by now. For meanwhile the Nazis have unleashed their devastating Blitz . . .

September 10, 1940: Yesterday I happened to find in a book store "La Fin du Potomak," Cocteau's last publication before the catastrophe. A loose conglomeration of narrative fragments, aphoristic notes, and poetry, it is undoubtedly lacking in the artistic éclat Jean commanded before. But a Cocteau in decline is still more exciting than, say, a Remarque at his best. . . . Infinite sadness throughout the book. In parts it is nothing but a whimper and stammer alluring and anticipating death.

> Voulez-vous que je vous aide?
> Peut-être serait-ce mieux.
> Mort êtes-vous belle ou laide?
> De vous je suis curieux.

The comparative awkwardness of these verses adds a new and persuasive note to Cocteau's repertoire. How brilliant and nimble he was when feigning tragedy! The experienced juggler hesitates and stumbles as he has to express real anguish.

The same day Bruno Frank read to me some impressive passages out of his story, "16,000 Francs." The most moving scene occurs towards the end of the composition. It takes place in Paris, at the Pantheon. A German refugee and upright man points out to his son the tombstones of France's immortality. He explains to the lad what Voltaire, Hugo, Zola have done for France and for mankind, and why they are truly great. Finally the boy asks his father this question: "A Pantheon like that, a vault of honor, there is no such thing in Germany, is there?"

"No," says the father, "there is none as yet."

While Bruno was reading to me, and he did it beautifully, I could not help thinking of another text that had startled and appalled me, only some hours before. It is a grand and grisly chapter of "La Fin du Potomak"—an uncanny hallucination, called "The Ruins of Paris."

September 13, 1940; San Francisco: Came here to approach some people who may be willing and able to do something on behalf of my magazine. But I can hardly think of anything except London and those murderous air raids. Would I worry that much, if the potential victims were "only" the British people and our cause? If Erika were not there?

September 20, 1940; New York: Word from Erika at last. Just three words: "Safe so far." A rather conditional comfort.

Golo and Heinrich in Lisbon.

Rumors that André Gide plans to come to this country.

September 25, 1940: The magazine project begins to take on a more definite shape. X has promised me a certain amount of money, which means a basis to start from. Seeing a lot of people—potential contributors, advisers, readers, promoters, angels, and enemies. The two first manuscripts I received for the opening number came from Bruno Walter and Aldous Huxley, which is an encouraging start. Muriel Rukeyser will contribute poetry. Christopher Lazare, whose subtle style and keen intelligence appeal greatly to me, takes over the art department. The theatrical column is, of course, the domain of Tom Curtiss . . . Extensive talks with Robert Nathan, W. H. Auden, Horace Gregory, Ernest Boyd, George Davis, Carson McCullers, Eleanor and Eunice Clark, Robert de Saint-Jean, Janet Flanner, and so forth: all of whom are willing to contribute. Some friends keep warning me to postpone the start until I have a really solid backing. But I don't want to wait. Now is the time for this venture. Besides I am convinced that the expenses will not necessarily be as colossal as generally presumed. And why should it not be possible to raise additional funds, once the magazine exists and has proved its function?

September 26, 1940: Letter from Mielein telling about Monika's ghastly experience. She was with Lanyi on the "City of Benares" sunk in the Atlantic, several days ago. Lanyi was drowned. Monika is back in London, safe so far . . .

October 13, 1940: Arrival of the Greek boat "Nea Hellas," with her cargo of refugee writers—including Heinrich Mann with his wife and Golo, Franz Werfel with Madame Alma Mahler Werfel, and many other familiar faces. At the pier to meet them—with Mielein, the Magician, and Frank Kingdon, who has done so much to make their coming possible. Most of the fugitives look surprisingly well-tanned and rested after the long journey. It seems, however, that they all had a tough and trying time before they reached Lisbon. Heinrich who is almost seventy—and looks it, too—was compelled to cross the French frontier secretly and by night, like a criminal; he had to climb a steep mountain path made for goats and smugglers but not for elderly novelists. As for Golo, he was in several French concentration camps and prisons to atone for his tactless gesture of joining the French ranks when Marshal Pétain and his friends had already decided to establish Fascism in France with the help of the German army.

October 14, 1940: Tea with H. G. Wells, in his apartment at the house of Thomas W. Lamont. A quaint old mansion—gloomy and dignified, in the grand old bourgeois style. Wells is still asleep when I arrive at the appointed hour, about five o'clock in the afternoon. The butler wakes him; then serves us tea and muffins, both of remarkable quality.

The master in his most aggressive vein. He peers at me out of pale, glacial eyes, and as I dare stammer something in reference to my humble magazine project he jerks with sarcasm and disapproval. Presently he discloses his profound contempt for little magazines. Never, under any circumstances, would he condescend to have any dealings with so preposterous an enterprise. I tell him that I appreciate his point of view, and help myself to another delicious muffin. While I relish my tea, he examines the list of my contributors, for each of whom he has some scathing crack. As I remain placid and composed, he changes the subject and dwells on the hideous character of the German people. All Germans, he insists, are tiresome bawlers and, furthermore, potential criminals. While refilling my cup with some more of the unusually aromatic tea, he announces that the Reich has to be dismembered, disarmed, and strictly policed by the Allied armies. I have no objection: whereupon he adds, somewhat irritated, that the German refugees are about as bad as the Nazis. I admit that there are quite a few bores among them. He pierces me with his look and observes that there is no such thing as German culture, really. German art hardly exists at all, and as for literature, it would be fatuous to compare the Teutonic trash with the lofty output of Britain.

"Right you are!" I exclaim cheerfully. "And yet you forget to mention the most ridiculous German delusion: that they possess anything one might possibly call music." Curiously enough, he joins in my laughter.

He keeps me for about an hour. I enjoy every minute of it. Not a word he says annoys me; for I realize he doesn't mean a single one of his rampant paradoxes. Why shouldn't he indulge in some baroque dislocations if it stimulates the circulation of his blood? A grand old man can certainly afford to be a little cranky. And a grand old man he is, beyond any doubt. I may be more critical now towards his novels and tales than I used to be as a young and responsive boy. At this point, his social and political essays seem more admirable to me than his narrative ventures. In fact, I consider his spirited blueprints more constructive and significant than most of those designed by younger, less whimsical gentlemen.

November 1, 1940: Erika back from England. But already she speaks of her next expedition to the "battlefield."

The atmosphere charged with tension on account of the Presidential elections. No doubt, the decision will be one of crucial gravity. No matter how smart and decent the individual Wendell Willkie may be, his victory over Roosevelt would inevitably imply a major defeat of our cause—a triumph and chance for Hitler.

November 4, 1940; New York: It was fun to spend the election night at that strictly Republican ladies' club where everybody whispered prayers for Willkie. The Daughters of the American Revolution almost lost their poise when the first returns poured in from all regions of these unpredictable States.

The uproar and clamor on Times Square were overwhelming—half-bedlam, half-carnival. Even those who had voted for and bet on Willkie seemed entirely overjoyed. I like the "I told you so"—gag. An amusing idea, to print in advance those posters quite independently of the eventual outcome of the historic duel. It proves a good-natured sense of humor—a tonic thing in these hectic and serious days.

Strolled about Broadway and Forty-second Street with Curt Riess and Ingrid. All of us in high spirits as if we had won a personal victory. "Aren't we happy?" shouted Diana Sheean as I discovered her, jammed amongst a lot of raving and roaring folks. It sounded touching, the way she twittered it, with that British accent of hers. But Jimmy Sheean, standing next to her, looked a hundred per cent American—tall and husky and a trifle tipsy: just enough to make him beam even more.

November 9, 1940: Last minute change of the magazine's name. When I told Glenway Wescott that I intended to call it "The Cross-Road," he said that sounded indeed most attractive: But didn't I think it might give the impression of a somewhat undecided attitude?—"Undecided?" I said "No, Sir. Not my magazine!" And, after a brief pause: "If Cross-Road sounds undecided, why, I'll call it DECISION."

December 14, 1940: Mielein and the Magician seem to take a faintly apprehensive view of my magazine venture. That is to say, they think the idea fine: if only I had a little bit more money . . .

Meanwhile "Decision" develops in an even more promising way than I dared anticipate. Curiously, I can't help feeling surprised when any proposition of mine is taken seriously by "the grown-ups." In this respect my attitude has hardly changed since the days of the "Zwölf-Uhr Mittagsblatt." When I was eighteen it tickled me to impersonate a theatrical critic. I never stopped wondering whether or not the printers would actually bother to set in type what I had written down. And later, when my own plays were produced, it seemed funny and flattering that veritable actors should go out of their way to memorize my lines. This time it's a magazine. But, amazingly, it materializes: people believe in it. There is something called "Decision Inc.," with officers, office and a bank account. The secretary looks exactly the way a real secretary should look—in fact, she is very pretty—and apparently fails to notice that I don't look like a boss.

The list of our sponsors and contributors becomes almost unduly glamorous. Some of the editorial advisers seem even willing to give me a bit of advice, occasionally. Ernest Boyd and Horace Gregory are those most keenly interested in what I try to do. Stefan Zweig, of course, proves as stimulating and helpful as ever. I also like G. A. Borgese's suggestion to carry a regular column surveying the various schemes of post-War organization.

Good contributions come in. William Carlos Williams, of whom I think very highly, has sent a remarkable story, and I am happy to have that fine treatise by Somerset Maugham on the prose style of Edmund Burke. What a delightful man Maugham is! For one reason or another I expected to meet a rather slick and snooty gentleman, and was most pleasantly surprised to find a bland and almost timid little chap, exceedingly delicate and entirely unassuming. Two charming moments occurred during our conversation. We discussed the literary rank of Winston Churchill, and after having praised his powerful eloquence, dwelt for a little while on certain mannerisms typical of his style. In this context I was tactless enough to refer to the Prime Minister as an elderly man who has a right to indulge occasionally in somewhat quaint rhetoric. I shall never forget the distrait and sorrowful way in which Maugham smiled at me while reminding me of the fact that the Prime Minister and he happen to be almost exactly the same age.

He had the same apologetic and yet faintly roguish smile when he asserted that, alas, there was nothing really worth while he could offer me as a contribution to my magazine. "That is to say," he added, looking very embarrassed, "the only paper I might let you see is so dull and dry that I am afraid you wouldn't want to use it . . ."

I am positive that his qualms were absolutely sincere.

. . . Noel Coward, whom I visited yesterday again, also promised to write something for "Decision," and to be helpful in every way he could. He, too, is a much nicer fellow than his legend suggests. His vanity is controlled by a keen intelligence and by natural courtesy. Besides he is attractive and gifted enough to risk certain poses which become embarrassing when aped by the would-be Noel Cowards.

December 18, 1940: The first issue in print.

I had scarcely believed that Sherwood Anderson would really give us a story. He didn't actually commit himself when I went to see him a couple of weeks ago. Now he has come through with an enchanting tale, "Girl by the Stove," a typical Anderson piece, with all that sensual persuasion and inconspicuous mastership he commands when he is at his best.

Among all the eminent American writers who have agreed to join our advisory board, he is the one I admire most and am the proudest to have. There is a particular aura around his work and name—a valid and simple glory. As far as popular appeal is concerned several others of our American sponsors may match or even surpass him— Vincent Sheean, for instance, or Robert Sherwood, or Stephen Vincent Benét. The last will act as my co-speaker in a symposium introducing "Decision" to the nation-wide audience of John T. Frederick's literary broadcasts. Everybody assures me that this is about the most effective break my venture could possibly get.

As for Robert Sherwood, he seems indeed on the point of becoming the official representative of American letters, together with Archibald MacLeish. The great success of "There Shall Be No Night" marks the beginning, but by no means the climax, of a career which may transcend the realm of literature in the strict, traditional sense.

And still Sherwood does not give the impression of an ambitious man. He is quiet, rather bashful; always slightly embarrassed, as it were, by his unusual tallness. When I saw him, just a few days ago, at an intimate dinner party given by Henri Bernstein, he resembled a shy, ungainly lad in the midst of self-assured adults. But, of course, even a well-trained conversationalist would be intimidated by the fireworks of M. Bernstein and the sweeping eloquence Dorothy Thompson displays, once she begins to talk. Howard Dietz—a spirited talker himself—gave up about two o'clock in the morning, yielding the floor to Henri and Dorothy. The two champions seemed of about equal tenacity until 3.30 A.M., when the Frenchman collapsed. Dorothy carried on—more dynamic than ever. It must have been five in the morning when she withdrew at last—to get two or three hours of sleep, as she told us, and then to compose her column.

What a stunning person she is! Every time I see her I am spellbound anew by that electrifying force she emanates—an emotional energy to which the efficacy of her manifestoes is due. No doubt, her flamboyant exposures of Hitlerism have been instrumental in enlightening and arousing American public opinion. But what I admire even more than her consistency in attacking what she knows to be evil or promoting what she knows to be right, is the bold determination she proves when abandoning those views and affiliations whose fallacy she has recognized. Her fight against the Nazis was surely an inspiring spectacle. But her crusade on behalf of Roosevelt's re-election was even more impressive from a moral point of view. For in the former case she rationalized and articulated an instinctive impulse—i.e., her natural hatred of an abject individual, Hitler—whereas in the latter instance, she overcame an old political opposition to much of the Roosevelt Administration for the sake of the general cause.

January 3, 1941: Curtiss shows up, in uniform. He enlisted with the National Guard last summer, and now is going to be marched off to Camp Stewart, Georgia. The boots, the coat, even the khaki shirt—everything looks as if it were too large and heavy for him. It gives me an odd feeling of embarrassment, indeed, of guilt to see him in this disguise. There are so many things he wants to do and is looking forward to, in connection with "Decision" for instance, and now he has to learn to shoot, instead. And why? Because those tiresome Teutons have a morbid penchant for guns. What a shame! What an inconceivable nuisance!—that they are strong and crazy enough to impose their ugly fixation on a civilized world which has other hobbies and aspirations.

Roosevelt's fireside chat to which I listened tonight—a most impressive piece of oratory, incidentally—reaffirms the inevitability of this country's entanglement in the Second World War.

January 10, 1941: The opening number of the magazine seems to be a success. Subscriptions and flattering comments pour in. But I am not quite satisfied with "Decision" as yet. Too many big names and big words; not enough youth and experimental endeavor. I suppose, however, this exhibition of "big shots" is indispensable to catch the public attention. After the second issue I may be in a position to take more hazardous chances.

January 26, 1941: The Magician, Mielein, and Erika are in Washington as the guests of the President and Mrs. Roosevelt. Erika sends me a note on the stationery of the White House—a fairly simple type of stationery, for that matter; but the place it comes from and the name it bears is the focus of vast developments, a house of destiny.

March 17, 1941: Spent last evening and this afternoon with Auden to prepare the radio dialogue scheduled for the day after tomorrow. "The function of the writer in the political crisis" is certainly too complex and ample a subject to be adequately covered in fifteen minutes or so. I think, however, our conversation may elucidate certain integral aspects of our respective views. Wystan—formerly much more of a political activist than I ever was—now feels that writers ought to avoid all political affiliations. Says W. H. Auden: "When I look back over the political activities of the literary world during the last ten years, I cannot help feeling that we might have been more effective if we hadn't been so hasty. In a modern liberal society, the artist if he is at all successful is in a peculiar position, in that more than anybody else he is free to do what he likes; he is not dictated to either by the State or by an employer. In some ways this makes him ill-suited to make political judgments, because he cannot understand at first hand the problem of political power and the role of force in Government. That is why, perhaps, he has such a weakness for extremist positions; why he tends either to become an anarchist or to look for a solution to the evils of society in a Good Dictator."

As he admonishes us to be "highly skeptical about any formula of ours being capable of representing the final and absolute truth," it is my turn to ask him this humble question: "On the other hand, wouldn't you agree, Mr. Auden, that there is an even greater danger of a paralyzing skepticism, in which everything is equally relative? While we should be aware of the limitations of our consciousness of the truth, we must keep our faith that it is possible to know something about the truth, and realize that some aspects are more relevant at some times than at others."

Wystan agrees and comes to the conclusion that "we have first of all to recover a sense of the unconditional; if we don't, it will be supplied to us in the form of an external tyranny."

April 8, 1941: No. 4 of "Decision" is almost satisfactory. Max Lerner's paper on "Democracy for a War Generation" contains incisive, irrefutable statements and demands. I am wholeheartedly with him when he urges the responsive leaders to give the world "an expression of war aims, in word and in deed. They must compass the kind of war this is, the enemies of every country against whom it is fought, the kind of men and the kind of ideas that can best fight it, and finally the kind of world that can arise out of it."

Maurice Samuels' contribution, "The Destruction of the Intelligence," is no less timely. What he has to say concerning propaganda testifies, once again, to his acute insight into the maze of Nazi psychology: "I submit that propaganda is therefore an end in itself. The ostensible objective of any propaganda campaign, whether it be the whipping up of hatred against a country, or of adoration for a Führer, is merely part of the instrument. The real objective is, always and continuously, the depression of the human intelligence . . ."

As for my extensive treatise on Walt Whitman, I can only hope it may communicate, in part at least, the profusion of feelings I tried to put into it. I wonder how Sherwood Anderson, an American of truly great stature, would have liked my attempt.

His "far-away death"—to quote Muriel Rukeyser's fine epitaph—has saddened me much more than seems reasonable, considering the casualness of our personal contact. But it is just this, perhaps, which makes me feel so baffled and dismayed: that I knew him so little, despite his friendliness.

I recall the afternoon when I went with Curtiss to see Anderson, at the Royalton. Curtiss had insisted that I take him along—the author of "Winesburg, Ohio" being one of his idols. I liked Anderson's face, as soon as I saw it, and I was even more fond of it after having watched his features, for half an hour or so. It was a face with wide spaces—somewhat slouching and bloated, but at the same time vigorous; a gentle, manly face, the face of a man who has experienced and understood many things, and is versed in all human impulses and desires, except those that are mean and petty. There was nothing petty about him. Everything was of generous proportions—large and kind and indulgent.

I don't think he made any noteworthy statements in the course of this afternoon chat. We talked shop—magazines and writers, what "The Dial" and "The Mercury" used to be like, and why Mencken writes such queer stuff nowadays. But there was always that bemused kindness in his look and smile—that paternal smirk, at once hardening and warning, as if he wanted to tell us: "Go ahead, boys!—why not. But take it easy! Don't expect too much! Literature is no gold mine, and as far as immortality is concerned . . . Never mind! You'll find out yourself . . ."

Before we left him he encouraged us to call on him again. But I didn't. And then he made that fatal trip to Panama.

April 20, 1941: Word from André Gide at last. He is in the South of France. The rumors concerning his plans to come to the U.S. turn out to be entirely incorrect. Evidently he has no intention of leaving France at this point. His wishes for "Decision" sound all the more cordial and sincere as he announces a contribution to one of the coming issues. The rest of his note, however, makes it only too plain that he is in a state of depression and, furthermore, handicapped by the censorship. "I shall try my best," he writes, "to send you a few pages before long. But I don't dare to promise anything; for I feel, four days out of five (if not nine out of ten) terribly remote from my work. Besides there are so many 'considerations' that slow down my writing . . ."

The quotation marks around the word "consideration" are more suggestive, alas, than anything he hazards to say in his letter.

June 2, 1941: The magazine involves much more labor than I anticipated. I don't mind it, though—on the contrary, I might enjoy it, if it were not for the cumbersome money problems. In fact, the financial situation becomes increasingly embarrassing. Several important investors I was counting on disappointingly failed to come through. How cruel and capricious are the rich! As soon as they realize that you are interested in their cash, they lose interest in you and in what they used to call "our common cause." . . . In my more serene moments I feel like writing a comedy entitled "The Fight with the Angels." At times, however, I am afraid it might turn out to be a tragedy.

June 7, 1941: Called on Louis Fischer. Delighted as ever by his sturdy wit and heartiness. Everything he says makes sense, is to the point, testifies to his good will and keen intelligence. There is something inspiring trust in his slow, sonorous speech and his firm, jovial regard.

He became eloquent and seemed extremely concerned when discussing the lack of political awareness he finds in American youth. What this country needs most urgently, according to him, is an effective and thorough scheme of positive anti-Fascist education in the camps to offset the outside pressure of Bundist, America-Firsters, and the like. The absence of spontaneous political discussion in the camps betrays apathy.

The inevitable question of war aims. Louis believes that the mere preservation of the status quo is not enough of a program to make soldiers out of the young men pouring into the training camps. So far, he feels, our war aims have been couched in vague defense generalities.

June 8, 1941: Who in one lifetime sees all causes lost,
         himself dismayed and beaten, cities down,
         love made monotonous fear, and the sad-faced
         inexorable armies and the falling plane,
         has sickness, sickness . . .

These terrifying lines are from a poem Muriel Rukeyser gave me for the forthcoming issue. If only I were somewhat less familiar with the anguish they articulate . . .

June 29, 1941: Hitler's attack on Russia is an event of such staggering implications that I don't dare to gauge them—not even in these unassuming notes. All I know, at this point, is that my spontaneous reaction is one of relief, rather than of dismay and apprehension. The air has become purer. The story of a colossal lie has finally reached its end.

Stalin and Hitler kept lying to each other for eighteen months. But we must not forget that the Nazis were also lying when they abused and slandered the Soviets before the deceitful Pact, while the Soviets happened to say the truth when abusing the Nazis. The Nazis will now exchange their pro-Soviet lies, model 1940, for the more familiar pattern of their anti-Soviet forgeries, model 1919-1939. Can we hope that the Soviet leaders may turn back at last from their furtive policy of the past two years to that valiant truthfulness which characterized Dimitroff's attitude during the Reichstag Fire trial at Leipzig?

The same day, later: No doubt, when Hitler turned against Stalin he forfeited his second decisive chance: the first one was Chamberlain's scheme of a semi-Fascist England collaborating with a Fascist Germany. Hitler might have ruled the world, with the Bank of England or with the Kremlin on his side. Without either of them he is doomed. He may still be very strong; but nobody is strong enough to meet the overpowering coalition of the British Commonwealth, the United States, and the Soviet Union: provided, of course, that it actually is a coalition—not a plot to prepare the world revolution or the encirclement of the Socialist ally.

August 10, 1941: At times the heat is so dazing that one can hardly breathe. Every step has to be paid for with sweat. I haven't been out of town since our Princeton household was dissolved—about the beginning of April, if I am not mistaken. Yet, curiously, New York never gets on my nerves. I am exceedingly fond of the place. I like it even when it becomes a parched and dusty inferno. I relish those sultry evenings when the vast masses of towered stones seem to exhale the accumulated glow of the day like tremendous stoves. I do not long for lush meadows, cool mountain valleys, and the salty breeze from the sea. It gives me a grim sort of pleasure to loiter around Times Square on a torrid August night. I do not seek company. I enjoy being by myself— all alone in the midst of a sweating, easy-going, weary, and sensual crowd.

I suppose this is the most lonely summer I've ever experienced. The city seems to be deserted by everybody I know. Erika is in England; my family in California. The only person I see is Muriel Rukeyser, who recently joined the staff of the magazine. She is a great help in these trying days. Probably I couldn't carry on "Decision" if it were not for her cheering and dynamic assistance.

But even she, the only comrade in this arid solitude, escapes to the country from Saturday until Monday: while I have to stay—paralyzed, as it were, by the demon of this fierce and relentless summer. At times I actually fear suffocation in the stifling hole that's my room.

The only comfort on those painful Sundays are the calls from Savannah. Curtiss grumbles and jokes on the phone—out there in that Southern town where he rests in a shady hotel room, for twenty-four hours or so, after the fatigue of a tough week in Camp Stewart. To him New York is the resort he dreams of when they make him sweat in the field or the kitchen. He keeps asking me about things that go on in his city—if I saw a new play, and what kind of material comes in for the magazine, and would I send him the volume H. L. Mencken just published. That he, in his martial exile, should take such lively interest in what we are doing here makes me feel so ashamed that I overcome my weariness and can finally work again.

The same day, later: To work again. . . . But what?

Such is the gravity of this hour, and so intense is my awareness of its magnitude, that I find no image adequate to express what at once dazes and stirs my mind. In such moments, all traditional devices tarnish and hesitate. The oft-tested pattern of fiction, the historical masquerades and poetic clichés become unbearably vapid. There is no invented scheme intimate and comprehensive enough to communicate my faith and anguish—the fears, the apprehension, the forebodings, the hopes and the repentance. Nothing will do, this time, but the plain, candid confession.

August 11, 1941: To tell the truth, the whole truth, and nothing but the truth. To tell my own story.

To tell the story of an intellectual in the period from 1920 to 1940—a character who spent the best time of his life in a social and spiritual vacuum; striving for a true community but never finding it; disconnected, restless, wandering; haunted by those solemn abstractions in which nobody else believes—civilization, progress, liberty.

To tell the story of a German who wanted to be a European: of a European who wanted to be a citizen of the world. Of an individualist equally opposed to standardization and anarchy.

Every testimony counts. Why should mine be worthless?

Every human life is at once unique and representative. Limited in its scope and molded by specific conditions; and yet full of infinite suggestions, transcending the range of its own problems and objectives, pointing to potentialities far beyond its empirical margin.

To tell my story, not despite the crisis, but because of it.

The same day, later: It is from the turning point that we should examine the path we have covered. In measuring its serpentine curves and paradoxical zigzags, we may learn something as to the next step to take. For one thing is certain at least, in the midst of so many staggering uncertainties: the next step will carry us into new land with landscapes and conditions as they have never been seen before. Nobody can foretell whether things will be worse or better in this transformed world to come. The horizons which, from now on, will surround our lives may be brighter or darker than the skies we knew. But surely the light will alter.

August 18, 1941: I don't want to lie anymore. I am fed up with all disguises and contrivances. Whom should I try to please or to impress? I am alone. I am free. I possess nothing nor do I wish to possess anything. Whatever I may have owned has been taken from me—even the language I used to consider mine. My moral consciousness does not veer according to the stock market, nor is it affected by the sex taboos of bourgeois or proletarian society, or by the hateful slogans of nationalism. I abominate nationalism,—the most devastating fallacy of modern man. I have abandoned my country disgusted with its boastful selfishness. I am not interested in countries and their spheres of influence. All I believe in is the indivisible, universal civilization to be created by man.

So this century is not the Germanic Century nor is it the American Century nor the Century of the Soviet Union. (I am fed up with lies!) It is the century to prepare the birth of the indivisible, universal civilization. It is the century of throes and convulsions; of vast transitions, disasters and resurrections. The grand strategy of Nazism is but a clumsy and reckless effort to falsify the intrinsic meaning and objective of this century—a meaning and an objective that have been dodged and disregarded by the democracies. Hitler's crimes are not only a peril but also a stimulus. Too transient and tawdry to discourage us, they are impressive enough to refute the validity of the status quo. His mad and abhorrent attempt to usurp universal hegemony compels us to accept, indeed, to fight for the concept of universal solidarity.

August 22, 1941: Moved and comforted as ever by the reading of Thomas Wolfe. No doubt, he is the only great and authentic voice to cry out the American dream after Melville and Whitman. Struck by the following lines:

"Each of us is all the sums he has not counted: subtract us into nakedness and night again, and you shall see begin in Crete four thousand years ago the love that ended yesterday in Texas. . . . Each moment is the fruit of forty thousand years. The minute-winning days, like flies, buzz home to death, and every moment is a window to all time."

Each moment then is a turning point—not only the fruit of an infinite past but also the bud, the chance, indeed, the promise of an infinite future. I recall this profound and tender invocation by Paul Valéry:

"Patience! patience! patience dans l'azur!
Chaque atôme de silence est la chance d'un fruit mûr."

The same day, later: Two sentences I would like to use as mottoes for my autobiography. The one, a diary note by Franz Kafka:

"Do not despair, not even at not despairing. When everything seems at a dead end, even then new forces draw up and march—and therein lies the significance of your being alive."

The other, out of André Gide's novel, "Strait Is the Gate":

"I imagine the celestial bliss, not as a fusion with God, but as an infinite, continuous approach. . . . In fact, if I were not afraid of playing with words, I might dare say that I would sneer at a bliss that is not progressive."

Without date: If God did not exist, we would have to invent Him. For it must be unspeakably bitter for God not to be, while His creation rampantly develops. Our sympathy should rescue Him from nothingness.

The same day, later: The fact that we are able to conceive the being of God implies in itself that He actually is. If His existence is conceivable, His non-existence becomes inconceivable. Only the divine intelligence can have been bold and potent enough to devise the concept of divinity.

Whence comes our creative impulse, if not from the Creator?

Yet God depends on man as His chosen instrument of self-identification. Our mortal kind has been assigned to mirror and materialize His immortal substance. Who is able to grasp the overpowering impact of such a task and privilege?

There are no "other worlds" to diminish or mitigate the stringent responsibility of our metaphysical mission. Those competing universes —presuming that they exist—have no relevancy to our drama: the thought of them carries distraction and discouragement.

The divine energy, even if spread throughout the spaces and galaxies, still is here with us, in its entirety. For, being omnipresent, He is indivisible. He is everywhere, and wherever He is, completely.

Our quest is also His pilgrimage. He partakes in our efforts, errors, and embraces. Our throbbing hearts echo His vast emotions. It is in our stammer that He recognizes His augury. Our disgrace is also His affliction; our progress upholds and reaffirms His cosmic equilibrium.

The more I think of God, the more I grasp the ultimate significance of our worldly affairs.

September 16, 1941: Occupied with editing a group of articles and poems, "The Other Germany," to be featured in our October issue. Stimulating talks with young Peter Viereck, who will contribute an essay on Stefan George. Among all young Americans I know, Peter is the most thoroughly versed in the mire of Nazi "ideology." His book, "Metapolitics: From the Romantics to Hitler," proves a remarkable insight into the labyrinth of the Teutonic soul. As for his own soul, I do not think that it has been contaminated by his intense study of Alfred Rosenberg and the like. A young man who has had the hard luck to be the son of a Nazi agent and still maintains his candor and integrity, is likely to be immune to all Nazoid germs and temptations.

The same day, later: This afternoon, in the bar of our hotel, an elderly gentleman lost his temper because Erika and I talked German. We watched him grumble and mumble, and his face turn purple; but we had no inkling what it was all about: until, all of a sudden, he got up and approached our table—staggering, a trembling fist raised against us. "I can't stand it!" he shouted. "That damned Nazi talk! That filthy gibberish! Stop it! Shut up! Or speak English!"

He kept raving and ranting, until Erika interrupted him. "Pleased to meet you, Sir," she said, with her most exquisite British accent. "I certainly appreciate your feelings. If American public opinion reacted as violently against Nazism as you do against the German language, the cause of democracy would be safe."

September 17, 1941: Three or five years ago, the idea of writing in a "foreign" language (that is to say, in any idiom save German) would have struck me as utterly absurd. I used to take it for granted that the innermost substance of my emotional and intellectual life is, and will always remain, indissolubly tied to that particular medium. To renounce my language—the only possession I cherished—seemed more of a sacrifice than I could possibly bear. But man is always inclined to underestimate his own adaptability and alertness.

Conditions rapidly deteriorated for the German writers in exile. In the end it became nonsensical to produce German books for which there would be no readers. As for translations, they are excellent instruments to spread the message and the fame of an author whose work already has its integral and undisputed place in the literature of his homeland. But how about an author who happens to have no home? An uprooted vagabond whose name has been forgotten in the country from which he comes, and is not established as yet in the land that shelters him now? He must not cling with stubborn nostalgia to his mother-tongue: the very people who speak it would be only too pleased to tear out his tongue and to kill him, along with his mother. The thing for him to do is to learn a new idiom to communicate a new identity. He will have to find a new vocabulary, a new set of rhythms and devices, a new medium to articulate his sorrows and emotions, his protests, and his prayers. The alternative confronting him is to become speechless, or adapt his speech to the tastes and traditions of his new fellowmen. If the writer in question has anything worthwhile to say, and, moreover, commands the indispensable degree of self-assurance, he is likely to take a chance, to make an effort, to venture on a new style. After a while he may realize, much to his own surprise, that the linguistic fixation which he once considered insurmountable is really nothing but another prejudice.

The same day, later: Julien Green told me the other day that he, too, is engaged in writing his autobiography, and that he writes it in English. Of course, his case is enviably exceptional, as he is really at home in two languages and two cultural spheres. He does not need to discover the rules and secrets of English (or American) prose: all he has to do is to rediscover the idiom of his own early years. Yet I recall having read in his diary—or rather, in his French "Journal"—that he feels quite at ease only when speaking or writing French. No doubt, his adventure is particularly delicate and, perhaps, more trying than even our experience. For while we are compelled to explore and conquer a new realm of speech and literature, he, on the contrary, has to abandon the human dialect which he once lovingly chose. The American-born lover of France is forced to give up his mistress and return to his family, which he left voluntarily, many a year ago. As for us German-born Americans, we quit our family—all fed up with its quarrelsome narrowness. While striving for a new speech—who knows?—we may find a mistress.

September 29, 1941: There is much I admire and love in Frederic Prokosch's new novel. True, "The Skies of Europe" falls short of "The Asiatics"—that amazing Odyssey of a visionary Narcissus. At the same time, however, his new book marks a definite step forward. For, while renouncing certain bewitching devices so lavishly employed in "The Asiatics," Frederic has also overcome some of his former shortcomings and limitations. He has become more responsible, more serious, more human. In "The Skies of Europe," there is an element of realistic sympathy that has been lacking before. His new work is apt to prove the sincerity of this fine and promising credo: "My greatest desire is to take part, however humbly, in the resurrection and growth of a truly international literature—an approach to writing which exceeds national limitations, both in matter and mentality."

November 27, 1941: My little secretary, Mary, begs me, all in tears, to have a talk with her boy friend and explain to him what's what, as far as this war is concerned. Johnny is a private in the U.S. armed forces, and doesn't like it a bit. Thinks the whole war is humbug and none of his business at all. Not that Mary, on her part, is fervently concerned with democracy, Hitler, and such as that. All she cares for is Johnny, and she doesn't want him to get himself into trouble. There may be plenty of trouble for him, if he continues to go over the hill and stay away from camp for a couple of weeks or so. So Mary urges me to give Johnny a lecture.

He is a Southerner—fair, tall and husky; disarmingly handsome and naïve. Reminds me somehow of my friend Willi L., in Berlin. But Johnny is not blasé or despondent. More on the radiant side.

He insists that life in camp is bad, "and that ain't good," he says. Of course, life with Mary is better. He doesn't get along with his sergeant, who is a "rat and a Jew." With Mary, on the contrary, he gets along just fine.

I tell him that I appreciate his point of view. But doesn't he realize that there is a war going on? "We ain't in it," he says. "Never will be, either. Let that guy Hitler conquer as much as he wants to. It's okay with me. I don't give a damn."

It may look ugly—written down, black on white. But the way he put it, it sounded differently. There is nothing ugly about the natural selfishness of a young chap who enjoys living and loving, rather than shooting and drilling. If only. . . . But what's the use of repeating here the arguments, which so utterly failed to convince Private Johnny? I know what it's all about. But Johnny doesn't believe me.

December 10, 1941: The office of the Coordinator of Information asked me to make a statement—in my capacity as an anti-Nazi of German extraction—concerning the recent developments. This is what I wrote:

"The formal declaration of war is but the legalization of a status that has long existed in reality. Yet it means a great, pivotal event. The German exiles—Hitler's first victims and his most implacable enemies—have experienced the truly diabolic character of the Nazi challenge. As we could not endure life in a country dominated and degraded by Hitler, the people of the United States could not live in a world subjugated by him.

"We were just a helpless minority of liberal intellectuals: the usurper found it easy to silence our grievous, indignant voices. To conquer the world is less convenient a task. Hitler will not succeed. The United States is not in the habit of losing wars. Germany is.

"I am proud to be in the country which will give the finishing stroke to the apocalyptic monster. My humble forces are at the disposal of the American Government. Wholeheartedly I join in the prayers of the

American people that the righteous cause may come out victorious—soon, and at not too dreadful a price."

December 11, 1941: "The Magic Flute," at the Metropolitan. Remarkable production, with Bruno Walter conducting. More spellbound than ever by the grandeur and loveliness of Mozart's music. Among all his works, this one has probably the widest scope of emotions and melodies. "The Magic Flute" surpasses even "Don Giovanni," in both dramatic boldness and musical inspiration. Also, I like the libretto, notwithstanding its obvious flaws and naïve dislocations. The blend of didactic and fantastic elements—freemasonry ethos plus fairy-tale devices—is original and suggestive. The sacerdotal common sense of Sarastro's attitude foreshadows Goethe's vision, whereas the stupendous variety of contrasting moods and images is truly akin to Shakespeare's cosmic hospitality.

Indeed, this miraculous opera echoes "A Midsummer Night's Dream," anticipates elements of the second "Faust," refutes Wagner, and altogether suggests an unprecedented type of musical theater—a ritual, solemn and serene, to be created and enjoyed by happier generations.

January 4, 1942: While the vast battle develops and spreads all over the globe, I have my own personal little struggle to keep the magazine going. The day after Pearl Harbor I made up my mind to discontinue "Decision." But I was only too willing to let people persuade me that I should make another effort, and must not give up as long as there is a faint chance to save and stabilize the review. They assure me—and I feel, rightly so—that the magazine has a real function, and that there is a warm and lively response to what we are trying to do. A new man, Charles Neider, who seems full of punch and confidence, offers me his services as managing editor, business manager, promoter, contributor, literary critic, and what not.

So let's make another effort!

January 8, 1942: Last night, Mary dropped in, along with her young husband, Johnny, who wanted to bid me farewell. They are going to ship him off: he doesn't know where to, but hopes it will be Bataan.

For he worships MacArthur and wants to "beat the hell out of them Japs."

His transformation is stunning, almost incredible. Since those "damned yellow-bellies" have had the nerve to bomb our stuff—out there, in Pearl Harbor—Johnny has decided that "they won't get away with their phony tricks." He'll give it to them—he, Johnny. Mary is proud and scared. Beaming and sobbing, she implores me to explain to Johnny the dangers involved in immoderate heroism. But I am not going to do anything of the kind. Why should I make an ass out of myself, once again? Johnny would laugh at me—just as he did, two or three months ago, when I tried to convince him that this is America's war. Besides I have a hunch that nothing will happen to him, anyway. He looks like a guy whom his good luck won't let down. He looks like a good guy to me.

January 14, 1942: In view of the astounding courage and discipline now displayed by the Soviet armies, I cannot help asking myself if I ought not to revise certain harsh opinions I harbored and pronounced at the time of the Hitler-Stalin Pact. But, again, I feel that my doubts in the political wisdom and integrity of the Comintern have nothing to do with the admirable morale of the Russian peasants and workers.

Yet there are certain widely accepted judgements or prejudices with regard to the Soviets, which should be reconsidered in the light of the new situation. How about those notorious trials staged by the Stalin régime? The fact that Russia seems free, at this point, of the pernicious Fifth Column bacillus is perhaps mainly due to the relentless purges of 1937. As for the Finnish war, was it really such an outrageous blunder as I considered it at the time? The present conduct of the "brave little northern republic" (they pay their debts: especially to the Nazis) almost justifies Moscow's preventive aggressiveness.

And, finally, can Stalin really be quite as unpopular with the Russian people as Hearst correspondents and the like kept telling us for ten years? I wonder if any conceivable nation would fight with such dogged tenacity to defend a régime they loathe.

(Hitler's authority was powerful enough to make the Germans invade and violate their unprotected neighbors. It remains to be seen if his halo will last, with the Russians seventy miles from Berlin, or the British and American troops in Cologne and Bremen.)

January 31, 1942: Everybody tells me the new double-number of "Decision" (January-February) is the best job we ever did. Too bad that it is the last one we are able to do. I have invested more love and labor in this thing than in any other venture before. It was all in vain. Not in vain, perhaps; for I don't think "Decision" an actual failure. But it has to remain a fragment, for want of some thousand dollars. The magazine could never live up to its inherent potentialities. It was never given a chance.

Does it make me feel better that other literary reviews are in a similar fix? No, it hardly means any comfort that "The Southern Review" has to suspend publication, while others may be compelled to do so before long. Quite the contrary, the disappearance of any congenial organ renders the loss of "Decision" all the more painful, and cannot but increase my misgivings as to the future role of creative writing in this war and this country.

The same day, later: There is no event without propitious and pleasant aspects: Truisms like this prove surprisingly true, in intricate and trying situations. The collapse of "Decision" means not only a bitter disappointment to me, but also a relief. For now I am free to concentrate on my book—without worrying about printers, engravers, secretaries, translators, poets, helpful friends, and other creditors.

February 23, 1942: The news of Stefan Zweig's suicide in Brazil was so utterly unexpected that I at first refused to believe it. Since I have read his farewell message and, moreover, reread some of the notes I received from him recently, the event seems less incredible but all the more saddening. I recall the despondent, troubled expression he had the last time I saw him, when he was in New York. He who used to be so buoyant and gregarious now showed his bewildered friends a new, ominous face—numbed and paled, as if by a sudden stroke of grief.

He had money, success, innumerable friends, and a young wife who loved him faithfully enough to follow him into death. Yet he did not want to go on. The humanist and zealous man of letters, the connoisseur and creator of subtle, lovable things—he could not bear the gruesome spectacle of a world bursting asunder.

March 3, 1942: Erika reminds me of the fact that this happens to be the tenth anniversary of our emigration from Germany. Ten years are a long time: more than half of my adult life up to now.

Shall I ever live in Germany again? I don't think so. Or rather, the question as such has lost its relevance as far as I am concerned.

I have gone far—too far, indeed, to go back. I must go further, forward—or else I shall go astray.

You can't go home again nor can you find a new home. The world will be your home, or you will be homeless, disconnected, doomed.

The world will be your home: if there is a world.

The issue, therefore, is not exile or return. The issue is whether there will be a world for people like us to live in, to work for. There might be, should be, will be, such a world: if the war and the peace can be won by the United Nations. And this world, if it comes into being, will accept and need our services: the services of men such as I—versed in various idioms and traditions, experienced go-betweens, mediators, and interpreters, fore-runners and agents of the super-national civilization to be constructed. The drama of our deracination may turn out to be the most effective training for the vast and delicate task ahead.

There is no tenth year of exile. Exile has reached its end. I don't feel in exile as long as I am allowed to stay here and contribute my tiny bit to the general effort. Nor would I feel uprooted in Britain or Soviet Russia or any other community engaged in this crucial struggle. We are all in one boat.

March 14, 1942: Tom Curtiss (who has recently been transferred to Governor's Island) told me today he is planning to write a satirical article on the ridiculous aspects of suicide. First I thought the approach somewhat frivolous and paradoxical. But as he explained his idea to me in a more detailed way, it struck me as pertinent and arresting. It may be most timely, just now, to debunk the romanticism of suicide. With death being so terribly close to all of us, the suicidal gesture appears pompous and obsolete. The lugubrious fuss of furtive preparations and farewell messages becomes disproportionate, indeed, a bit fatuous, considering the prefunctory apocalypse of mechanized modern warfare. Under the circumstances, the impatience for death seems as nonsensical as the fear of it. Why accelerate its coming? We have a good chance to be shortly caught, anyhow. On the other hand, why be afraid of its touch and soothing embrace? Life, I should think, is indeed fearful enough to make us overcome our puerile fear of death.

The same day, later: Jean Cocteau once told me that suicide, in his opinion, is the most dreary triviality conceivable. That is, perhaps, why he has allegedly become a "collaborationist." For confronted with the alternative to commit either a treacherous or a trivial act, Jean would decide in favor of treachery.

According to what I hear, he has managed to settle down rather cozily amongst the Ruins of Paris.

March 15, 1942: Cocteau's compliance in Nazi barbarism is a melancholy event but was to be foreseen and, therefore, should neither surprise nor hurt me. But it would have been almost unbearable to see Gide contaminated by the European plague.

Jean is not a free man but enslaved in a double way—by his vanity and by opium. Addicted to pipes and to publicity, he is at the mercy of the Nazi masters, who could deprive him of both.

Besides Field Marshal Hermann Göring, an experienced dope fiend himself, ought to be lenient on Cocteau's morbid vagaries.

I visualize Jean Cocteau performing his magic gags in the snowy twilight of a chaotic hotel room. The air around him is imbued with the unmistakable scent of the Chinese drug. While he prepares another "petite pipette," a portly gentleman on the couch helps himself to a little morphine injection. The jolly giant—massive and glittering—is nobody less than Göring relaxing in Jean's boudoir. He guffaws—all vociferous cordiality—as his sprightly host produces some of his oft-tested clowneries. Jean imitates Marlene Dietrich, a parrot, and Adolf Hitler. Hermann has the time of his life. Convulsed with laughter, he even forgets to attend the merry mass execution scheduled for midnight sharp.

It is four o'clock in the morning when the monstrous Marshal finally retires—leaving Cocteau in a state of utter weariness and agitation. In the wan light of the early hour he looks like a nervous mummy—fidgety, withered, all corroded by his vices, vanities, and visions.

"Adieu!" he beckons—exhausted and yet coquettish, while withdrawing to the inner sanctum of his apartment, the place where he treasures his finest pipes, Radiguet's portrait, some pebbles Picasso gave him in Rome—twenty-five years ago—and the rubber gloves by means of which Heaven touched him without dirtying itself.

"Adieu, lecteur. Je me couche.

"Je suis ravagé par la poésie comme certains docteurs par l'emploi des rayons X."

If Cocteau's skin is parched by mystic, corrosive rays, Gide's face is tanned by sunshine and salty breezes.

To think of Jean is bitterly amusing. The thought of André Gide is refreshing and comforting.

I imagine him walking along the Mediterranean beach, somewhere between Nice and Cannes—slightly stooping but still elastic; an ageless wanderer in his dark pelerine. What is he looking for, in the floating haze of the dawn? What mystery puzzles him? What promise makes him smile? Sober and inspired he seems all absorbed in the auguries of the beginning day—the savage cries of the gulls, the rhythm of the waves, the traces in the sand.

He is confident, I don't doubt it. To him, it cannot be difficult to overcome the bitterness of past frustrations, to endure the gloom and misery of the present. For what was means less to him than what is: what is, less than what could be and will be.

April 10, 1942: At the Czech General Consulate. Long conversation with X concerning the growing anti-Nazi activities in our country. (I still am a citizen of Czechoslovakia, and proudly so, too . . .)

Similar news from all occupied zones in Europe.

Curt Riess showed me yesterday a heap of documents out of which he compiled the material for his impressive book, "Underground Europe." Such is the profusion of encouraging facts and figures that he could include but portions of them in his voluminous survey.

Skeptics admonish us, and rightly so, not to overrate the political significance of this widespread discontent. Certainly, the secret groups and foolhardy individuals who dare to defy Hitlerism, everywhere between Spitzbergen and the Isle of Crete, have no fighting chance, for the time being. Now, their devious obstruction may have but a negligible nuisance value. But how about tomorrow? When the Allied armies succeed in invading the Hitler-dominated continent—who will be their allies, if not those powerless saboteurs? Their present martyrdom not only prepares but actually guarantees the vast upheaval to come.

April 11, 1942: There are so many things I would like to re-read: "La Chartreuse de Parme" (which André Gide thinks the greatest French novel) and "Anna Karenina" (which is, perhaps, the greatest of all novels: though I don't consider Tolstoi the greatest of all novelists). Yes, and "Wilhelm Meister," and "Gulliver's Travels," and maybe "Moll Flanders." I should have time for Hawthorne (whom I scarcely know) and for Mark Twain (whom I begin to forget). And why not test, once again, old passions like "Wuthering Heights," or Gogol's "Dead Souls," or "Le Père Goriot" by Balzac?

I am sometimes afraid the constant preoccupation with politics might eventually corrupt or obfuscate my mind, and in the end could distract me from those problems and pleasures which really are my natural métier—the only domain where I can hope to accomplish something worth while.

April 21, 1942: The American raid on Tokyo is encouraging news. So are the bombardments of Lübeck by the RAF. . . . How odd this is!—that I don't even need to overcome any humanitarian qualms to approve of as gruesome an event as is an air bombardment. My spontaneous reaction is one of downright enjoyment when I learn that the Axis has been weakened or hurt anywhere. I do not think of the women and children, the hospitals and cathedrals. All things and beings within the realm of those dictatorships are potentially inimical, until the day of their rebellion and liberation.

The same day, later: To be firm, unyielding; relentless, if necessary. But not to become callous! Not violent and obtuse.

Not to become Nazi-like while fighting Nazism!

April 22, 1942: President Roosevelt's idea of calling this war the War for Survival may involve certain technical disadvantages. For this formula seemingly suggests that the sole task confronting us is to save our skins and the status quo, which would be hardly a very inspiring goal.

On second thought, however, Roosevelt's slogan connotes a vast program and promise—far beyond the scope of a merely static and defensive policy. For our imperiled civilization has no chance to survive, unless it improves and moves, reaffirms its faith, reorganizes its structure, becomes dynamic, revolutionary. In other words, the War of Survival can be won only if it is also a war for progress and international solidarity, the prelude to reconstruction. The battle-cry of Survival implies the Four Freedoms and the Bill of Rights extended to all peoples, everywhere; it postulates the rejuvenation of Democracy, the end of nationalism, the beginning of a truly New Order.

The President is a matchless authority in all questions of tact and timing. His instinct is almost infallible when it comes to gauging and anticipating the degree of public responsiveness to certain issues or requirements. Once again he proves his diplomatic (or pedagogical?) intuition by not indulging, at this point, in boisterous phrases and ornate generalities. It would be easy, and therefore a trifle cheap, to label the present tribulation as a Crusade for Liberty, the Battle for a Free World, or something along these lines. But Mr. Roosevelt—more subtle and yet more candid than political leaders are in general—contents himself with a deliberate understatement. For he realizes that the big words and gestures have been abused too long. They no longer express the essential realities and demands of life.

It is the grand strategy of Life always to take the offensive against man's cowardice and inertia. It may occur, in the most critical hour, that the great ideals and vistas seem to pall upon a weary, derelict generation. In such moments of utmost danger, Life brings forth, surprisingly, a new compulsion, a challenge unprecedented. With all abstractions worn out or refuted, there remains but one cogent, irrefutable argument: that we must awaken, struggle, and have confidence, or we are doomed to perish.

"Who speaks of victory?" says Rainer Maria Rilke. "To survive is all."

April 23, 1942: Working all day long.

April 24, 1942: This morning, a note from the Local Board No. 15-23 of the Selective Service, to the effect that "the case of K.M., Order No. 454, has been reopened . . . The board intends to make a new determination of the registrant's classification."

This perfunctory announcement, if it means business, may mark a turning point in my life. To be admitted to the American Army, at this juncture of history, would imply a test and a chance without parallel in my experience up to now. For too many years I contented myself with the role of a commentator, warner, propagandist, and critic. Whatever I had to say in reference to the present crisis I did say long ago. The truth, when repeated too often, can degenerate into a truism or a bumptious cliché. Of course, there is nothing wrong with truism or clichés, as long as they boost the morale of a fighting nation. But, then, there are plenty of gentlemen eager and able to stimulate the people's spirit and to make it plain to them what the war is about. No doubt, they do an essential, indispensable job—those professional spokesmen and instructors of public opinion. For one reason or another, however, I do not feel like joining their assiduous clique. For the first time in my life, I want to belong to the rank and file. I am avid for subordination—hankering for anonymity.

The obsession that haunted me when I was a child—the paralyzing fear of moral and physical isolation—never ceased to perturb me. Always detached and free, I remained always afraid of becoming lonely and disconnected. In puerile fantasies I tried to deny and overcome the intrinsic law of my nature, which prevented me from belonging to the enviable, if pain-stricken masses. Infinitely more grisly than any actual pain is the danger of being excluded from the collective adventure. To be an outsider is the one unbearable humiliation.

But this time I do not need to exclude myself. I recognize the necessity of this war. And so I conclude my reply to the Selective Service Board with these words:

"I want to notify you of my willingness, indeed, my eagerness to join the U.S. forces, even before my naturalization has actually taken place. It is my earnest desire to serve your country and our cause in whatever capacity the Board may deem appropriate. Will you, please, consider these lines as a formal application. I trust that you may find it possible to change my classification right now."

May 28, 1942: Preliminary physical examination. A civil doctor—very gentle and uncle-like—retains some of my blood to test its qualification. He promises me that I shall be called to Governors Island, in a fortnight or so.

"Of course, they'll take you," he says as I ask him whether he thinks me suitable for military service. "There is nothing wrong with you, as far as I can see. They'll take you, all right."

I was as proud and pleased as if he had told me that I write like Shakespeare or that I look like General MacArthur.

June 2, 1942: Impatient for news from Governors Island. Yet I'll have to wait for another week or so.

The spring days are long and sultry. I don't know what to do with my many hours. I don't want to start on something new, as I might be inducted before having finished it. Besides I feel strangely languid and depleted since I am through with the autobiography. It was a big and absorbing job. Now it's done. I have told my story. What is there I could add? Never before have words seemed as stale and meaningless to me as they do just now. I am longing for silence and for service.

Yes, I want to give up my privacy and to become a private.

The same day, later: Reading T. S. Eliot. His vision, like Rainer Maria Rilke's, seems to transcend at times the scope of our earth-bound perception. Both Eliot and Rilke are somehow initiated into that magic silence where "the unspoken word, the Word unheard, the Word without a word" unfolds its ultimate, unspeakable validity.

"At the still point, there the dance is . . ." Eliot's augury could occur in the "Sonnets to Orpheus."

It strikes me as odd and depressing that most people consider Eliot's poems, and those of Rilke's last and purest period, cryptic and intricate. To my ear, they have the bland persuasion of simple prayers and songs. Only cerebral abstractions or vulgarities can be incomprehensible. The truly poetic message may be dark; for so is Life, from the heart of which it emanates. To call this streaming shadowiness "obscure" means to disparage or ignore the secrets and revelations inherent in "this brief transit where the dreams cross, the dreamcrossed twilight between birth and dying."

June 4, 1942: The uncertainty continues. I am told that it may take weeks, if not months, until I shall be inducted—presuming that I am found acceptable by the military physicians and psychologists. So the decision I was looking forward to has been postponed, once again.

I can hardly bear the sight of my room any longer. During the last twenty-one months I haven't spent more than five nights outside the Bedford Hotel. I may go to California to stay some time with my parents, whom I have not seen for ages. Of course, it might be that I shall be called back East, almost immediately upon my arrival in Pacific Palisades. It could also be that I would reach the West Coast just in time to witness a Japanese air raid or an attempt to invade this country. The bombardments of Alaska are ominous signs. The word "invasion" occurs more and more frequently in the papers. (I don't think they would dare, though. But we have got accustomed to all sorts of dire and incredible surprises.)

June 6, 1942: Today is the Magician's sixty-seventh birthday. When I first met him, he was younger than I am now. There is something unspeakably weird about the passing of time. Hugo von Hofmannsthal is one of the few poets who have not only grasped but also formulated this tremendous feeling of transitoriness. Whenever I think of the chimerical change of all mortal stuff, I recall Hofmannsthal's verse:

> Dies ist ein Ding, das keiner voll aussinnt
> Und viel zu grauenvoll als dass man klage:
> Dass alles gleitet und vorüberrinnt . . .

"This is a thing nobody quite conceives, and horrifying beyond lament: that everything fleets and flits away . . ."

Last night, Christopher Lazare and I had a good time listening to a cycle of "Rosenkavalier" records. Hofmannsthal's libretto is undoubtedly one of the finest things ever written for the queer medium which is opera. The moment that struck us most was when the aging Marschallin confides to her young lover that sometimes she would get up, in the middle of the night, and stop all clocks in her house— overpowered by a sudden dismay. Time flies, she is no longer young, she has to renounce her love, she will die.

It is all very simple. The simplest things are the most mysterious ones. The basic facts of our lives are horrifying beyond lament:

The same day, later: Rummaging my papers I am surprised by the profusion of notes and sketches I meant to use in various contexts. But the articles and stories I was planning, at the time, never came into being. What a waste of labor and material!

I am sorry I did not go through with the piece about Picasso as a representative of our epoch—its grandeur and its disintegration.

The fragments about musical subjects might have yielded interesting stories. I may keep the outline for an essay on George Gershwin, and also the notes about Czech composers—Dvorak, Smetana, and so forth.

The treatise on Kossuth's journey through the United States was almost finished when I stopped working on it for one reason or another. The quotations I compiled are indeed timely and instructive enough. The Hungarian leader, pleading for the cause of his country, employed all arguments used by the interventionists, in 1940. His Isolationist opponents used—in 1851!—almost literally the same phrases known to us from the speeches of Lindbergh, Wheeler, Walsh, etc. To describe how certain principles, that were cogent in 1770 and even in 1800, became disputable in 1850, lost all validity in 1940.

Why did I fail to conclude the article about the Church and Reconstruction? "Horizon" carried a story dealing with the same topic. But it confirmed and amplified my remarks, rather than repeated them.

There remains a good deal to be said concerning the prospects of closer collaboration between unorthodox left-wing groups and progressive Christians. To point out how dangerously the development of a new humanistic philosophy has been hindered by the obtuse materialism of the Marxian gospel, and by the retrogressive moral and social views to which the clergy still adhere in too many cases. Both obstacles must be overcome to create a new pattern of ethical behavior, and to revitalize man's vision of his own potential dignity.

Highly significant subject. Additional notes. To be continued.

THE END

An American Soldier
Revisiting His
Former Homeland

You can't go home again...: It was a great American writer, the late Thomas Wolfe, who chose this phrase as title for one of his novels.

You can't go home again...: These words were in my mind—haunting me like a nostalgic tune, a melancholy leitmotiv—while I was touring occupied Germany, in 1945 and 1946.

More than twelve years had elapsed since I had left the country, together with my family. That was back in 1933—the fatal year of Hitler's coming to power. While the vast majority of our former compatriots was jubilant about the enthronement of their beloved "Führer," while the blinded, misguided nation hailed the establishment of the gangster regime, a handful of clear-sighted people recognized the tragic gravity of the situation. To us, exile was a matter of course, under the circumstances. We simply felt quite incapable of breathing the air in our Nazi-infested homeland.

Did we hope to return?

Well, in the beginning we may have indulged in illusions. Yes, it was an illusion to believe—as we tried to do, for some time—that the Germans would ever revolt against Hitler, that they wished to get rid of him. The awful truth is that the Germans adored their Führer—in fact, quite a few of them have remained faithful to him up to the present day and would be only too happy if they could have him back...

The war Hitler waged against the civilized world was in fact the war of the German people. They supported him wholeheartedly, with a steadfastness, an enthusiasm that would have been worthy of a better cause.

By 1939 and 1940, even the most dogged optimists had to give up their long-cherished hope for a German revolution. Clearly, the Germans were neither willing nor able to liberate themselves and the world from Hitler and Hitlerism. More firmly established than ever within the aggressive Reich, Hitler and Hitlerism had to be defeated from without.

Of course, we German refugees — the first victims and most inexorable enemies of Nazism — were eager to contribute our bit to the fight against the Brown Plague. I was happy and proud, therefore, to join the army of my new country, the United States of America, and to be sent overseas — first to North Africa, then to Italy, where I served with General Clark's Fifth Army. Subsequently, I was transferred to the editorial staff of the American military newspaper, The Stars & Stripes, Mediterranean Edition, then stationed in Rome, Italy.

It was that newspaper — a publication, incidentally, of remarkably high journalistic standards — which sent me to my former homeland, Germany, as a soldier-correspondent. That was early in May, 1945, just a few days before the official German surrender. I went over the Alps by jeep, and, after short stops in Innsbruck, Salzburg and Berchtesgaden, approached Munich, the city where I was born and spent my entire childhood.

What a strange, nightmarish experience! — to walk through those once-familiar streets, now reduced to masses of ruins and rubble...With most of the characteristic landmarks missing, I could hardly find my way from the city center to the suburban district on the Isar River where our former home is situated.

As the residential outskirts have in general been spared by Allied bombs — in Munich as well as in other German towns — I hoped to find our house intact. It was a spacious and handsome villa my father had had built for himself, shortly before the outbreak of World War I. In 1933, the Nazis took it away from us, along with everything else we owned in Germany. Maybe some Party big shot was still occupying our former home. If so, it certainly would be fun to throw him out in person!

But I was to be disappointed. The building — even though it appeared fairly well-preserved at the first look — turned out to be an empty shell, with its inside all burnt out, its roof destroyed, its staircase in pieces. What a pity! I would not have the pleasure of expelling any Nazi invaders. No human being could possibly live in these ruins.

But as I was standing there in the garden, contemplating somewhat nostalgically what used to be the happy home of my youth, I discovered, not without surprise, that the place was not quite deserted, after all! There was a girl on the balcony just in front of my former room on the second floor. She was watching me suspiciously.

"What are you doing up there, Fräulein?" I asked her in German, but with a slight American accent.

She shrugged her shoulders, sullen and distrustful. As I repeated my question, she said, still with the same peevish and weary expression: "Why, I'm living here—can't you see that? I'm bombed out; my parents are dead, my fiancé too—killed in Russia; I have no place to stay. This balcony is all right, as long as it doesn't rain... Want to come up?" she suggested with a wry, yet inviting smile.

I wondered how I could reach the second floor since the staircase was gone; but she pointed out to me a kind of ladder—quite an ingenious device she had constructed herself, as she informed me not without pride.

"Do you know whose house this used to be?" I enquired, having joined her on the balcony.

"I suppose it belonged to some writer," she explained, rather indifferently. "One of those who didn't get along with the Nazis—so of course, he couldn't keep the house. Then the SS took it over; they had a *Lebensborn* established here."

Much to her suprise, I didn't know the meaning of that romantic-sounding German term—*Lebensborn*. According to her explanation, a *Lebensborn* was a place where racially qualified young men and equally well-bred young women collaborated in the interest of the German nation.—"There was nothing frivolous about it," the girl assured me—speaking maybe out of personal experience. "They didn't do it for the fun of it—just for the propagation of our Nordic race. Many fine babies were begotten and born in this house..."

"So that's what they were using this house for," I said. "Interesting. *Very* interesting indeed."

"Yes, a *Lebensborn* certainly was an interesting place," the girl agreed, and added: "You can stay here overnight, if you don't feel like going back to your billets. It's really quite cozy here. Almost like home, you know..."

I thanked her for her kind invitation which, unfortunately, I could not accept. It is true, my good old balcony was rather a cozy place; but for one reason or other, it didn't quite look like home to me...

Strolling through the bleak, deserted city, I could not help wondering whether it would be possible to locate any of my old friends in these ruins. Did I really want to find any of them? How could I know how they had behaved, during those past years of terror and disgrace? There were indeed good reasons to suspect that most of them had conducted themselves in a more or less objectionable fashion...

But then, I was in Germany as a reporter — not as a private tourist. I had to get some stories for The Stars & Stripes...

Dutifully, I remembered that Emil Jannings, the movie actor, had his home not very far from Munich — on the Lake of St. Wolfgang, near Salzburg. He and his attractive wife, Gussy Holl — formerly married to Conrad Veidt — used to be great friends of ours. An interview with old Jannings, I thought, would certainly make good copy. So I drove out in my jeep.

"Now listen, Emil," I said to him, right as I entered his house, "I'm here as a newspaper man — *not* as a friend! I don't know whether you were a Nazi, and frankly, I don't care. I want a story — that's all."

Far from being hurt or insulted, he overwhelmed me with his cordiality. How *happy* he was to see me! Didn't I remember the fun we had had together? That Christmas Eve in Hollywood, eighteen years ago? And that delightful carnival in Munich? Yes, those were the days...!

A Nazi — *he*, Emil Jannings? How utterly absurd! How ridiculous! — "It is true," he admitted, "I played in one of those Nazi propaganda films, *Ohm Krüger*. But I was *forced* to do so — don't you see? Dr. Göbbels himself *blackmailed* me into accepting the role. He *hated* me — Göbbels did! It would have been suicide to disobey his orders. Don't forget, I have a Jewish grandmother..."

Did I believe his tales? Well, not altogether, but to a certain extent. Jannings is a pretty good actor...Besides, it was somehow touching to see the jolly old fellow again. The atmosphere of his house where I had spent many a pleasant weekend, Gussy's amusing chat, the exquisite Rhine wine to which he treated me — all this was liable to soften my attitude, to render me more gentle and conciliatory than I had meant to be.

The article on Jannings I wired to my paper was certainly not a eulogy, but it may have been rather on the mild and lenient side. I ventured to suggest that Jannings had probably been *as* anti-Nazi as he *could* without jeopardizing his position and bank account.

As a result of my story in The Stars & Stripes, I got an avalanche of letters from people who had followed Jannings' career during the Hitler years. Had I gone mad?—those correspondents asked me indignantly, or had Mr. Jannings bribed me with a handsome amount of money? Why else should I try to whitewash that notorious scoundrel? Didn't I *know* that he had been one of the worst? With one of the angry letters I found a booklet enclosed—a biography of "Ohm Krüger," the anti-British hero of the Boer War. The pamphlet opened with an introduction, written by Emil Jannings, in which the actor expressed in the most fervent and flowery terms his profound gratitude to the Minister of Propaganda and Enlightenment, Dr. Paul Joseph Göbbels, under whose auspices, and thanks to whose generosity, he, Jannings, had had the privilege of appearing in that great, patriotic film...And so forth, in the same servile vein.

And with the author of that shameful document I had had a friendly chat and a bottle of wine! The idea was positively sickening.

I decided to be more careful, from now on. *Beware of old friends!*

When I went to see Richard Strauss—again for strictly journalistic purposes—I preferred to remain anonymous, or rather, to introduce myself as "War Correspondent Smith from Chicago." I hoped the old gentleman, to whom I had once been presented many years before, would not recognize me in American uniform—which, in fact, he didn't.

The conversation with Strauss took place in the garden of his beautiful villa in Garmisch, near Munich. The great composer—looking remarkably well-preserved, considering his advanced age—received my companion and me with a kind of patronizing graciousness, all smiling self-assurance.

"Yes, I'm feeling fine," he cheerfully answered our polite question. No, the Nazis had never bothered him. — "That is to say," he corrected himself, "they have never given me any serious trouble. Of course, there were minor nuisances—some of them quite disturbing. For instance, they wanted me to put up a bombed-out family from Munich here in my private residence." He pointed at the large house which he was then occupying with his son and daughter-in-law. "Imagine! Strangers in *my* home! Outrageous, isn't it?"

There was something at once disarming and amazing about his naive selfishness. To him, nothing in the world seemed to matter, except the personal affairs of Dr. Richard Strauss—his comforts, his income, his fame.—"Baldur von Schirach was an excellent man," he would say, unblushingly. "He really appreciated my music. Frank was a good fellow, too—full of understanding for my work." (The gentleman he referred to was Governor Frank of Poland, the high Nazi official personally in charge of the gas chambers of Auschwitz. Composer Strauss once wrote a beautiful hymn praising the virtues of War Criminal Frank.)

Hitler? No, Dr. Strauss didn't think that Hitler was so good. "His musical tastes were deplorably one-sided. Wagner, and Wagner again! Hardly ever did he go to hear any of my operas..."

I looked at him, flabbergasted. Could I ever enjoy *Rosenkavalier* and *Salomé* again, having listened to his shockingly callous talk?

What a strange country this was, where even the creative artists, even the geniuses seemed to have forgotten the language of humanity!

Well, I would go on exploring that mysterious land which is Occupied Germany, in the hope of finding men more sincere than the great actor Jannings, more humane and generous than Richard Strauss, the master composer. But even if I met, or *re*-met, some people whose thoughts and words were still intelligible, still acceptable to me, they would constitute just a tiny minority of congenial souls within the vast mass of strangers.

Yes, I felt a stranger in my former fatherland. There was an abyss separating me from those who used to be my countrymen. Wherever I went in Germany, the melancholy tune and nostalgic leitmotiv followed me:

YOU CAN'T GO HOME AGAIN...

Index of Names

Bracketed numbers refer to introduction